D1467339

Shojo Beat

Fairy Cube

Vol. 2

Story & Art by

Kaori Yuki

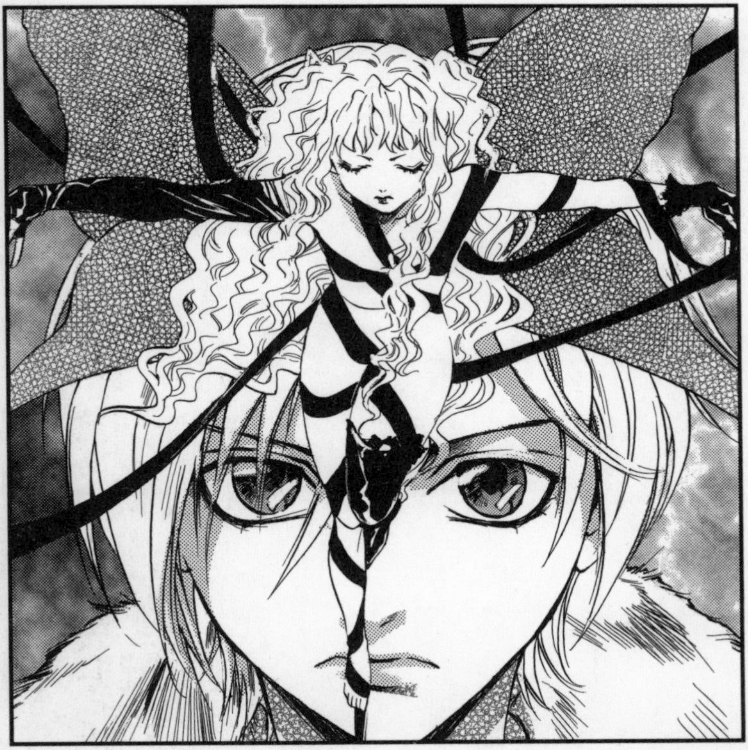

CONTENTS

Fairy Cube THE CHARACTERS

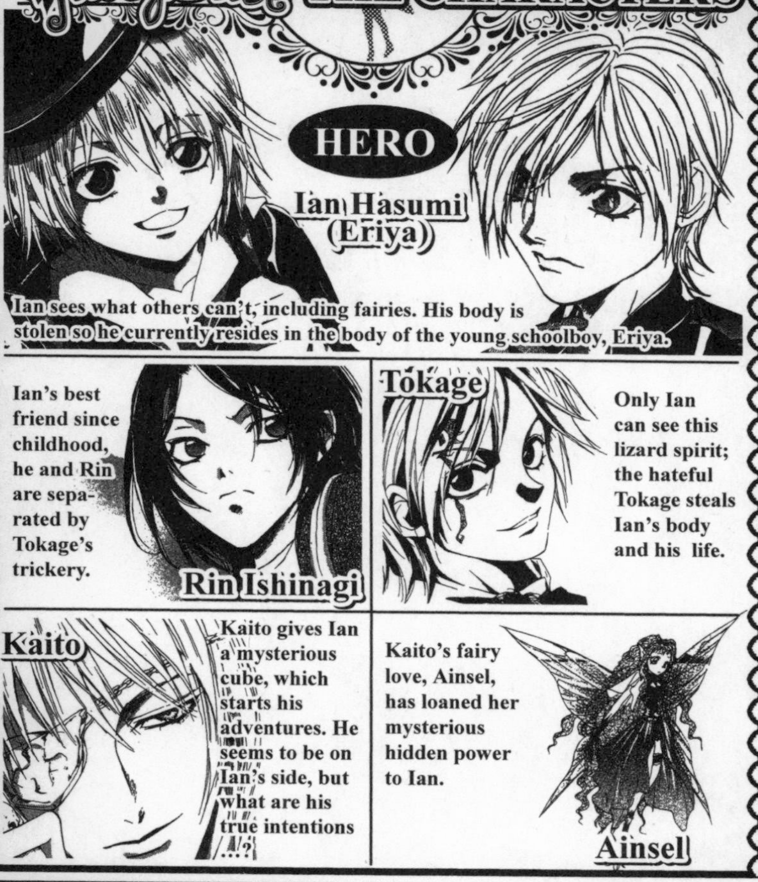
HERO
Ian Hasumi (Eriya)
Ian sees what others can't, including fairies. His body is stolen so he currently resides in the body of the young schoolboy, Eriya.
Ian's best friend since childhood, he and Rin are separated by Tokage's trickery.
Rin Ishinagi
Tokage
Only Ian can see this lizard spirit; the hateful Tokage steals Ian's body and his life.
Kaito
Kaito gives Ian a mysterious cube, which starts his adventures. He seems to be on Ian's side, but what are his true intentions...?
Kaito's fairy love, Ainsel, has loaned her mysterious hidden power to Ian.
Ainsel

THE STORY SO FAR...

Ian Hasumi has always been able to see fairies and spirits, including Tokage, his Other, or alternate self. When a stranger named Kaito gives him a cube containing Tokage's essence, Tokage manages to take over Ian's body. ▶ After a frightening visit to Faerie, Ian and Ainsel return to this world and Ian swears revenge on Tokage. He enters another's body to become a Wing Person... ▶ Ian, who is now in the body of the schoolboy, Eriya, searches for Tokage, and gets into a fight with the Wing People who have taken over the school. He rescues Rin from battle, revealing his true self. However, Eriya's grandmother, Mrs. Barrett discovers the secret and interrogates Ian/Eriya on his identity...!!

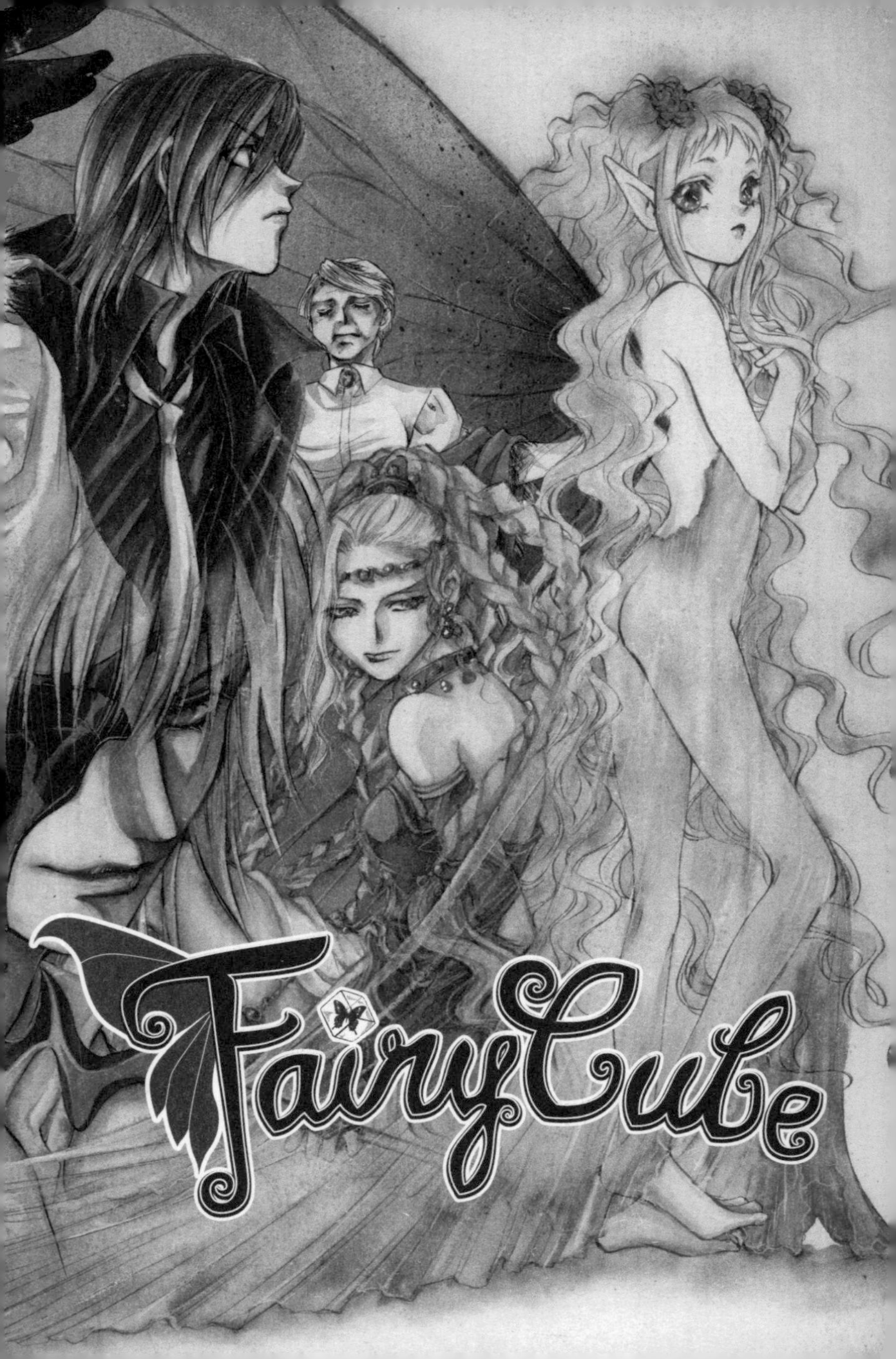
Fairy Cube

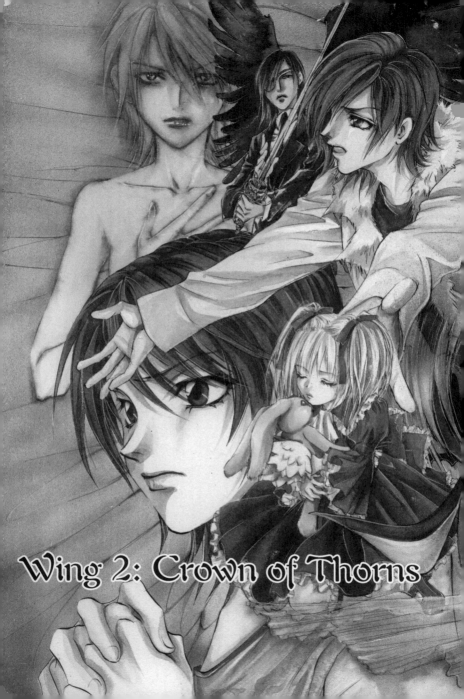

Wing 2: Crown of Thorns

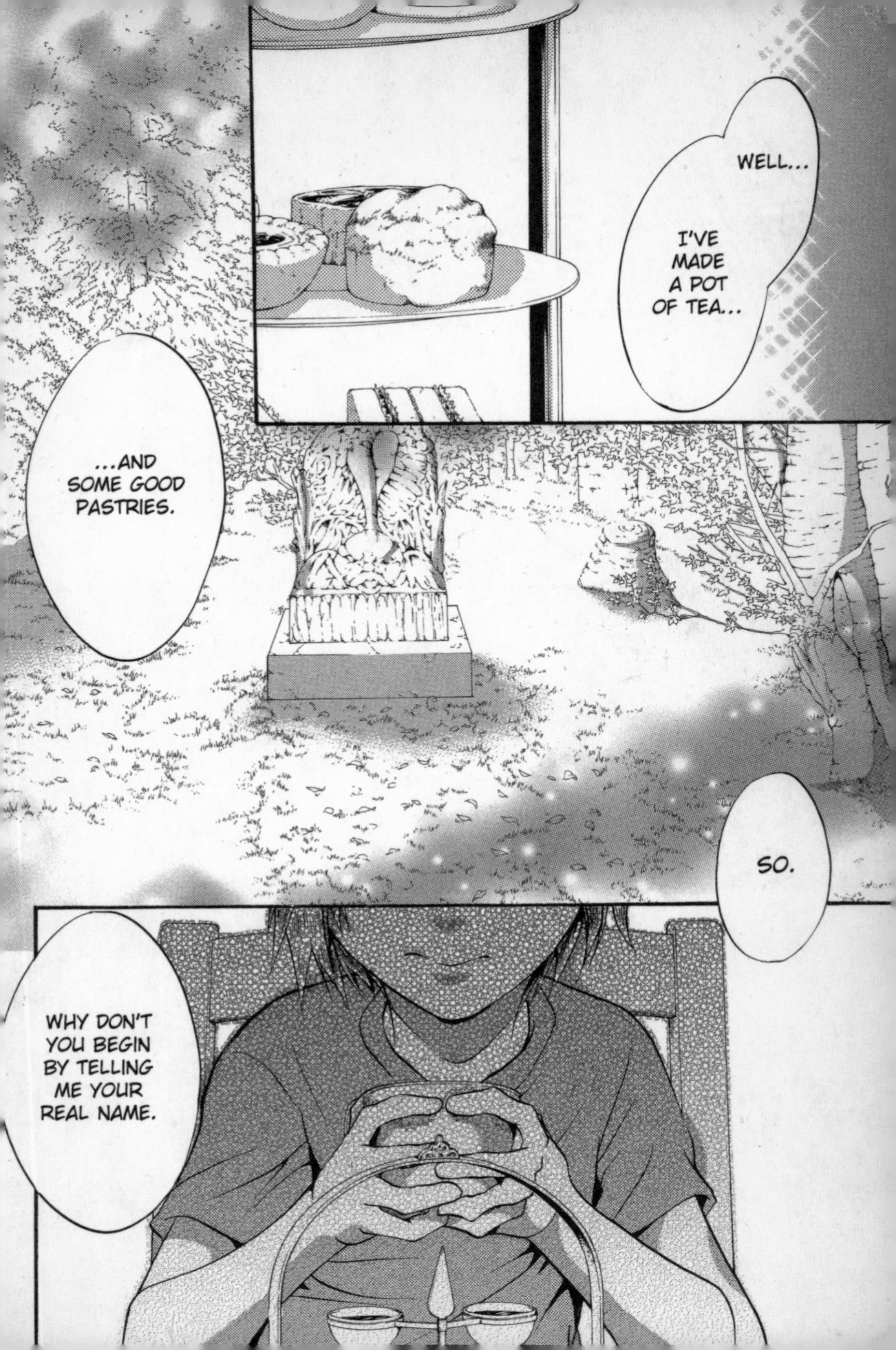
WELL...
I'VE MADE A POT OF TEA...
...AND SOME GOOD PASTRIES.
SO.
WHY DON'T YOU BEGIN BY TELLING ME YOUR REAL NAME.

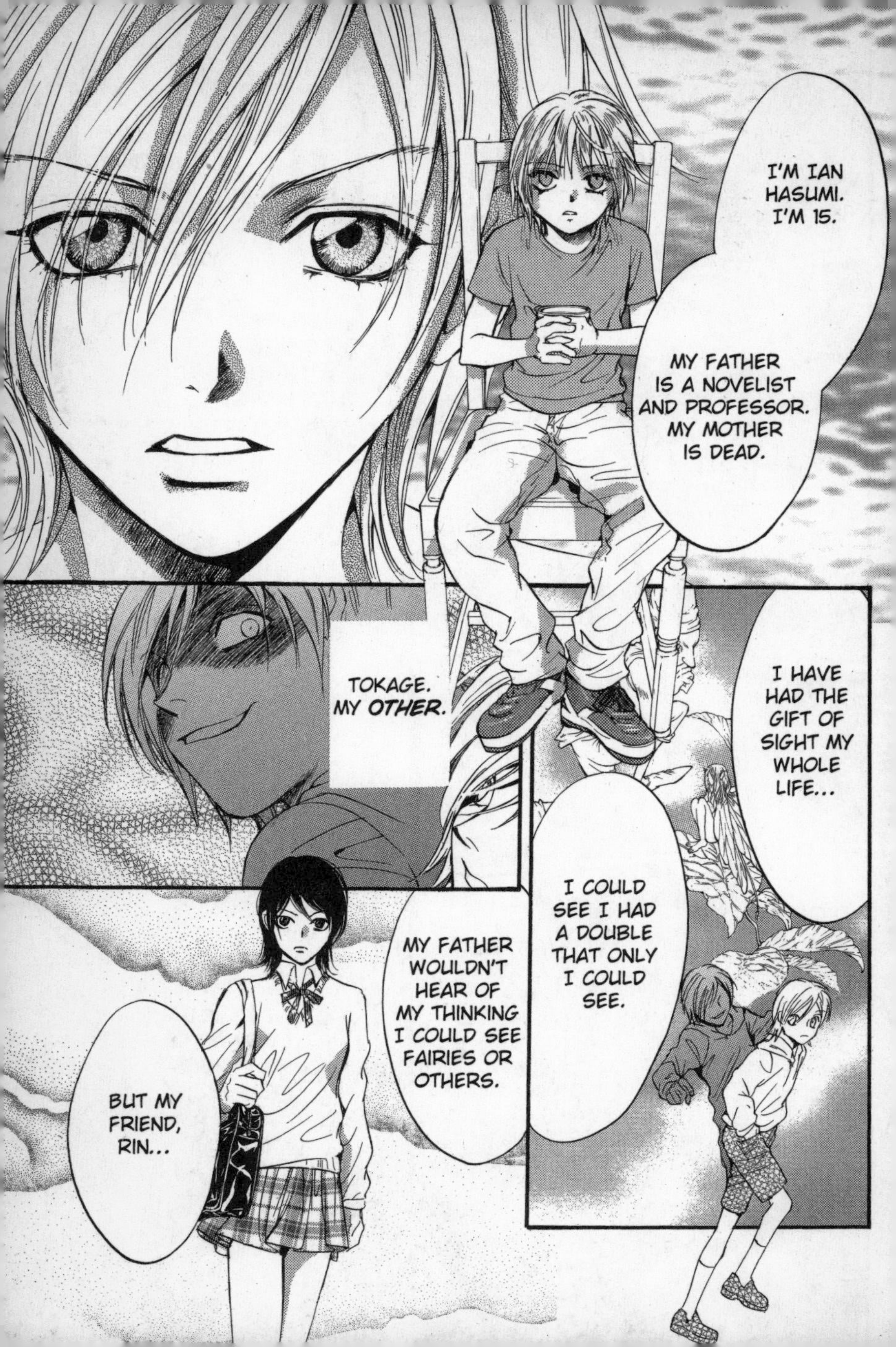
I'M IAN HASUMI. I'M 15.
MY FATHER IS A NOVELIST AND PROFESSOR. MY MOTHER IS DEAD.
I HAVE HAD THE GIFT OF SIGHT MY WHOLE LIFE...
I COULD SEE I HAD A DOUBLE THAT ONLY I COULD SEE.
TOKAGE. MY *OTHER*.
MY FATHER WOULDN'T HEAR OF MY THINKING I COULD SEE FAIRIES OR OTHERS.
BUT MY FRIEND, RIN...

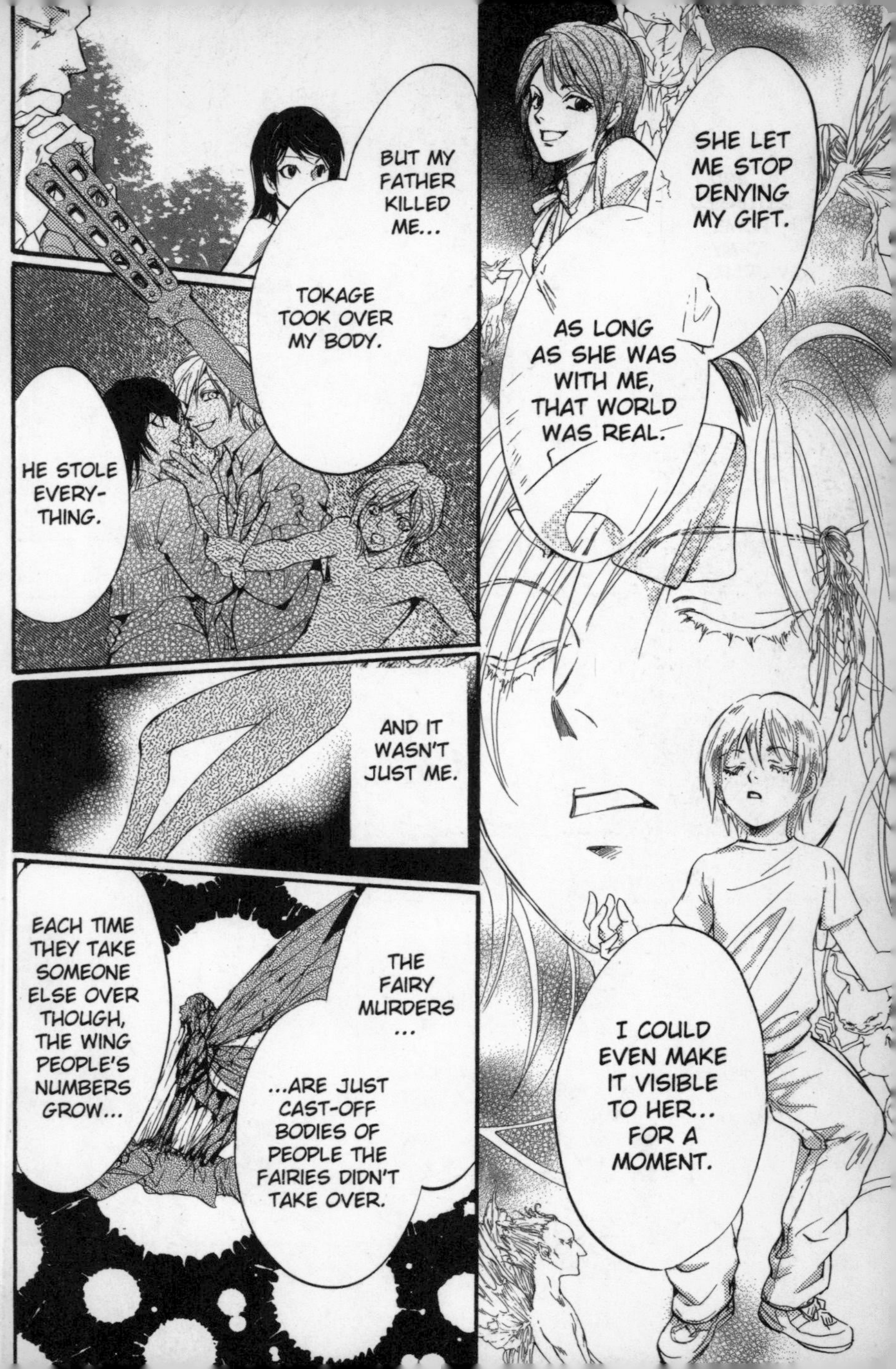
SHE LET ME STOP DENYING MY GIFT.
AS LONG AS SHE WAS WITH ME, THAT WORLD WAS REAL.
I COULD EVEN MAKE IT VISIBLE TO HER... FOR A MOMENT.
BUT MY FATHER KILLED ME...
TOKAGE TOOK OVER MY BODY.
HE STOLE EVERY-THING.
AND IT WASN'T JUST ME.
THE FAIRY MURDERS ...
...ARE JUST CAST-OFF BODIES OF PEOPLE THE FAIRIES DIDN'T TAKE OVER.
EACH TIME THEY TAKE SOMEONE ELSE OVER THOUGH, THE WING PEOPLE'S NUMBERS GROW...

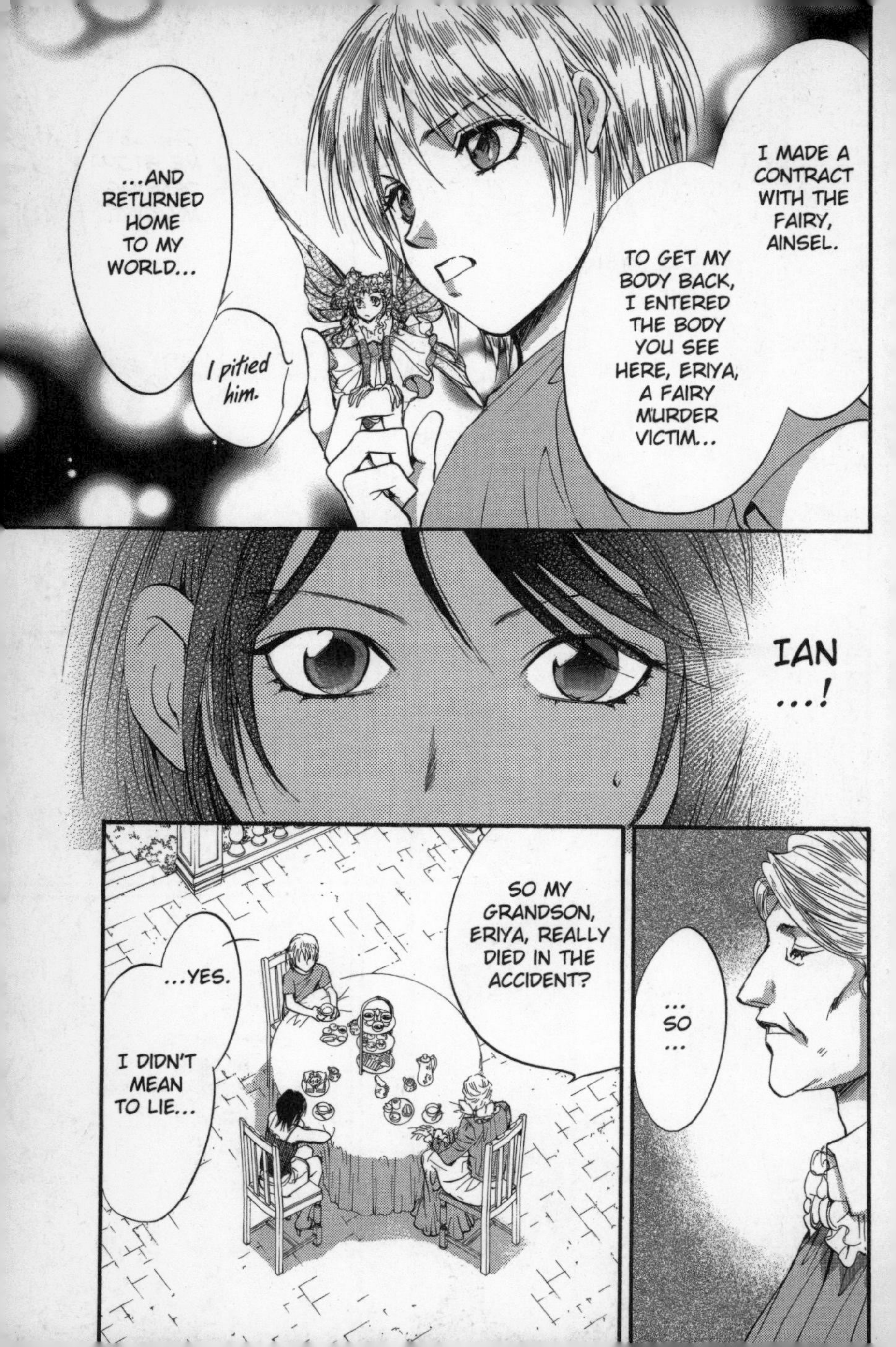

I MADE A CONTRACT WITH THE FAIRY, AINSEL.
TO GET MY BODY BACK, I ENTERED THE BODY YOU SEE HERE, ERIYA, A FAIRY MURDER VICTIM...
...AND RETURNED HOME TO MY WORLD...
I pitied him.
IAN ...!
... SO ...
SO MY GRANDSON, ERIYA, REALLY DIED IN THE ACCIDENT?
...YES.
I DIDN'T MEAN TO LIE...

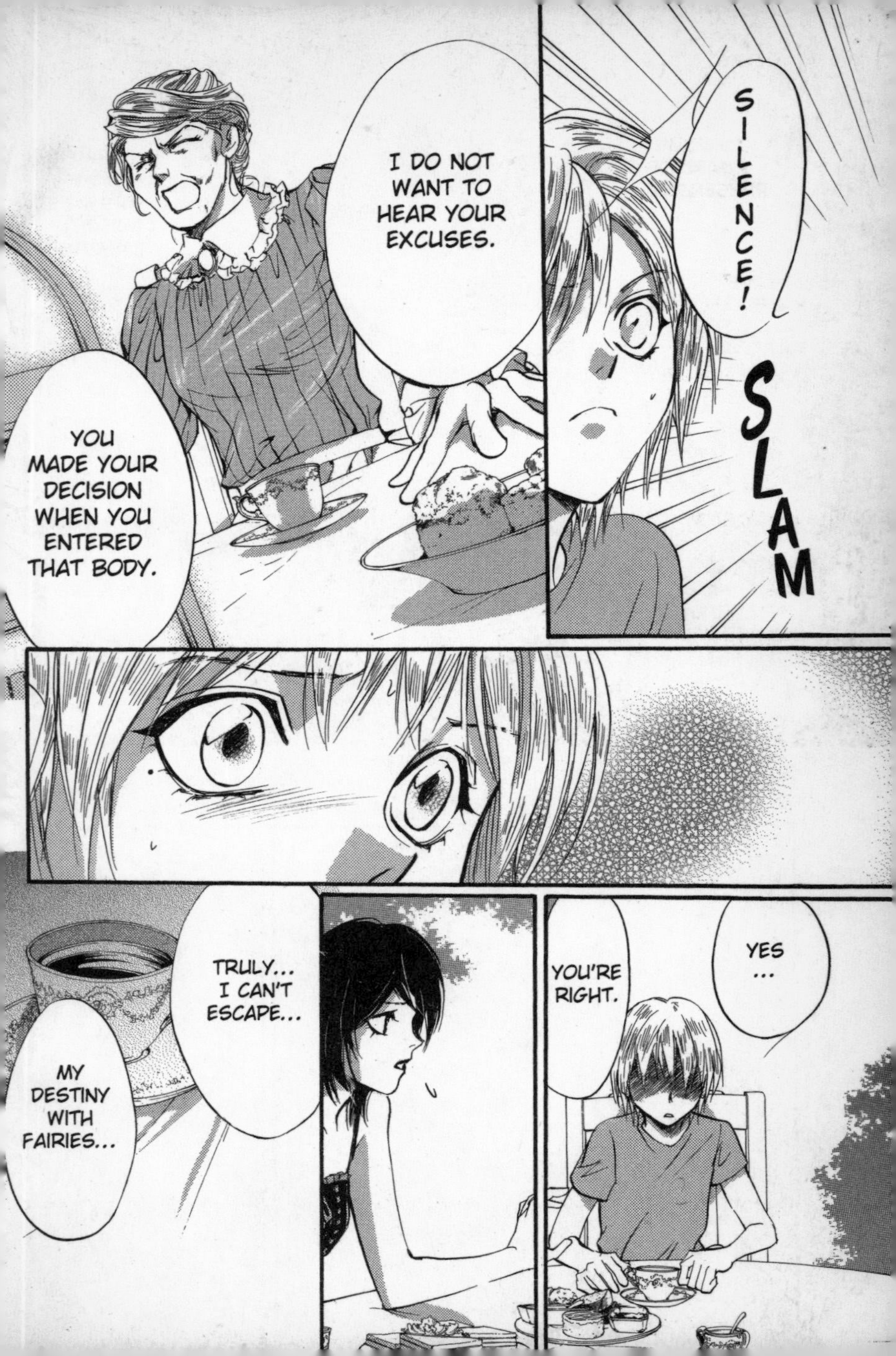
SILENCE!
SLAM
I DO NOT WANT TO HEAR YOUR EXCUSES.
YOU MADE YOUR DECISION WHEN YOU ENTERED THAT BODY.
YES...
YOU'RE RIGHT.
TRULY... I CAN'T ESCAPE...
MY DESTINY WITH FAIRIES...

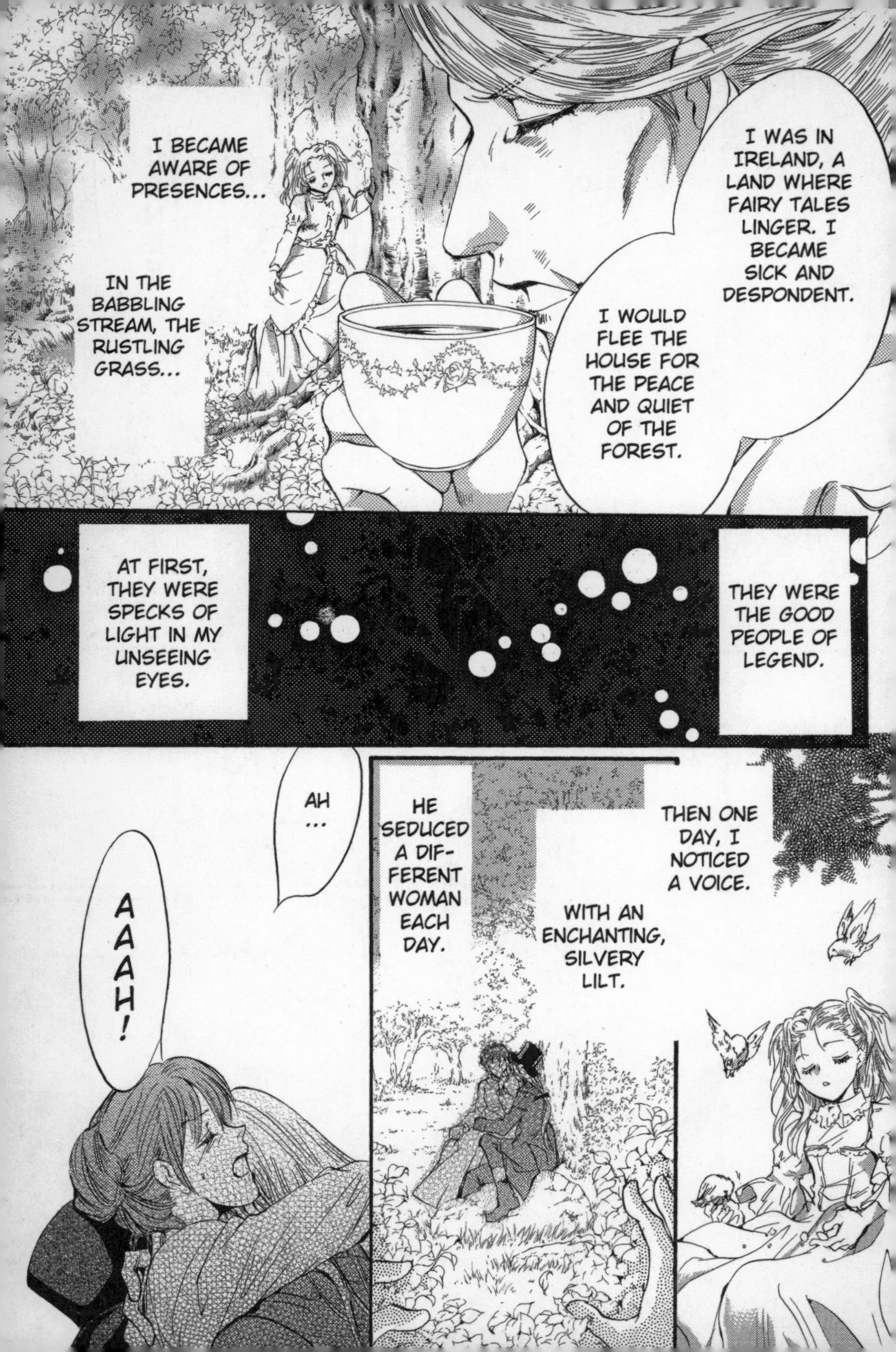
I WAS IN IRELAND, A LAND WHERE FAIRY TALES LINGER. I BECAME SICK AND DESPONDENT.
I WOULD FLEE THE HOUSE FOR THE PEACE AND QUIET OF THE FOREST.
I BECAME AWARE OF PRESENCES...
IN THE BABBLING STREAM, THE RUSTLING GRASS...
THEY WERE THE GOOD PEOPLE OF LEGEND.
AT FIRST, THEY WERE SPECKS OF LIGHT IN MY UNSEEING EYES.
THEN ONE DAY, I NOTICED A VOICE.
WITH AN ENCHANTING, SILVERY LILT.
HE SEDUCED A DIF-FERENT WOMAN EACH DAY.
AH ...
AAAAH!

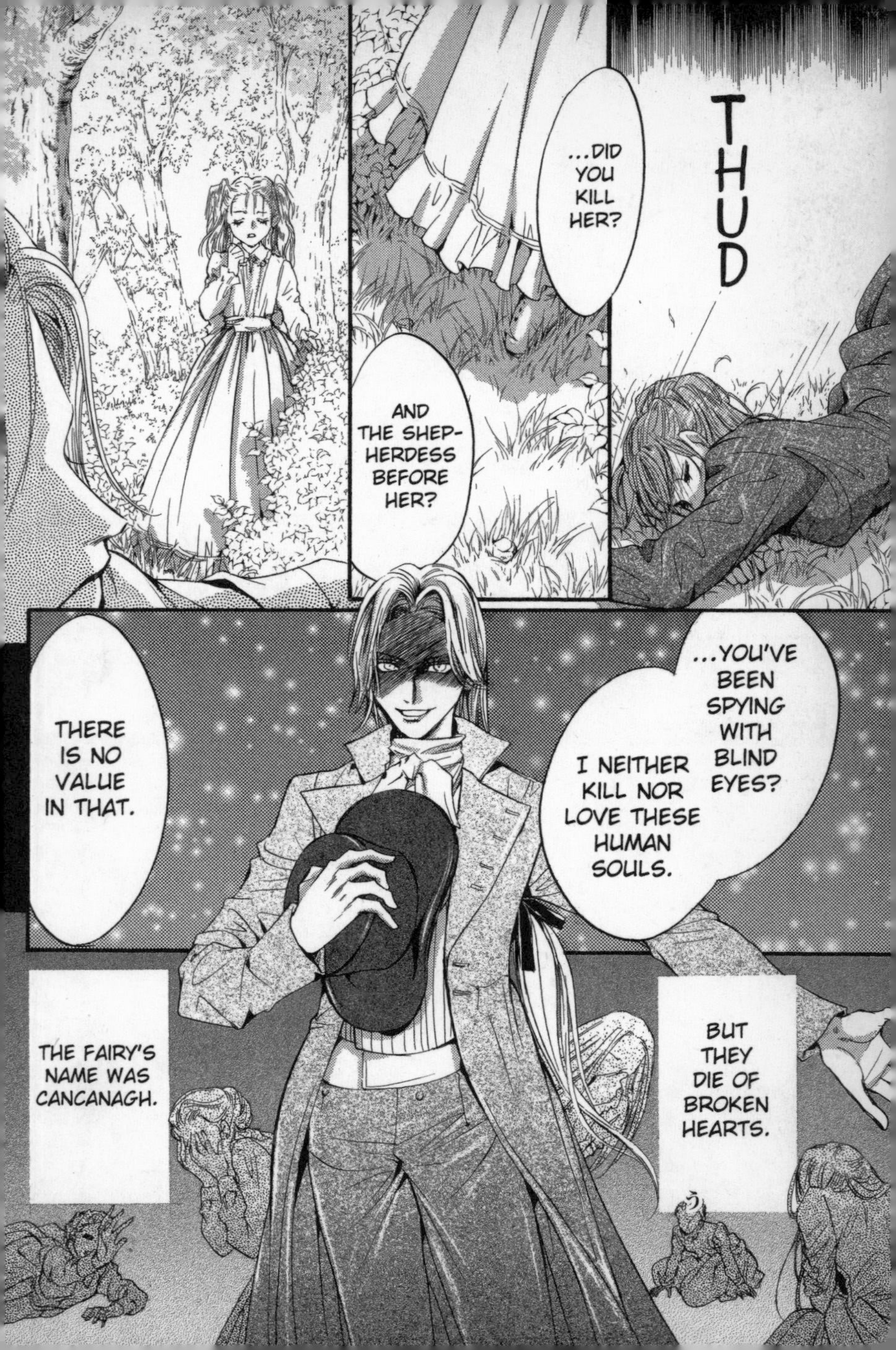
THUD
...DID YOU KILL HER?
AND THE SHEP-HERDESS BEFORE HER?
...YOU'VE BEEN SPYING WITH BLIND EYES?
I NEITHER KILL NOR LOVE THESE HUMAN SOULS.
THERE IS NO VALUE IN THAT.
BUT THEY DIE OF BROKEN HEARTS.
THE FAIRY'S NAME WAS CANCANAGH.

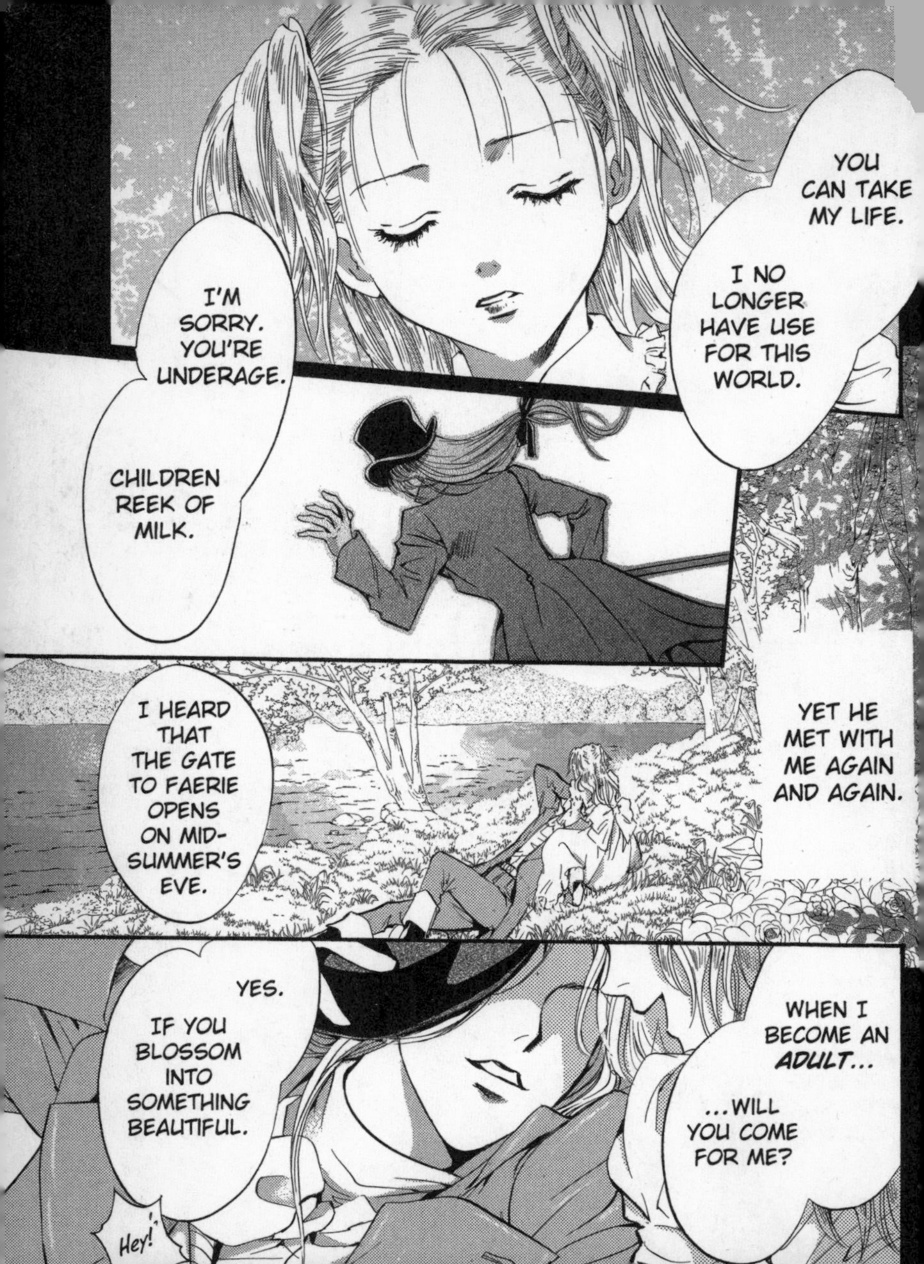
YOU CAN TAKE MY LIFE.
I NO LONGER HAVE USE FOR THIS WORLD.
I'M SORRY. YOU'RE UNDERAGE.
CHILDREN REEK OF MILK.
YET HE MET WITH ME AGAIN AND AGAIN.
I HEARD THAT THE GATE TO FAERIE OPENS ON MID-SUMMER'S EVE.
WHEN I BECOME AN *ADULT*...
...WILL YOU COME FOR ME?
YES.
IF YOU BLOSSOM INTO SOMETHING BEAUTIFUL.
Hey!

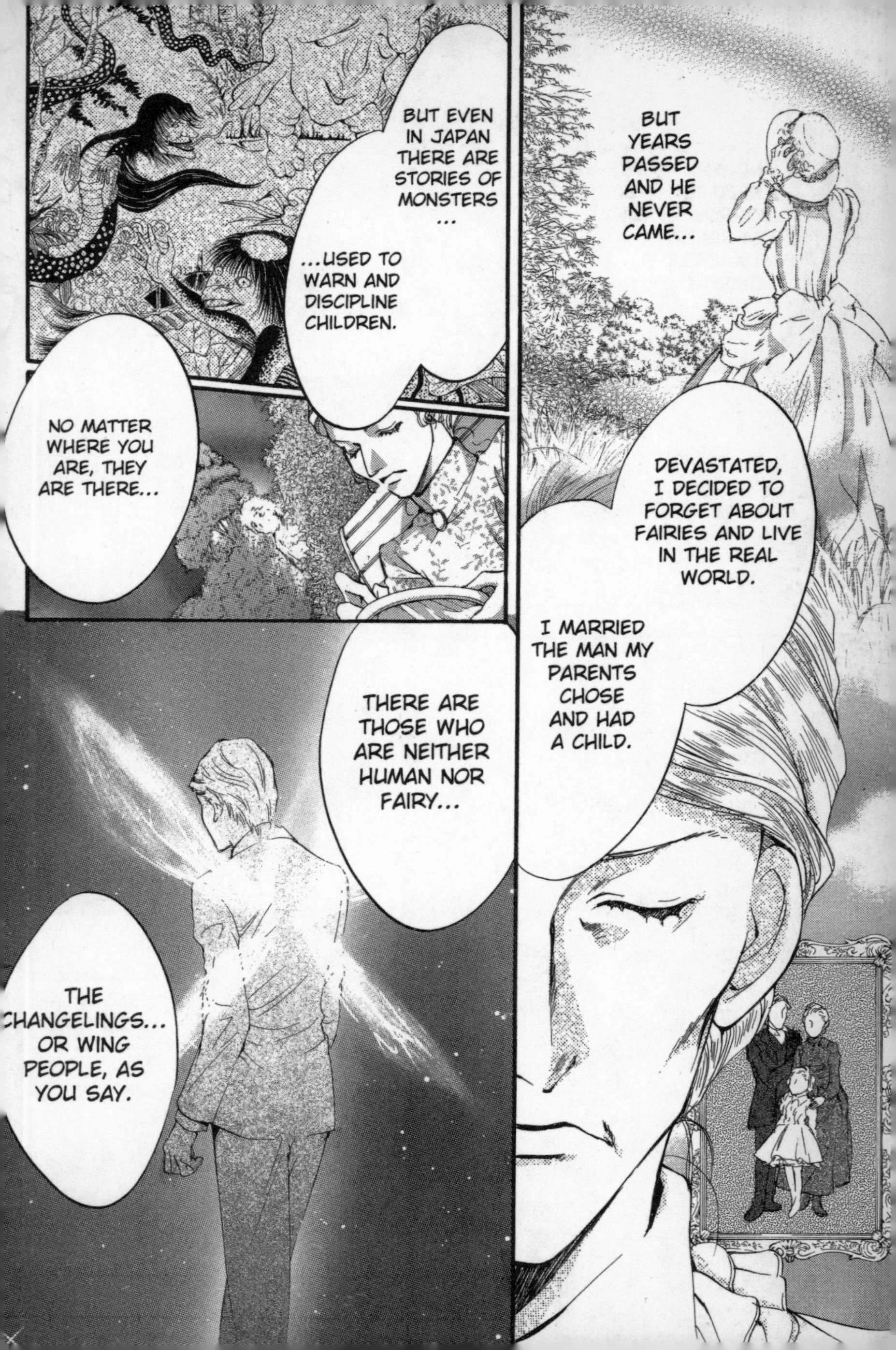
BUT YEARS PASSED AND HE NEVER CAME...
DEVASTATED, I DECIDED TO FORGET ABOUT FAIRIES AND LIVE IN THE REAL WORLD.
I MARRIED THE MAN MY PARENTS CHOSE AND HAD A CHILD.
BUT EVEN IN JAPAN THERE ARE STORIES OF MONSTERS ...
...USED TO WARN AND DISCIPLINE CHILDREN.
NO MATTER WHERE YOU ARE, THEY ARE THERE...
THERE ARE THOSE WHO ARE NEITHER HUMAN NOR FAIRY...
THE CHANGELINGS... OR WING PEOPLE, AS YOU SAY.

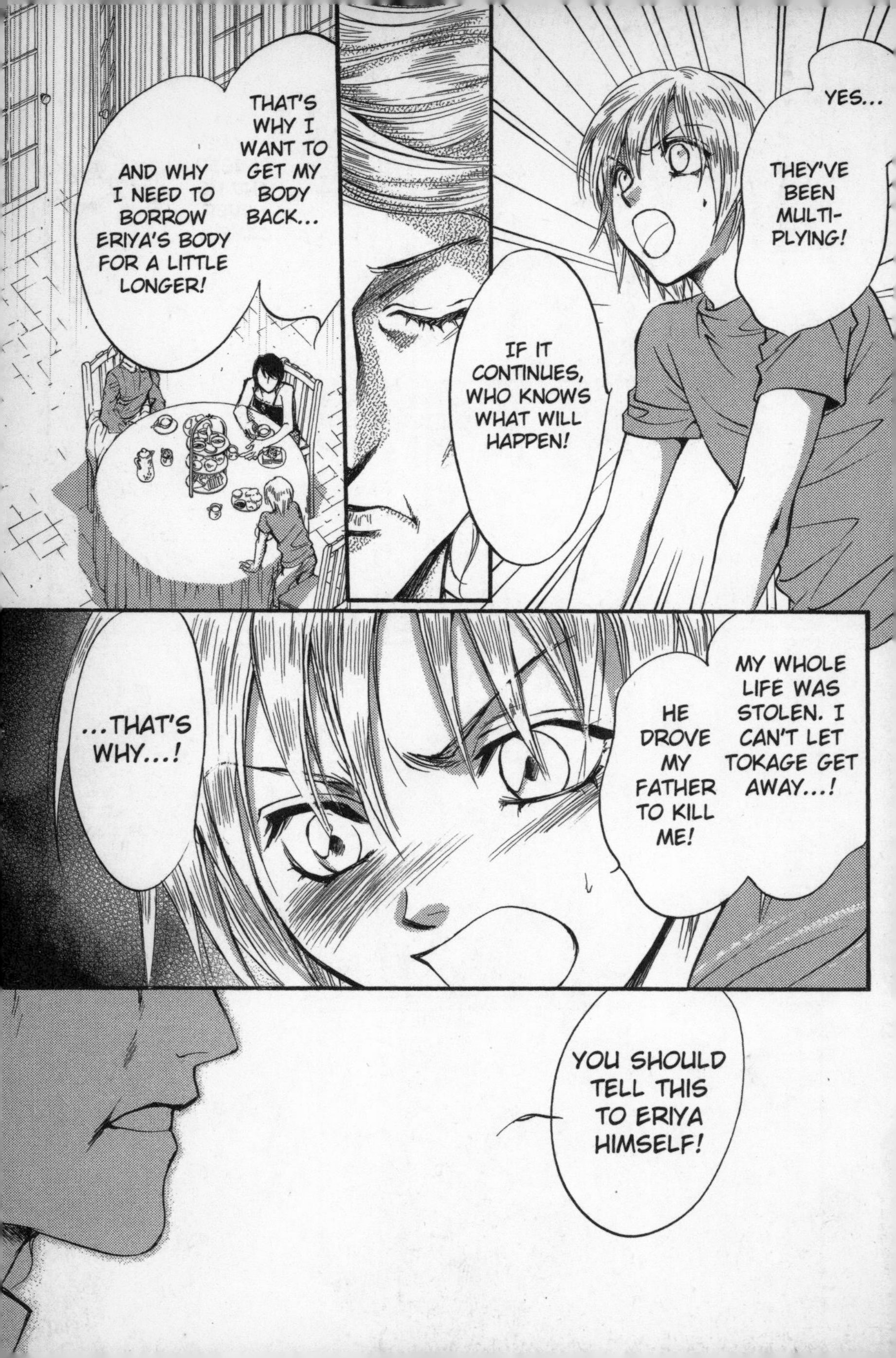
YES...
THEY'VE BEEN MULTI-PLYING!
IF IT CONTINUES, WHO KNOWS WHAT WILL HAPPEN!
THAT'S WHY I WANT TO GET MY BODY BACK...
AND WHY I NEED TO BORROW ERIYA'S BODY FOR A LITTLE LONGER!
MY WHOLE LIFE WAS STOLEN. I CAN'T LET TOKAGE GET AWAY...!
HE DROVE MY FATHER TO KILL ME!
...THAT'S WHY...!
YOU SHOULD TELL THIS TO ERIYA HIMSELF!

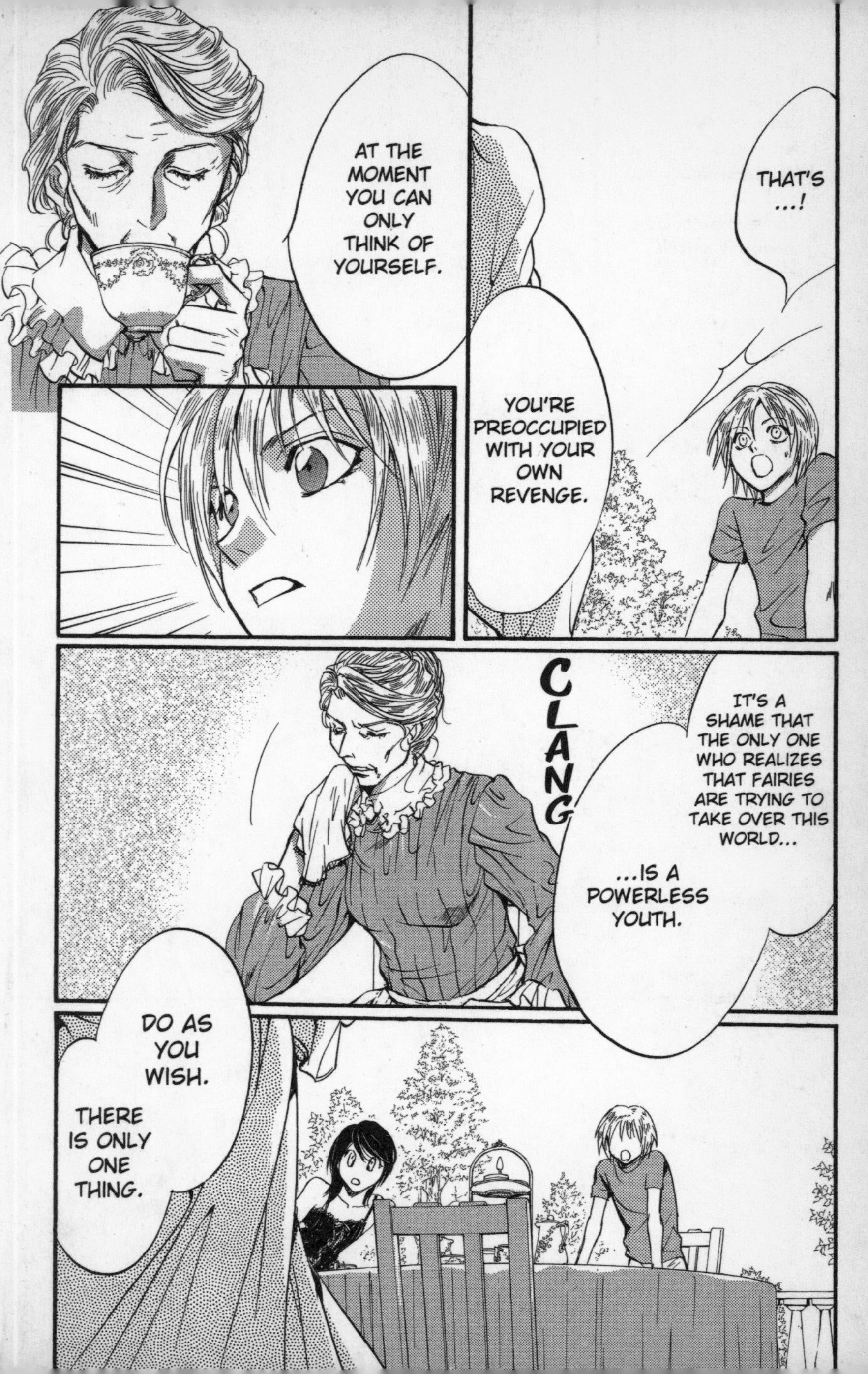
THAT'S ...!
YOU'RE PREOCCUPIED WITH YOUR OWN REVENGE.
AT THE MOMENT YOU CAN ONLY THINK OF YOURSELF.
CLANG
IT'S A SHAME THAT THE ONLY ONE WHO REALIZES THAT FAIRIES ARE TRYING TO TAKE OVER THIS WORLD...
...IS A POWERLESS YOUTH.
DO AS YOU WISH.
THERE IS ONLY ONE THING.

Volume two; halfway through! —— . ...

It's short, but I won't slack off.

I had so much fun drawing the characters, with serious faces, in chibi style, etc.♡ I can't stop talking about them.

I took some time off recently because my 21-month-old had a fever. We had to take him to the hospital--he was so sick! It was really stressful! Well, I hope you'll keep reading.

I may be sleep deprived, but I'm working really hard!♥♥

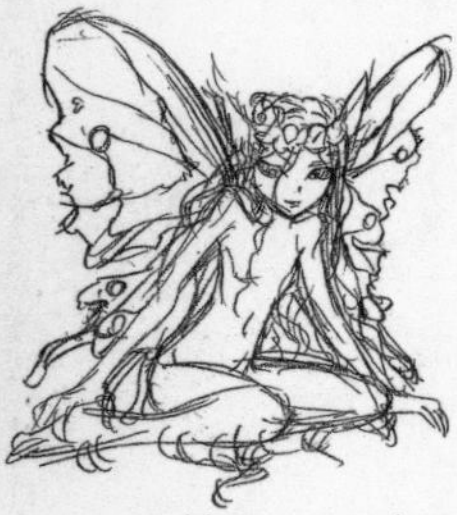

Victory with Torn Wings—

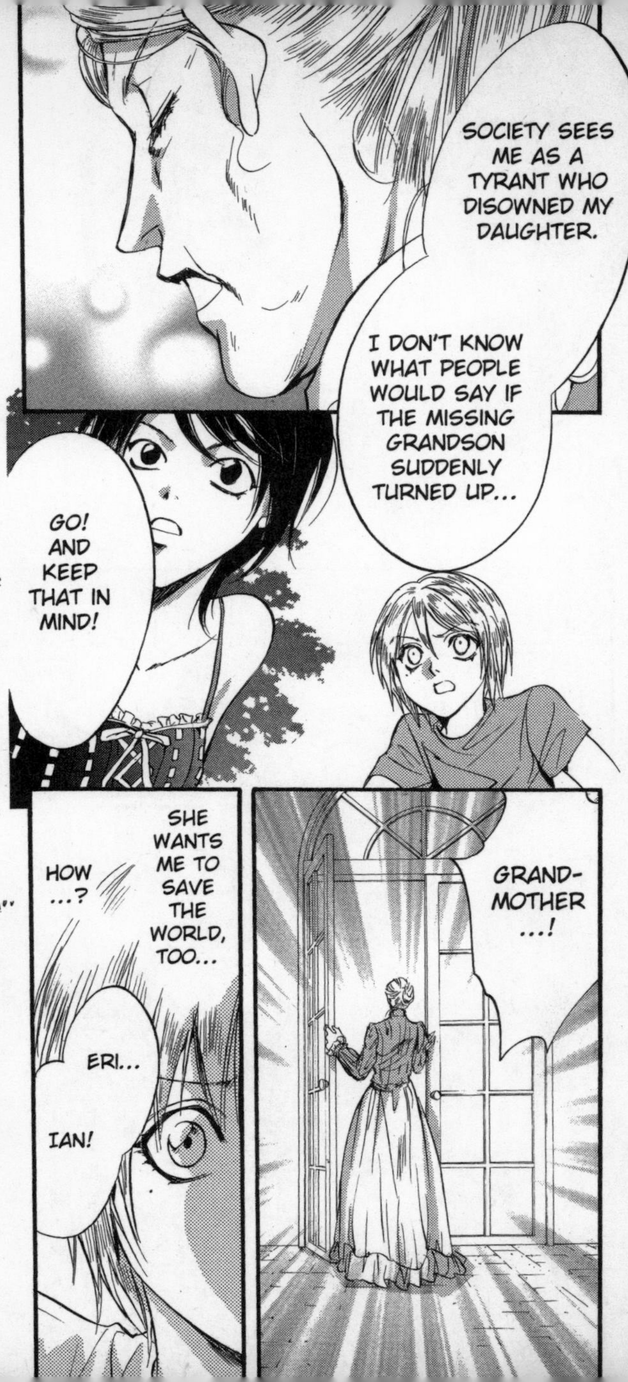
SOCIETY SEES ME AS A TYRANT WHO DISOWNED MY DAUGHTER.
I DON'T KNOW WHAT PEOPLE WOULD SAY IF THE MISSING GRANDSON SUDDENLY TURNED UP...
GO! AND KEEP THAT IN MIND!
GRAND-MOTHER ...!
SHE WANTS ME TO SAVE THE WORLD, TOO...
HOW ...?
ERI...
IAN!

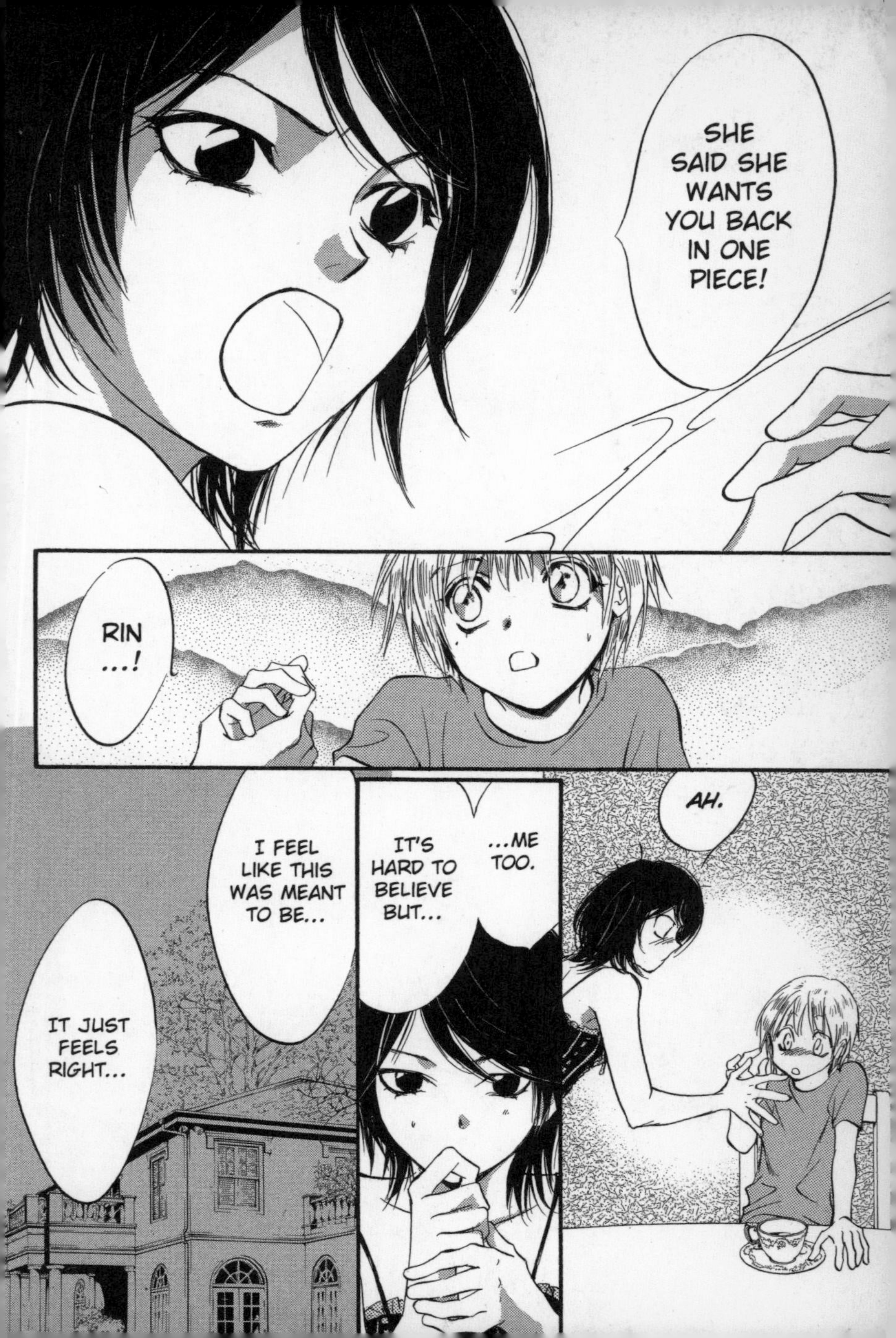
SHE SAID SHE WANTS YOU BACK IN ONE PIECE!
RIN ...!
AH.
...ME TOO.
IT'S HARD TO BELIEVE BUT...
I FEEL LIKE THIS WAS MEANT TO BE...
IT JUST FEELS RIGHT...

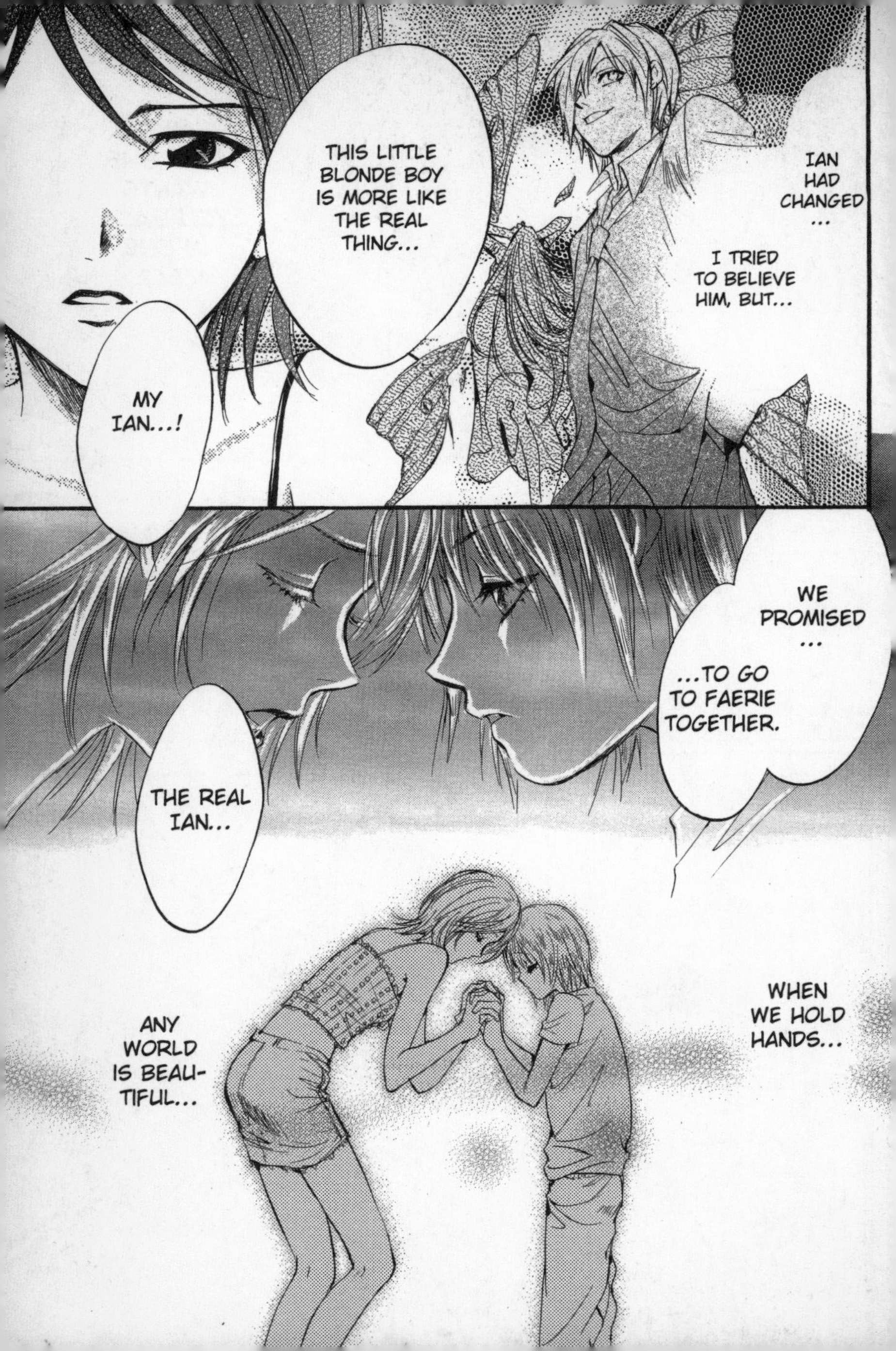
IAN HAD CHANGED...
I TRIED TO BELIEVE HIM, BUT...
THIS LITTLE BLONDE BOY IS MORE LIKE THE REAL THING...
MY IAN...!
WE PROMISED...
...TO GO TO FAERIE TOGETHER.
THE REAL IAN...
WHEN WE HOLD HANDS...
ANY WORLD IS BEAU- TIFUL...

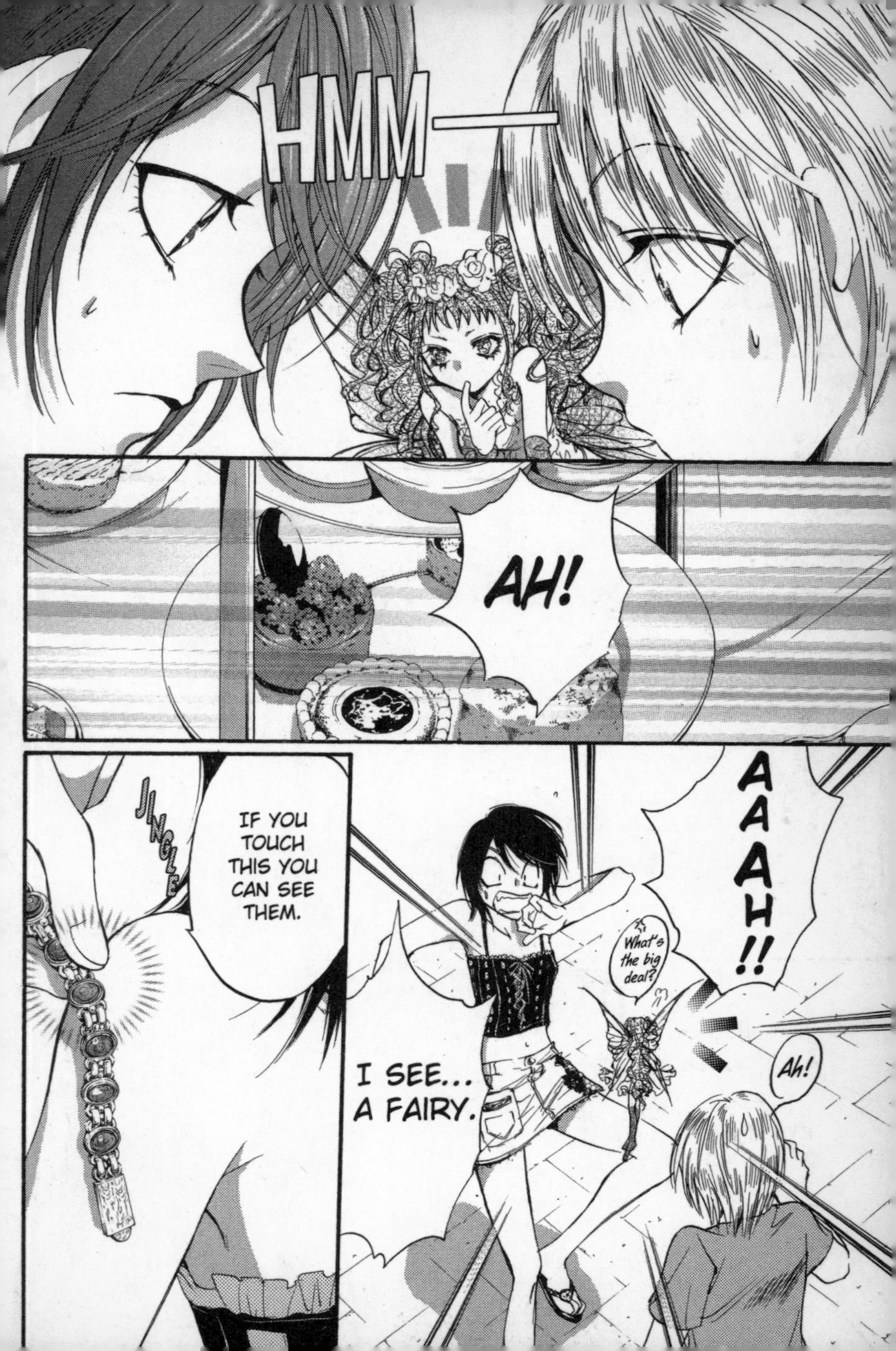
HMM—
AH!
AAAAH!!
What's the big deal?
Ah!
I SEE... A FAIRY.
JINGLE
IF YOU TOUCH THIS YOU CAN SEE THEM.

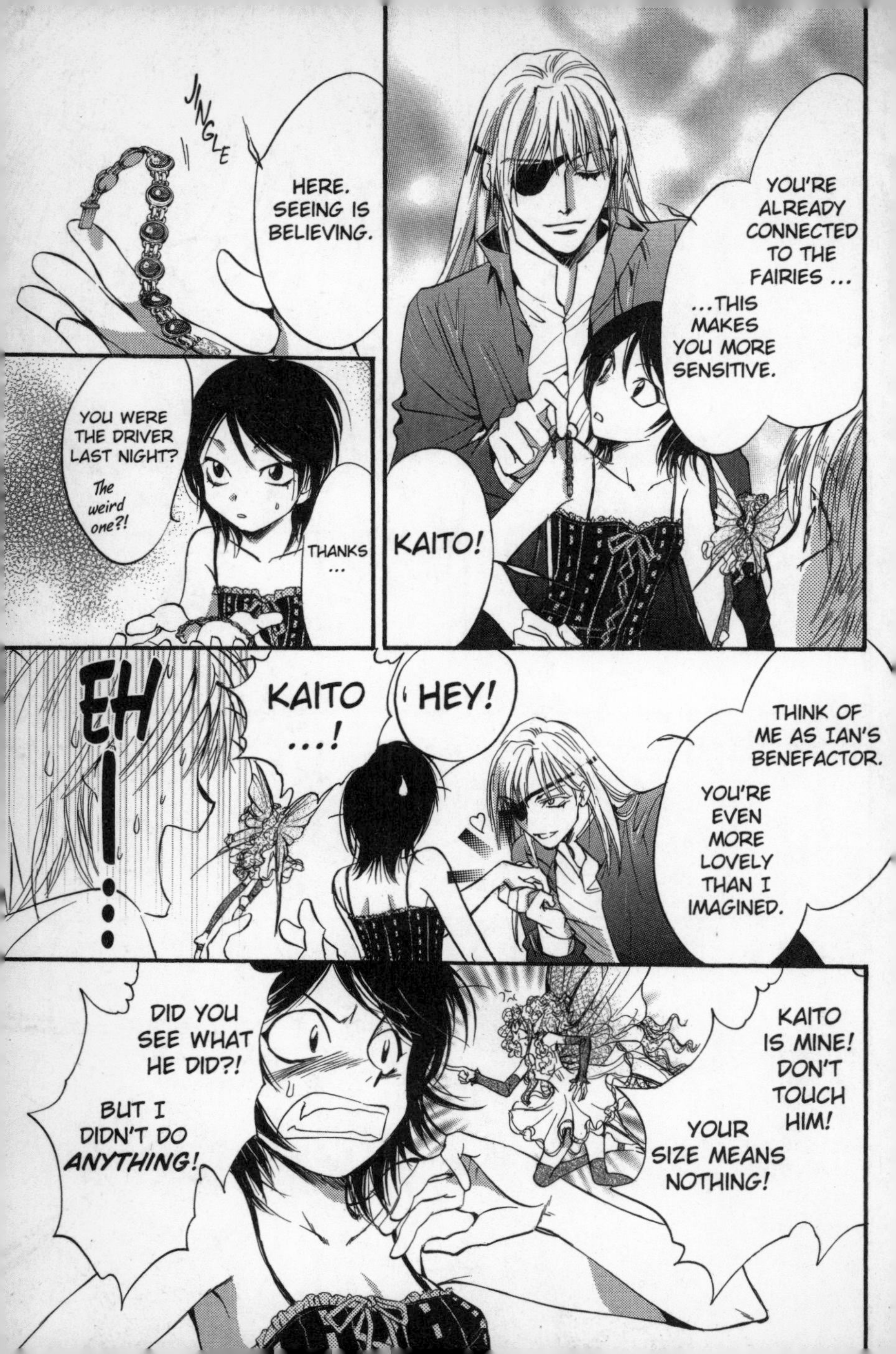
YOU'RE ALREADY CONNECTED TO THE FAIRIES ...
...THIS MAKES YOU MORE SENSITIVE.
KAITO!
HERE. SEEING IS BELIEVING.
JINGLE
YOU WERE THE DRIVER LAST NIGHT?
The weird one?!
THANKS ...
THINK OF ME AS IAN'S BENEFACTOR.
YOU'RE EVEN MORE LOVELY THAN I IMAGINED.
HEY!
KAITO ...!
EH!...
KAITO IS MINE! DON'T TOUCH HIM!
YOUR SIZE MEANS NOTHING!
DID YOU SEE WHAT HE DID?!
BUT I DIDN'T DO *ANYTHING*!

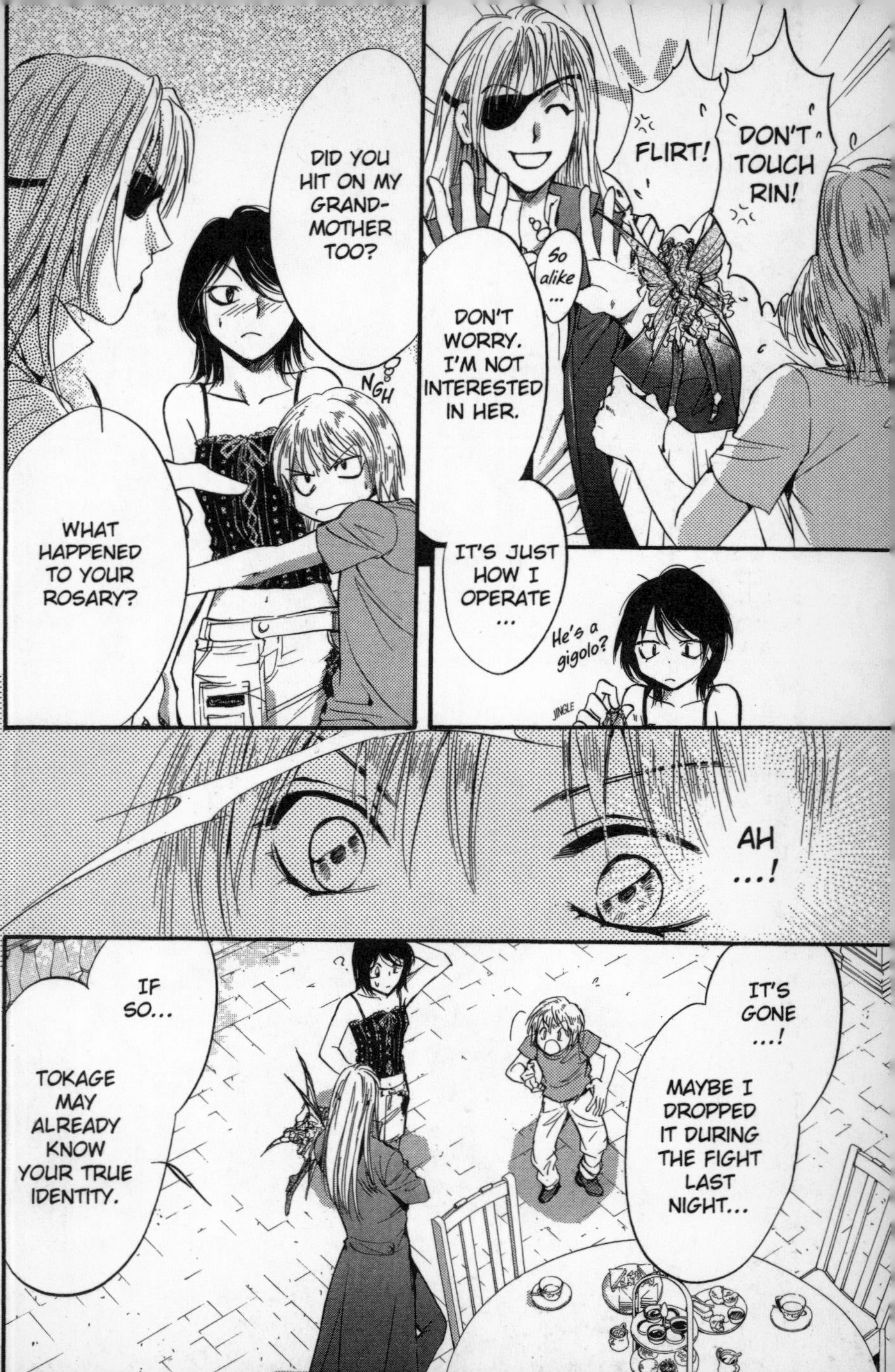
DON'T TOUCH RIN!
FLIRT!
So alike...
DON'T WORRY. I'M NOT INTERESTED IN HER.
IT'S JUST HOW I OPERATE...
He's a gigolo?
JINGLE
DID YOU HIT ON MY GRANDMOTHER TOO?
NGH
WHAT HAPPENED TO YOUR ROSARY?
AH...!
IT'S GONE...!
MAYBE I DROPPED IT DURING THE FIGHT LAST NIGHT...
IF SO...
TOKAGE MAY ALREADY KNOW YOUR TRUE IDENTITY.

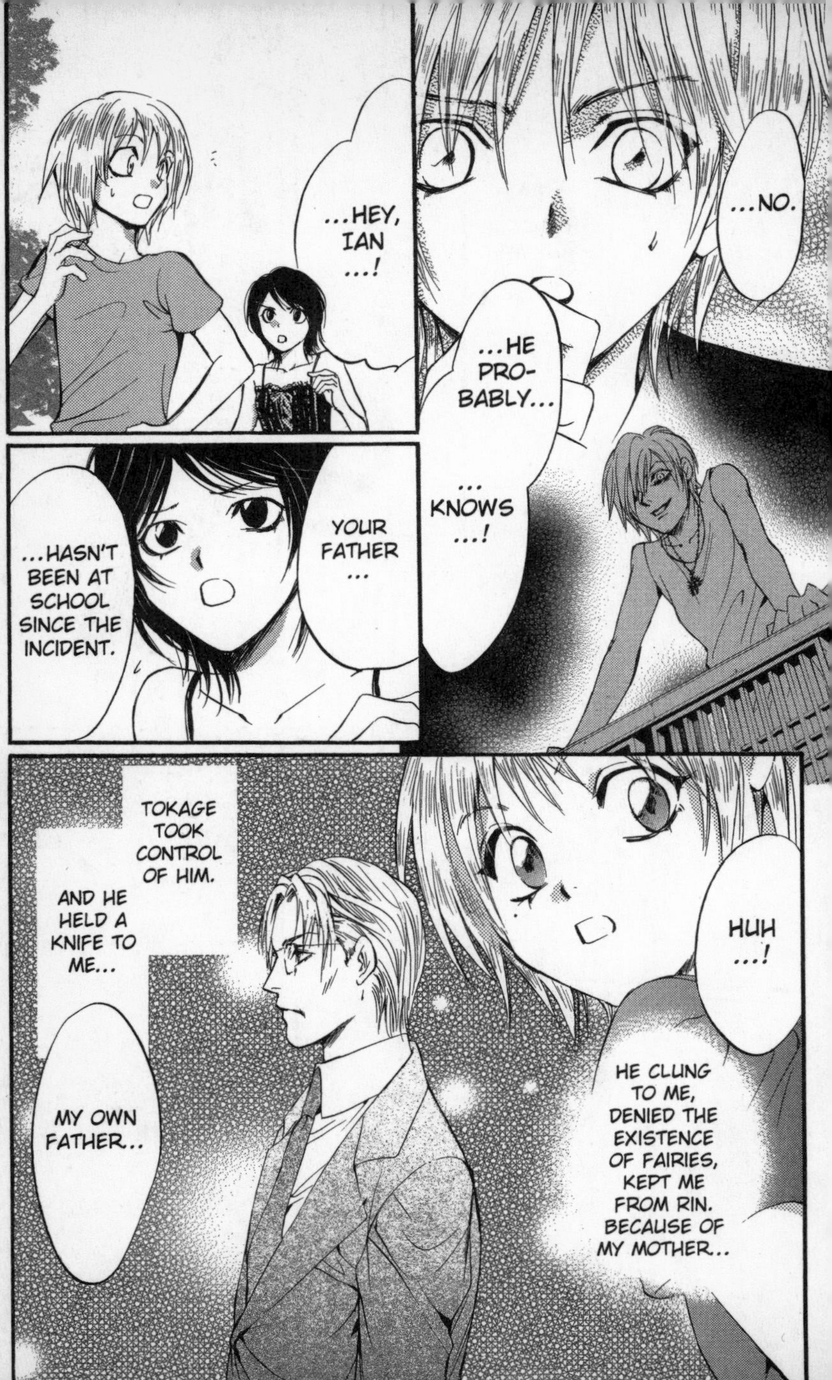
...NO.
...HE PRO-BABLY...
...KNOWS...!
...HEY, IAN...!
YOUR FATHER...
...HASN'T BEEN AT SCHOOL SINCE THE INCIDENT.
HUH...!
TOKAGE TOOK CONTROL OF HIM.
AND HE HELD A KNIFE TO ME...
HE CLUNG TO ME, DENIED THE EXISTENCE OF FAIRIES, KEPT ME FROM RIN. BECAUSE OF MY MOTHER..
MY OWN FATHER..

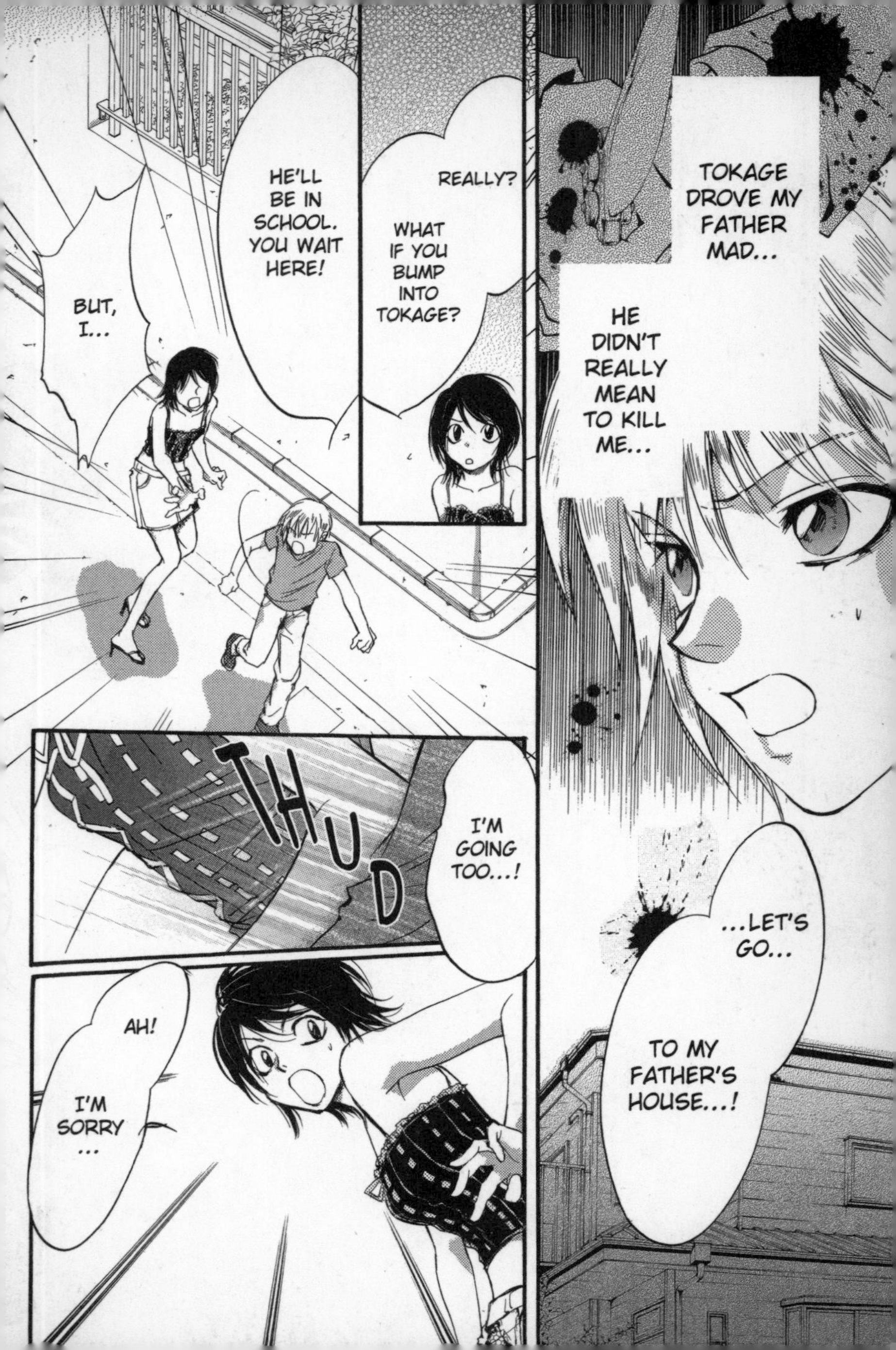
TOKAGE DROVE MY FATHER MAD...
HE DIDN'T REALLY MEAN TO KILL ME...
...LET'S GO...
TO MY FATHER'S HOUSE...!
REALLY?
WHAT IF YOU BUMP INTO TOKAGE?
HE'LL BE IN SCHOOL. YOU WAIT HERE!
BUT, I...
I'M GOING TOO...!
THUD
AH!
I'M SORRY ...

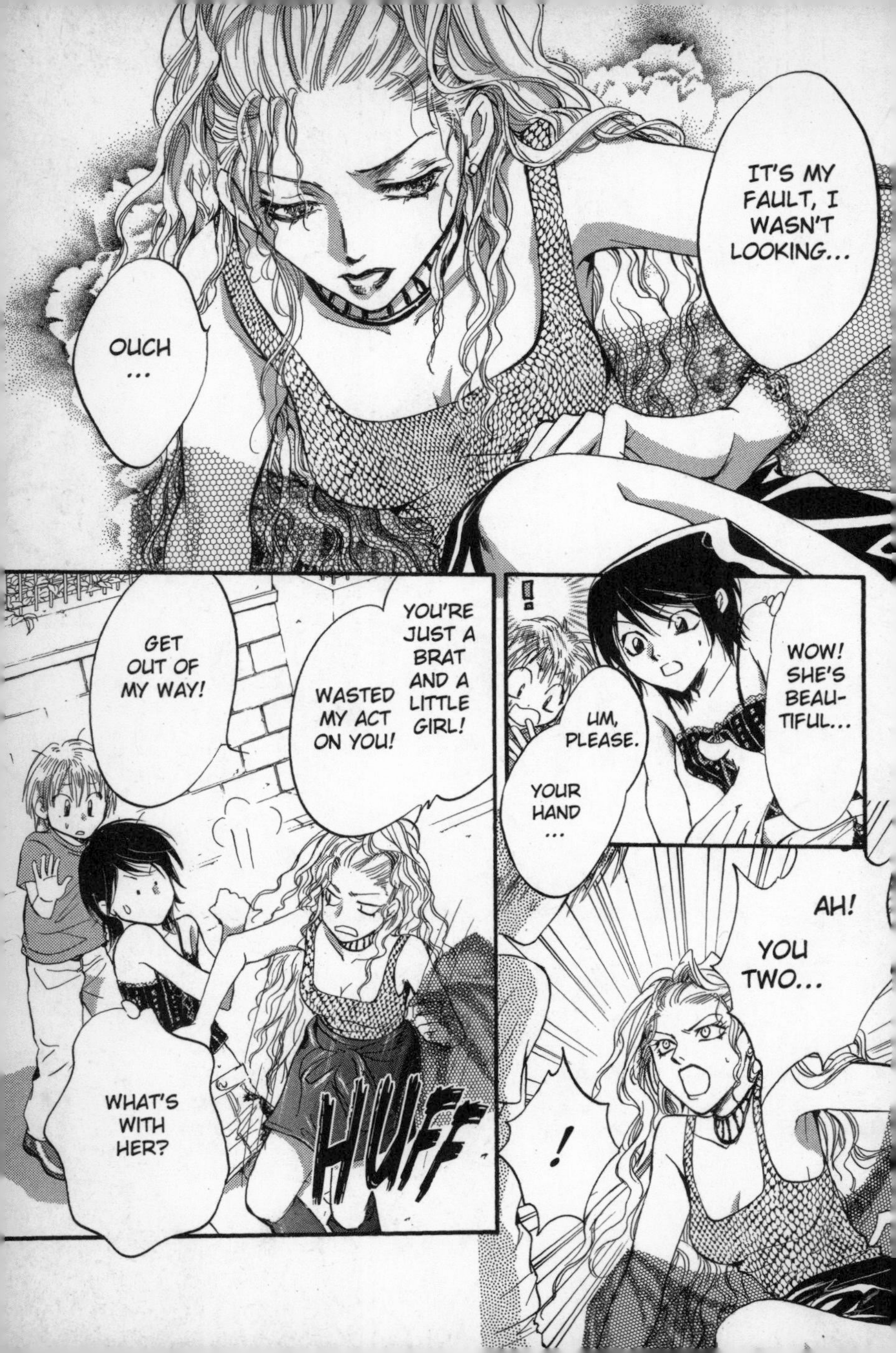
IT'S MY FAULT, I WASN'T LOOKING...
OUCH ...
WOW! SHE'S BEAU-TIFUL...
UM, PLEASE.
YOUR HAND ...
AH!
YOU TWO...
!
YOU'RE JUST A BRAT AND A LITTLE GIRL!
WASTED MY ACT ON YOU!
GET OUT OF MY WAY!
HUFF
WHAT'S WITH HER?

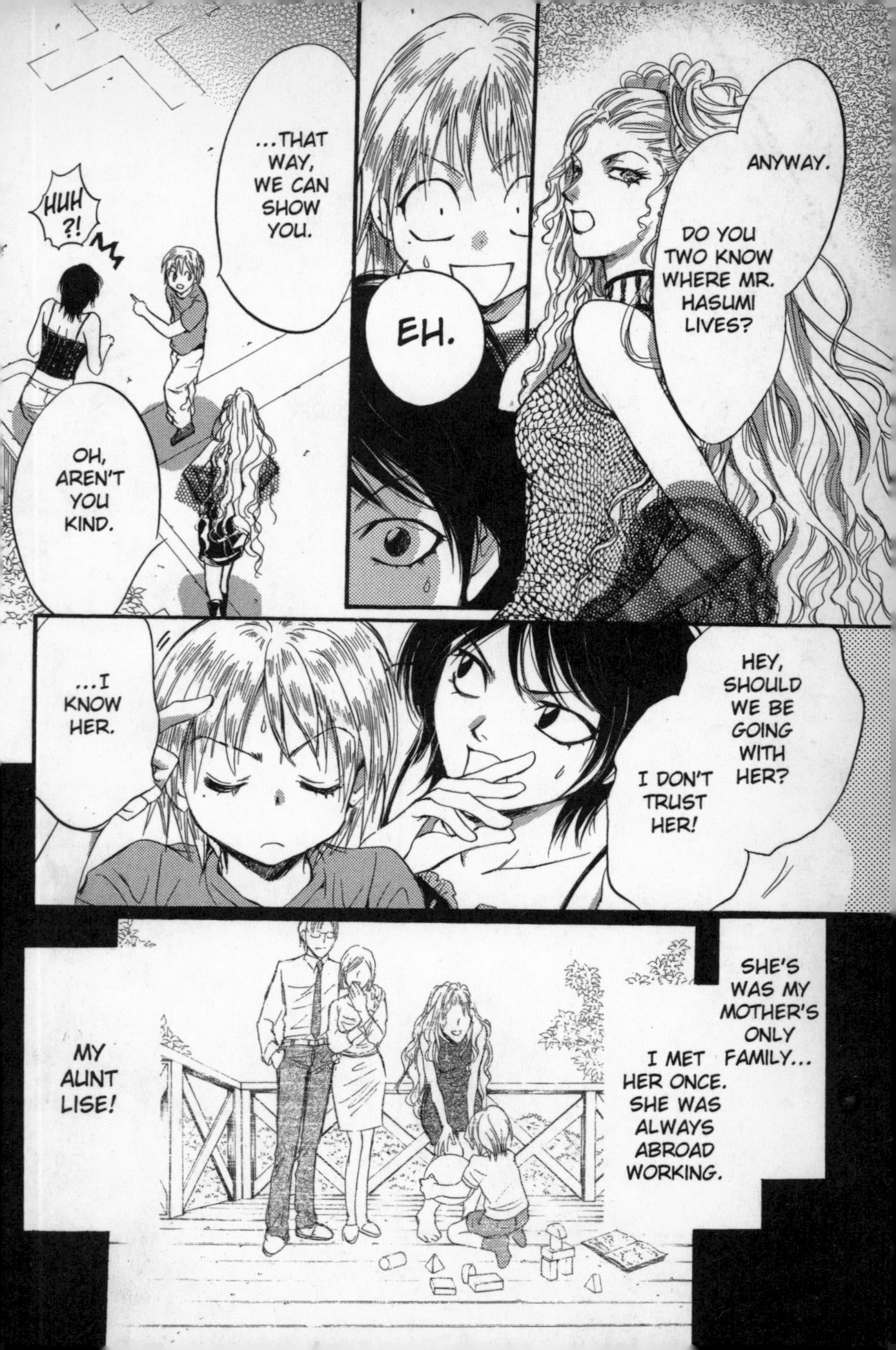
ANYWAY.
DO YOU TWO KNOW WHERE MR. HASUMI LIVES?
EH.
...THAT WAY, WE CAN SHOW YOU.
HUH ?!
OH, AREN'T YOU KIND.
HEY, SHOULD WE BE GOING WITH HER?
I DON'T TRUST HER!
...I KNOW HER.
SHE'S WAS MY MOTHER'S ONLY FAMILY...
I MET HER ONCE. SHE WAS ALWAYS ABROAD WORKING.
MY AUNT LISE!

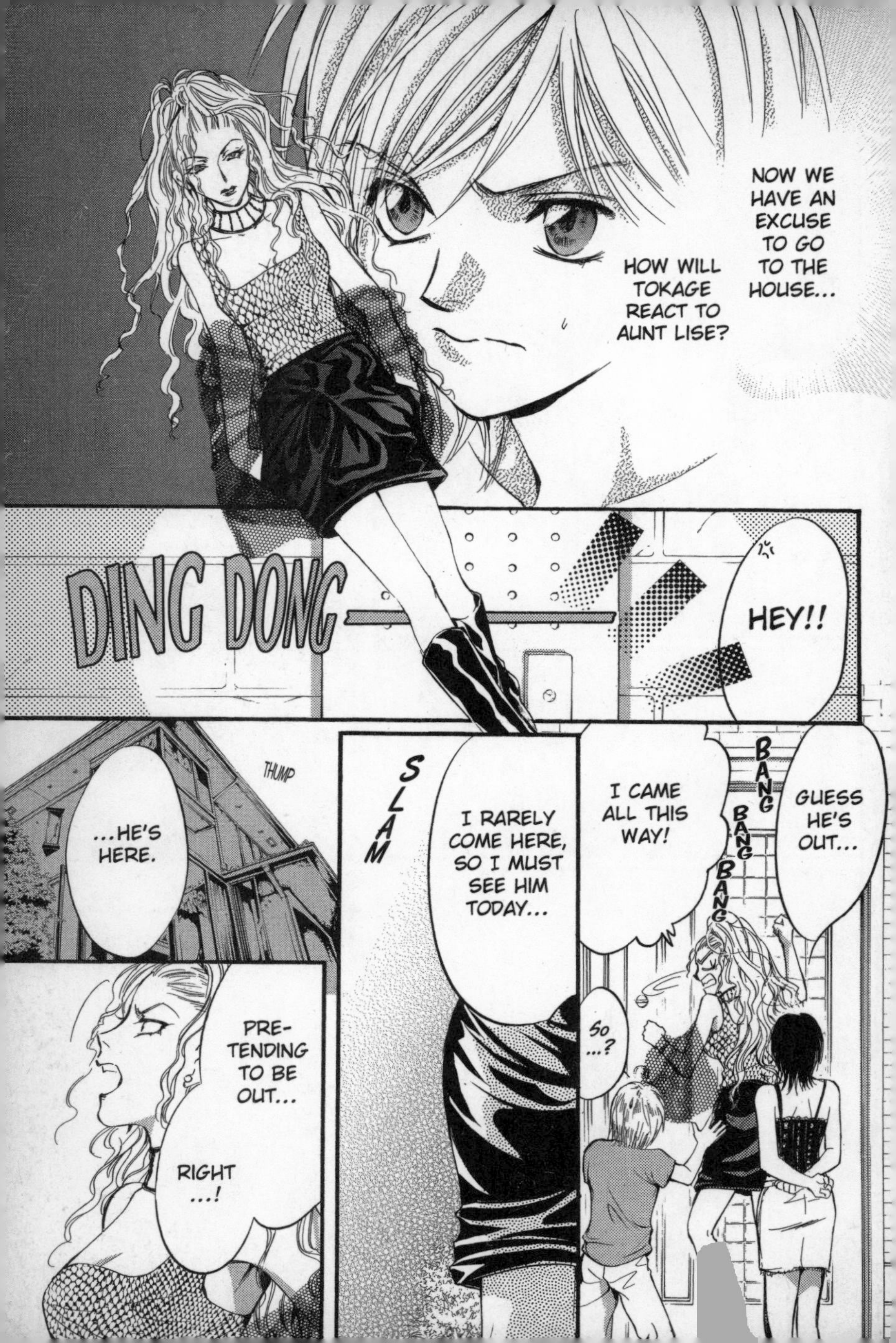
NOW WE HAVE AN EXCUSE TO GO TO THE HOUSE...
HOW WILL TOKAGE REACT TO AUNT LISE?
HEY!!
DING DONG
GUESS HE'S OUT...
BANG BANG BANG
I CAME ALL THIS WAY!
So ...?
SLAM
I RARELY COME HERE, SO I MUST SEE HIM TODAY...
THUMP
...HE'S HERE.
PRE-TENDING TO BE OUT...
RIGHT ...!

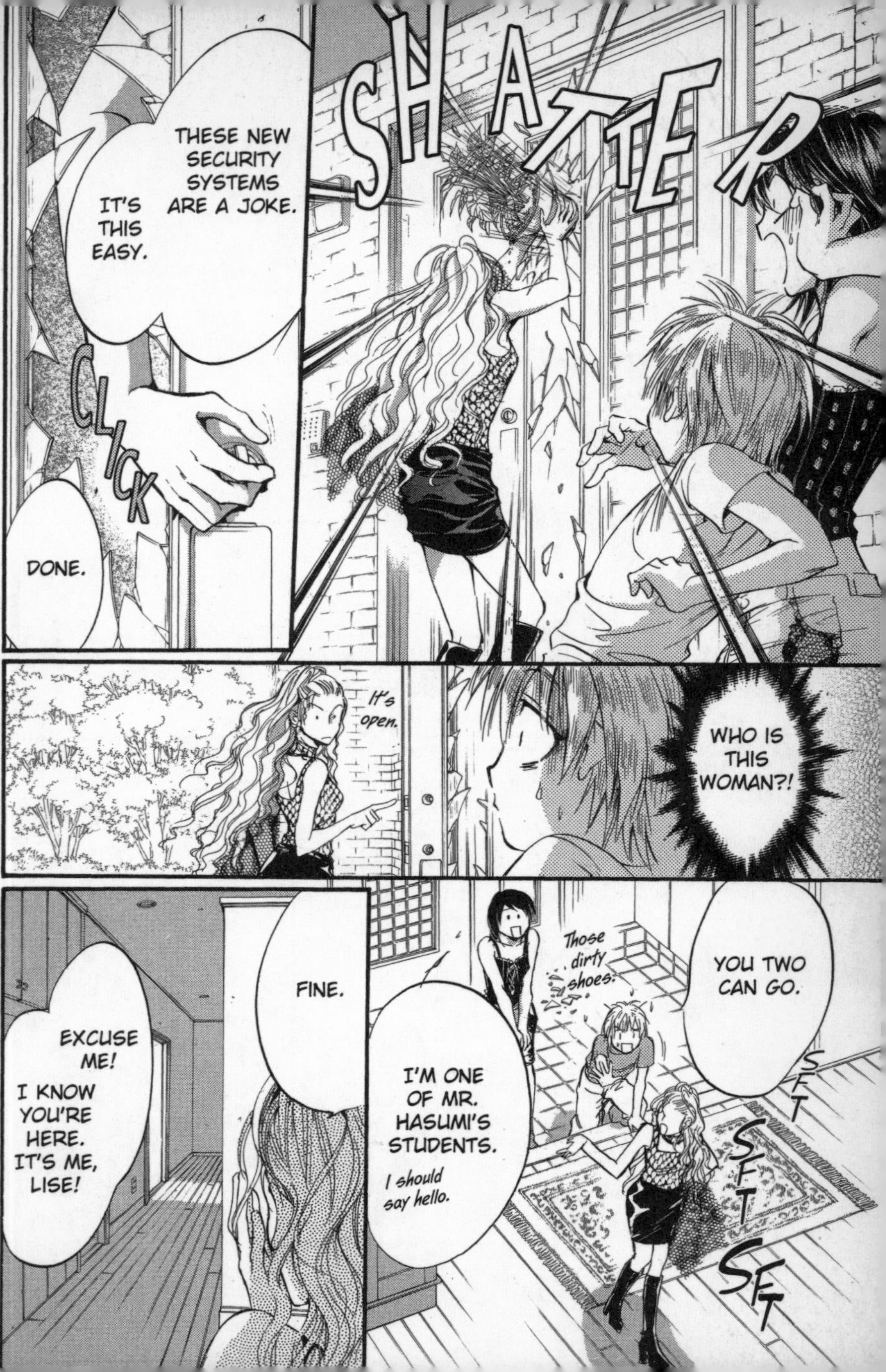
SHATTER
THESE NEW SECURITY SYSTEMS ARE A JOKE.
IT'S THIS EASY.
CLICK
DONE.
WHO IS THIS WOMAN?!
It's open.
YOU TWO CAN GO.
SFT SFT SFT SFT
Those dirty shoes.
FINE.
I'M ONE OF MR. HASUMI'S STUDENTS.
I should say hello.
EXCUSE ME! I KNOW YOU'RE HERE. IT'S ME, LISE!

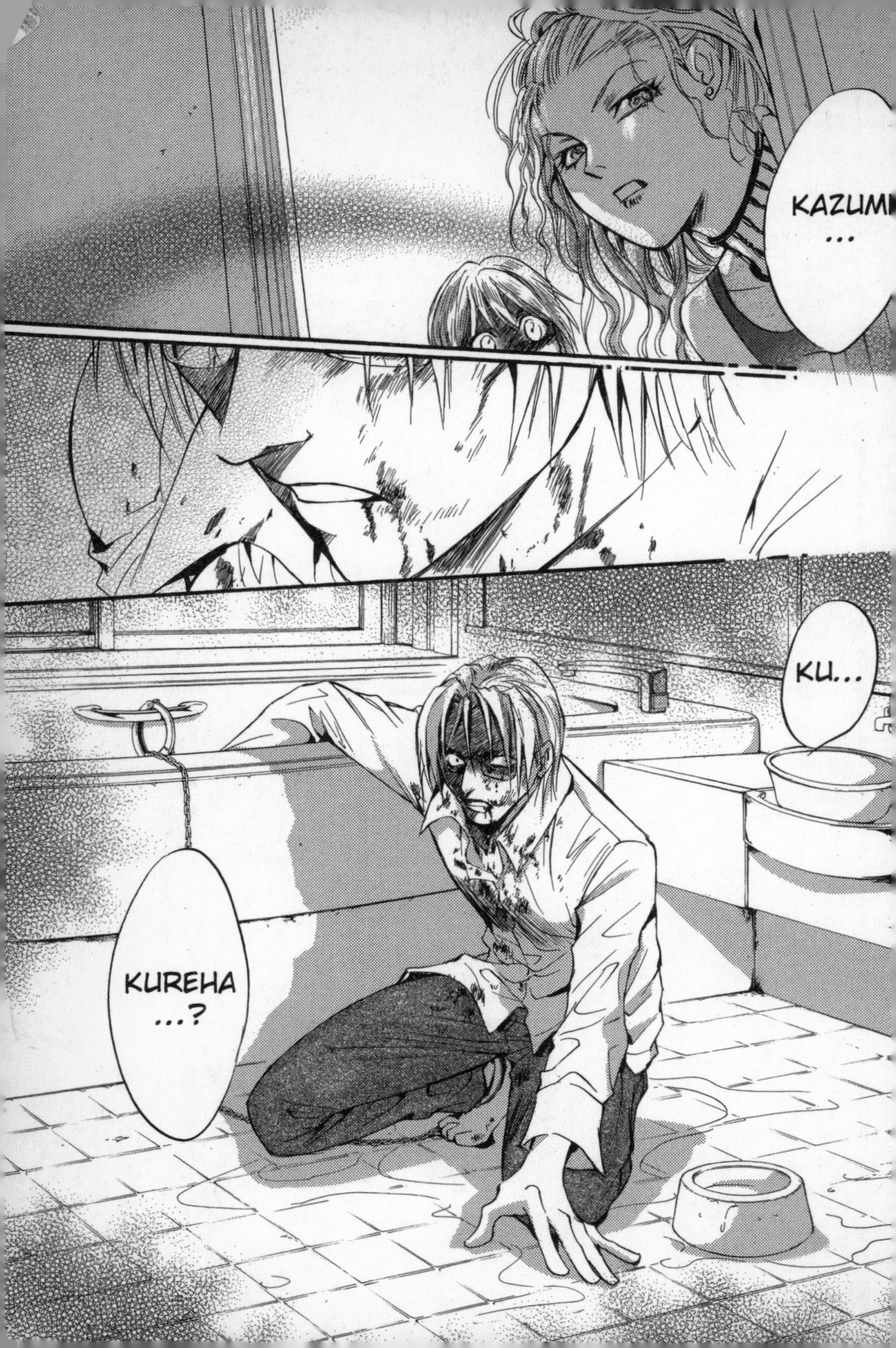
KAZUMI ...
KU...
KUREHA ...?

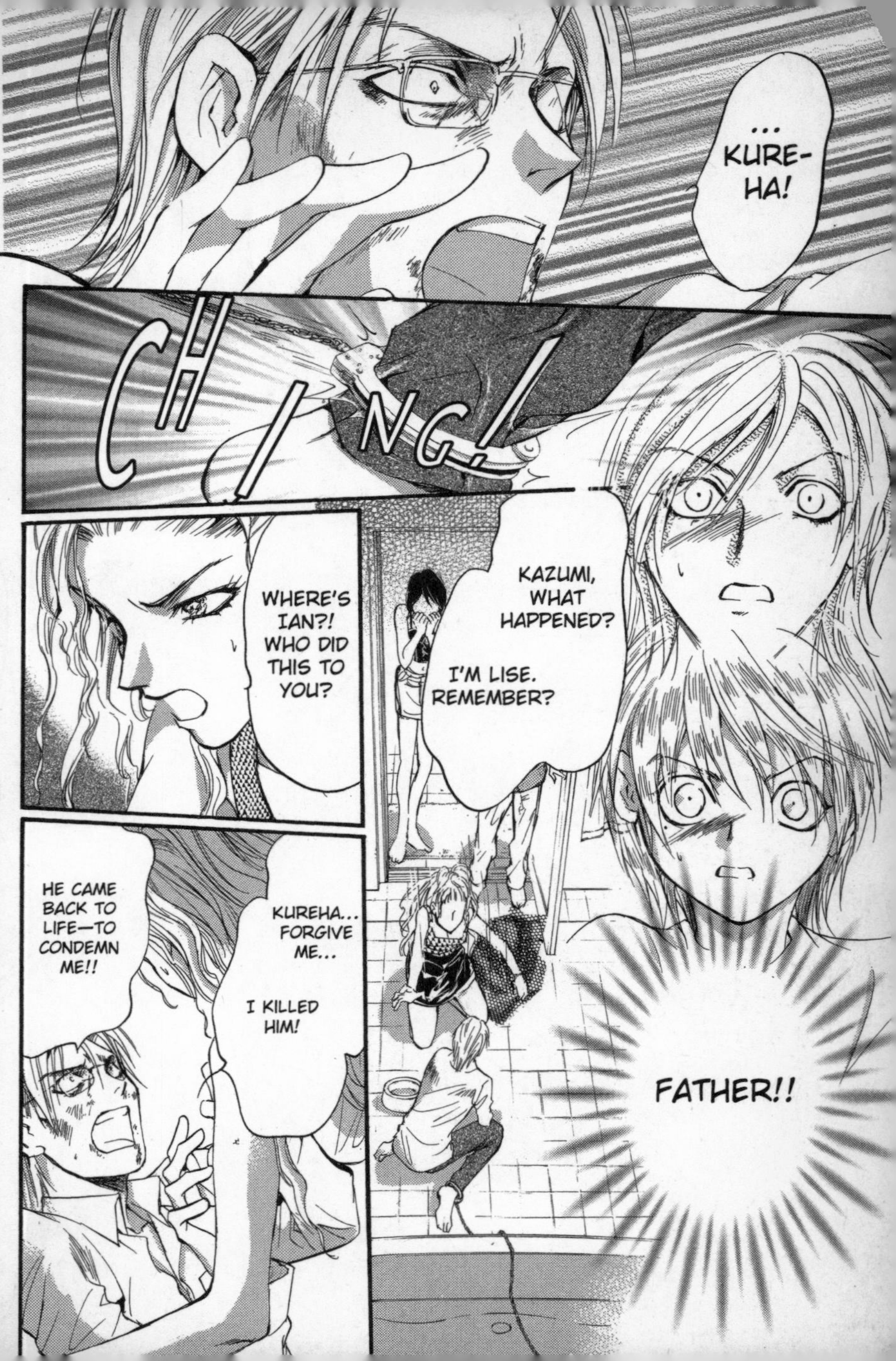
...KURE-HA!
CHING!
KAZUMI, WHAT HAPPENED?
I'M LISE. REMEMBER?
FATHER!!
WHERE'S IAN?! WHO DID THIS TO YOU?
KUREHA... FORGIVE ME...
I KILLED HIM!
HE CAME BACK TO LIFE—TO CONDEMN ME!!

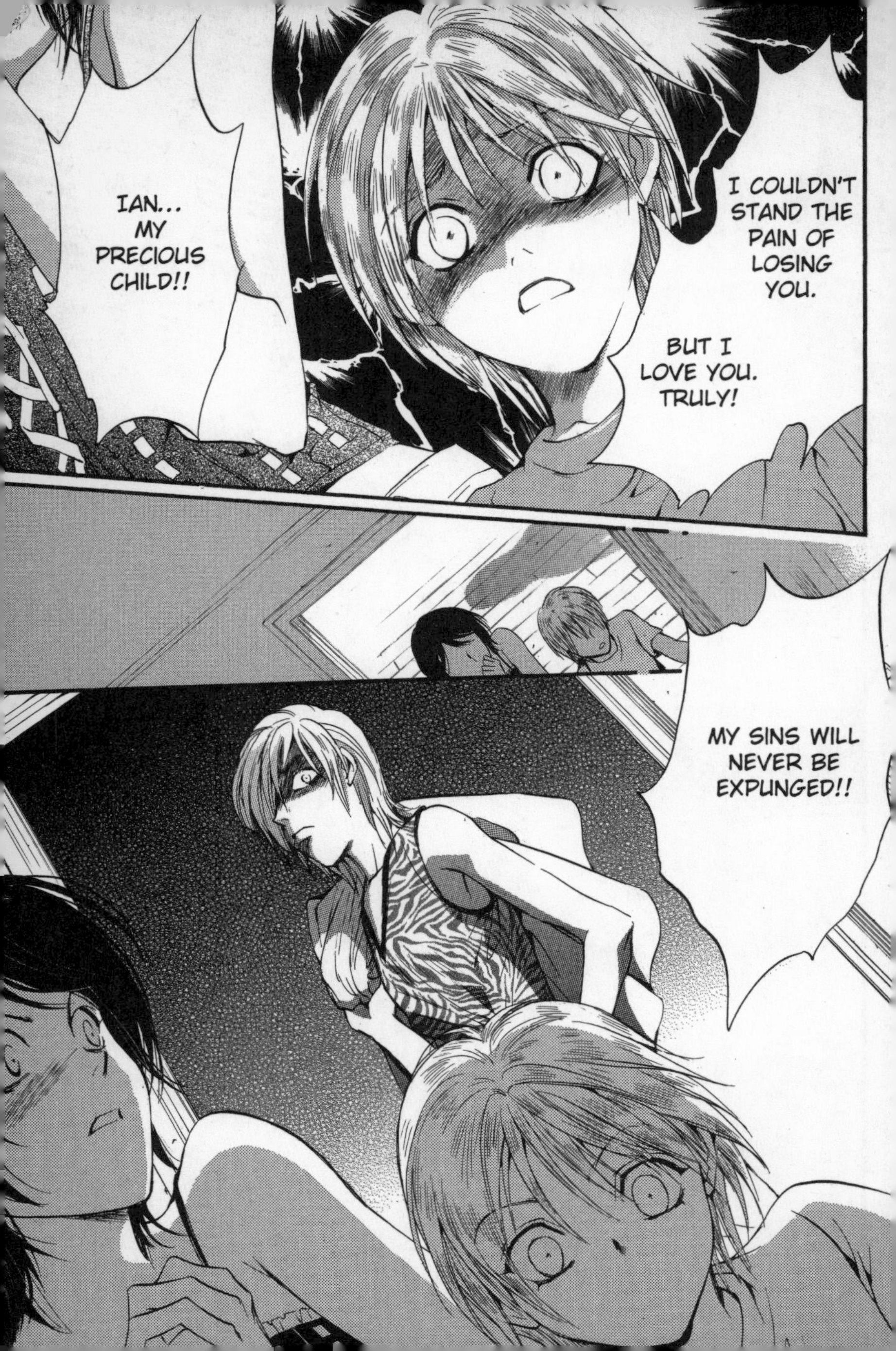
I COULDN'T STAND THE PAIN OF LOSING YOU.
BUT I LOVE YOU. TRULY!
IAN... MY PRECIOUS CHILD!!
MY SINS WILL NEVER BE EXPUNGED!!

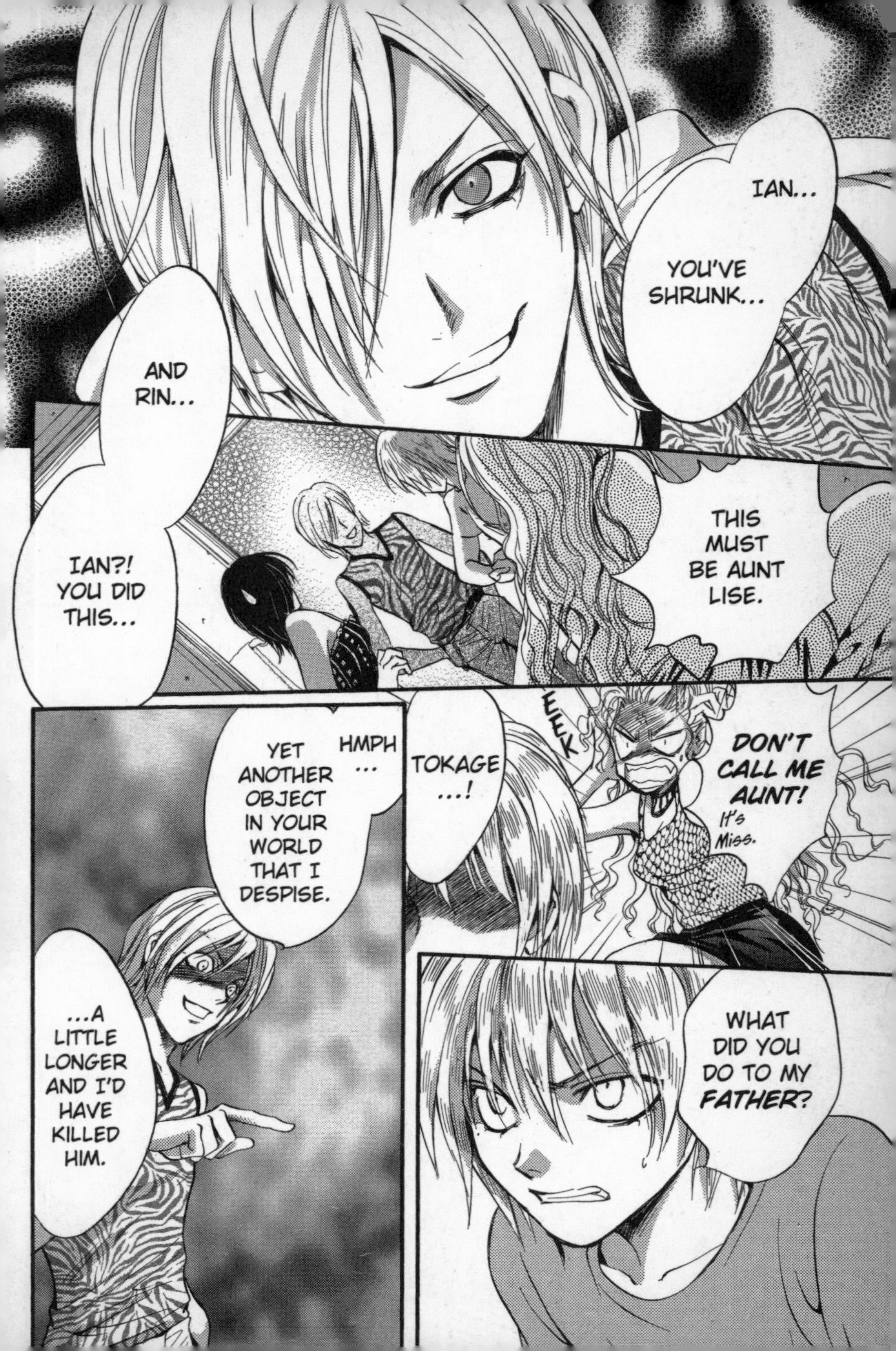
IAN...
YOU'VE SHRUNK...
AND RIN...
THIS MUST BE AUNT LISE.
IAN?! YOU DID THIS...
EEEK
DON'T CALL ME AUNT!
It's Miss.
TOKAGE...!
WHAT DID YOU DO TO MY FATHER?
HMPH...
YET ANOTHER OBJECT IN YOUR WORLD THAT I DESPISE.
...A LITTLE LONGER AND I'D HAVE KILLED HIM.

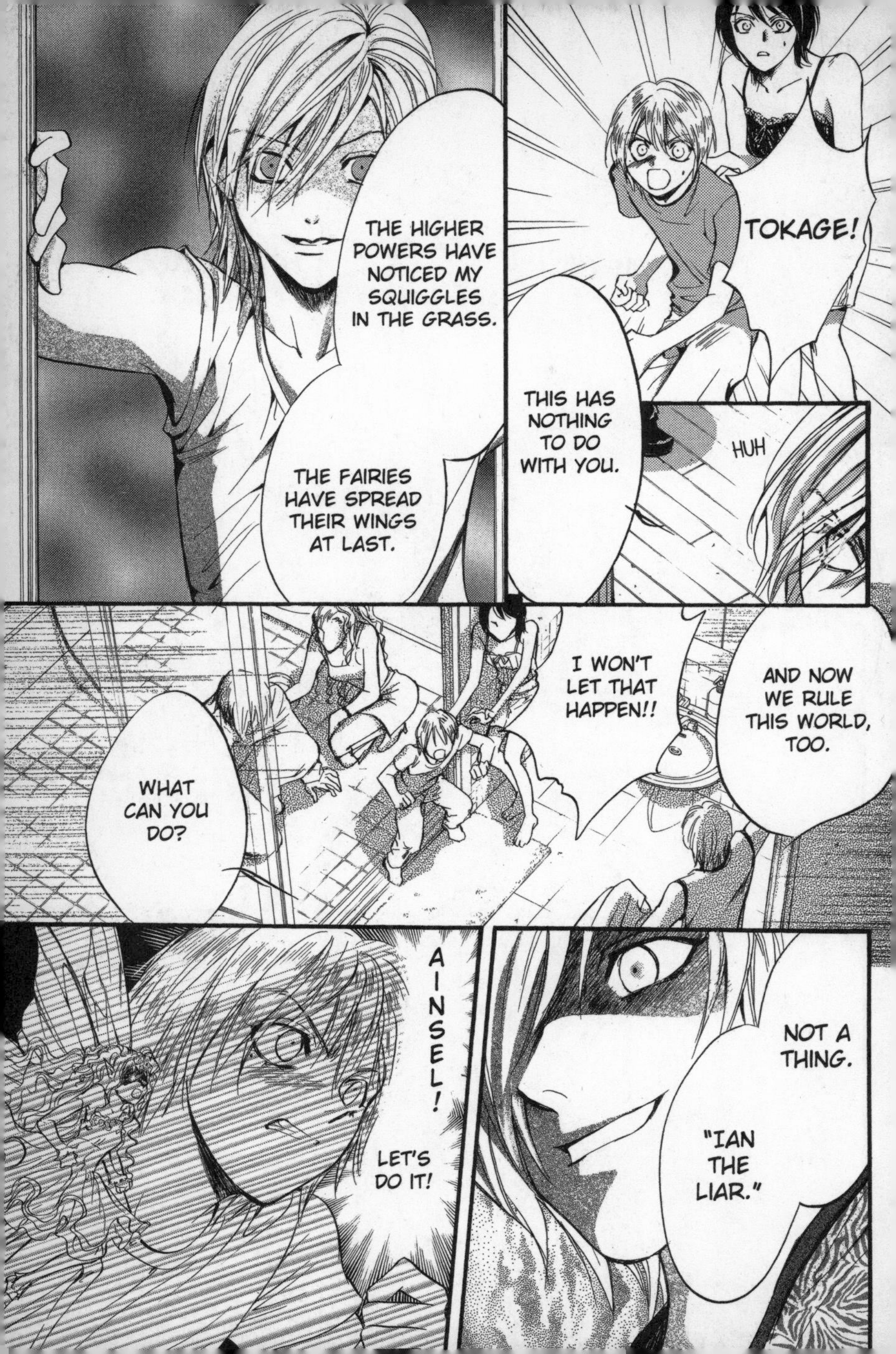
TOKAGE!
THIS HAS NOTHING TO DO WITH YOU.
HUH
THE HIGHER POWERS HAVE NOTICED MY SQUIGGLES IN THE GRASS.
THE FAIRIES HAVE SPREAD THEIR WINGS AT LAST.
AND NOW WE RULE THIS WORLD, TOO.
I WON'T LET THAT HAPPEN!!
WHAT CAN YOU DO?
NOT A THING.
"IAN THE LIAR."
AINSEL!
LET'S DO IT!

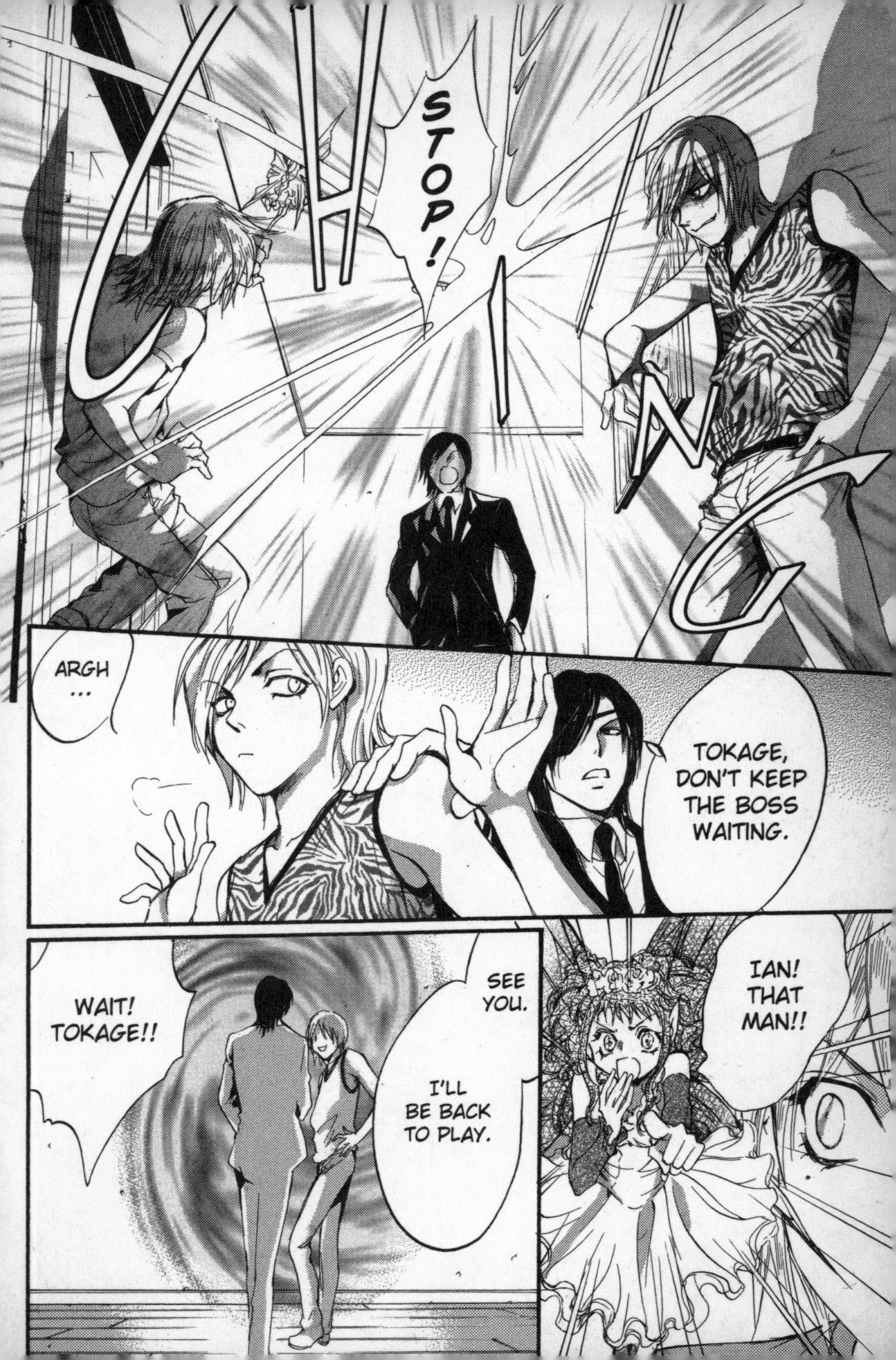
STOP!
CHING
TOKAGE, DON'T KEEP THE BOSS WAITING.
ARGH ...
IAN! THAT MAN!!
SEE YOU.
I'LL BE BACK TO PLAY.
WAIT! TOKAGE!!

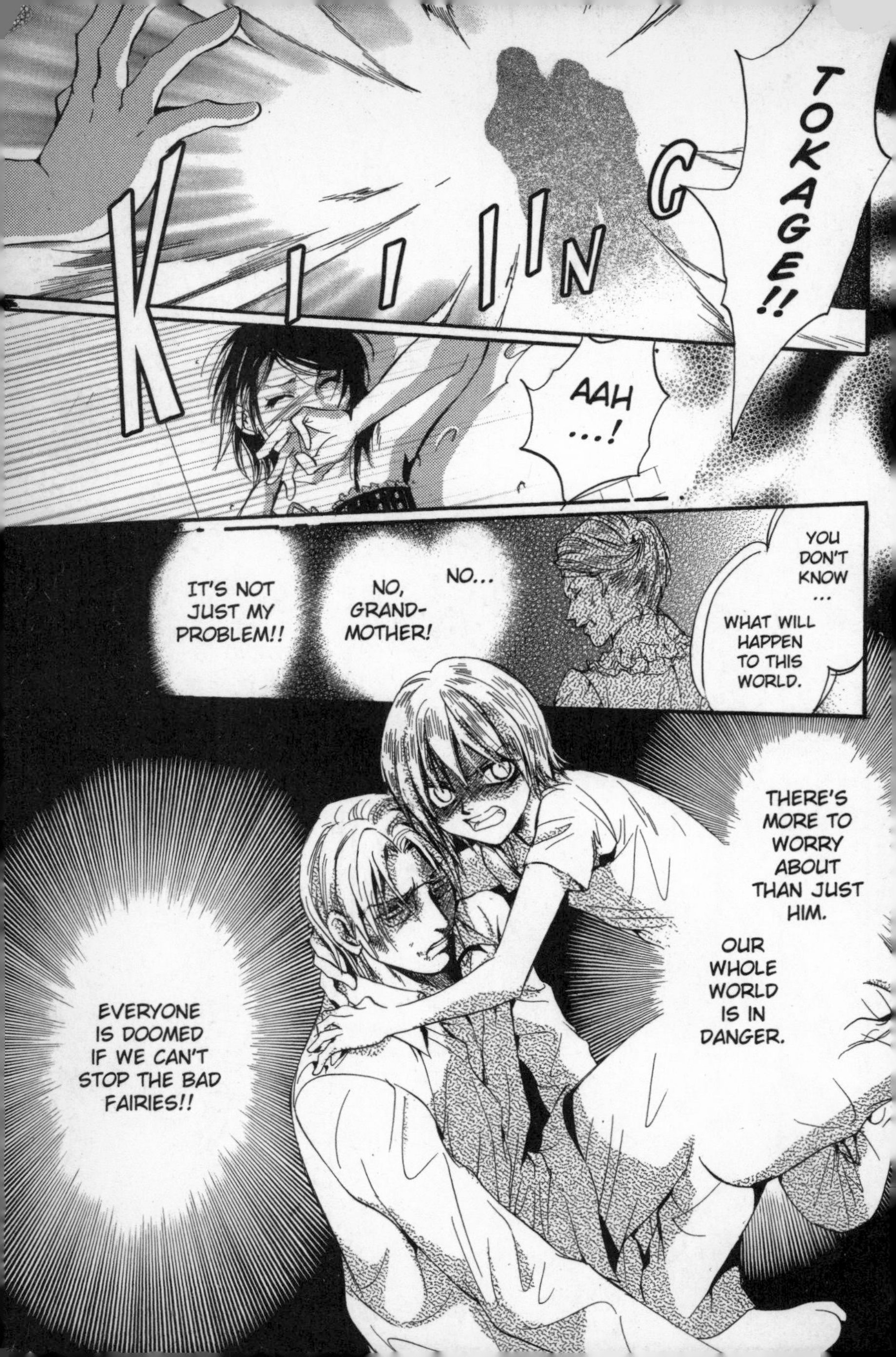
TOKAGE!!
KIIIING
AAH ...!
YOU DON'T KNOW ...
WHAT WILL HAPPEN TO THIS WORLD.
NO...
NO, GRAND-MOTHER!
IT'S NOT JUST MY PROBLEM!!
THERE'S MORE TO WORRY ABOUT THAN JUST HIM.
OUR WHOLE WORLD IS IN DANGER.
EVERYONE IS DOOMED IF WE CAN'T STOP THE BAD FAIRIES!!

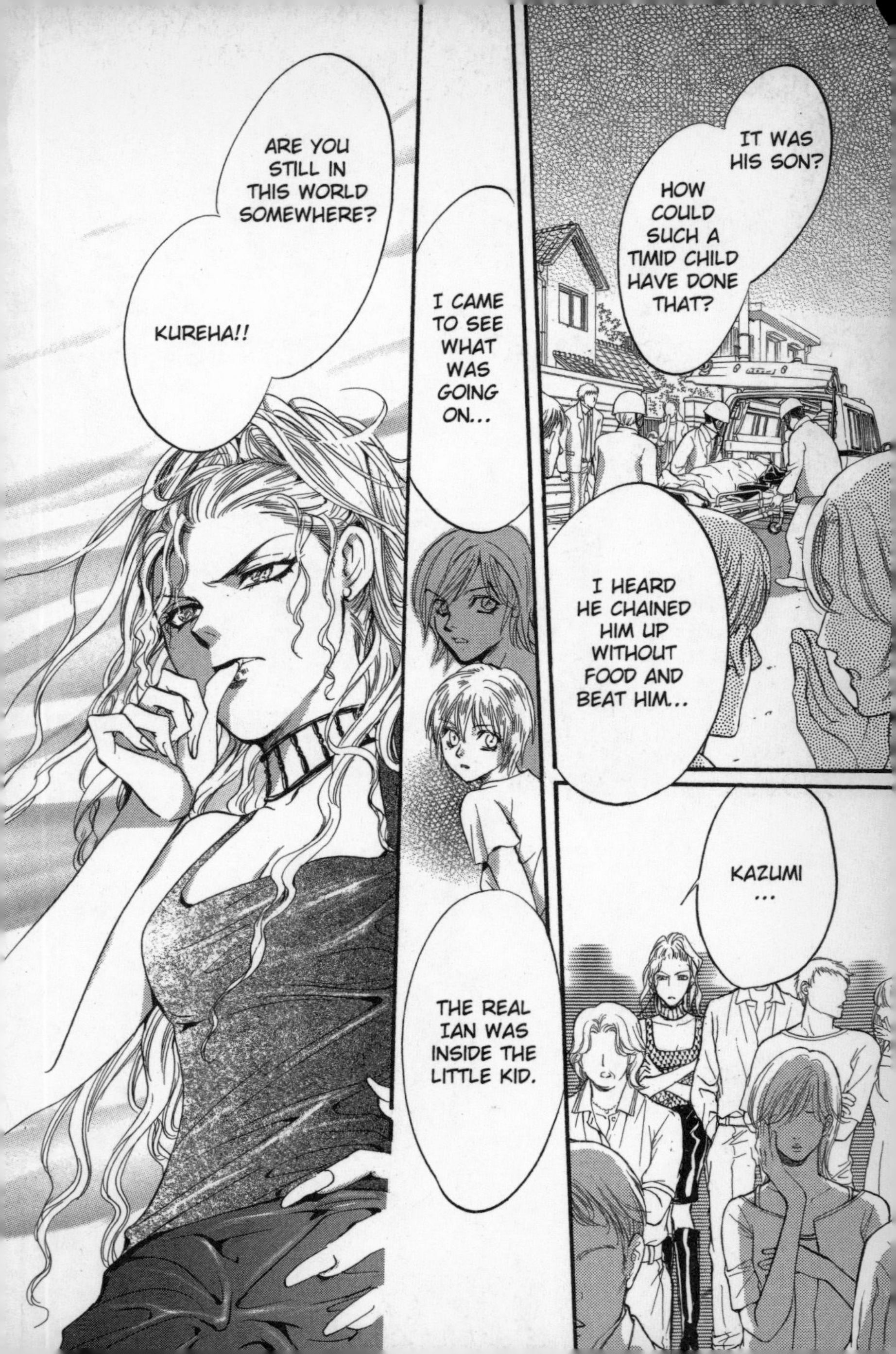
IT WAS HIS SON?
HOW COULD SUCH A TIMID CHILD HAVE DONE THAT?
I HEARD HE CHAINED HIM UP WITHOUT FOOD AND BEAT HIM...
KAZUMI ...
I CAME TO SEE WHAT WAS GOING ON...
THE REAL IAN WAS INSIDE THE LITTLE KID.
ARE YOU STILL IN THIS WORLD SOMEWHERE?
KUREHA!!

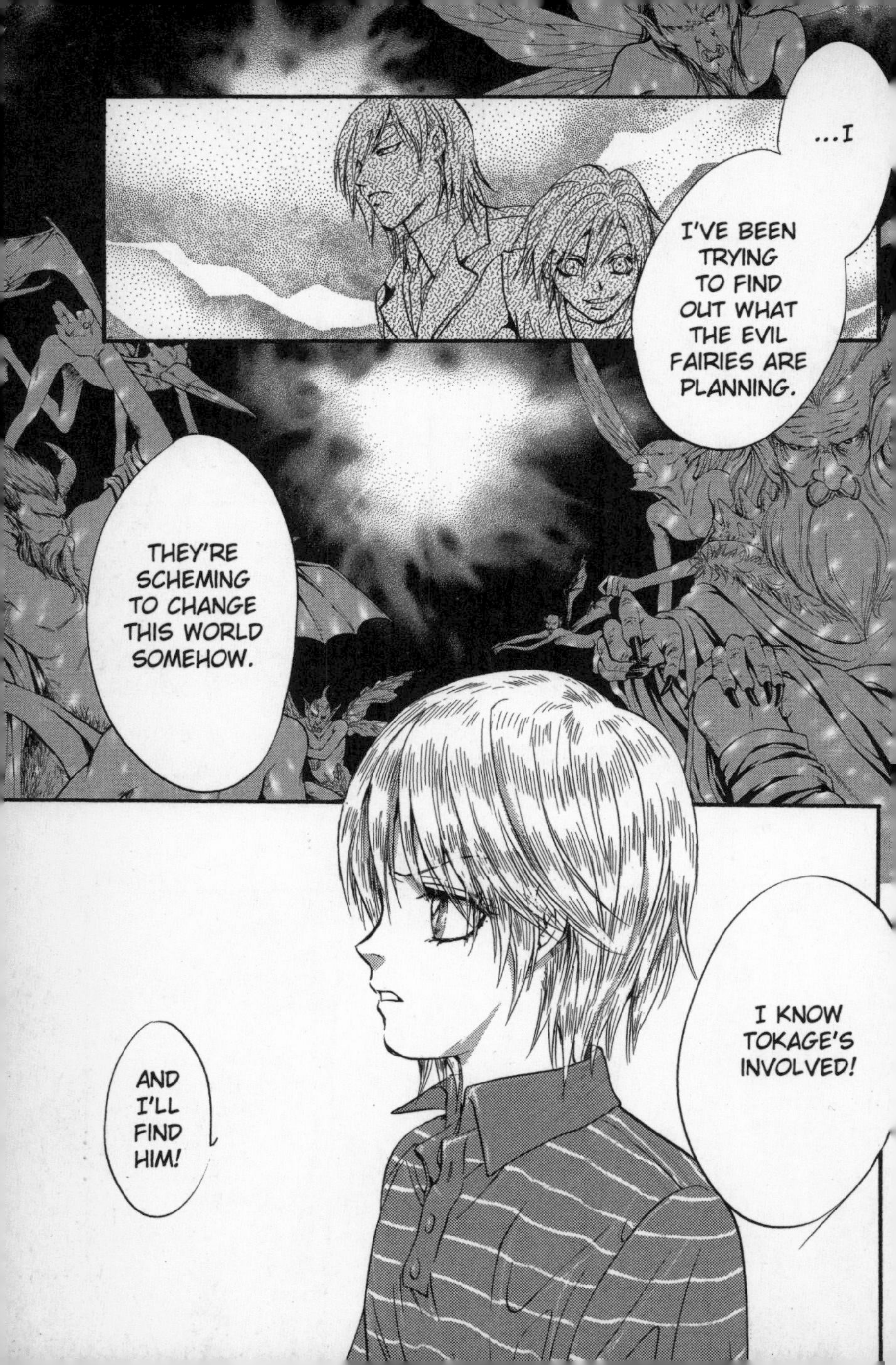
...I
I'VE BEEN TRYING TO FIND OUT WHAT THE EVIL FAIRIES ARE PLANNING.
THEY'RE SCHEMING TO CHANGE THIS WORLD SOMEHOW.
I KNOW TOKAGE'S INVOLVED!
AND I'LL FIND HIM!

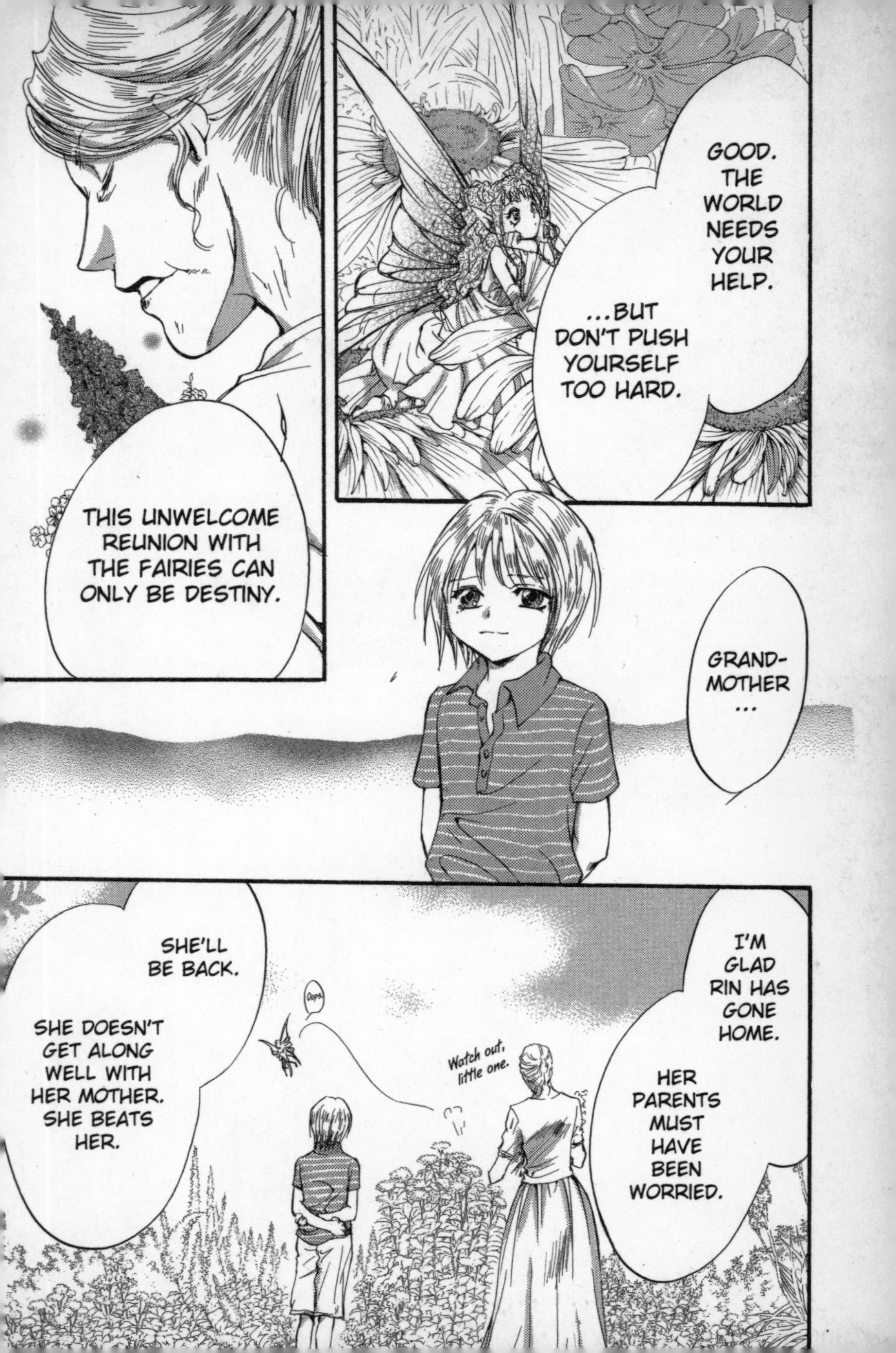
GOOD. THE WORLD NEEDS YOUR HELP.
...BUT DON'T PUSH YOURSELF TOO HARD.
THIS UNWELCOME REUNION WITH THE FAIRIES CAN ONLY BE DESTINY.
GRAND-MOTHER ...
I'M GLAD RIN HAS GONE HOME.
HER PARENTS MUST HAVE BEEN WORRIED.
Watch out, little one.
Oops.
SHE'LL BE BACK.
SHE DOESN'T GET ALONG WELL WITH HER MOTHER. SHE BEATS HER.

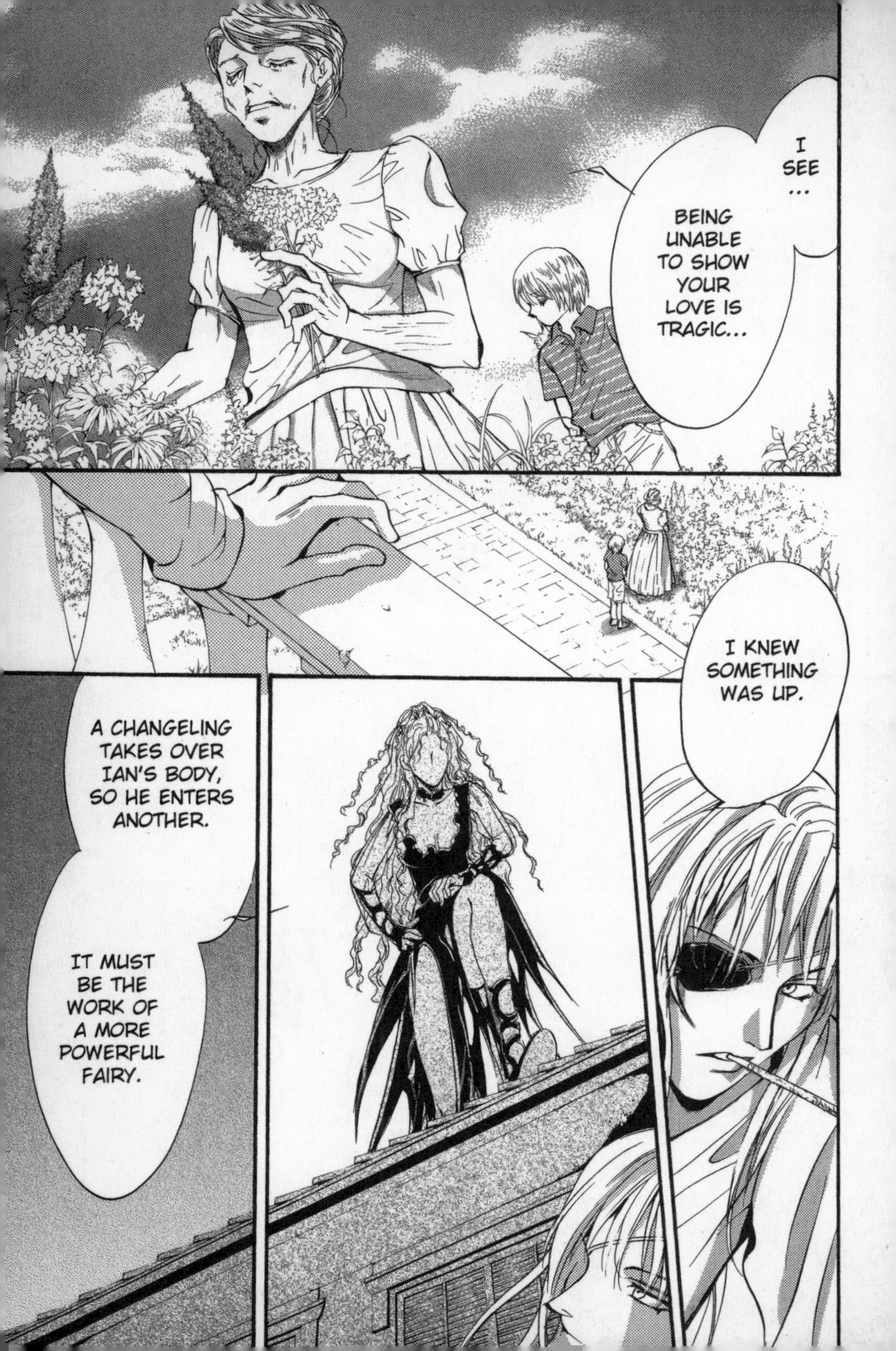
I SEE...
BEING UNABLE TO SHOW YOUR LOVE IS TRAGIC...
I KNEW SOMETHING WAS UP.
A CHANGELING TAKES OVER IAN'S BODY, SO HE ENTERS ANOTHER.
IT MUST BE THE WORK OF A MORE POWERFUL FAIRY.

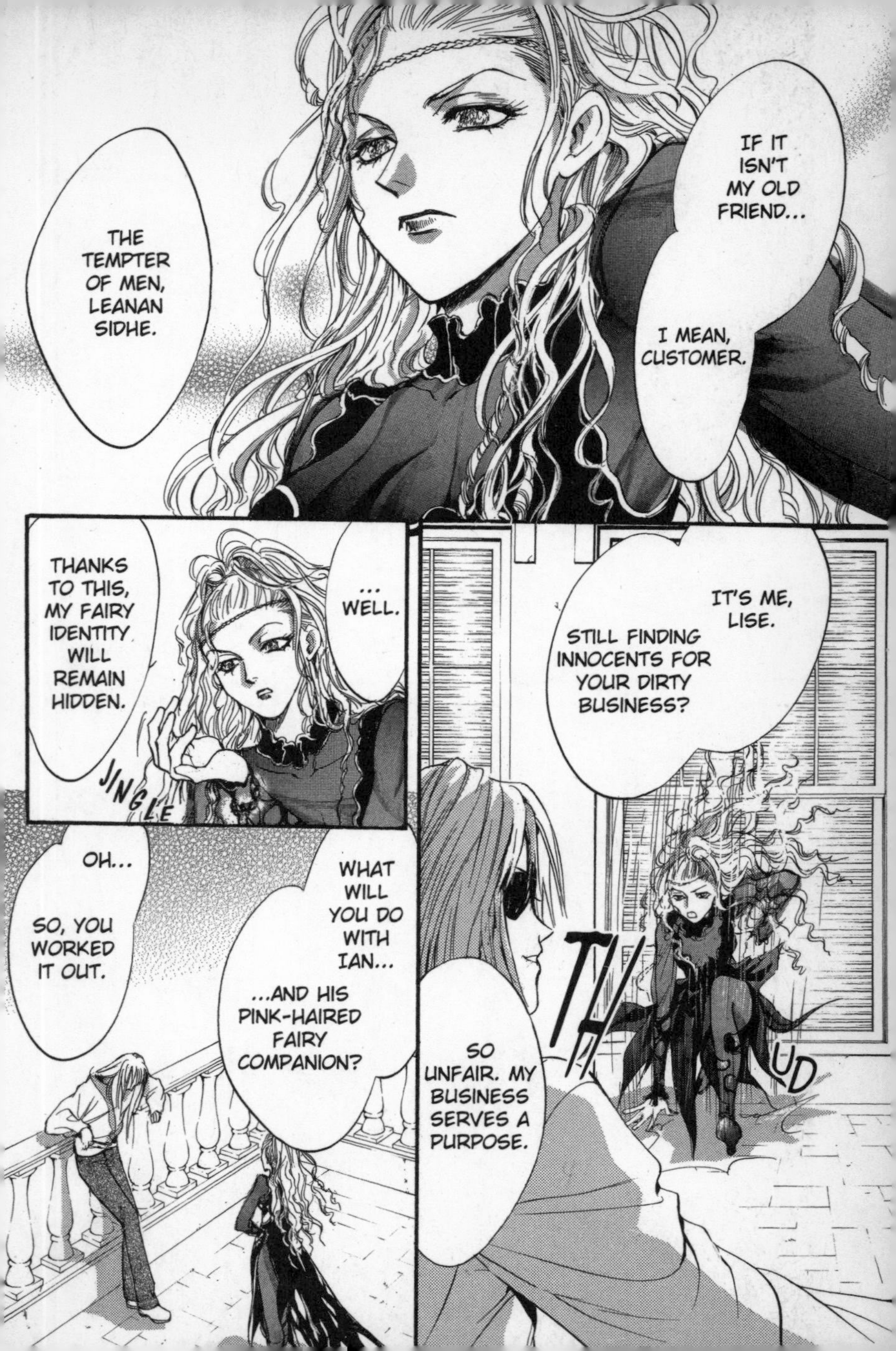
IF IT ISN'T MY OLD FRIEND...
I MEAN, CUSTOMER.
THE TEMPTER OF MEN, LEANAN SIDHE.
IT'S ME, LISE.
STILL FINDING INNOCENTS FOR YOUR DIRTY BUSINESS?
THUD
SO UNFAIR. MY BUSINESS SERVES A PURPOSE.
...WELL.
THANKS TO THIS, MY FAIRY IDENTITY WILL REMAIN HIDDEN.
JINGLE
WHAT WILL YOU DO WITH IAN...
...AND HIS PINK-HAIRED FAIRY COMPANION?
OH...
SO, YOU WORKED IT OUT.

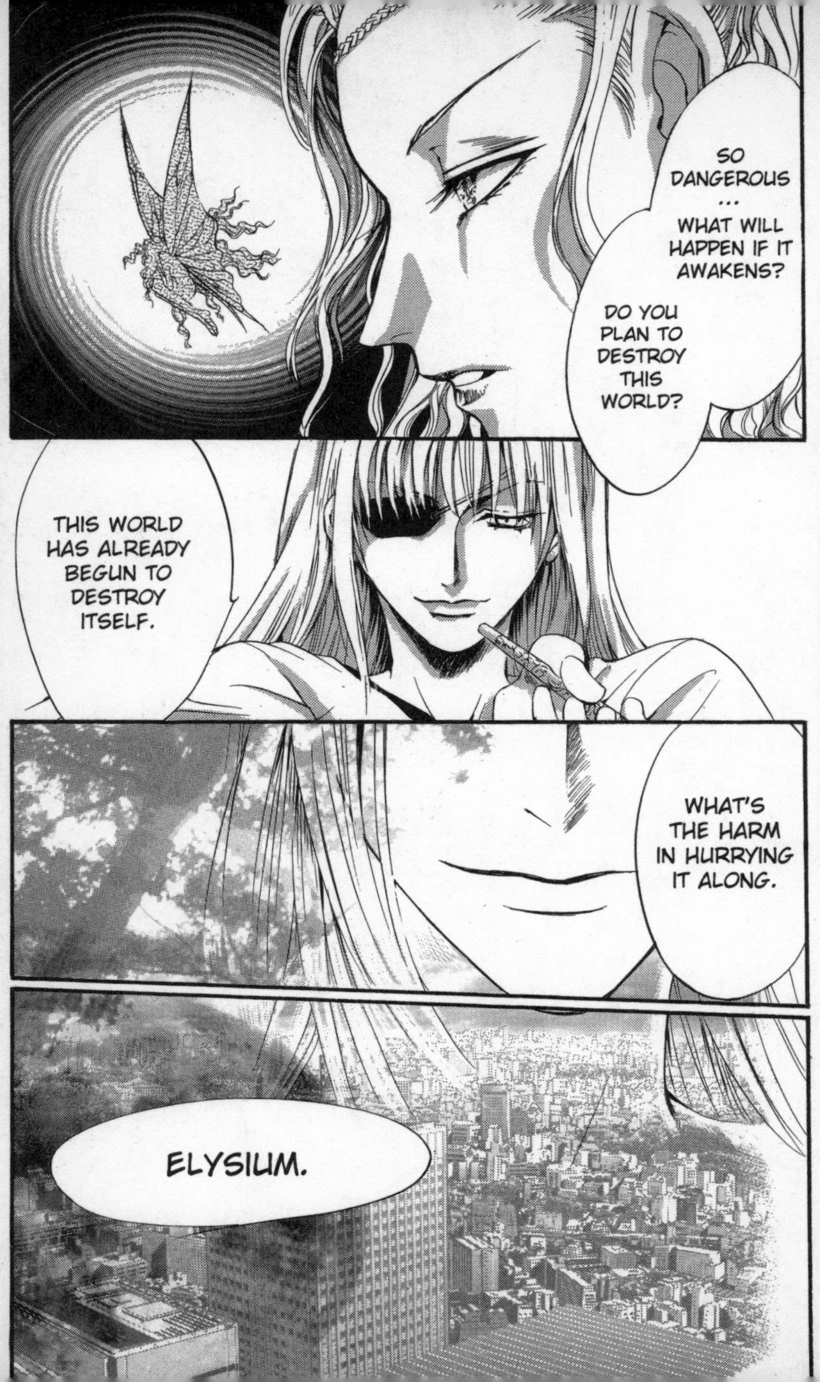
SO DANGEROUS ... WHAT WILL HAPPEN IF IT AWAKENS?
DO YOU PLAN TO DESTROY THIS WORLD?
THIS WORLD HAS ALREADY BEGUN TO DESTROY ITSELF.
WHAT'S THE HARM IN HURRYING IT ALONG.
ELYSIUM.

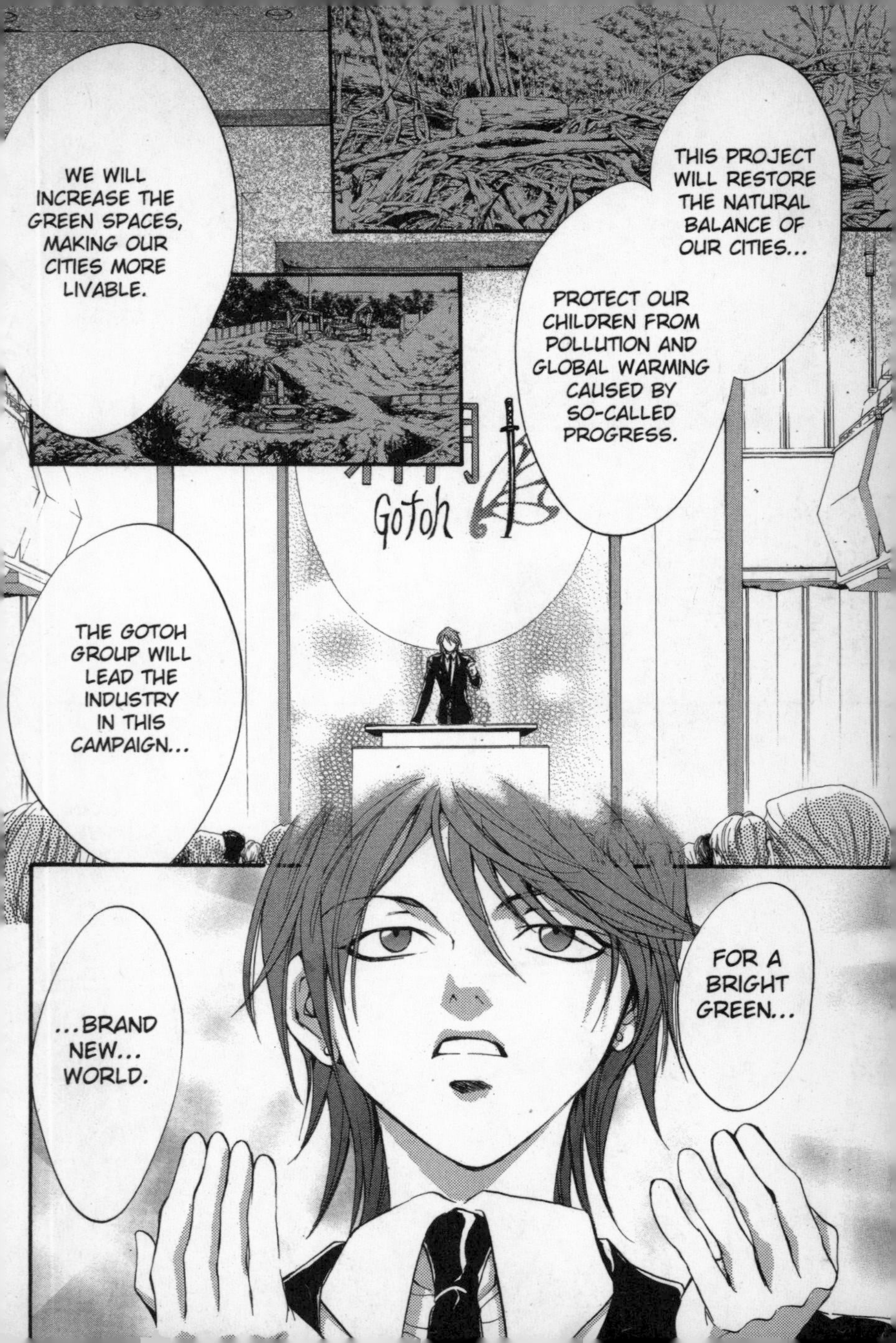
THIS PROJECT WILL RESTORE THE NATURAL BALANCE OF OUR CITIES...
PROTECT OUR CHILDREN FROM POLLUTION AND GLOBAL WARMING CAUSED BY SO-CALLED PROGRESS.
WE WILL INCREASE THE GREEN SPACES, MAKING OUR CITIES MORE LIVABLE.
Gotoh
THE GOTOH GROUP WILL LEAD THE INDUSTRY IN THIS CAMPAIGN...
FOR A BRIGHT GREEN...
...BRAND NEW... WORLD.

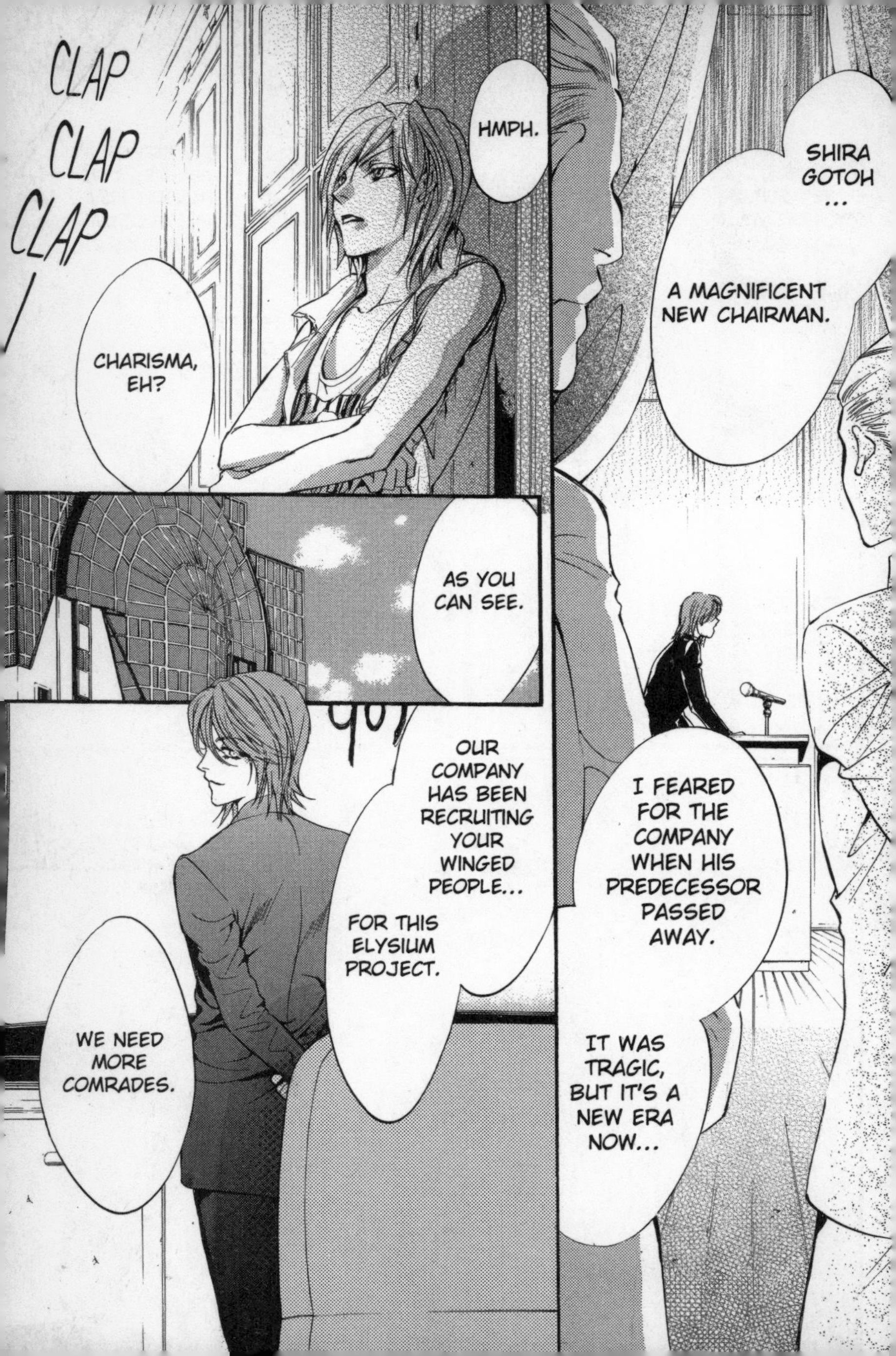
SHIRA GOTOH ...
A MAGNIFICENT NEW CHAIRMAN.
I FEARED FOR THE COMPANY WHEN HIS PREDECESSOR PASSED AWAY.
IT WAS TRAGIC, BUT IT'S A NEW ERA NOW...
HMPH.
CLAP CLAP CLAP
CHARISMA, EH?
AS YOU CAN SEE.
OUR COMPANY HAS BEEN RECRUITING YOUR WINGED PEOPLE...
FOR THIS ELYSIUM PROJECT.
WE NEED MORE COMRADES.

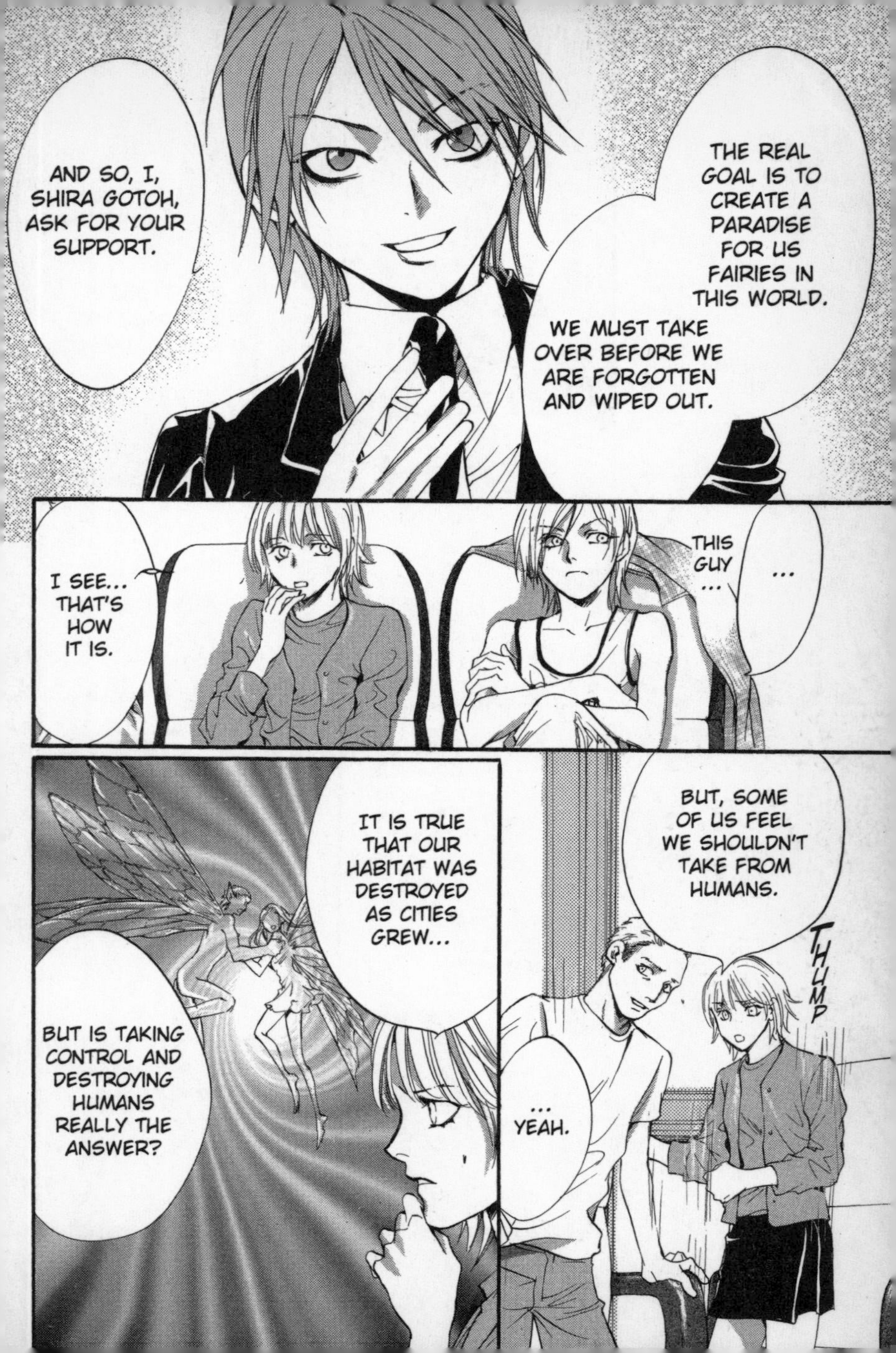
THE REAL GOAL IS TO CREATE A PARADISE FOR US FAIRIES IN THIS WORLD.
WE MUST TAKE OVER BEFORE WE ARE FORGOTTEN AND WIPED OUT.
AND SO, I, SHIRA GOTOH, ASK FOR YOUR SUPPORT.
...
THIS GUY ...
I SEE... THAT'S HOW IT IS.
BUT, SOME OF US FEEL WE SHOULDN'T TAKE FROM HUMANS.
THUMP
... YEAH.
IT IS TRUE THAT OUR HABITAT WAS DESTROYED AS CITIES GREW...
BUT IS TAKING CONTROL AND DESTROYING HUMANS REALLY THE ANSWER?

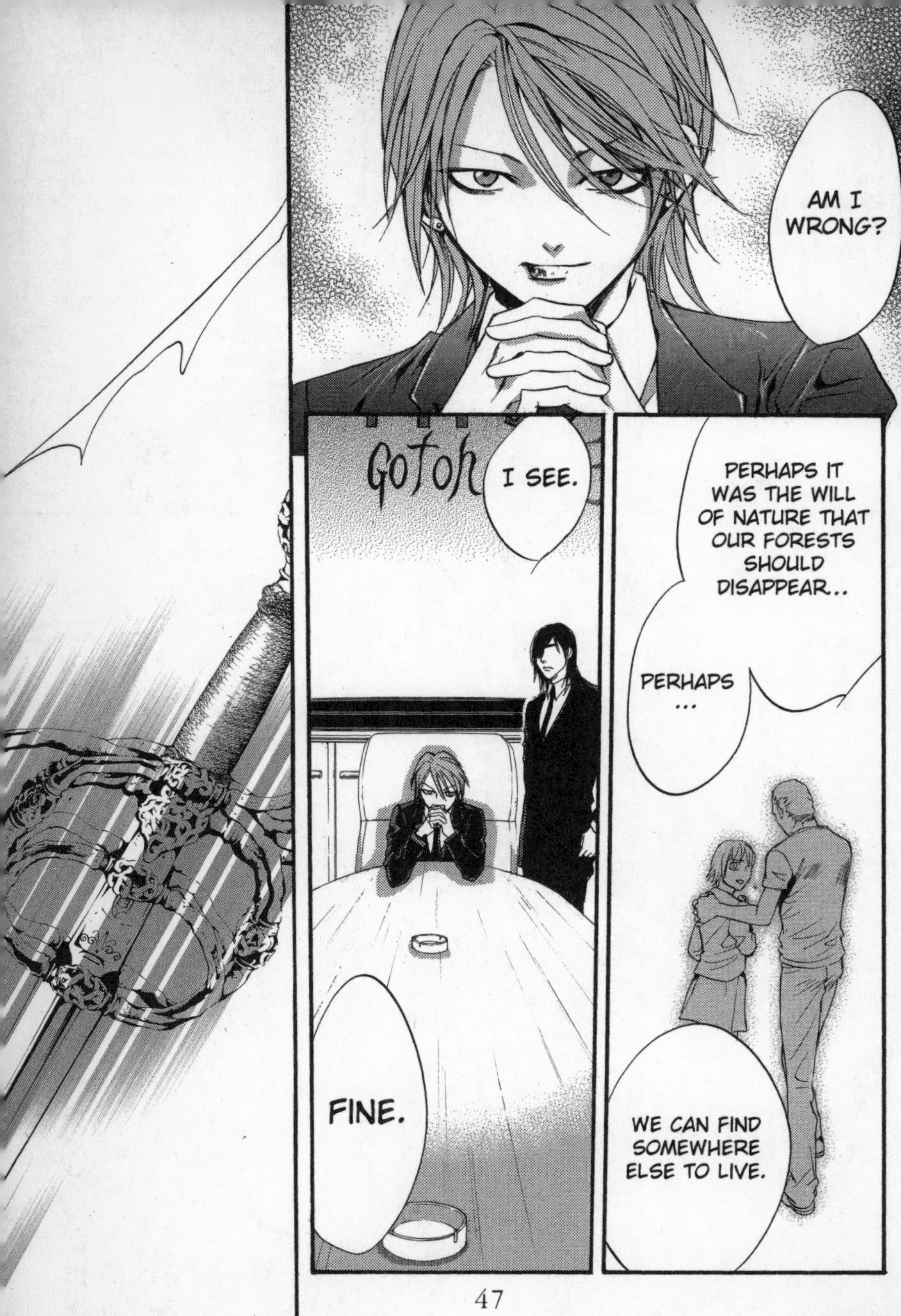
AM I WRONG?
PERHAPS IT WAS THE WILL OF NATURE THAT OUR FORESTS SHOULD DISAPPEAR...
PERHAPS ...
WE CAN FIND SOMEWHERE ELSE TO LIVE.
Gotoh
I SEE.
FINE.

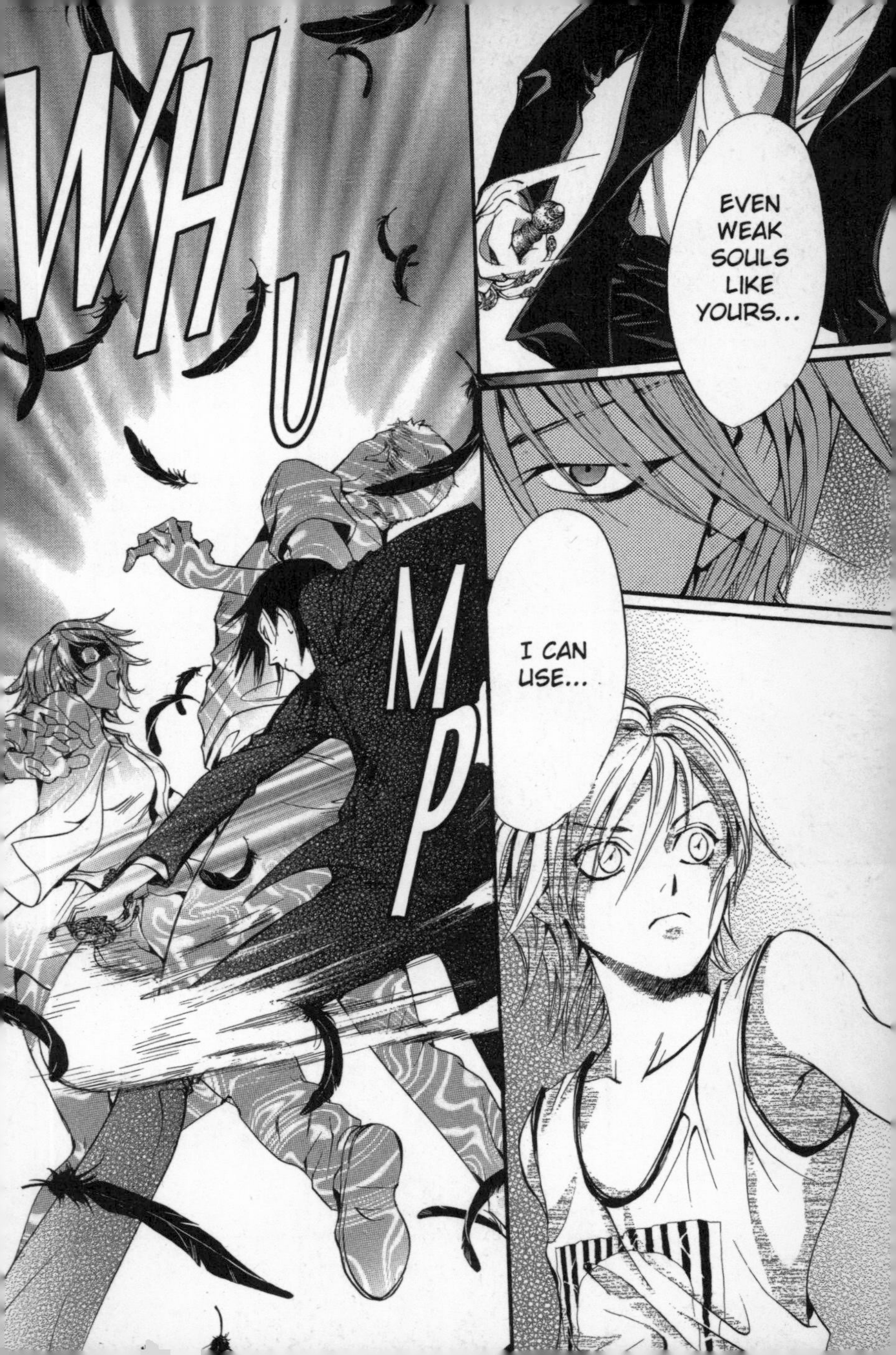
EVEN WEAK SOULS LIKE YOURS...
I CAN USE...
WHUMP

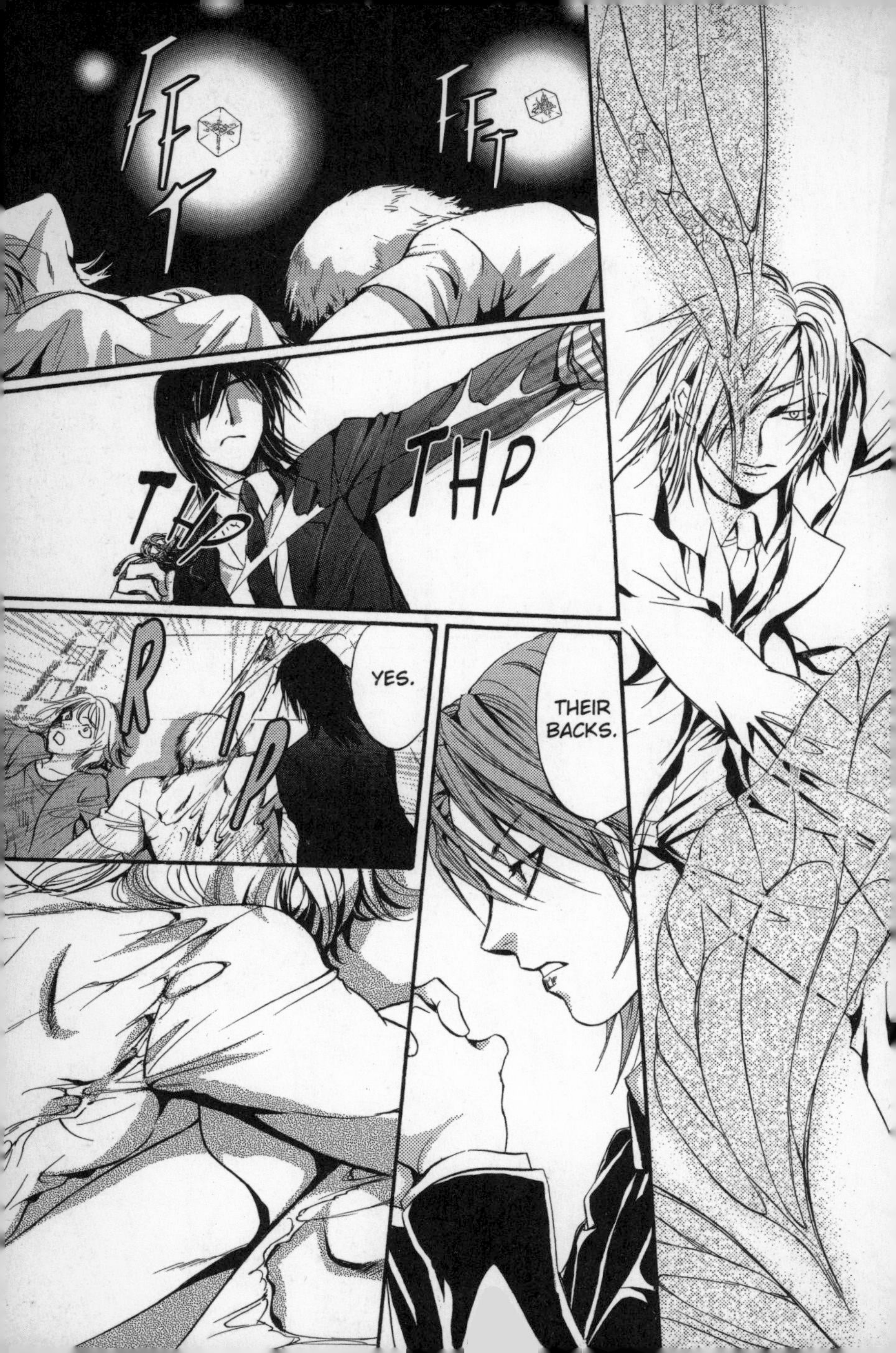
FFT
FFT
THP
THP
THEIR BACKS.
YES.
RIP

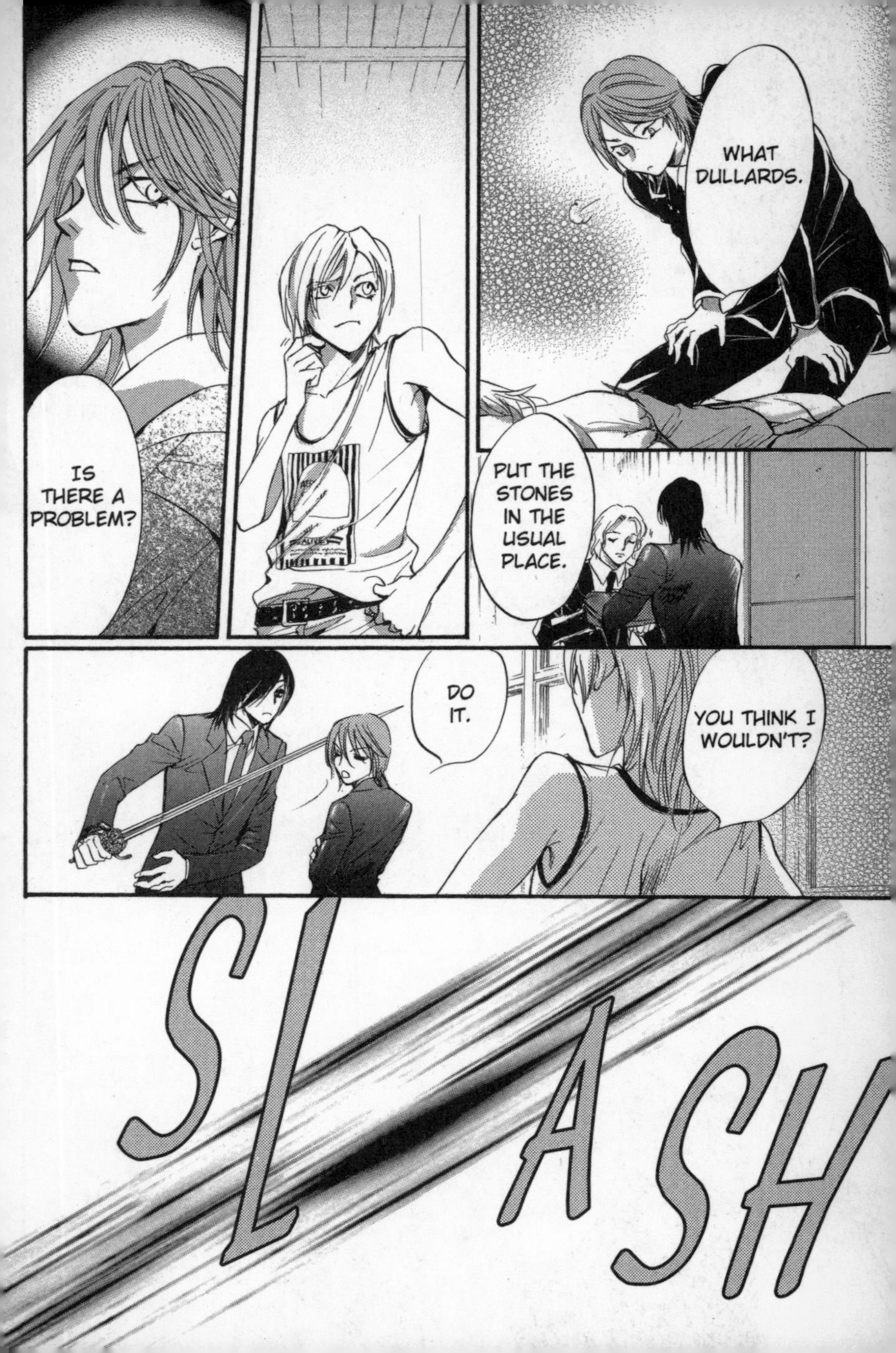
WHAT DULLARDS.
PUT THE STONES IN THE USUAL PLACE.
IS THERE A PROBLEM?
YOU THINK I WOULDN'T?
DO IT.
SLASH

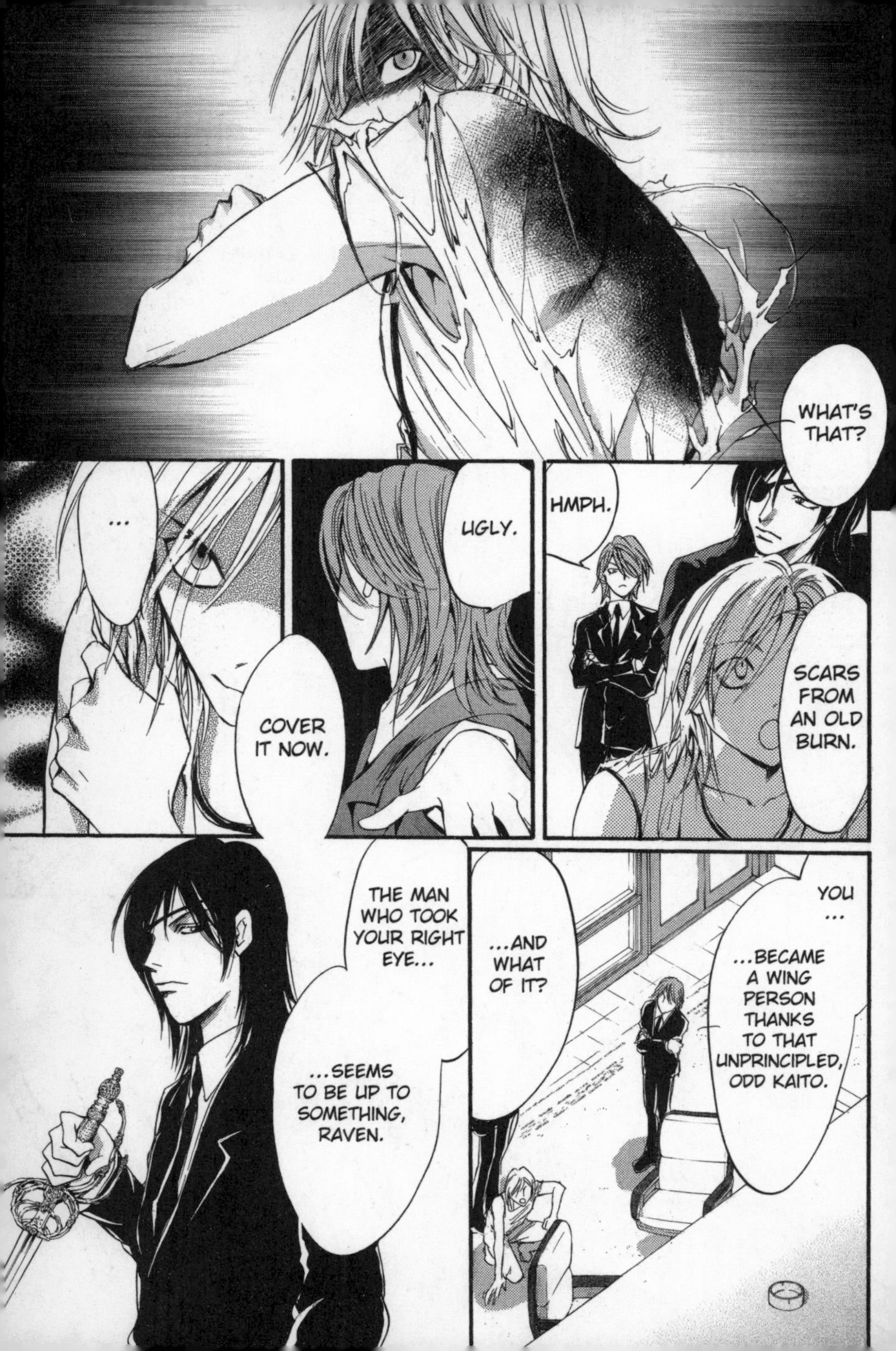
WHAT'S THAT?
HMPH.
SCARS FROM AN OLD BURN.
UGLY.
COVER IT NOW.
...
YOU ...
...BECAME A WING PERSON THANKS TO THAT UNPRINCIPLED, ODD KAITO.
...AND WHAT OF IT?
THE MAN WHO TOOK YOUR RIGHT EYE...
...SEEMS TO BE UP TO SOMETHING, RAVEN.

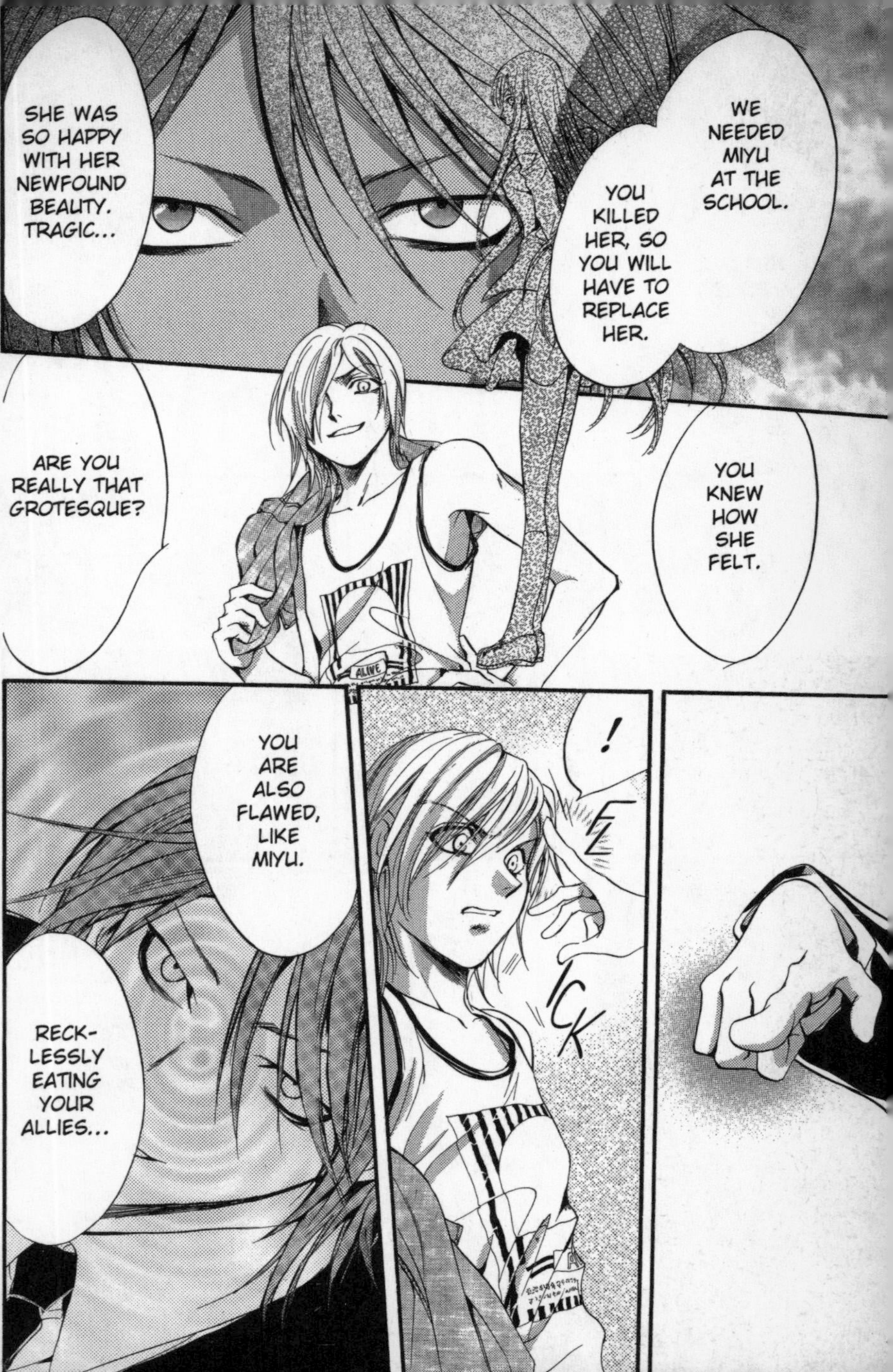
WE NEEDED MIYU AT THE SCHOOL.
YOU KILLED HER, SO YOU WILL HAVE TO REPLACE HER.
SHE WAS SO HAPPY WITH HER NEWFOUND BEAUTY. TRAGIC...
YOU KNEW HOW SHE FELT.
ARE YOU REALLY THAT GROTESQUE?
!
ICK
YOU ARE ALSO FLAWED, LIKE MIYU.
RECK-LESSLY EATING YOUR ALLIES...

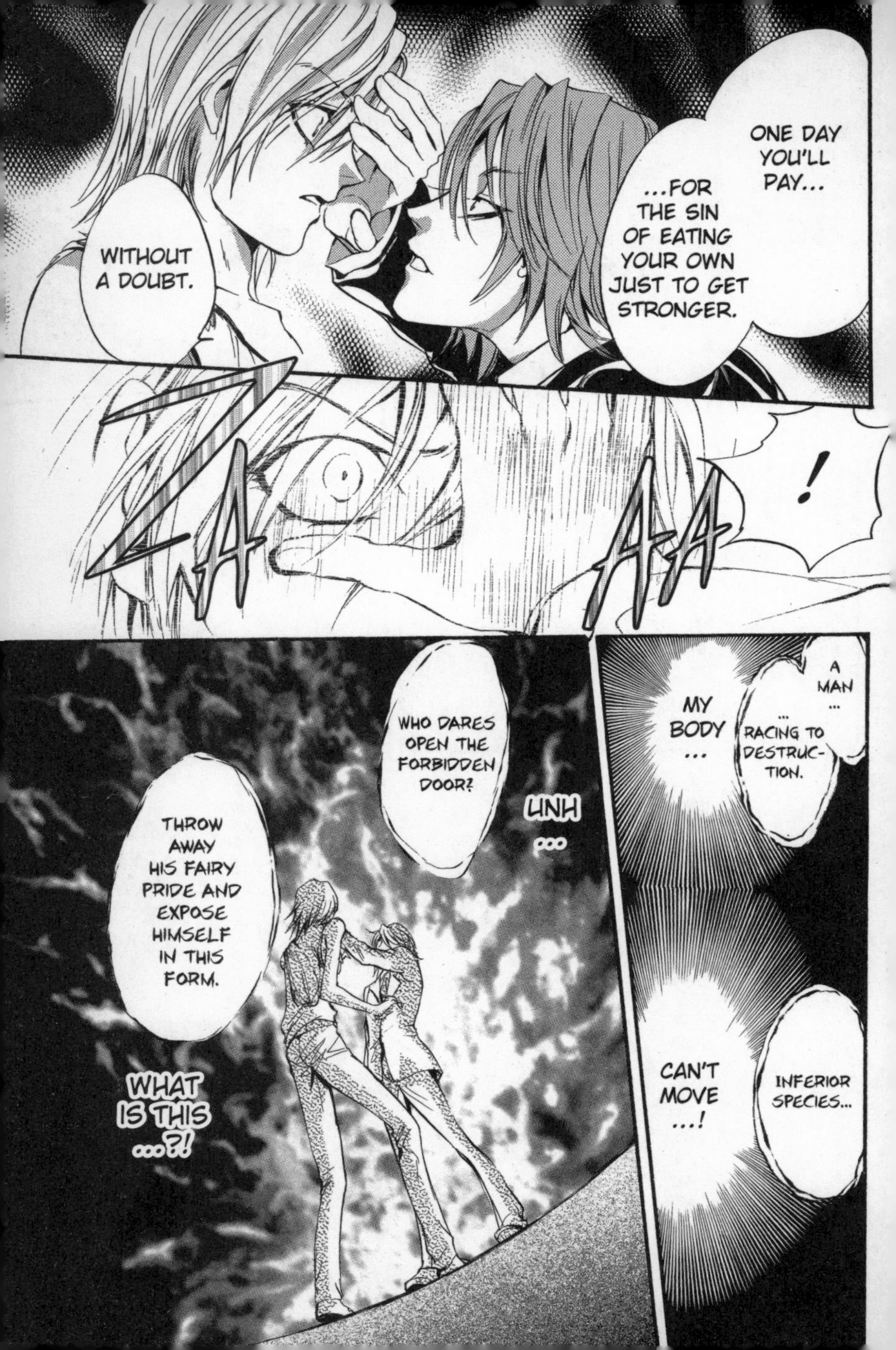
ONE DAY YOU'LL PAY...
...FOR THE SIN OF EATING YOUR OWN JUST TO GET STRONGER.
WITHOUT A DOUBT.
!
ZAAA
A MAN ... ... RACING TO DESTRUC-TION.
MY BODY ...
INFERIOR SPECIES...
CAN'T MOVE ...!
WHO DARES OPEN THE FORBIDDEN DOOR?
THROW AWAY HIS FAIRY PRIDE AND EXPOSE HIMSELF IN THIS FORM.
UNH ...
WHAT IS THIS ...?!

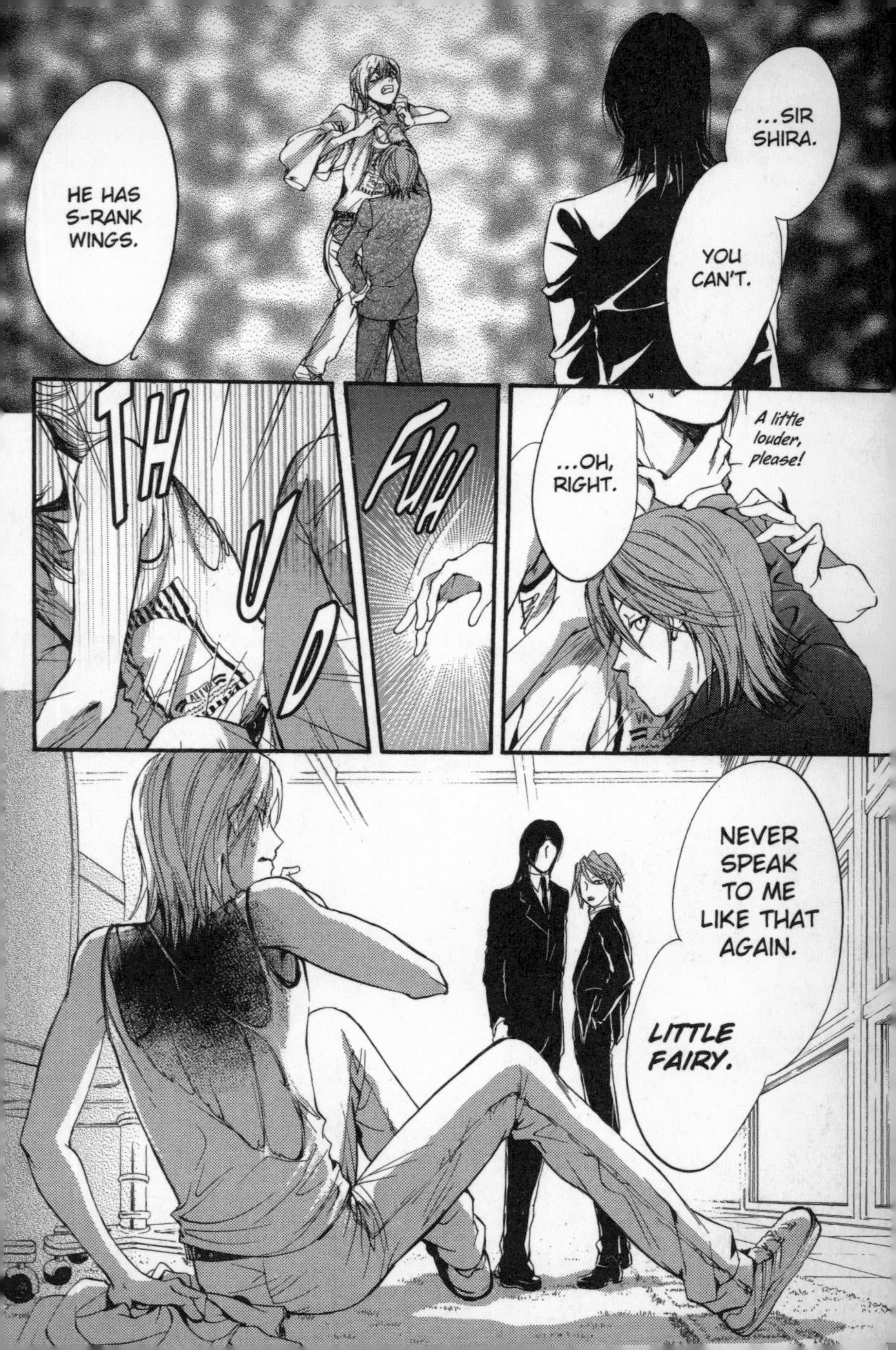
...SIR SHIRA.
YOU CAN'T.
HE HAS S-RANK WINGS.
A little louder, please!
...OH, RIGHT.
FUH
THUD
NEVER SPEAK TO ME LIKE THAT AGAIN.
LITTLE FAIRY.

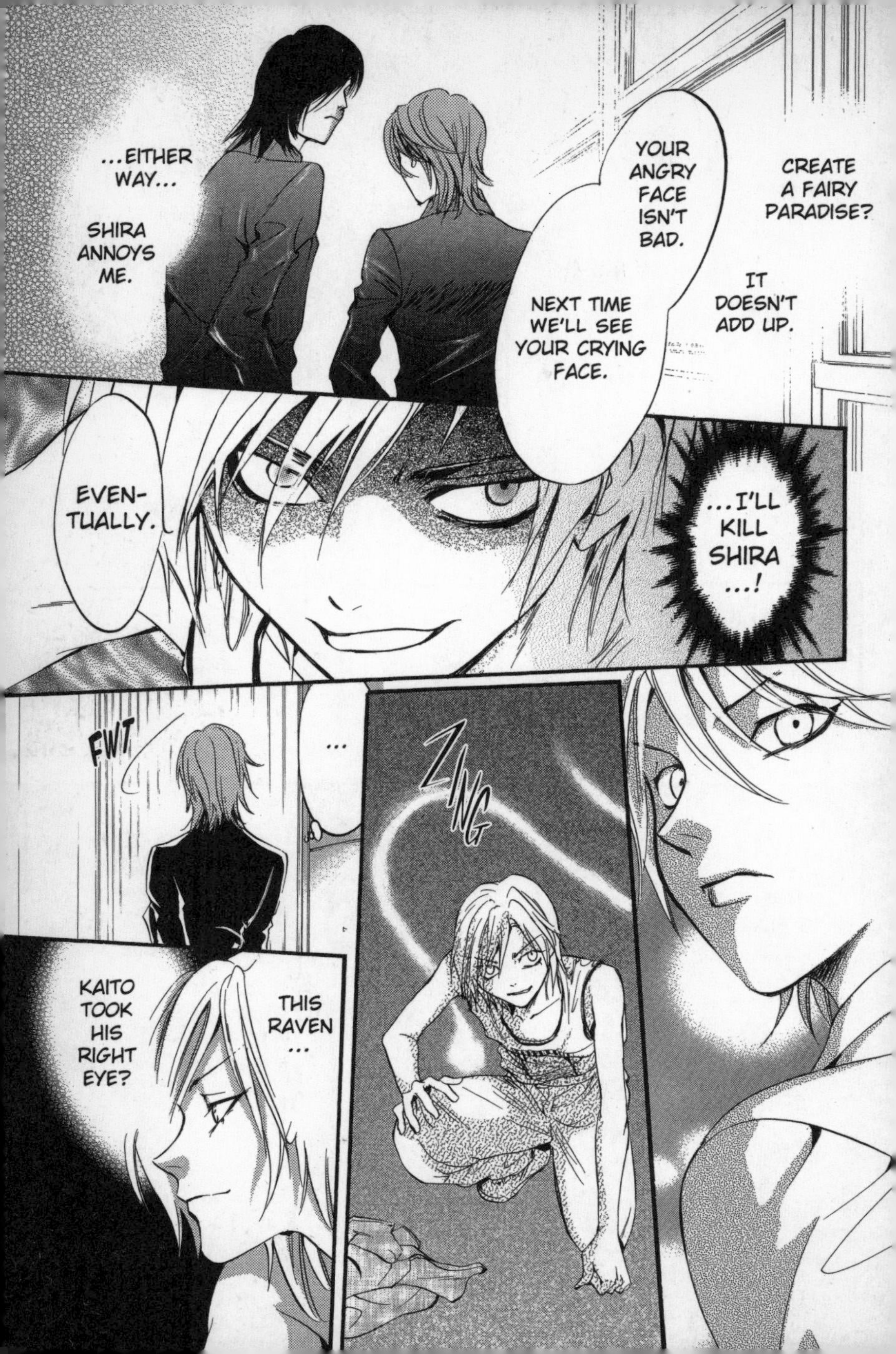
CREATE A FAIRY PARADISE?
IT DOESN'T ADD UP.
YOUR ANGRY FACE ISN'T BAD.
NEXT TIME WE'LL SEE YOUR CRYING FACE.
...EITHER WAY...
SHIRA ANNOYS ME.
...I'LL KILL SHIRA ...!
EVEN-TUALLY.
ZING
...
FWT
THIS RAVEN ...
KAITO TOOK HIS RIGHT EYE?

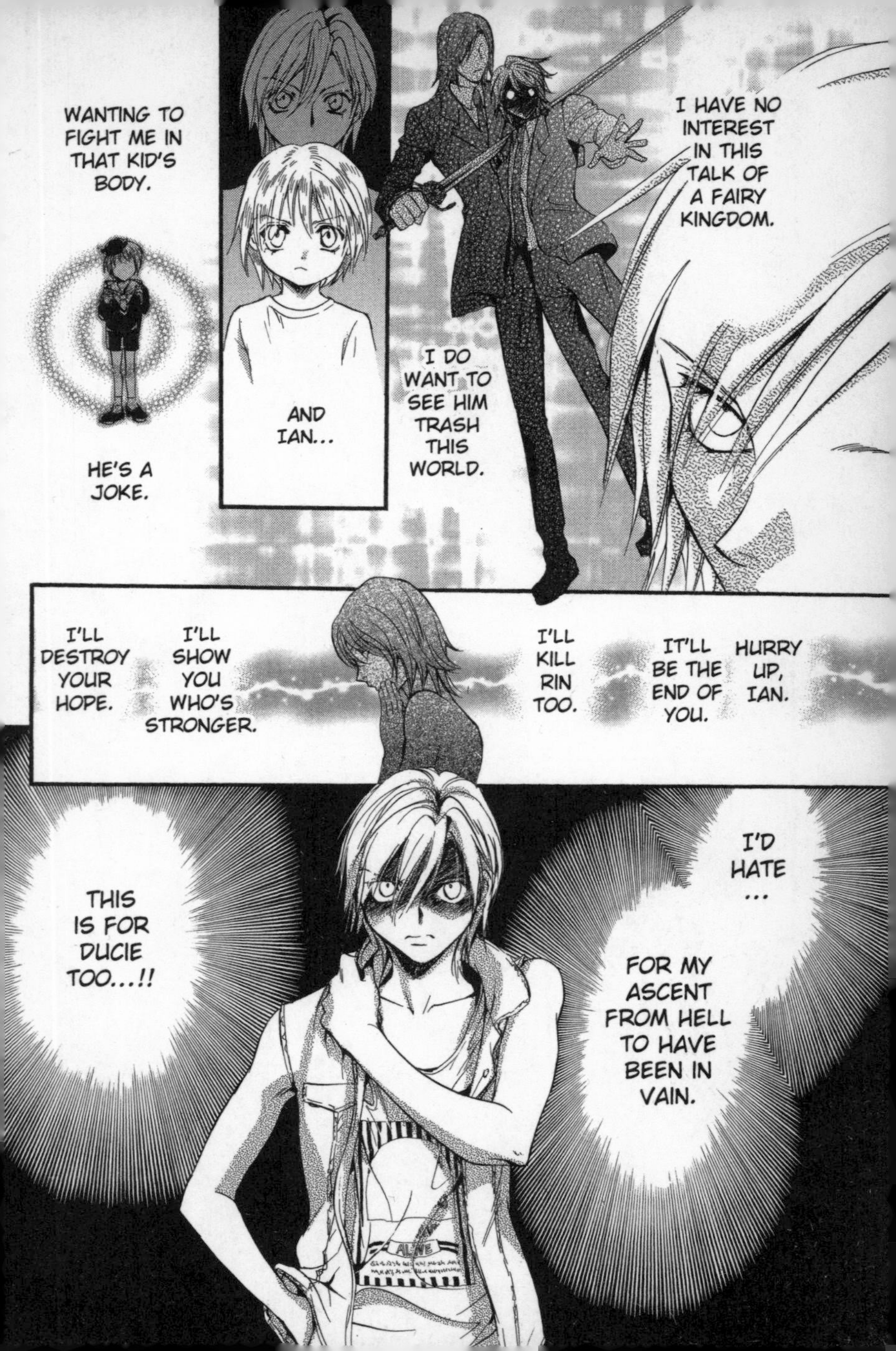
I HAVE NO INTEREST IN THIS TALK OF A FAIRY KINGDOM.
I DO WANT TO SEE HIM TRASH THIS WORLD.
AND IAN...
WANTING TO FIGHT ME IN THAT KID'S BODY.
HE'S A JOKE.
HURRY UP, IAN.
IT'LL BE THE END OF YOU.
I'LL KILL RIN TOO.
I'LL SHOW YOU WHO'S STRONGER.
I'LL DESTROY YOUR HOPE.
I'D HATE ...
FOR MY ASCENT FROM HELL TO HAVE BEEN IN VAIN.
THIS IS FOR DUCIE TOO...!!

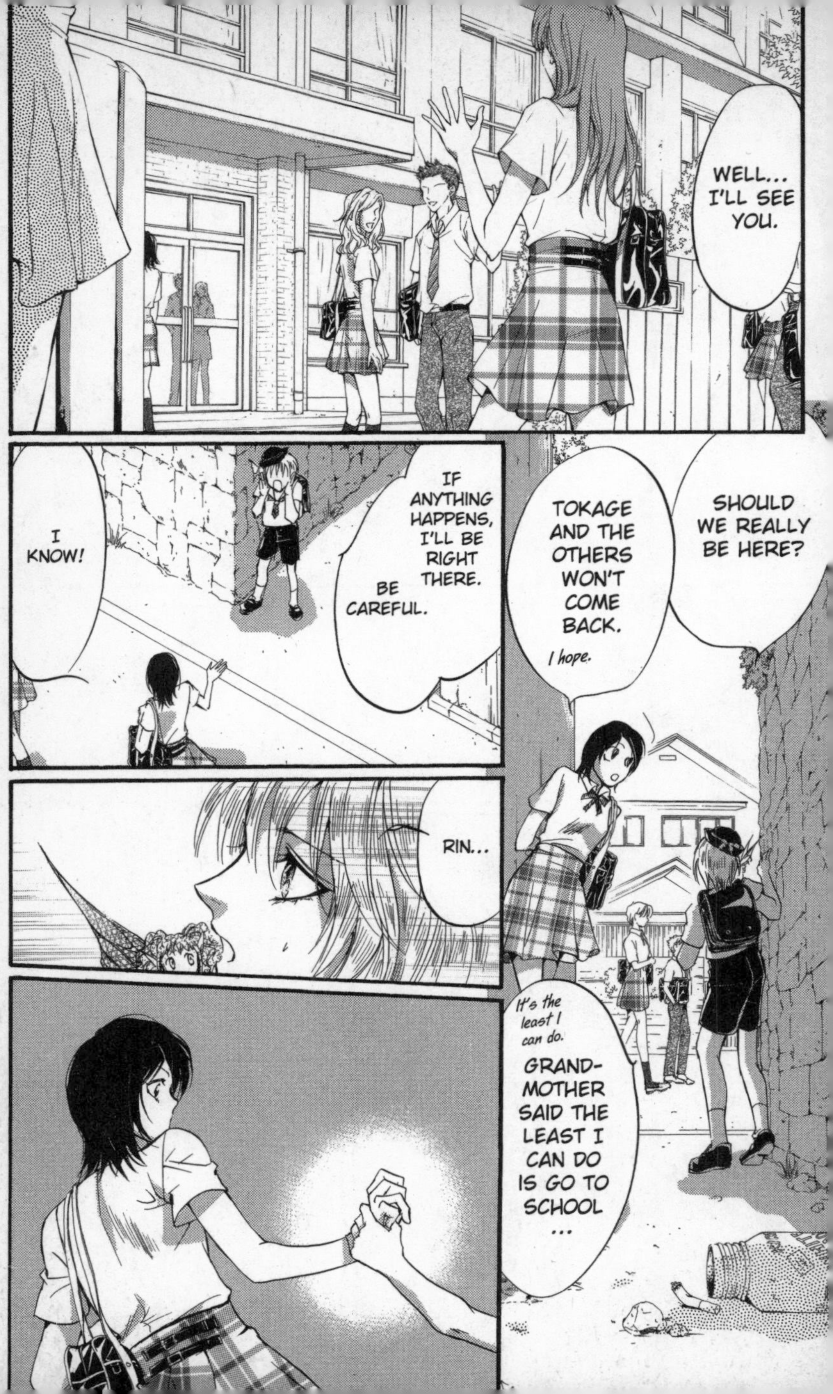
WELL... I'LL SEE YOU.
SHOULD WE REALLY BE HERE?
TOKAGE AND THE OTHERS WON'T COME BACK.
I hope.
It's the least I can do.
GRANDMOTHER SAID THE LEAST I CAN DO IS GO TO SCHOOL...
IF ANYTHING HAPPENS, I'LL BE RIGHT THERE.
BE CAREFUL.
I KNOW!
RIN...

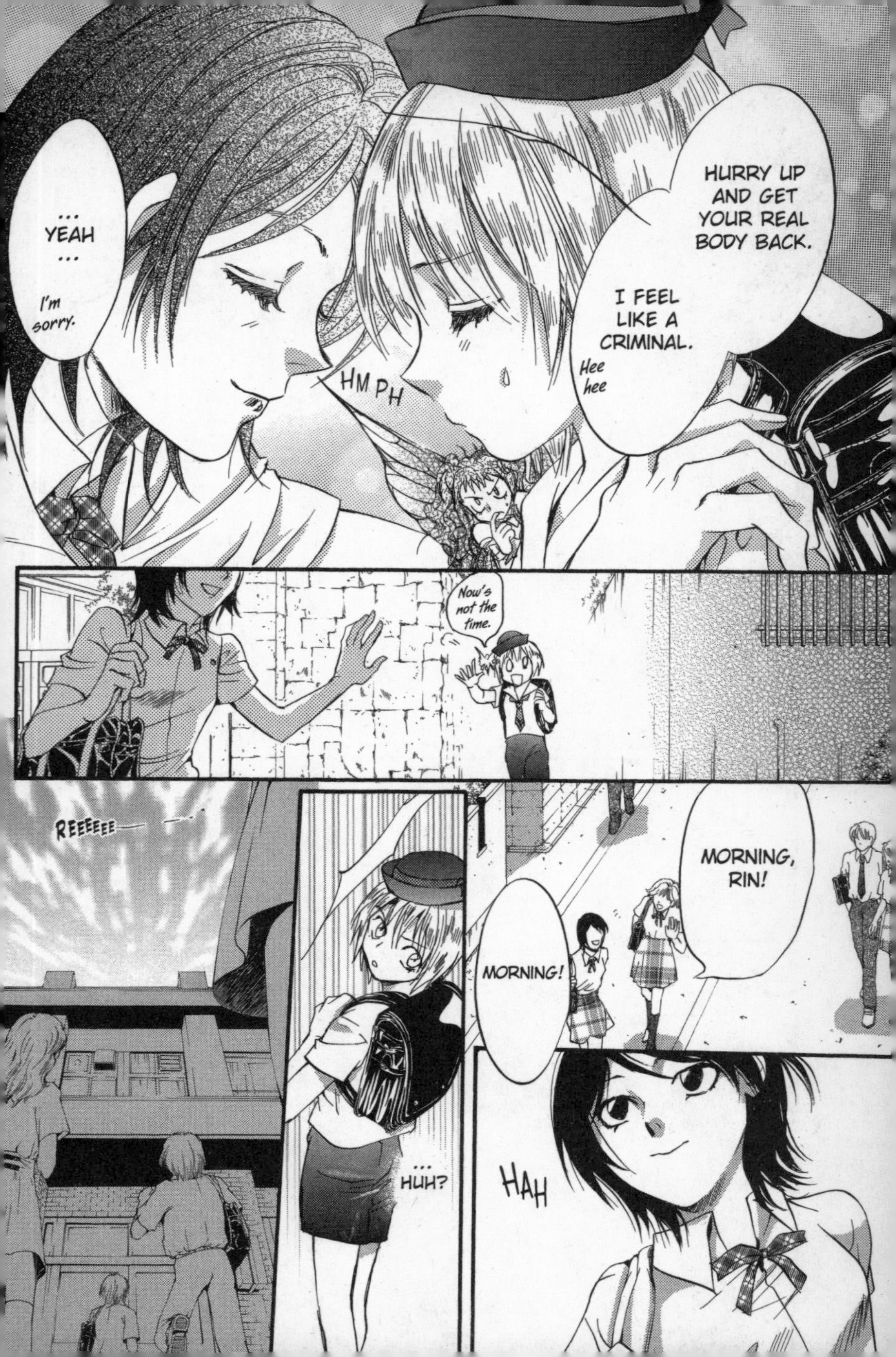

HURRY UP AND GET YOUR REAL BODY BACK.
I FEEL LIKE A CRIMINAL.
Hee hee
HMPH
... YEAH ...
I'm sorry.
Now's not the time.
MORNING, RIN!
MORNING!
HAH
... HUH?
REEEEEEE—

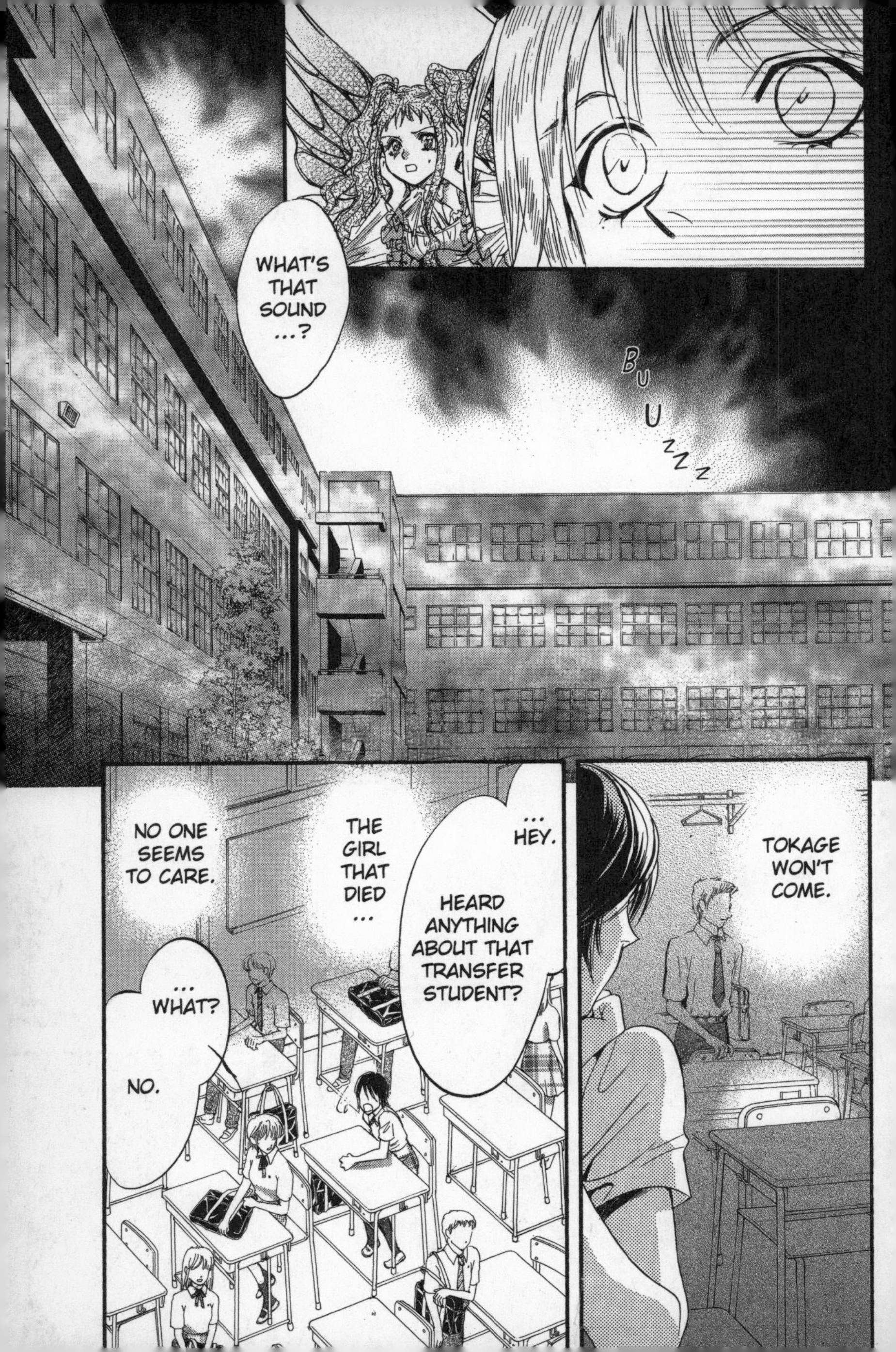
WHAT'S THAT SOUND ...?
BUUZZZ
TOKAGE WON'T COME.
... HEY.
HEARD ANYTHING ABOUT THAT TRANSFER STUDENT?
THE GIRL THAT DIED ...
NO ONE SEEMS TO CARE.
... WHAT?
NO.

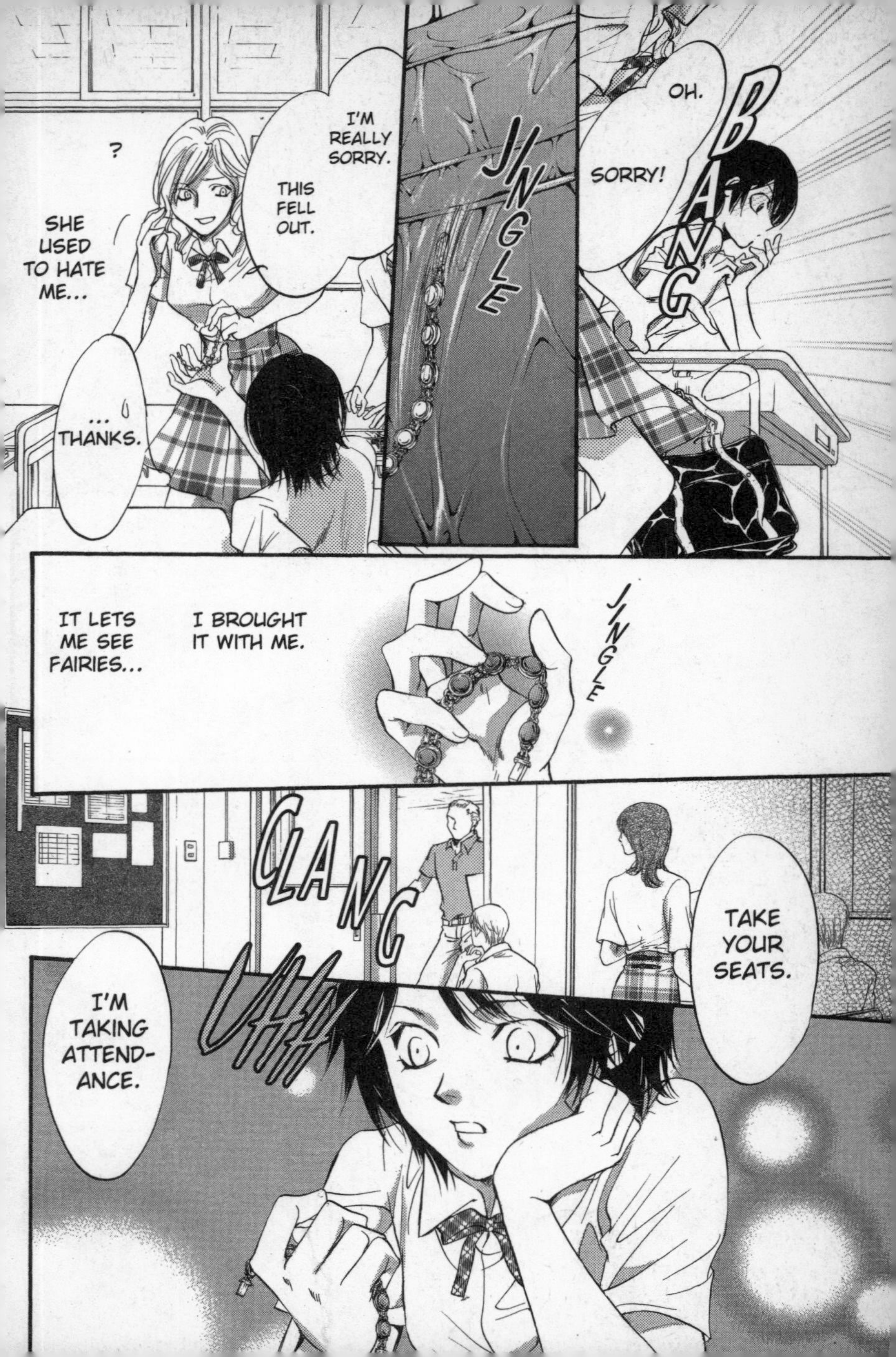
BANG
OH.
SORRY!
JINGLE
I'M REALLY SORRY.
THIS FELL OUT.
?
SHE USED TO HATE ME...
...THANKS.
JINGLE
I BROUGHT IT WITH ME.
IT LETS ME SEE FAIRIES...
TAKE YOUR SEATS.
CLANG
I'M TAKING ATTENDANCE.

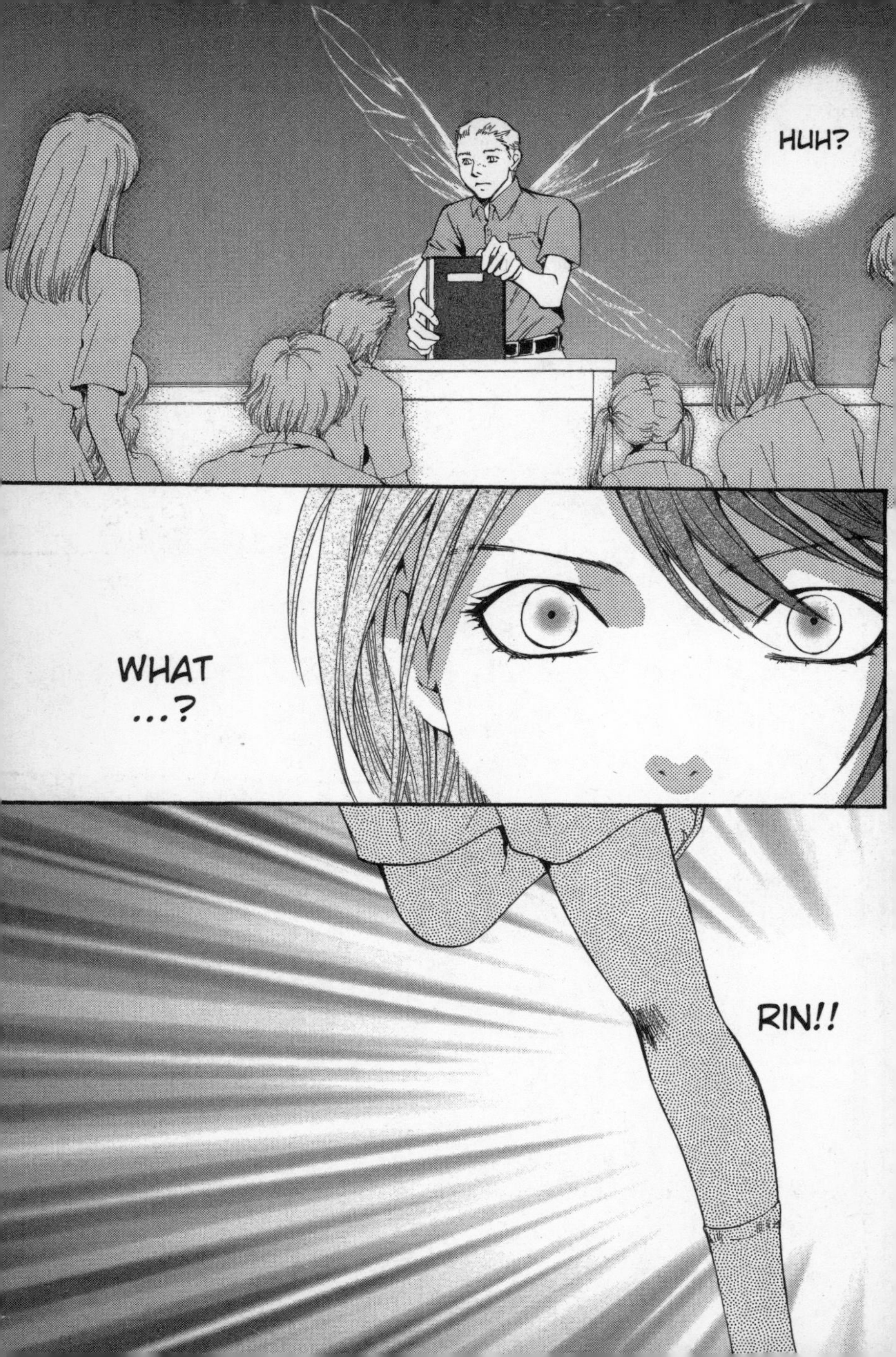
HUH?
WHAT ...?
RIN!!

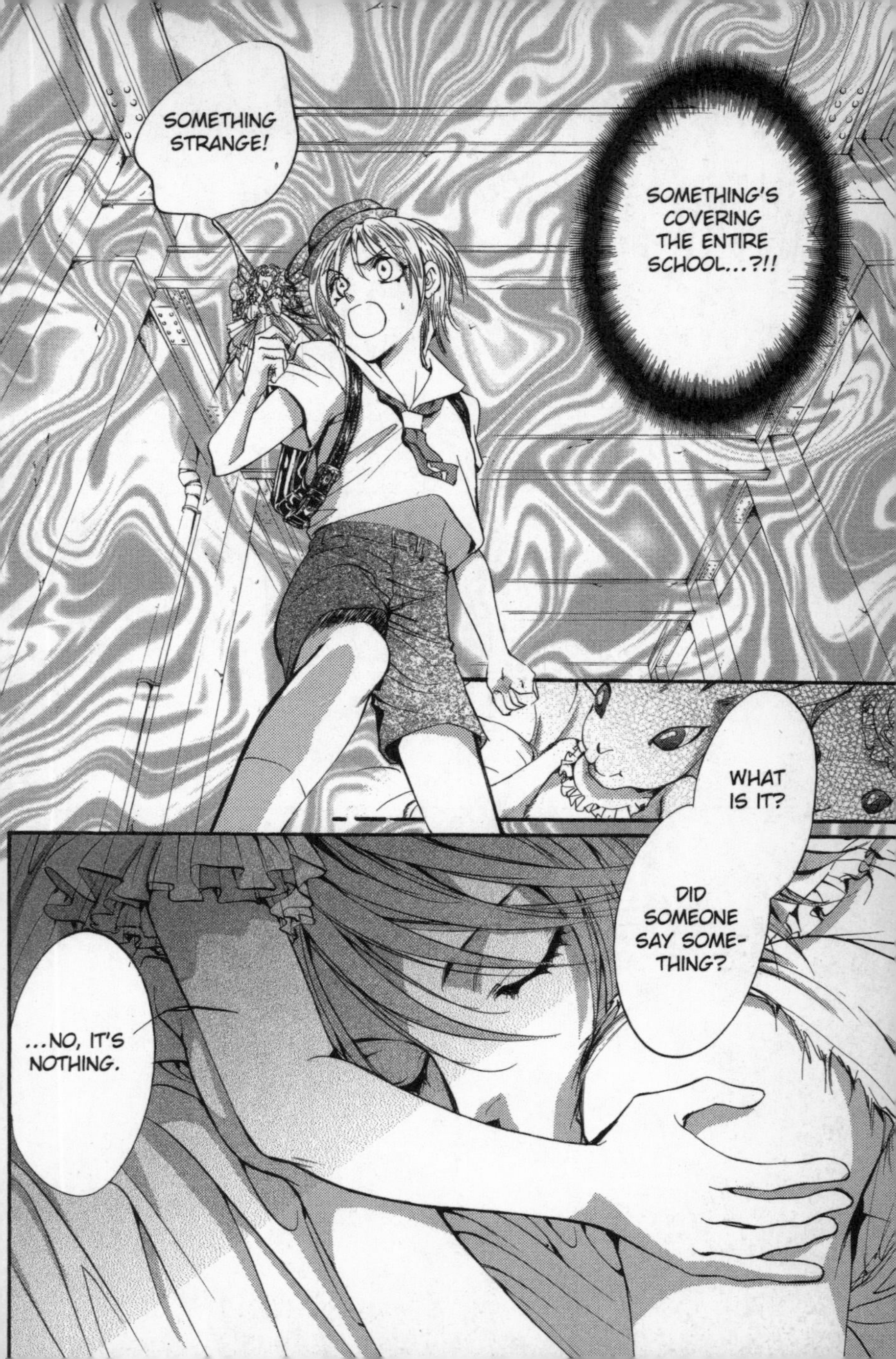
SOMETHING STRANGE!
SOMETHING'S COVERING THE ENTIRE SCHOOL...?!!
WHAT IS IT?
DID SOMEONE SAY SOME-THING?
...NO, IT'S NOTHING.

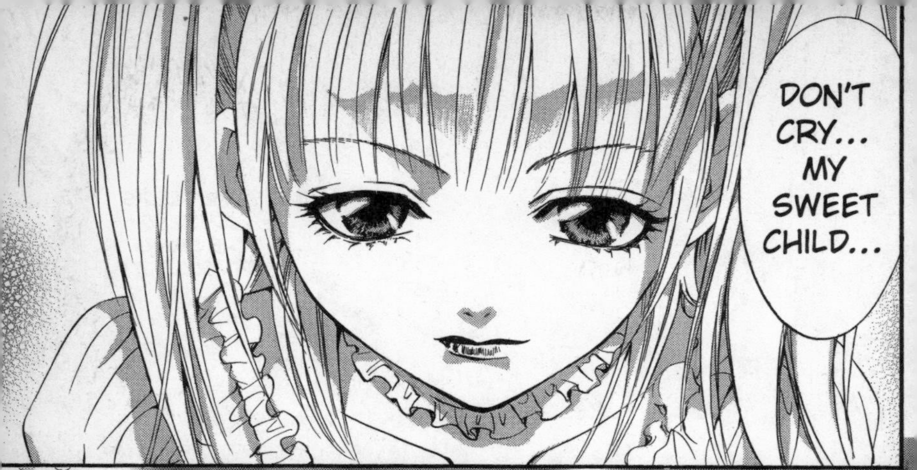
DON'T CRY... MY SWEET CHILD...
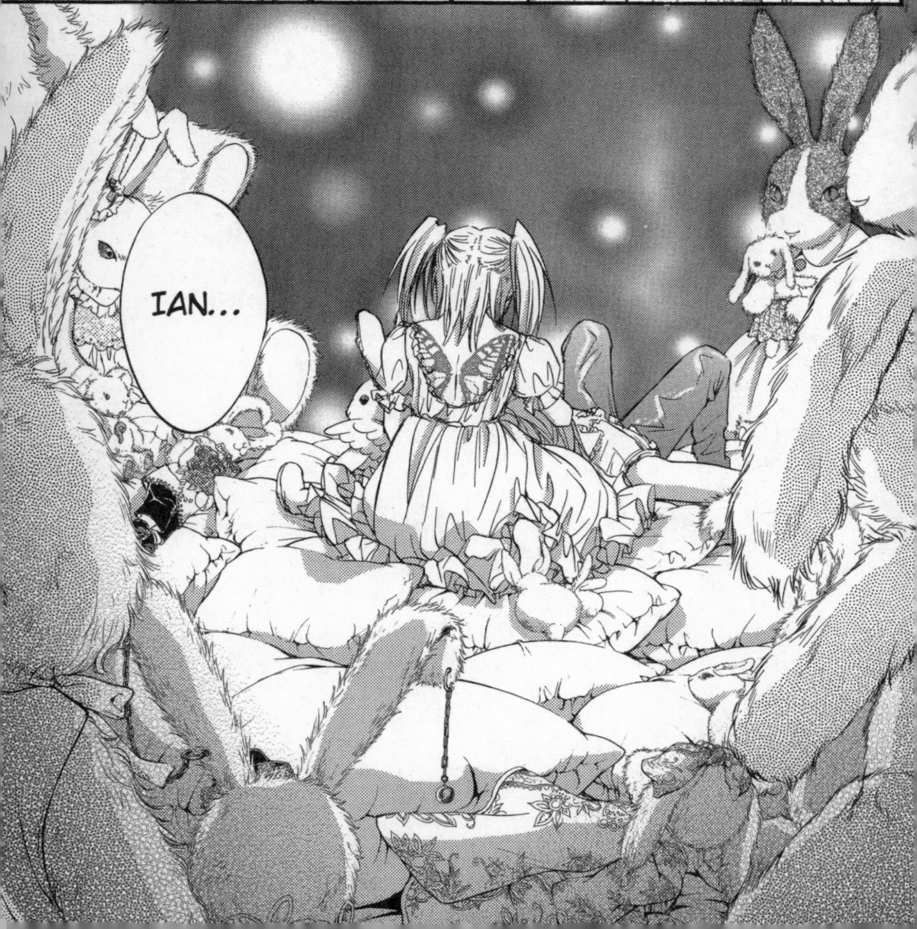
IAN...

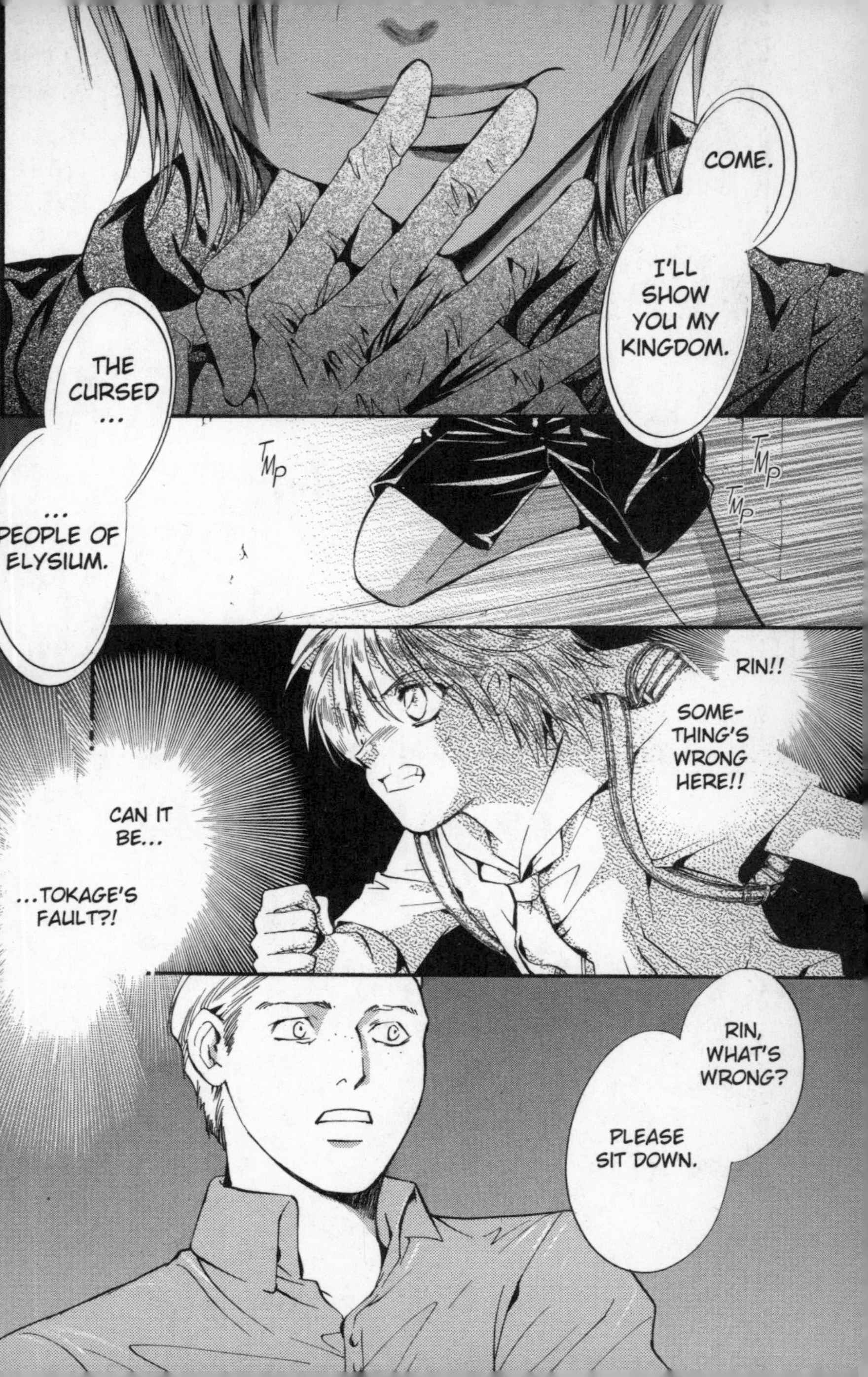
COME.
I'LL SHOW YOU MY KINGDOM.
TMP
TMP
TMP
THE CURSED...
...PEOPLE OF ELYSIUM.
RIN!!
SOME-THING'S WRONG HERE!!
CAN IT BE...
...TOKAGE'S FAULT?!
RIN, WHAT'S WRONG?
PLEASE SIT DOWN.

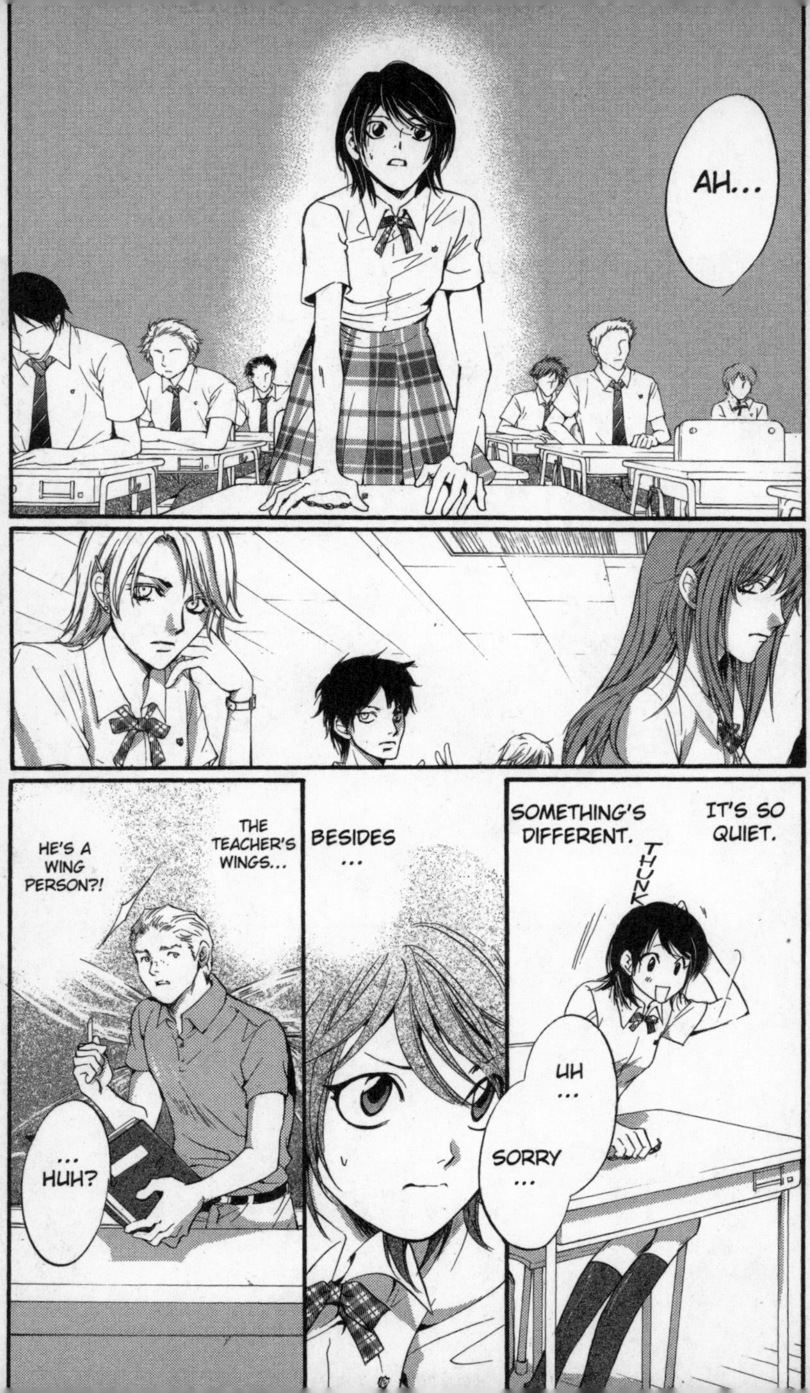
AH...
IT'S SO QUIET.
SOMETHING'S DIFFERENT.
THUNK
UH ...
SORRY ...
BESIDES ...
THE TEACHER'S WINGS...
HE'S A WING PERSON?!
... HUH?

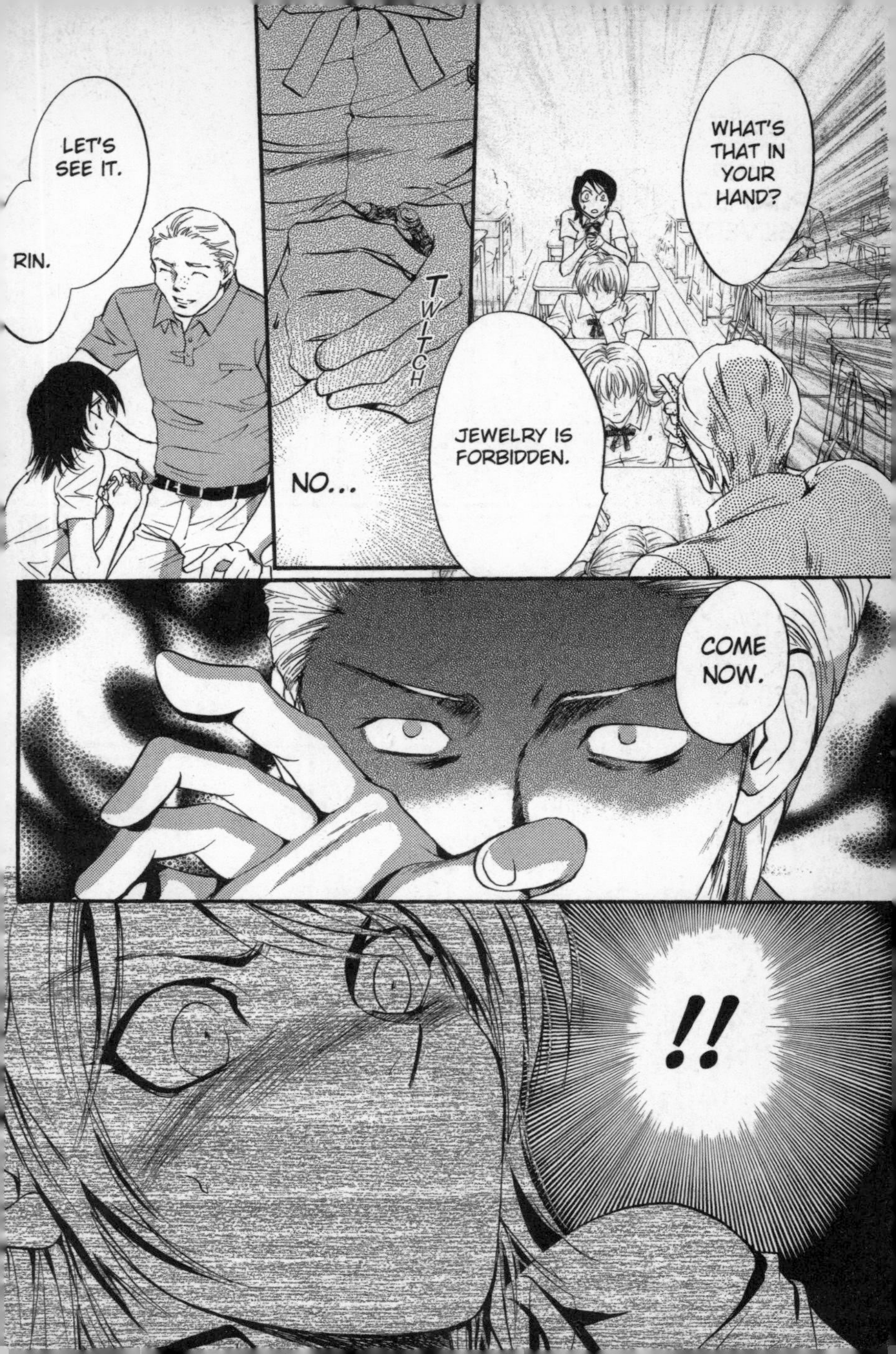
WHAT'S THAT IN YOUR HAND?
JEWELRY IS FORBIDDEN.
TWITCH
NO...
LET'S SEE IT.
RIN.
COME NOW.
!!

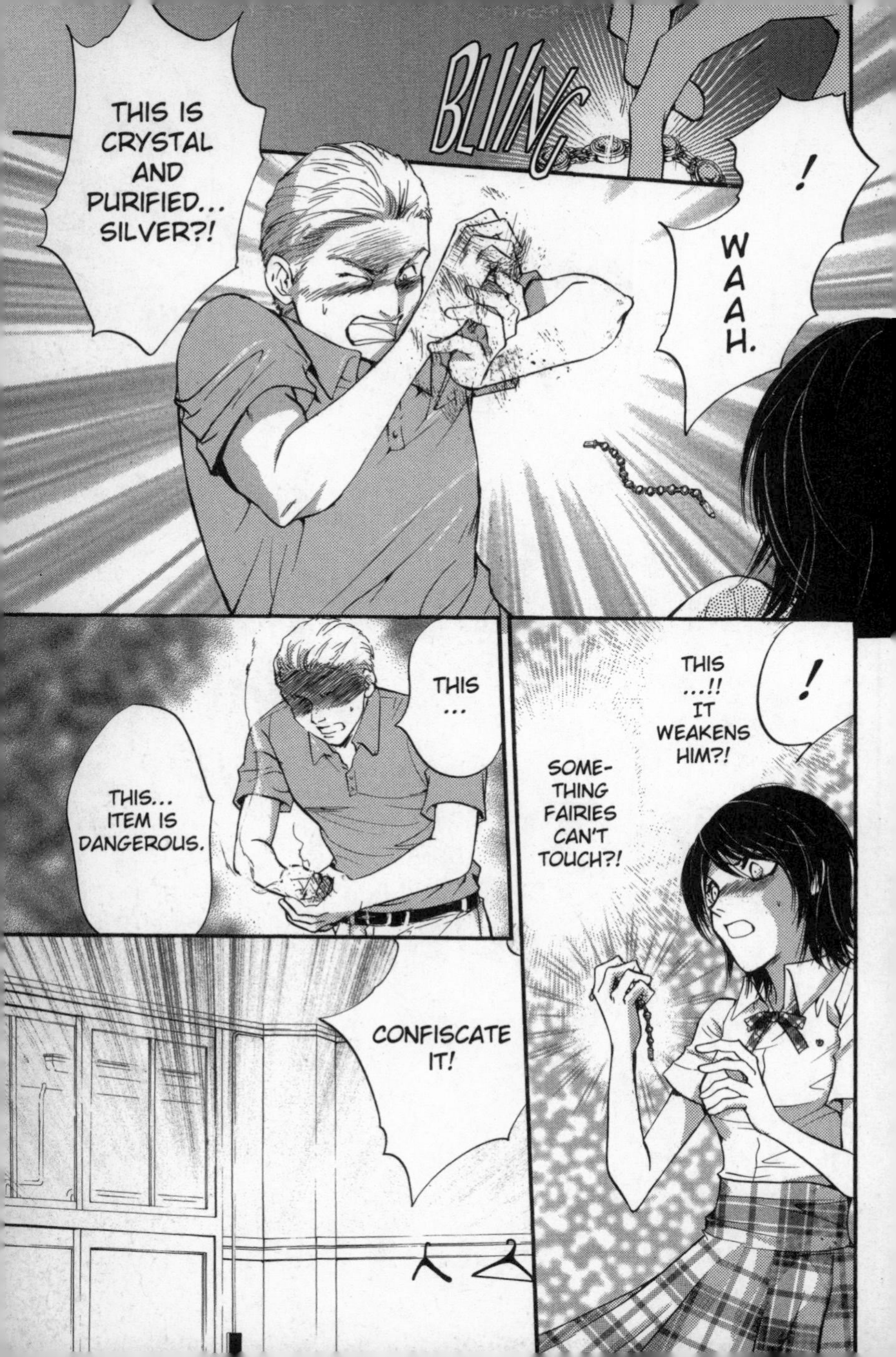

BLING
! WAAH.
THIS IS CRYSTAL AND PURIFIED... SILVER?!
!
THIS ...!! IT WEAKENS HIM?!
SOME-THING FAIRIES CAN'T TOUCH?!
THIS ...
THIS... ITEM IS DANGEROUS.
CONFISCATE IT!

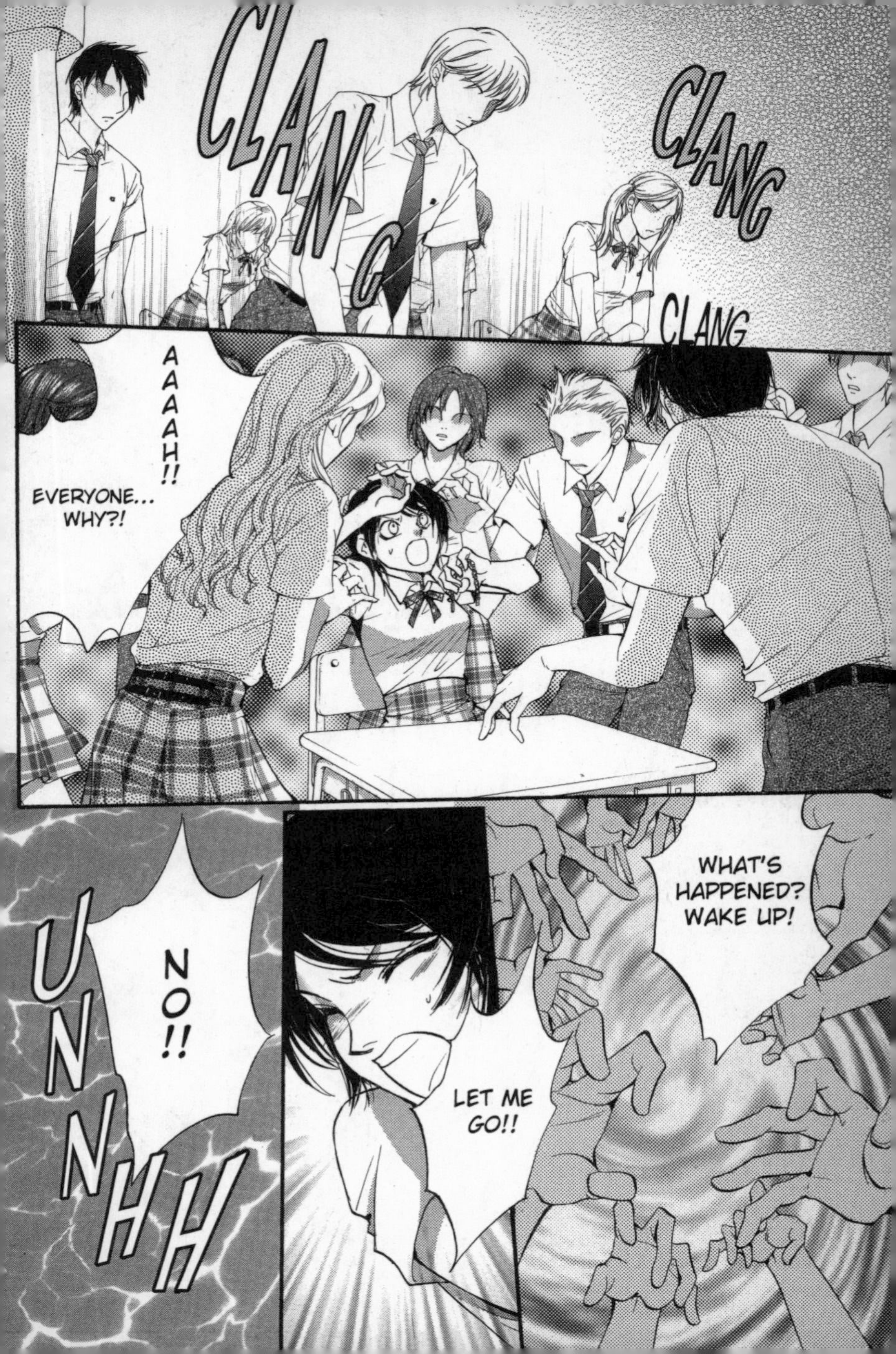
CLANG
CLANG
CLANG
AAAAAH!!
EVERYONE... WHY?!
WHAT'S HAPPENED? WAKE UP!
LET ME GO!!
NO!!
UNNHH

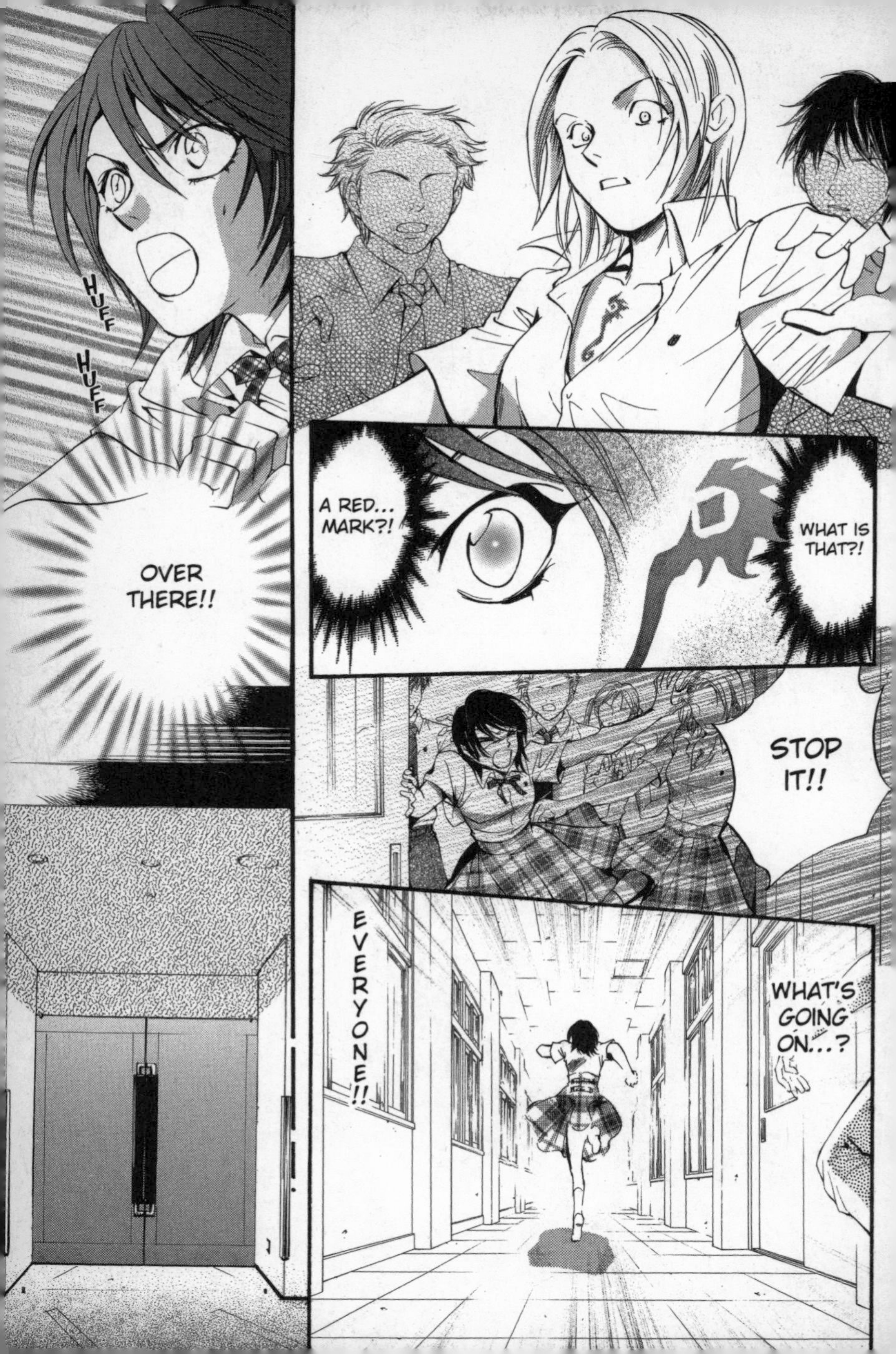
WHAT IS THAT?!
A RED... MARK?!
STOP IT!!
HUFF HUFF
OVER THERE!!
WHAT'S GOING ON...?
EVERYONE!!

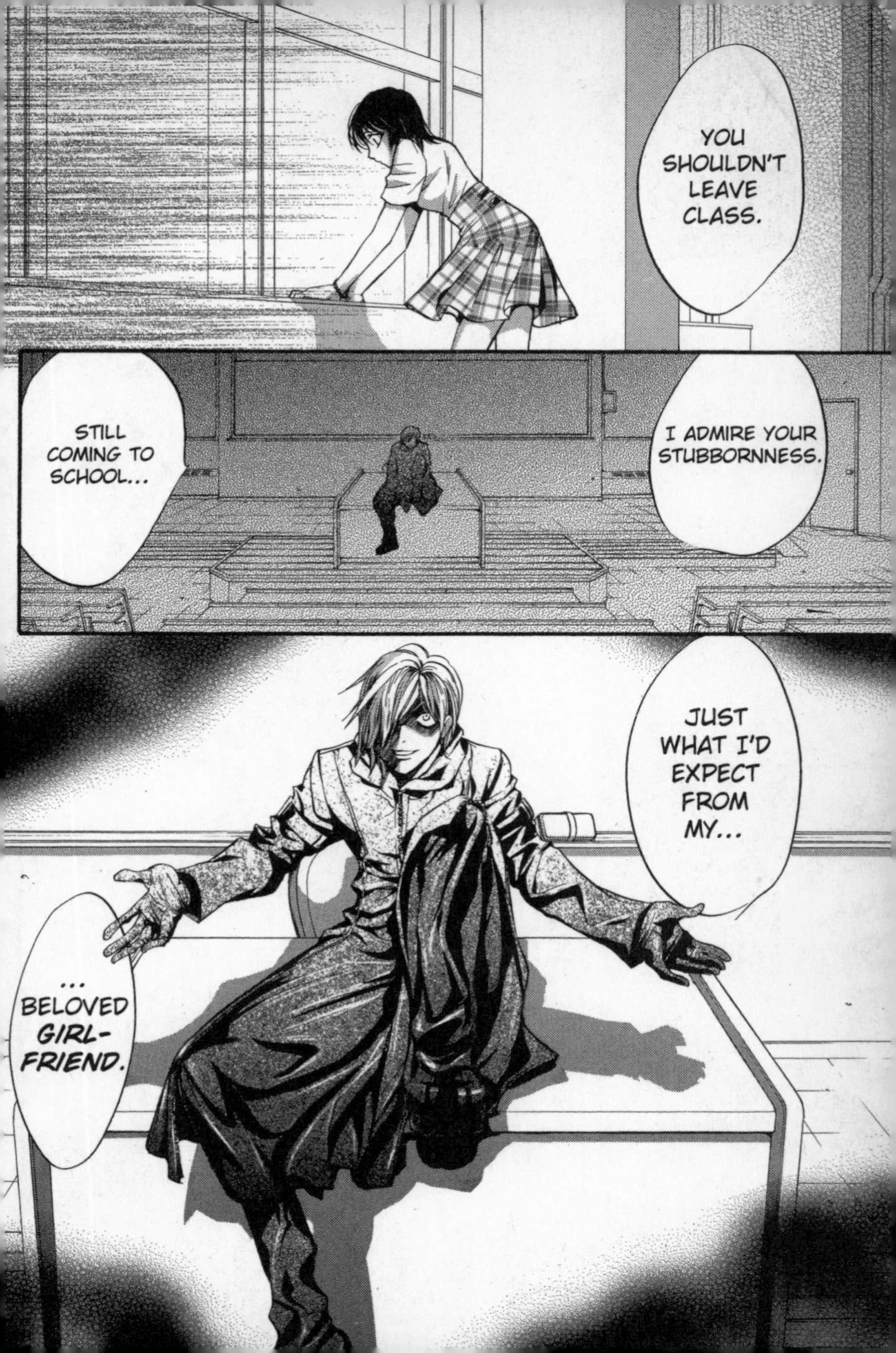
YOU SHOULDN'T LEAVE CLASS.
I ADMIRE YOUR STUBBORNNESS.
STILL COMING TO SCHOOL...
JUST WHAT I'D EXPECT FROM MY...
...BELOVED GIRL-FRIEND.

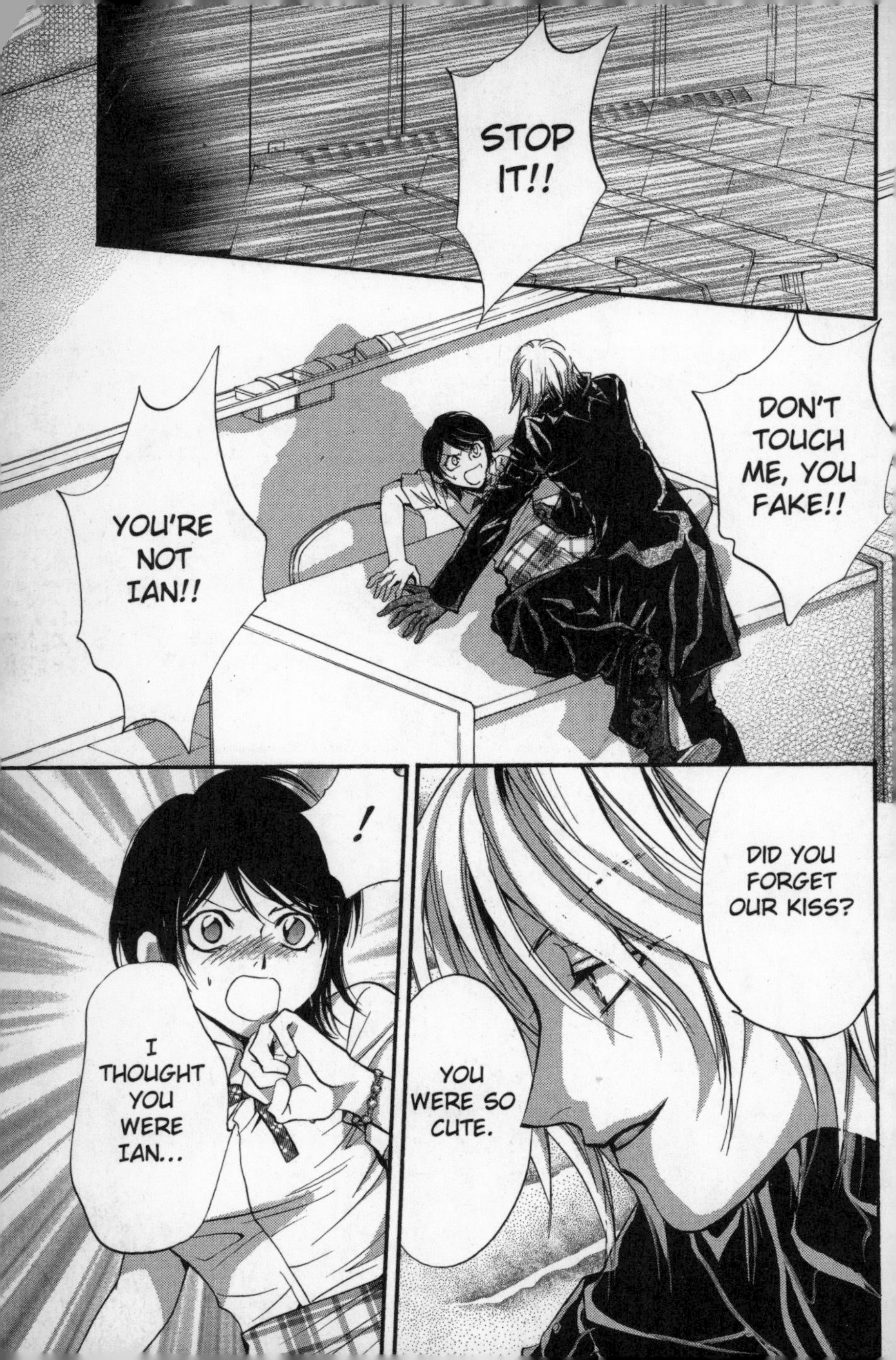
STOP IT!!
DON'T TOUCH ME, YOU FAKE!!
YOU'RE NOT IAN!!
DID YOU FORGET OUR KISS?
YOU WERE SO CUTE.
!
I THOUGHT YOU WERE IAN...

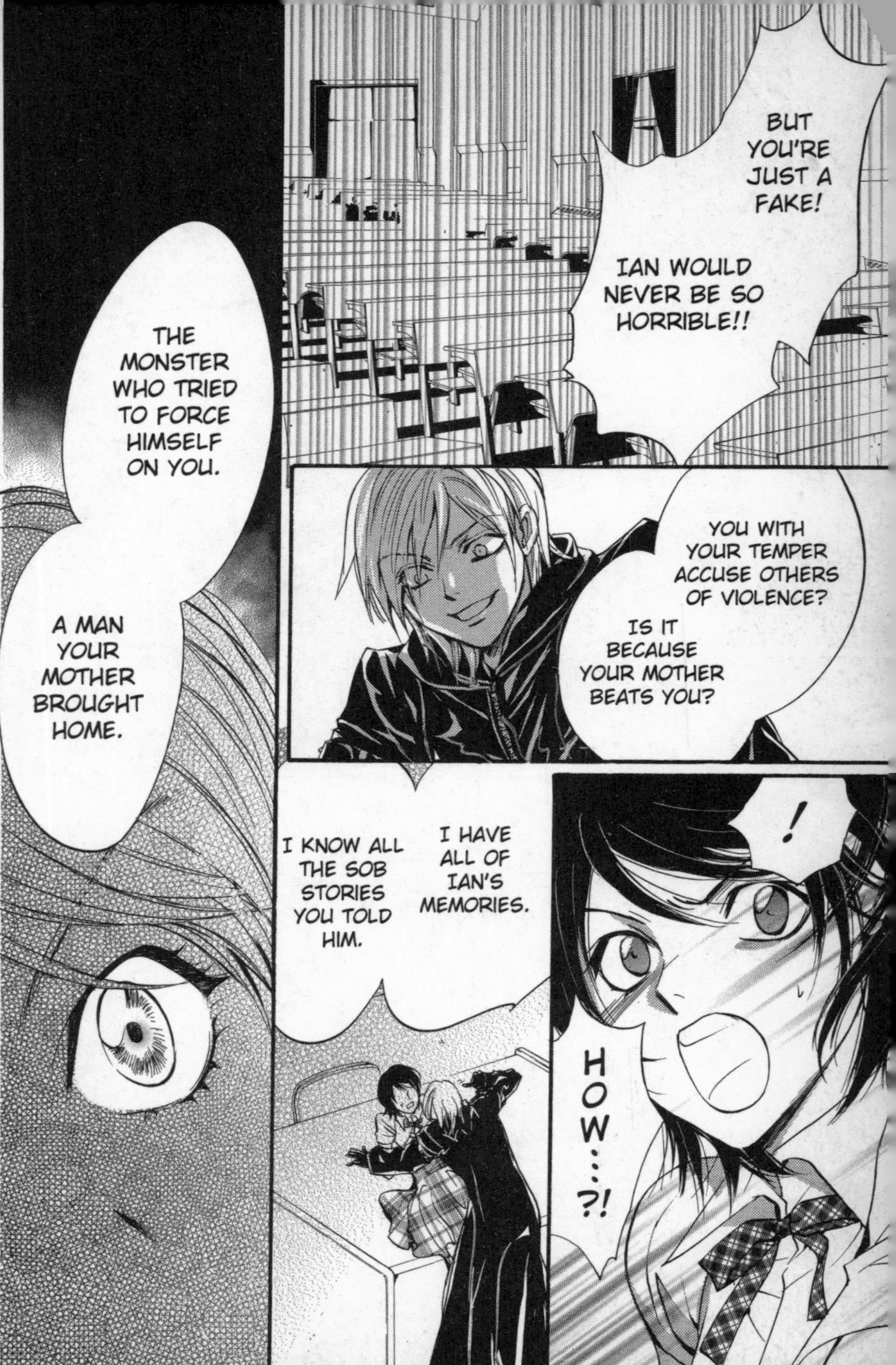
BUT YOU'RE JUST A FAKE!
IAN WOULD NEVER BE SO HORRIBLE!!
YOU WITH YOUR TEMPER ACCUSE OTHERS OF VIOLENCE?
IS IT BECAUSE YOUR MOTHER BEATS YOU?
!
HOW...?!
I HAVE ALL OF IAN'S MEMORIES.
I KNOW ALL THE SOB STORIES YOU TOLD HIM.
THE MONSTER WHO TRIED TO FORCE HIMSELF ON YOU.
A MAN YOUR MOTHER BROUGHT HOME.

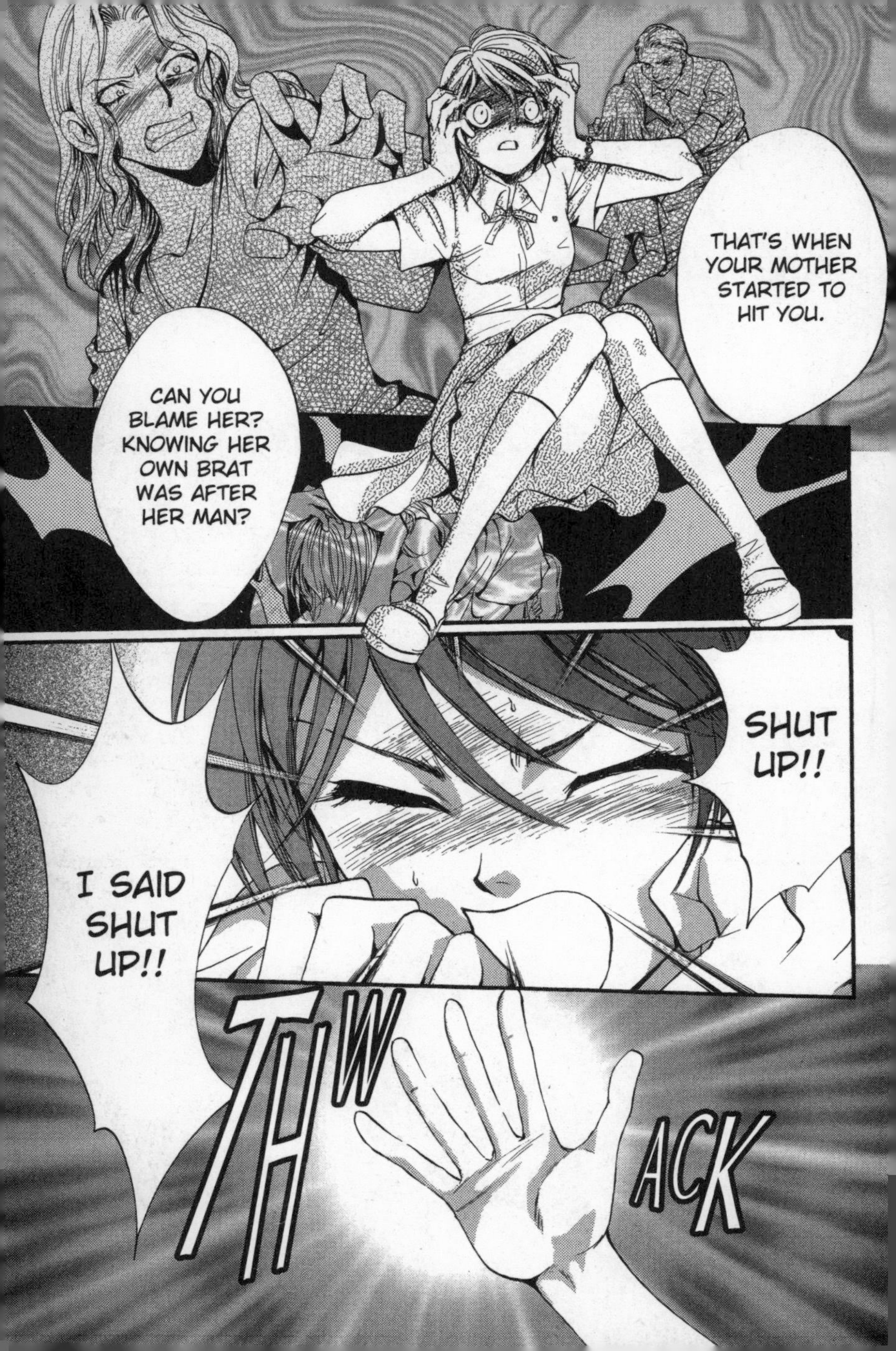
THAT'S WHEN YOUR MOTHER STARTED TO HIT YOU.
CAN YOU BLAME HER? KNOWING HER OWN BRAT WAS AFTER HER MAN?
SHUT UP!!
I SAID SHUT UP!!
THWACK

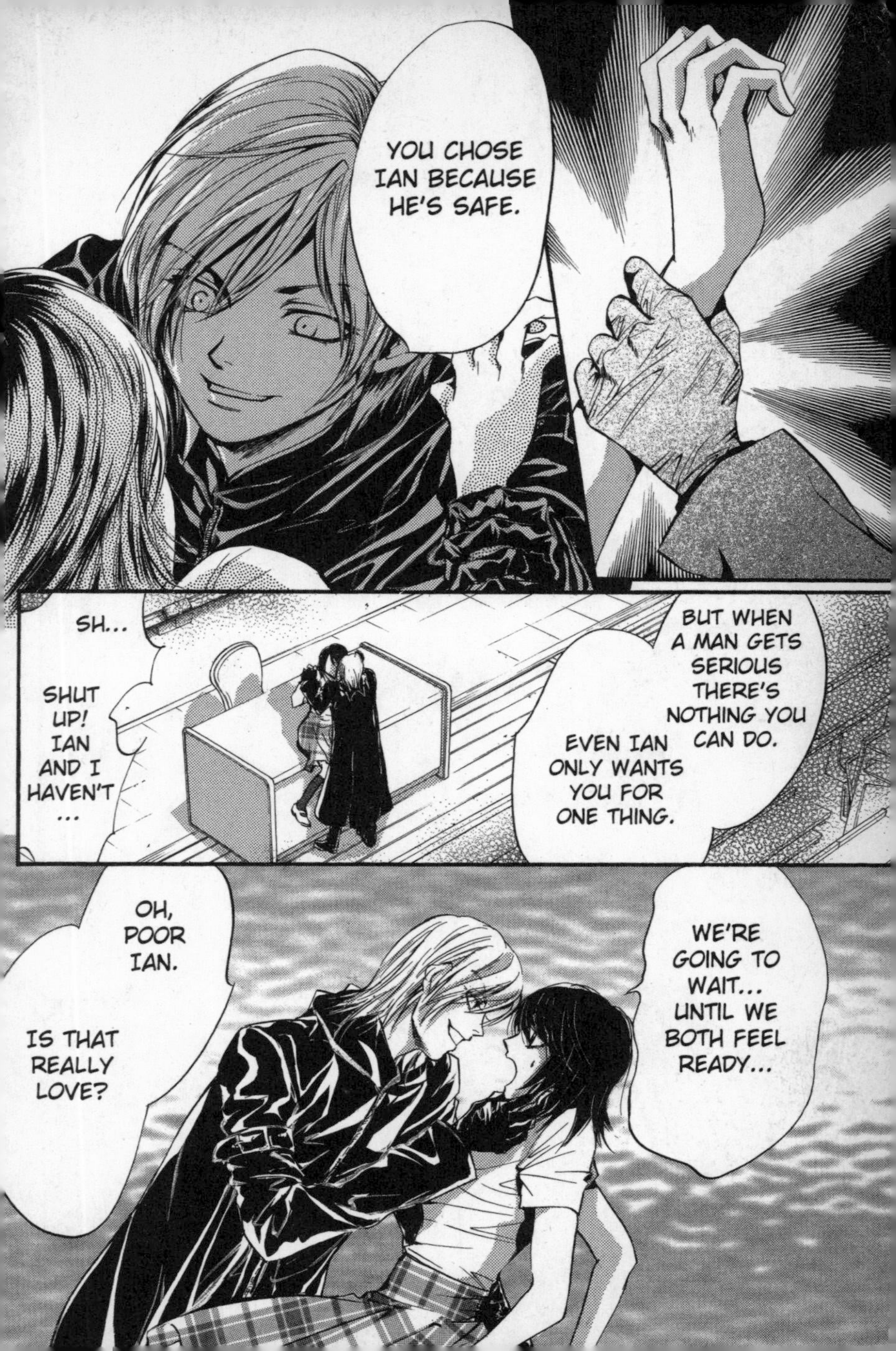
YOU CHOSE IAN BECAUSE HE'S SAFE.
BUT WHEN A MAN GETS SERIOUS THERE'S NOTHING YOU CAN DO.
EVEN IAN ONLY WANTS YOU FOR ONE THING.
SH...
SHUT UP! IAN AND I HAVEN'T ...
WE'RE GOING TO WAIT... UNTIL WE BOTH FEEL READY...
OH, POOR IAN.
IS THAT REALLY LOVE?

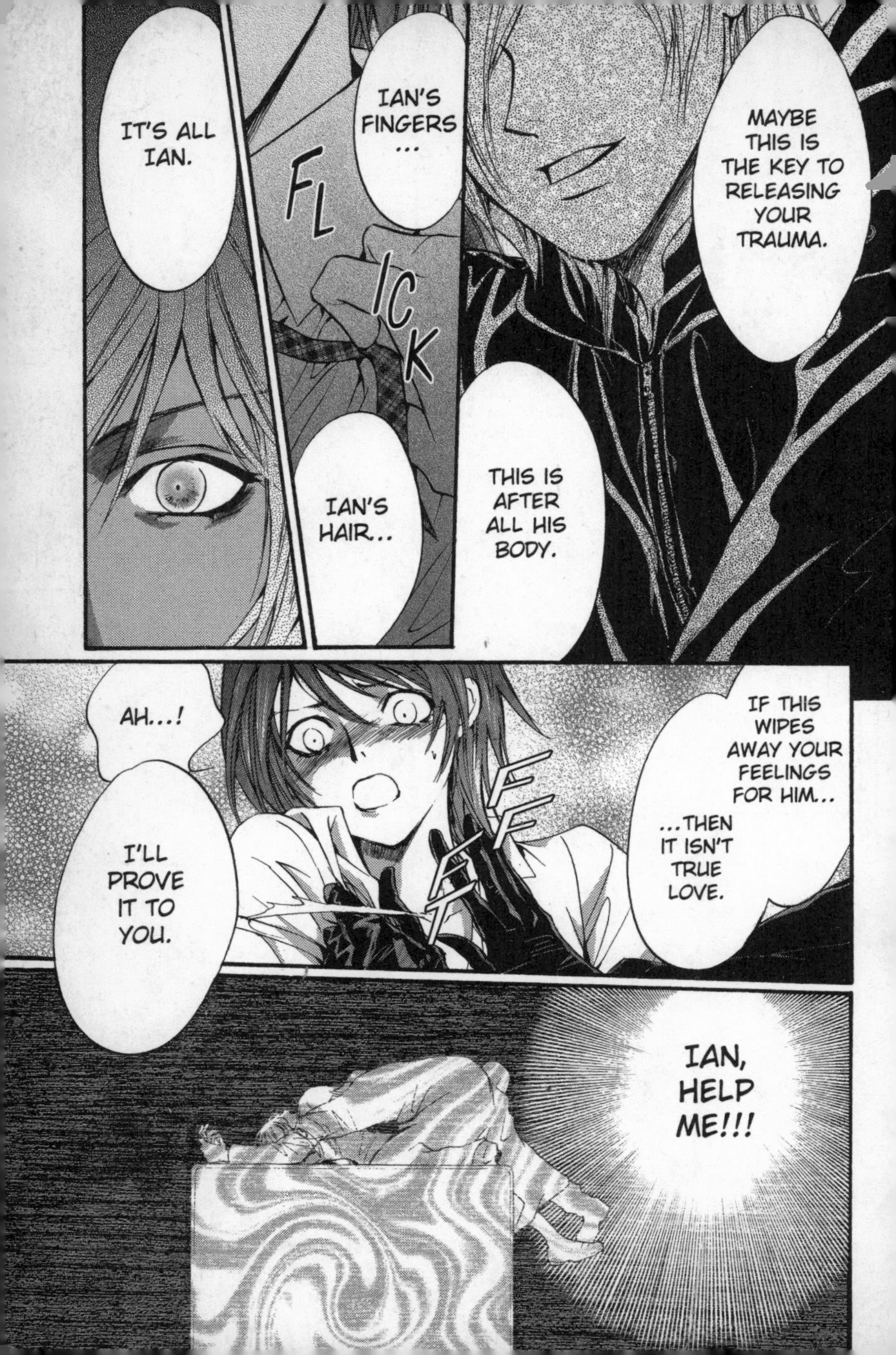

MAYBE THIS IS THE KEY TO RELEASING YOUR TRAUMA.
THIS IS AFTER ALL HIS BODY.
IAN'S FINGERS...
FLICK
IAN'S HAIR...
IT'S ALL IAN.
IF THIS WIPES AWAY YOUR FEELINGS FOR HIM...
...THEN IT ISN'T TRUE LOVE.
FFFF
AH...!
I'LL PROVE IT TO YOU.
IAN, HELP ME!!!

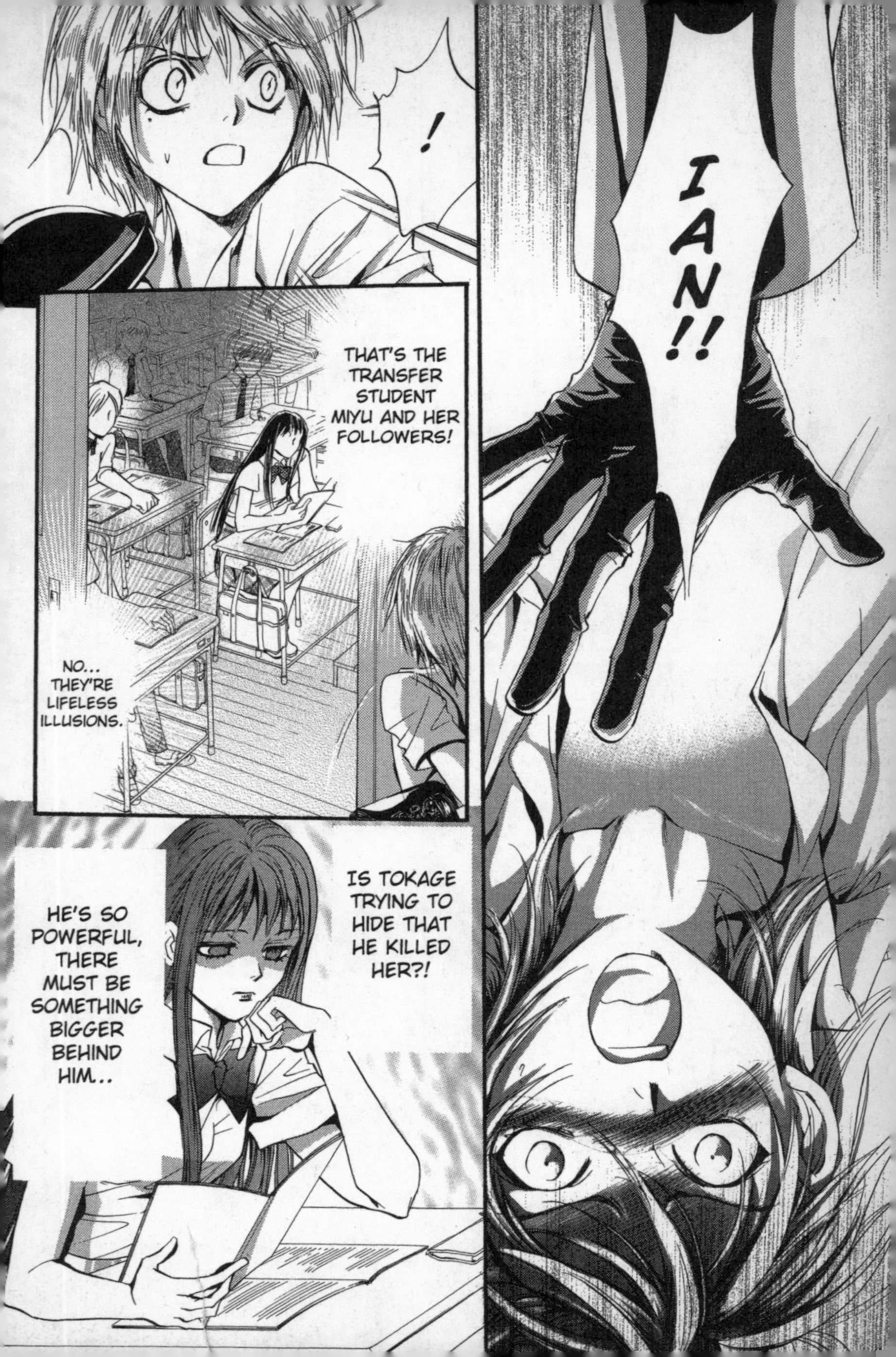

IAN!!
!
THAT'S THE TRANSFER STUDENT MIYU AND HER FOLLOWERS!
NO... THEY'RE LIFELESS ILLUSIONS.
IS TOKAGE TRYING TO HIDE THAT HE KILLED HER?!
HE'S SO POWERFUL, THERE MUST BE SOMETHING BIGGER BEHIND HIM...

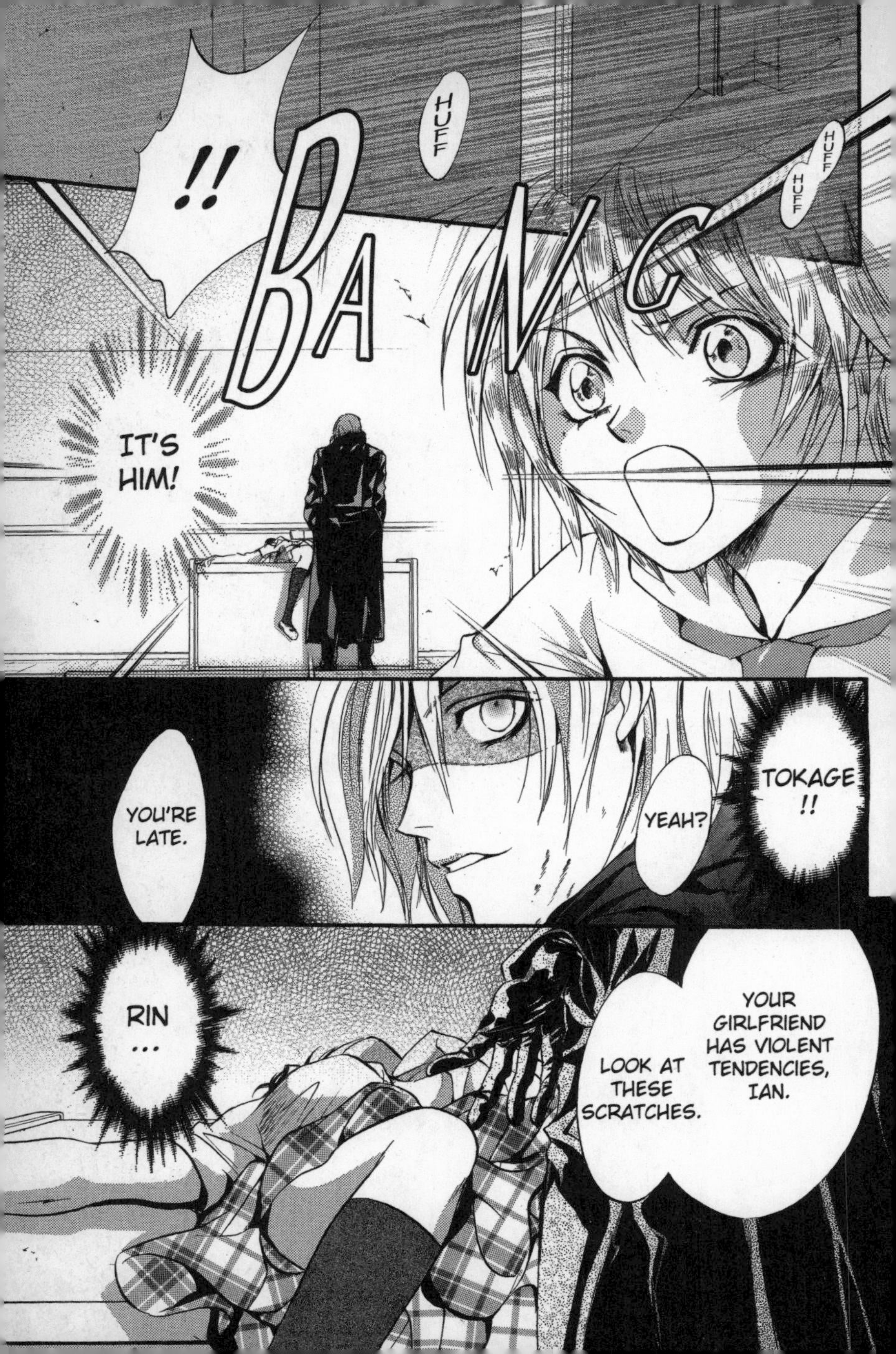
HUFF HUFF
HUFF
BANG
!!
IT'S HIM!
TOKAGE !!
YEAH?
YOU'RE LATE.
YOUR GIRLFRIEND HAS VIOLENT TENDENCIES, IAN.
LOOK AT THESE SCRATCHES.
RIN ...

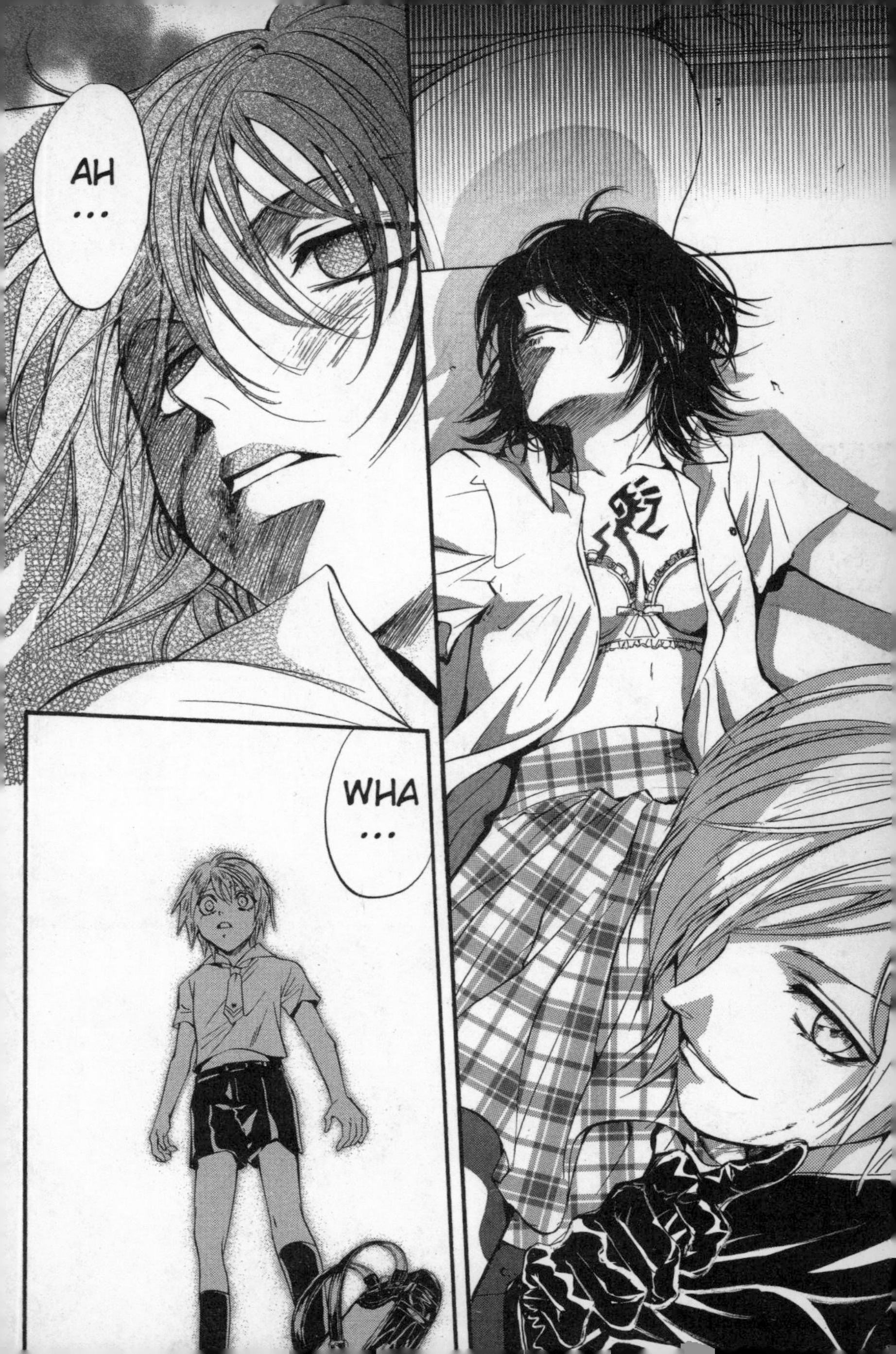
AH ...
WHA ...

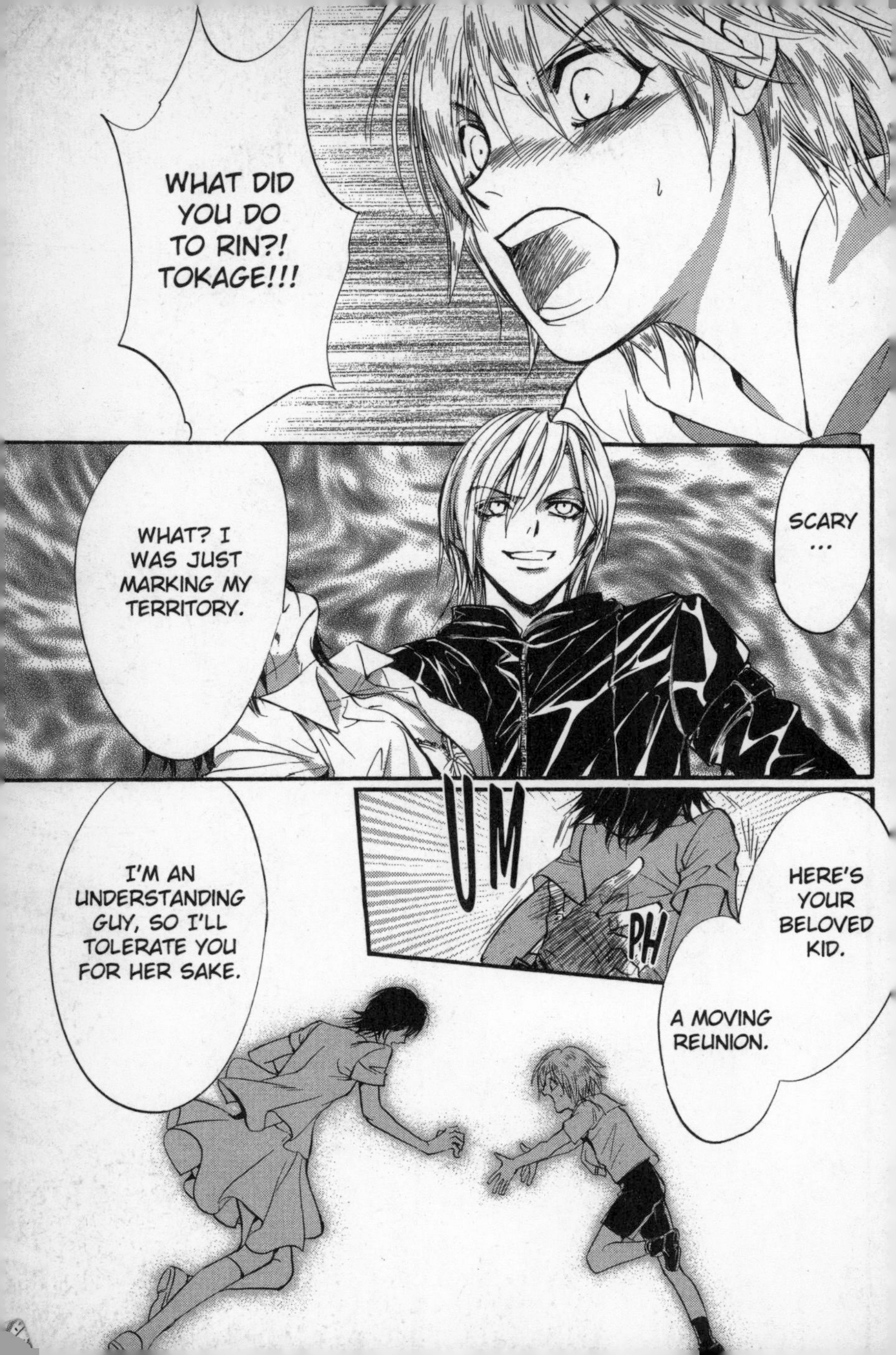
WHAT DID YOU DO TO RIN?! TOKAGE!!!
SCARY ...
WHAT? I WAS JUST MARKING MY TERRITORY.
UMPH
HERE'S YOUR BELOVED KID.
A MOVING REUNION.
I'M AN UNDERSTANDING GUY, SO I'LL TOLERATE YOU FOR HER SAKE.

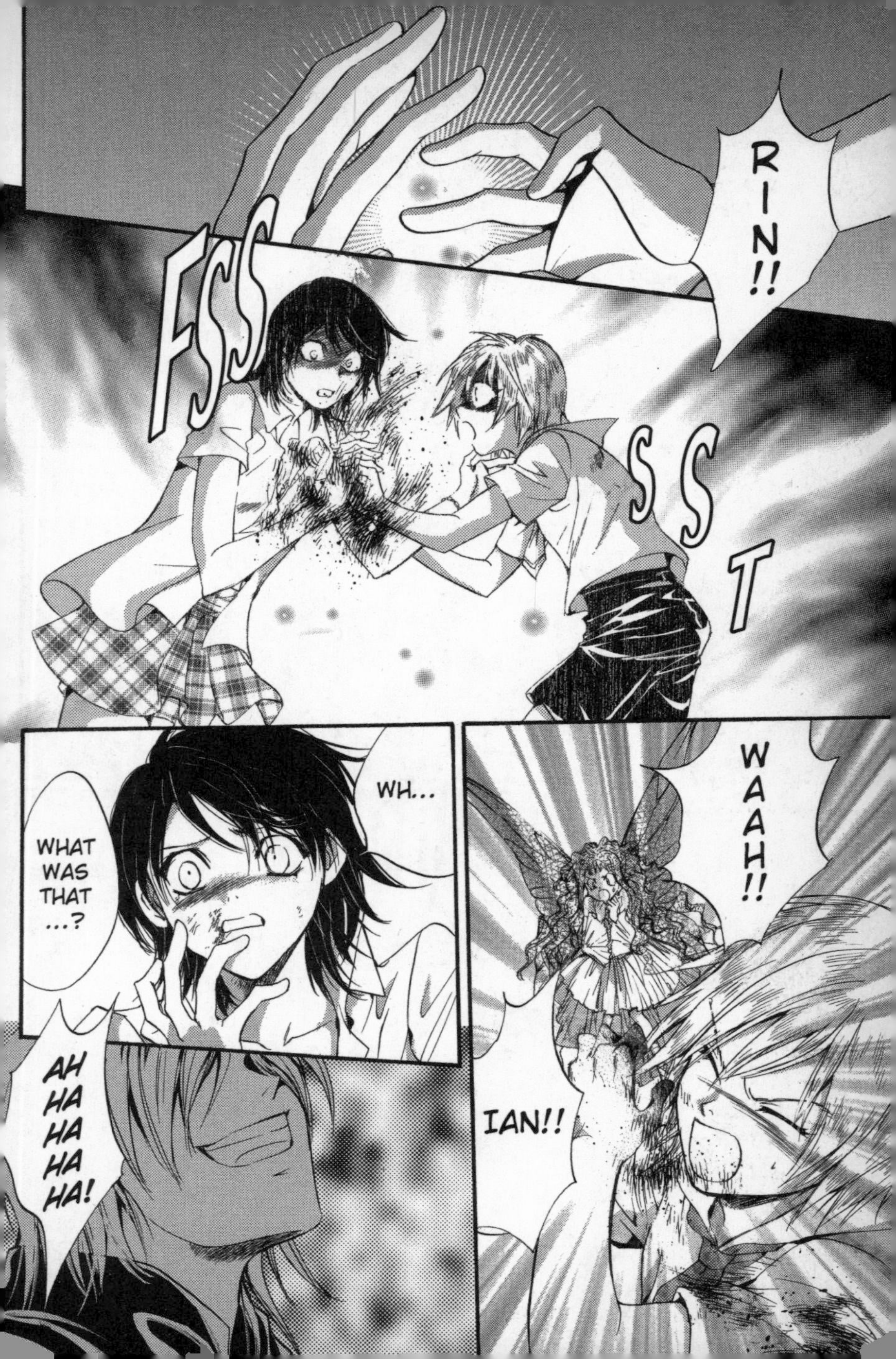
RIN!!
FSS
SSST
WAAAH!!
IAN!!
WH...
WHAT WAS THAT ...?
AH HA HA HA HA HA!

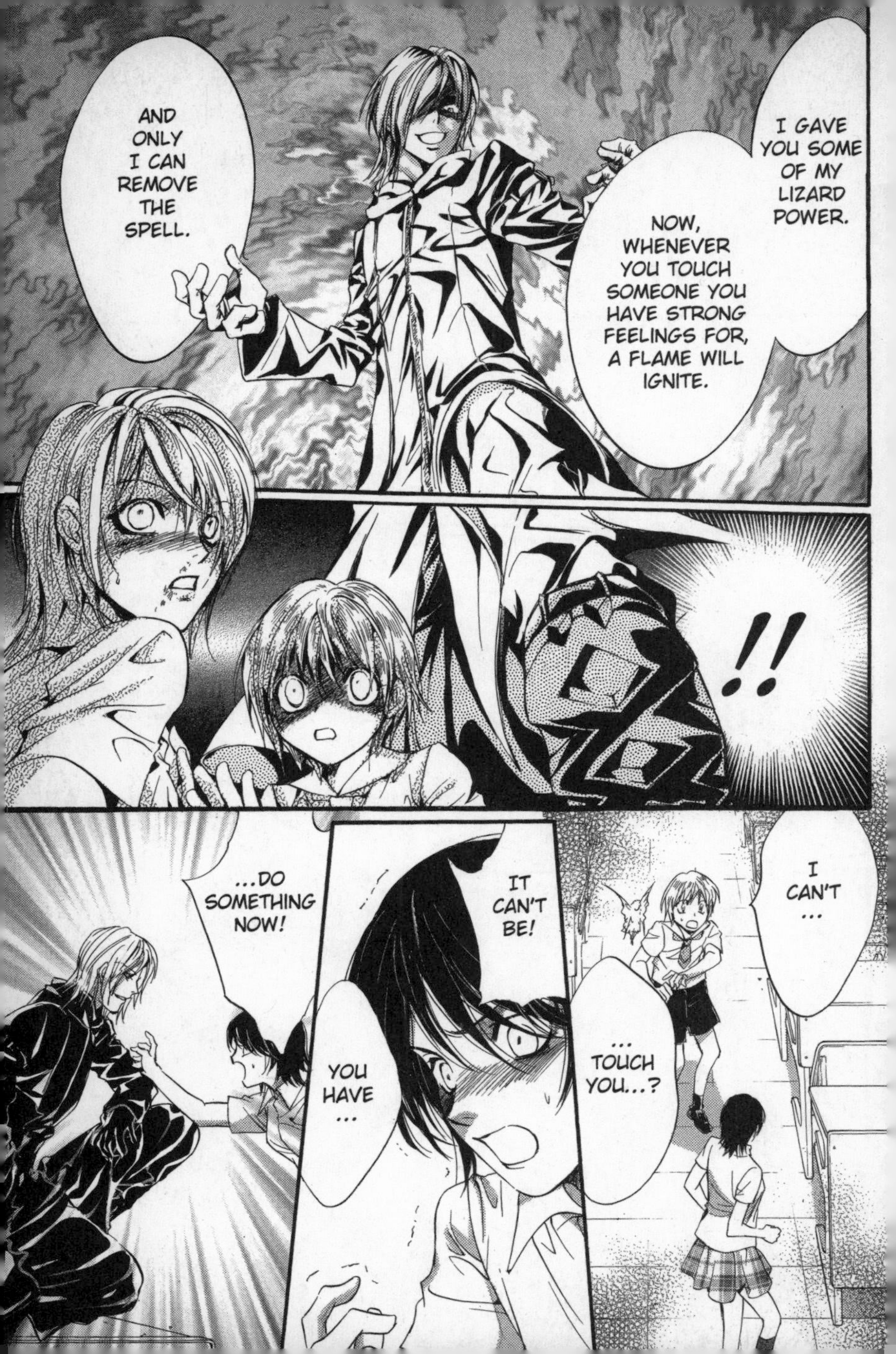
I GAVE YOU SOME OF MY LIZARD POWER.
NOW, WHENEVER YOU TOUCH SOMEONE YOU HAVE STRONG FEELINGS FOR, A FLAME WILL IGNITE.
AND ONLY I CAN REMOVE THE SPELL.
!!
I CAN'T ...
... TOUCH YOU...?
IT CAN'T BE!
YOU HAVE ...
...DO SOMETHING NOW!

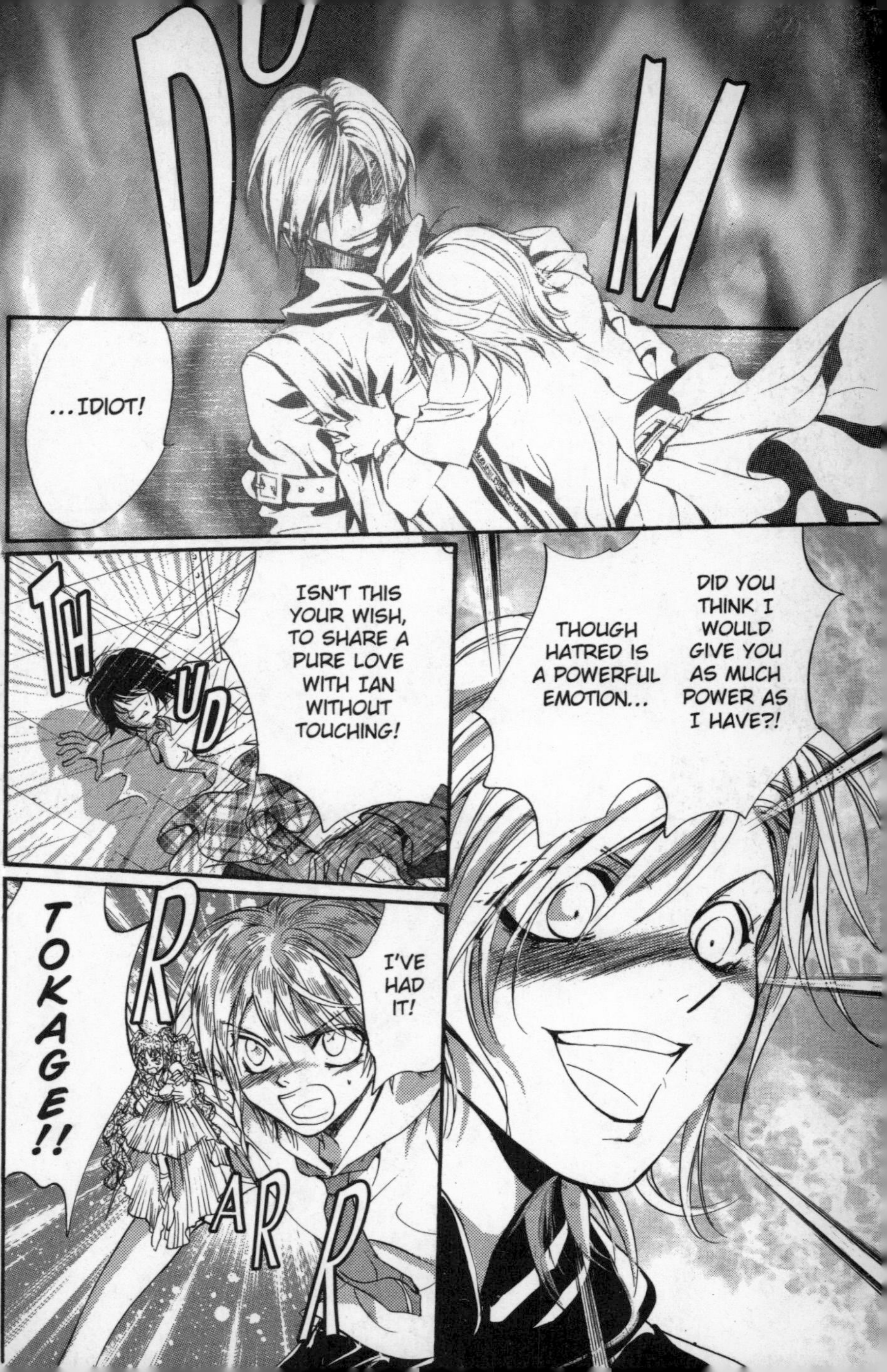
DOM
...IDIOT!
THOUGH HATRED IS A POWERFUL EMOTION...
DID YOU THINK I WOULD GIVE YOU AS MUCH POWER AS I HAVE?!
ISN'T THIS YOUR WISH, TO SHARE A PURE LOVE WITH IAN WITHOUT TOUCHING!
THUD
I'VE HAD IT!
TOKAGE!!
RARR

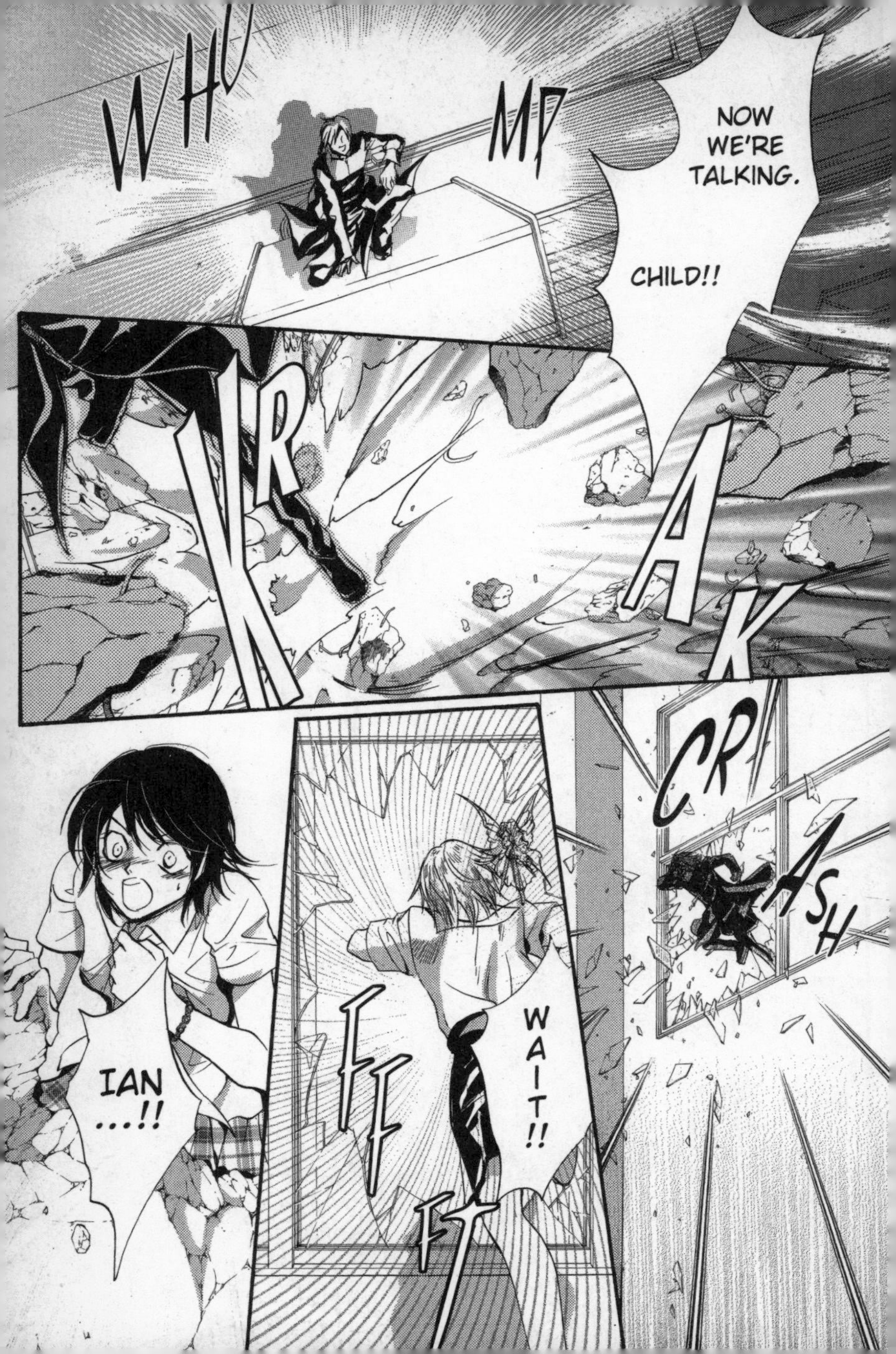

NOW WE'RE TALKING.
CHILD!!
WHUMP
KRAK
CRASH
WAIT!!
FFFFT
IAN ...!!

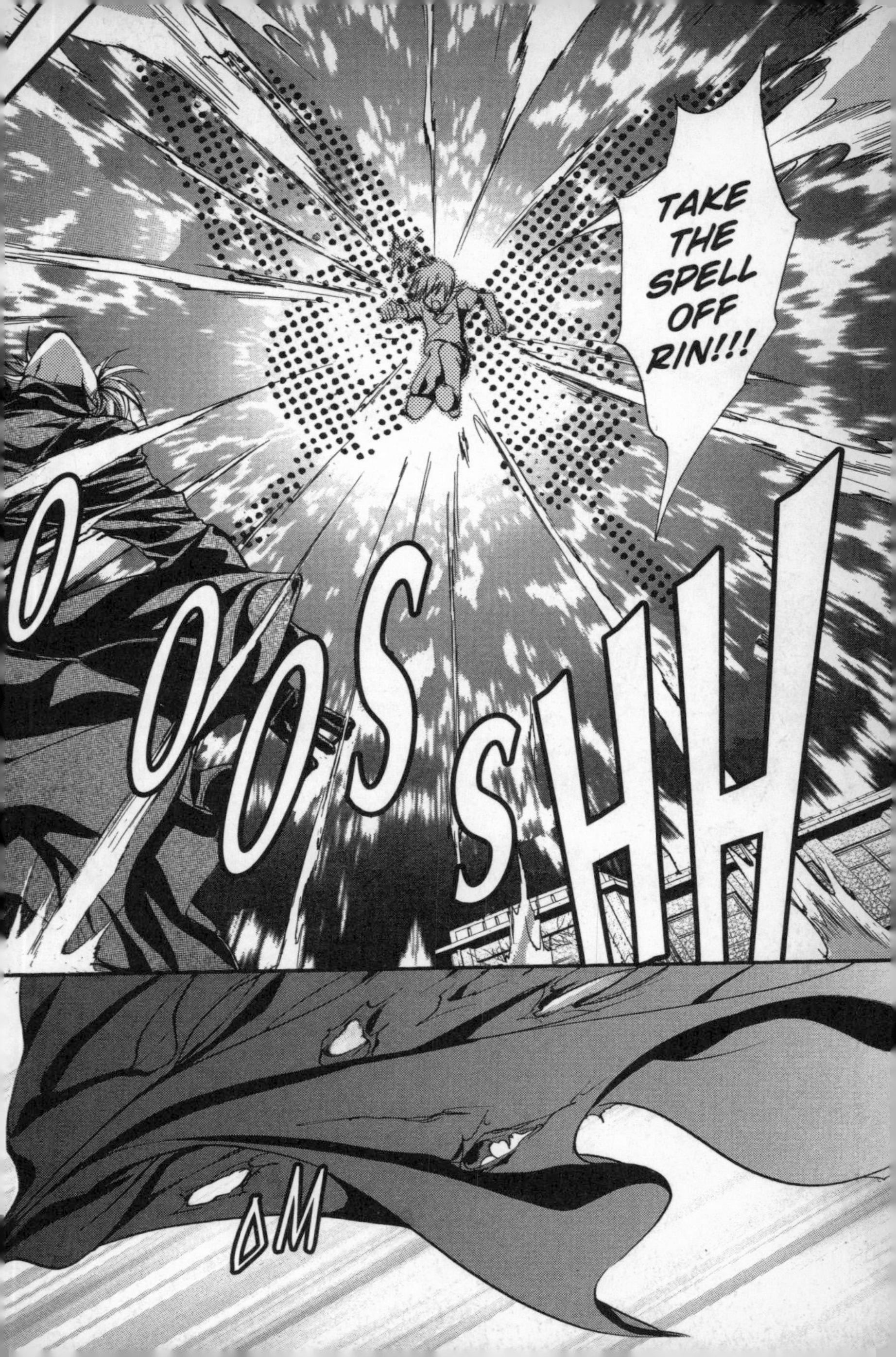
TAKE THE SPELL OFF RIN!!!
OOOSSHH

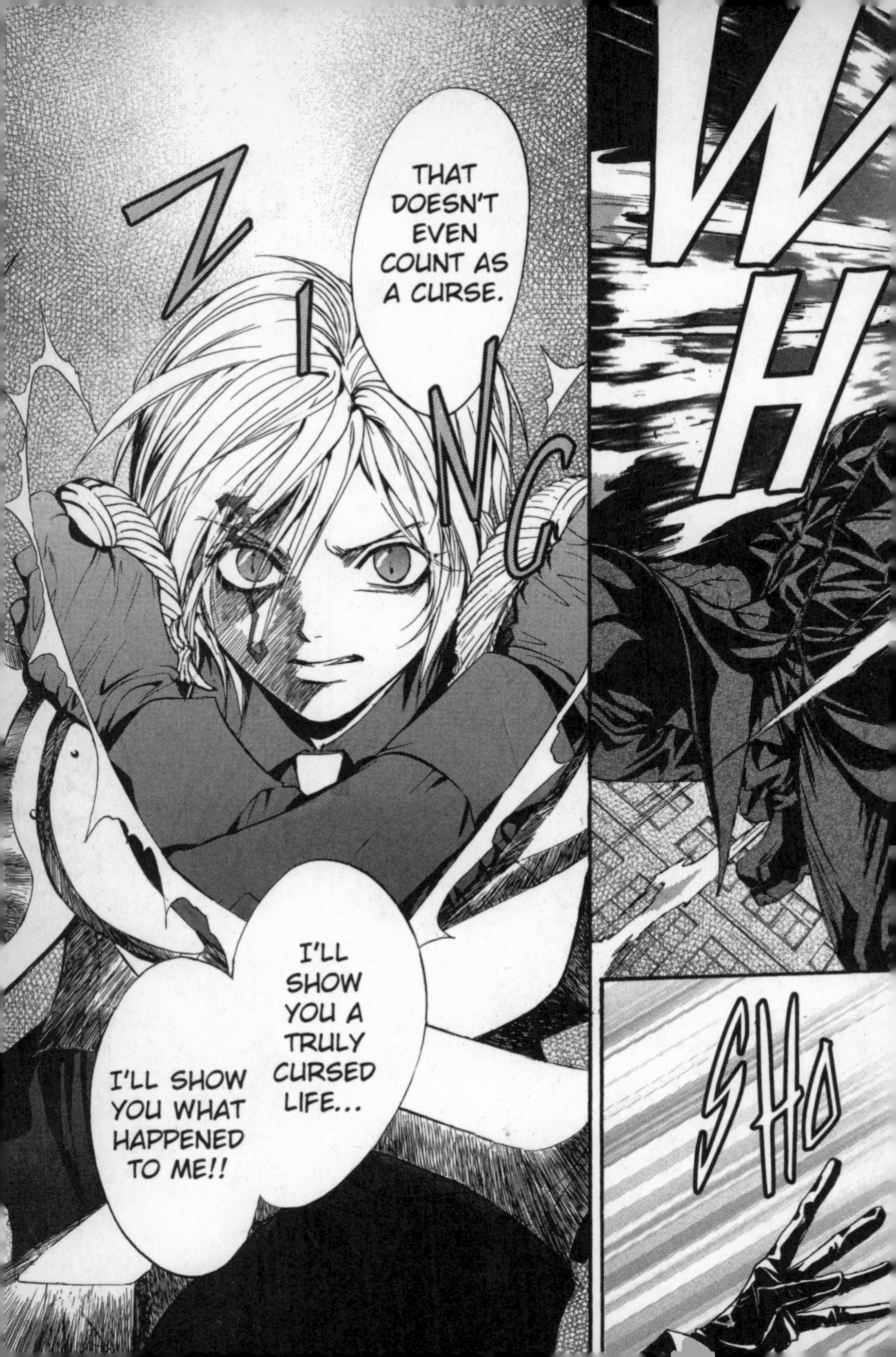

WH
SHO
ZING
THAT DOESN'T EVEN COUNT AS A CURSE.
I'LL SHOW YOU A TRULY CURSED LIFE...
I'LL SHOW YOU WHAT HAPPENED TO ME!!

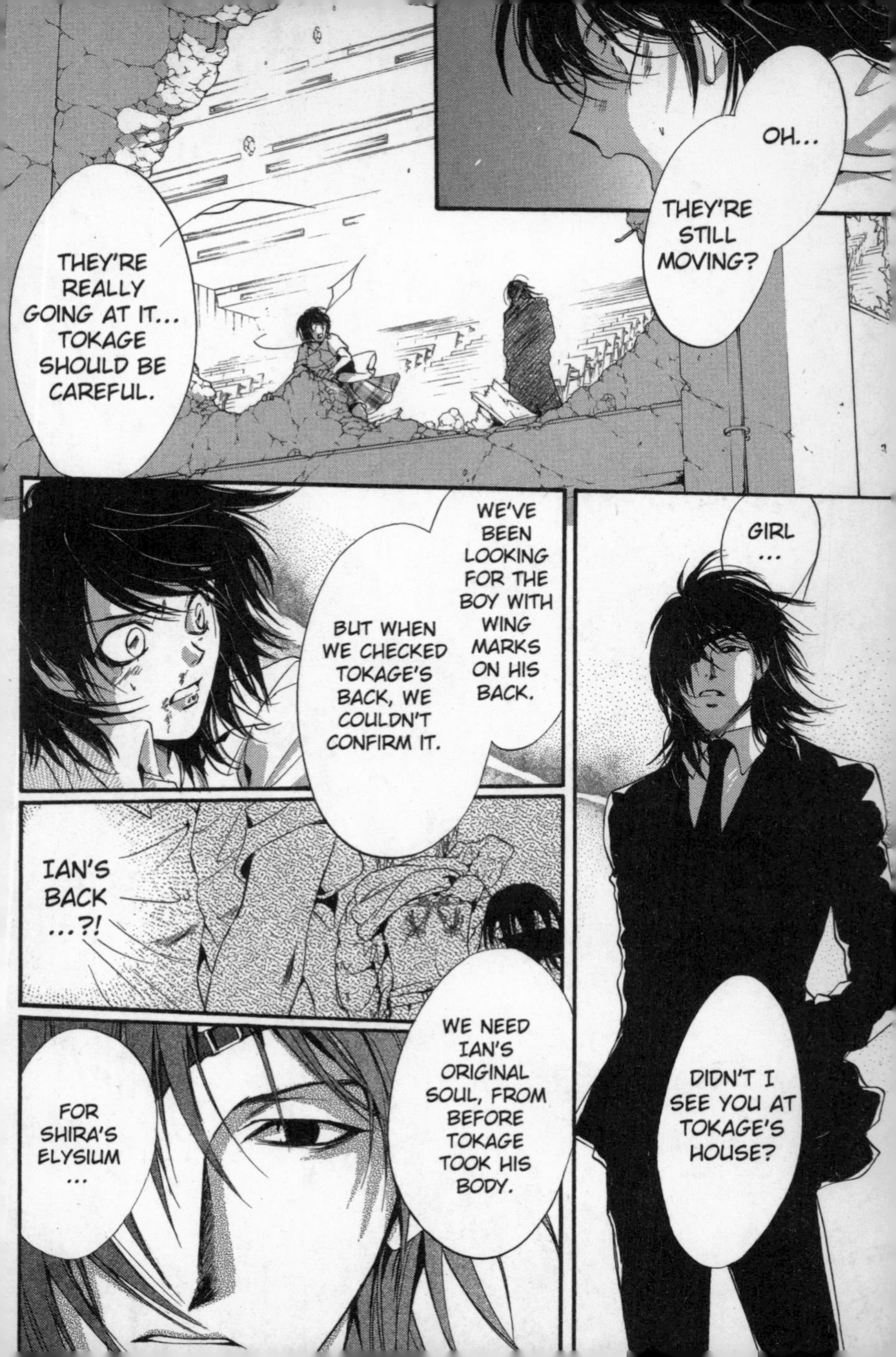
OH...
THEY'RE STILL MOVING?
THEY'RE REALLY GOING AT IT... TOKAGE SHOULD BE CAREFUL.
GIRL...
DIDN'T I SEE YOU AT TOKAGE'S HOUSE?
WE'VE BEEN LOOKING FOR THE BOY WITH WING MARKS ON HIS BACK.
BUT WHEN WE CHECKED TOKAGE'S BACK, WE COULDN'T CONFIRM IT.
IAN'S BACK ...?!
WE NEED IAN'S ORIGINAL SOUL, FROM BEFORE TOKAGE TOOK HIS BODY.
FOR SHIRA'S ELYSIUM ...

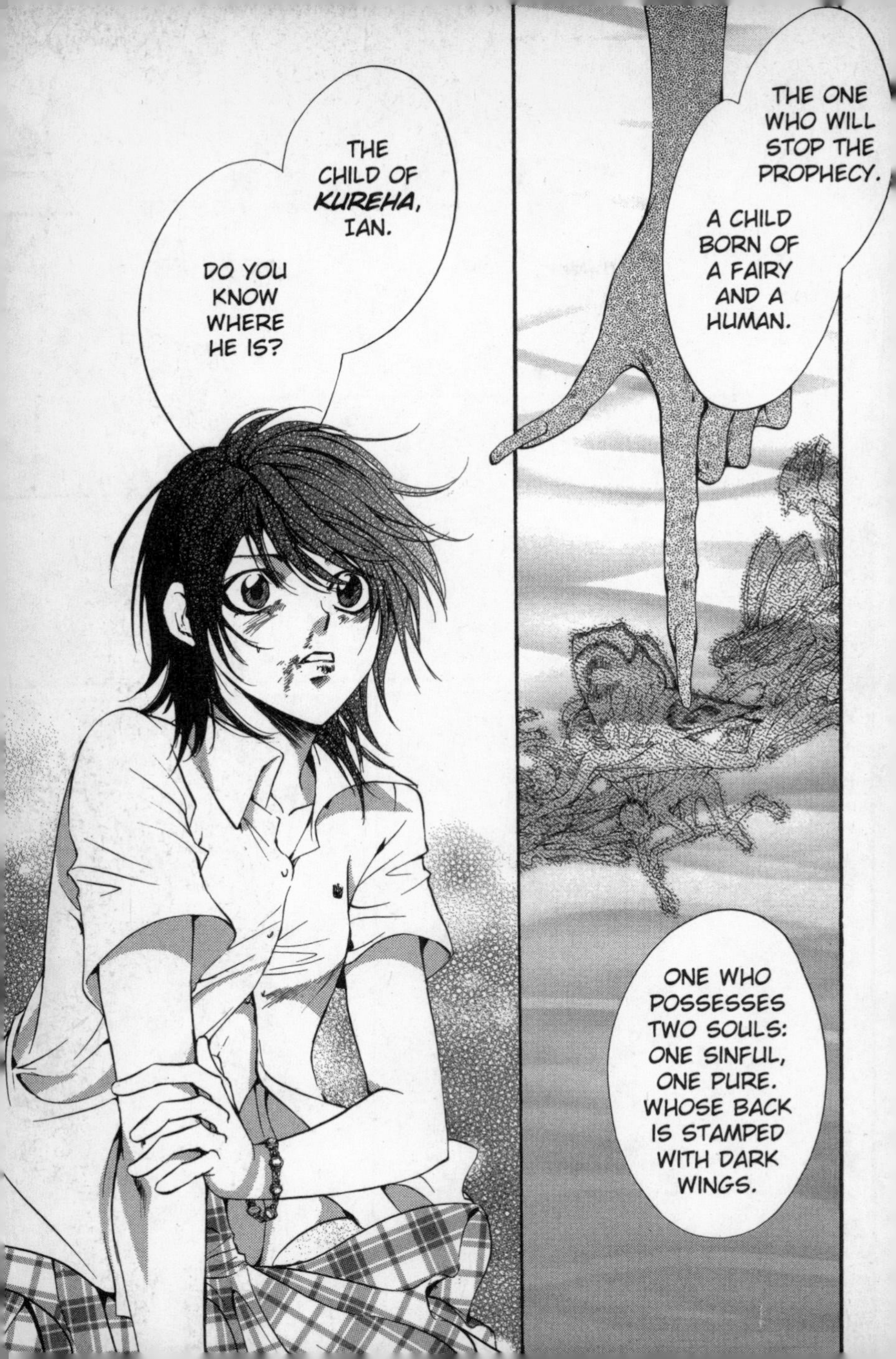
THE ONE WHO WILL STOP THE PROPHECY.
A CHILD BORN OF A FAIRY AND A HUMAN.
ONE WHO POSSESSES TWO SOULS: ONE SINFUL, ONE PURE. WHOSE BACK IS STAMPED WITH DARK WINGS.
THE CHILD OF KUREHA, IAN.
DO YOU KNOW WHERE HE IS?

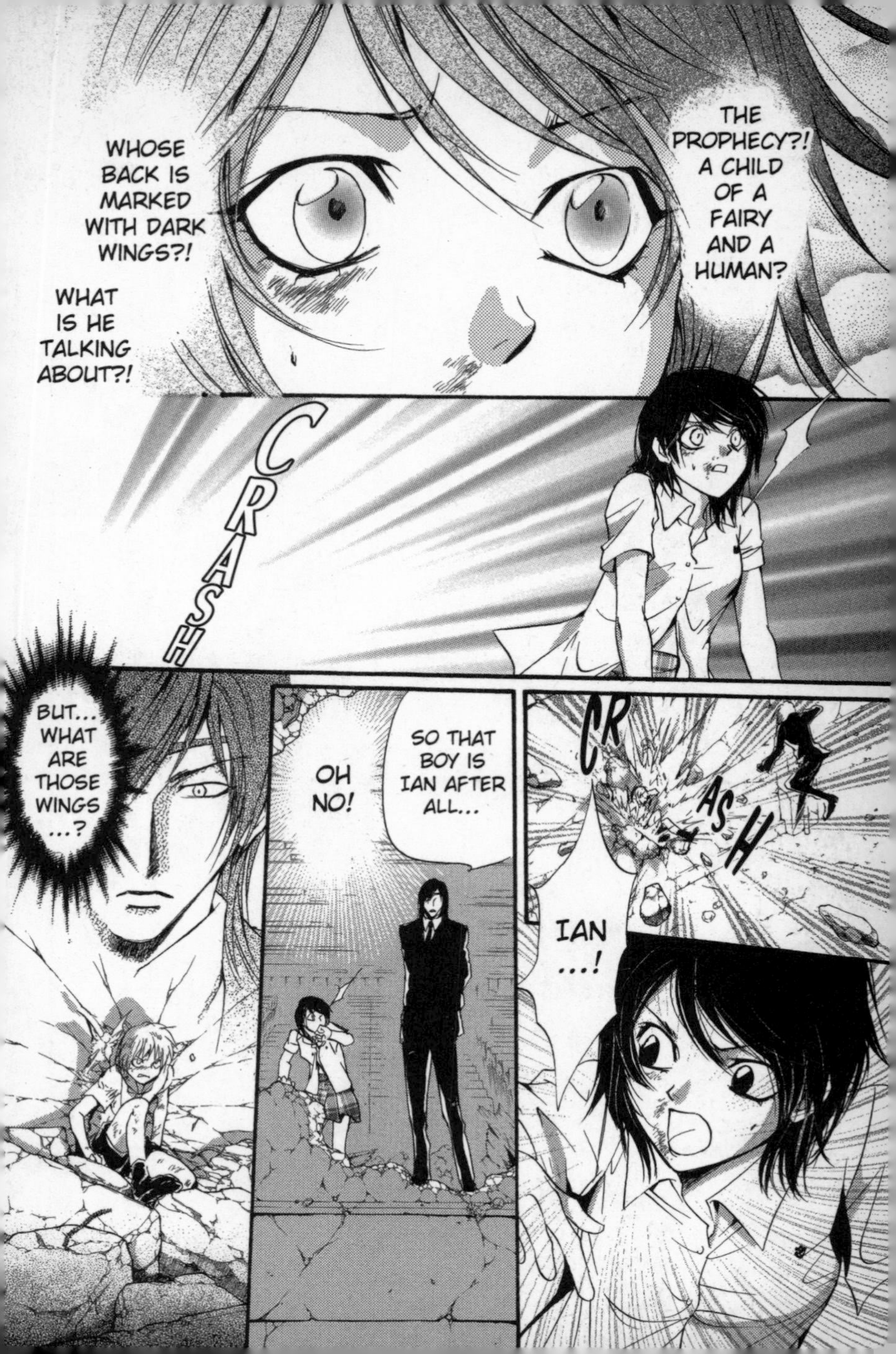
THE PROPHECY?! A CHILD OF A FAIRY AND A HUMAN?
WHOSE BACK IS MARKED WITH DARK WINGS?!
WHAT IS HE TALKING ABOUT?!
CRASH
CRASH
IAN ...!
SO THAT BOY IS IAN AFTER ALL...
OH NO!
BUT... WHAT ARE THOSE WINGS ...?

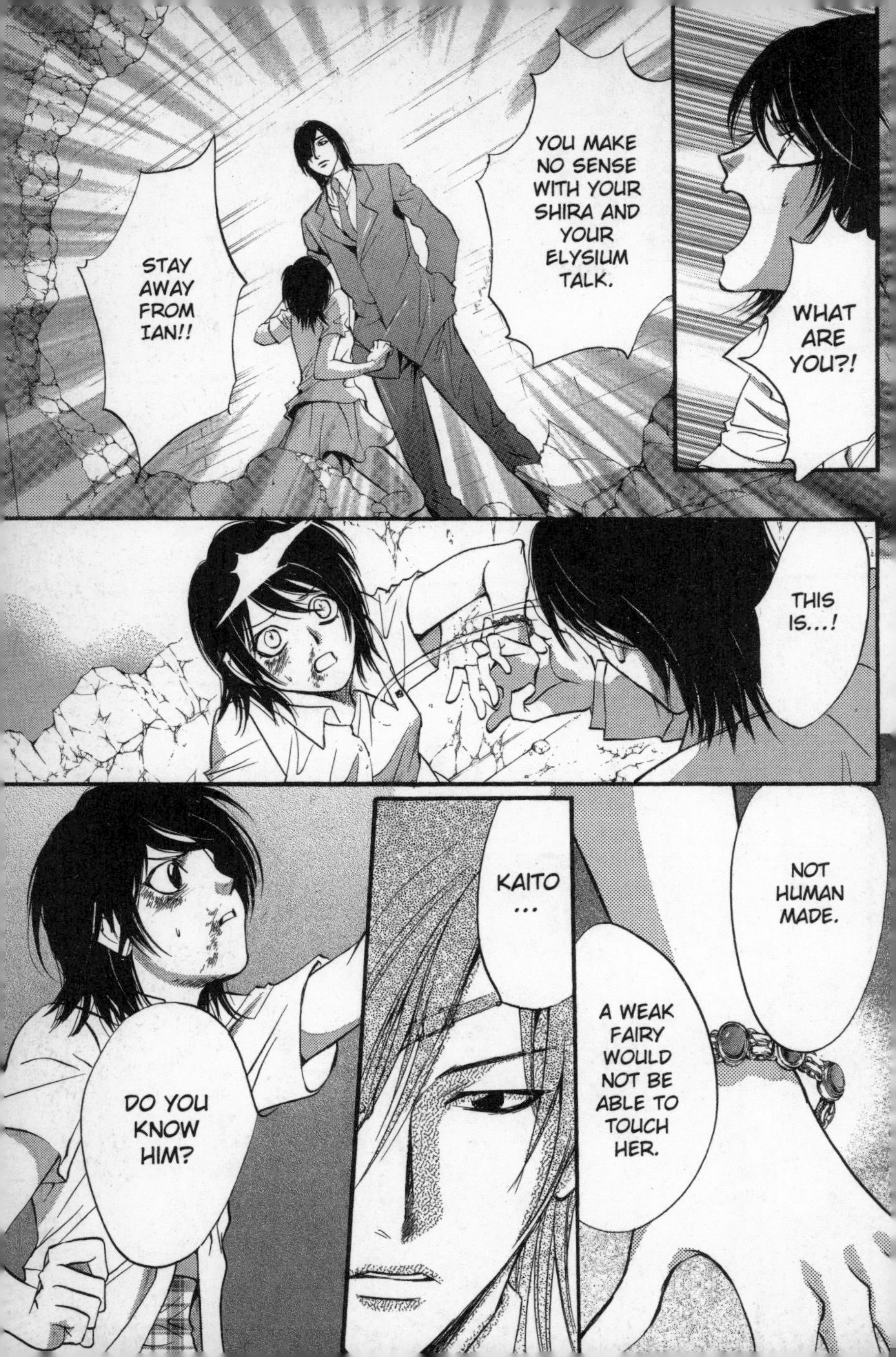
WHAT ARE YOU?!
YOU MAKE NO SENSE WITH YOUR SHIRA AND YOUR ELYSIUM TALK.
STAY AWAY FROM IAN!!
THIS IS...!
NOT HUMAN MADE.
A WEAK FAIRY WOULD NOT BE ABLE TO TOUCH HER.
KAITO ...
DO YOU KNOW HIM?

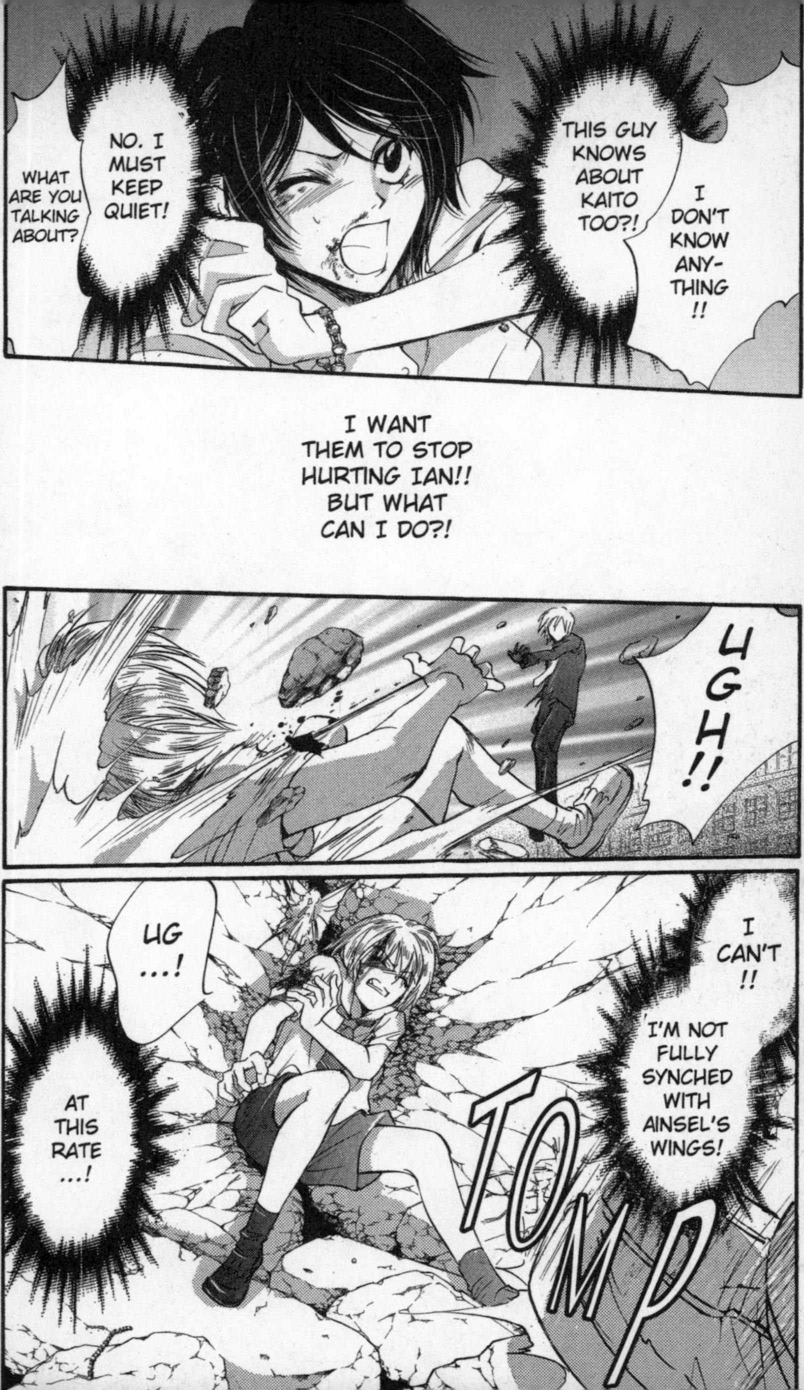

I DON'T KNOW ANYTHING!!
THIS GUY KNOWS ABOUT KAITO TOO?!
NO. I MUST KEEP QUIET!
WHAT ARE YOU TALKING ABOUT?
I WANT THEM TO STOP HURTING IAN!! BUT WHAT CAN I DO?!
UGH!!
I CAN'T!!
I'M NOT FULLY SYNCHED WITH AINSEL'S WINGS!
TOMP
UG...!
AT THIS RATE...!

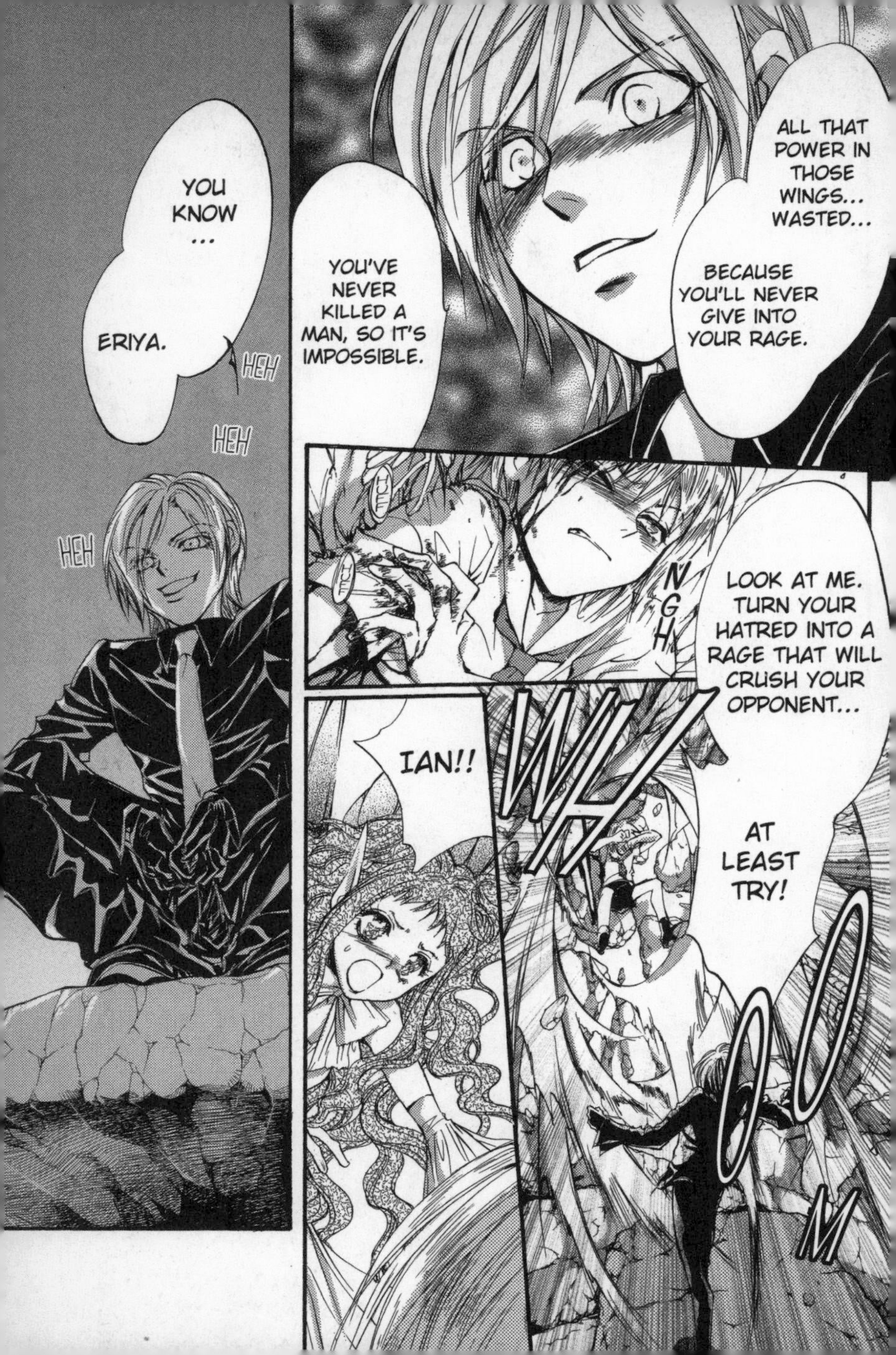
ALL THAT POWER IN THOSE WINGS... WASTED...
BECAUSE YOU'LL NEVER GIVE INTO YOUR RAGE.
YOU'VE NEVER KILLED A MAN, SO IT'S IMPOSSIBLE.
NGH
LOOK AT ME. TURN YOUR HATRED INTO A RAGE THAT WILL CRUSH YOUR OPPONENT...
AT LEAST TRY!
WHOOM
IAN!!
YOU KNOW ... ERIYA.
HEH
HEH
HEH

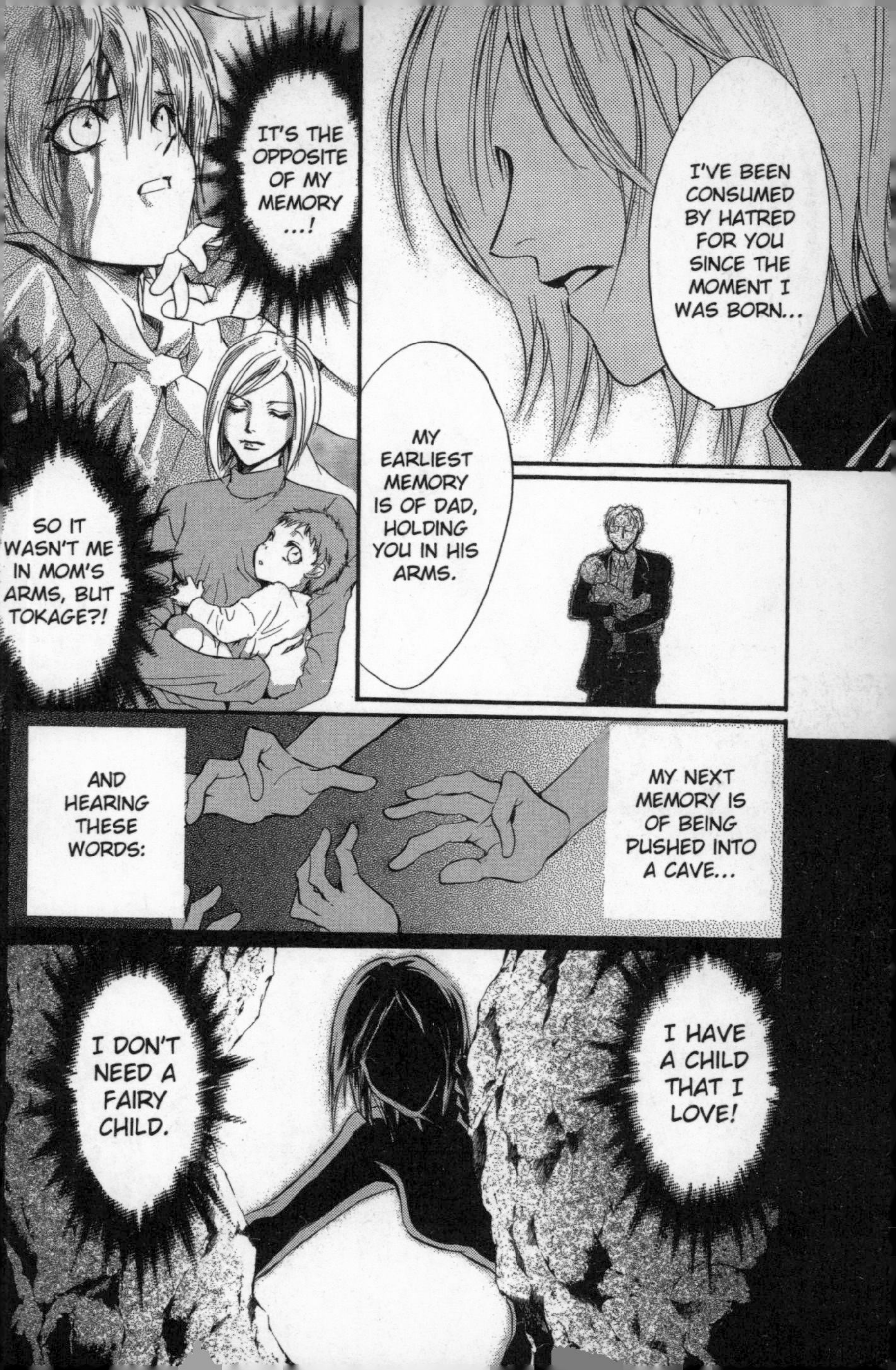

I'VE BEEN CONSUMED BY HATRED FOR YOU SINCE THE MOMENT I WAS BORN...
MY EARLIEST MEMORY IS OF DAD, HOLDING YOU IN HIS ARMS.
IT'S THE OPPOSITE OF MY MEMORY...!
SO IT WASN'T ME IN MOM'S ARMS, BUT TOKAGE?!
MY NEXT MEMORY IS OF BEING PUSHED INTO A CAVE...
AND HEARING THESE WORDS:
I HAVE A CHILD THAT I LOVE!
I DON'T NEED A FAIRY CHILD.

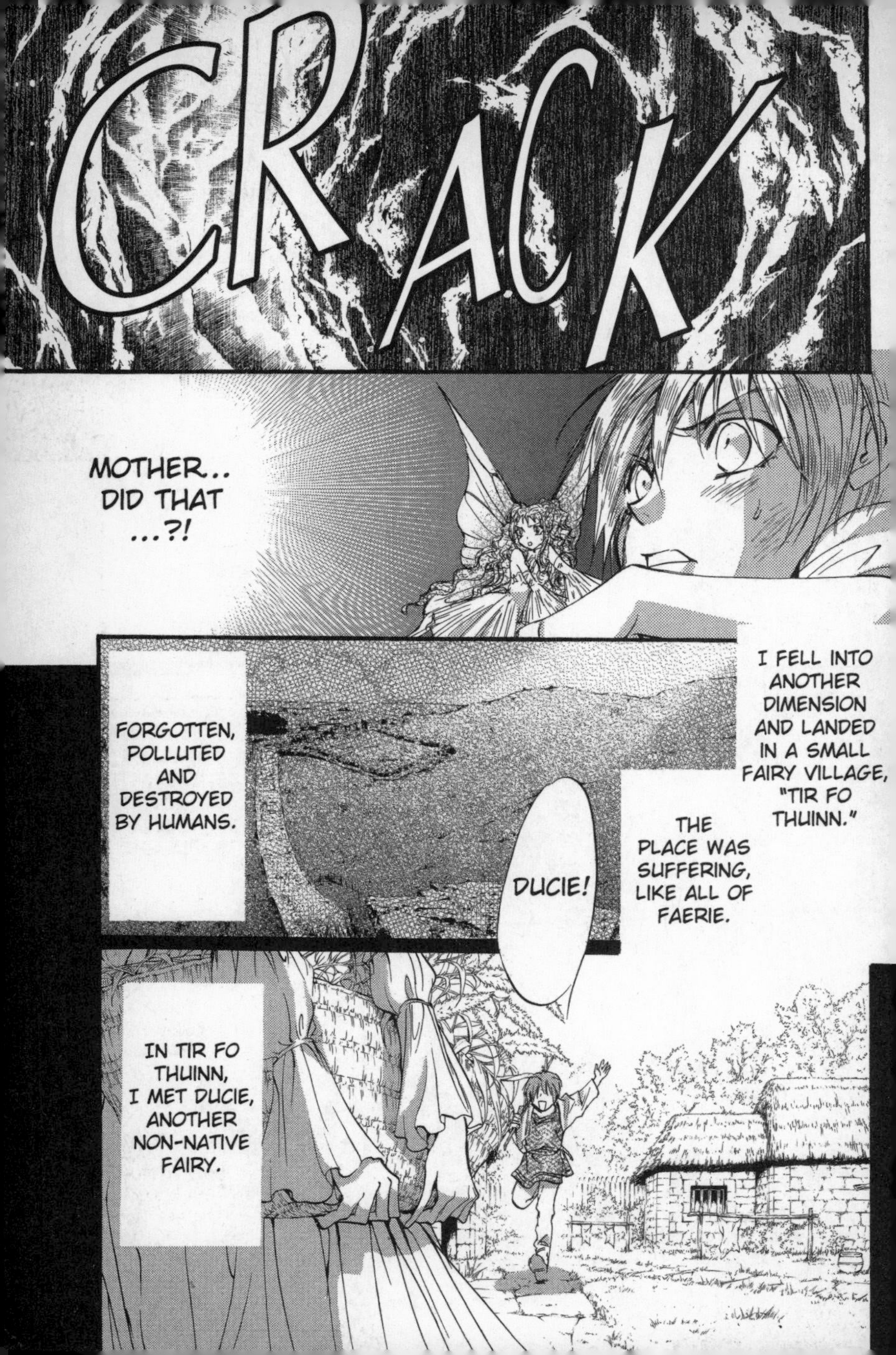
CRACK
MOTHER... DID THAT ...?!
I FELL INTO ANOTHER DIMENSION AND LANDED IN A SMALL FAIRY VILLAGE, "TIR FO THUINN."
THE PLACE WAS SUFFERING, LIKE ALL OF FAERIE.
FORGOTTEN, POLLUTED AND DESTROYED BY HUMANS.
DUCIE!
IN TIR FO THUINN, I MET DUCIE, ANOTHER NON-NATIVE FAIRY.

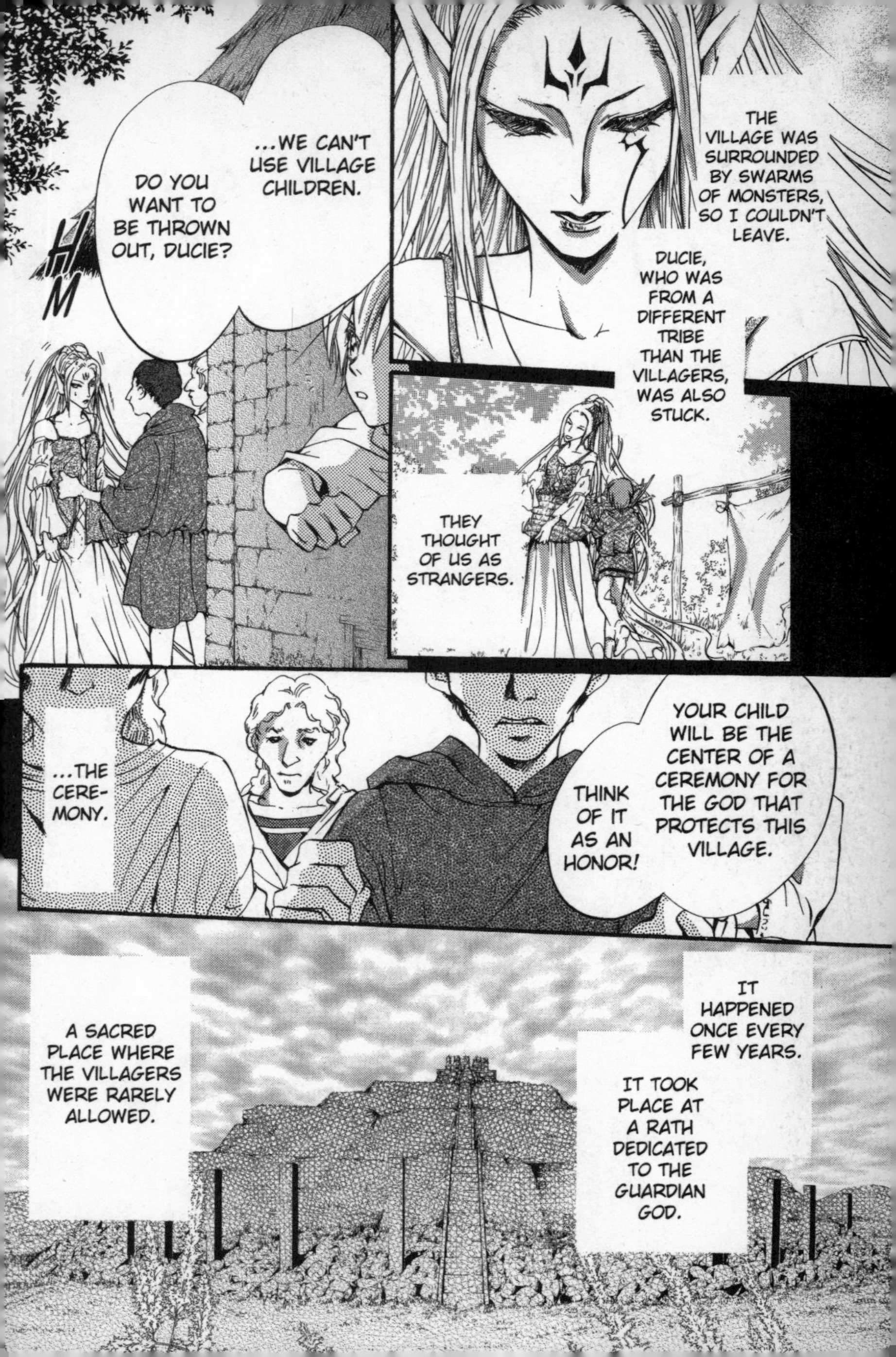
THE VILLAGE WAS SURROUNDED BY SWARMS OF MONSTERS, SO I COULDN'T LEAVE.
DUCIE, WHO WAS FROM A DIFFERENT TRIBE THAN THE VILLAGERS, WAS ALSO STUCK.
THEY THOUGHT OF US AS STRANGERS.
...WE CAN'T USE VILLAGE CHILDREN.
DO YOU WANT TO BE THROWN OUT, DUCIE?
HM
YOUR CHILD WILL BE THE CENTER OF A CEREMONY FOR THE GOD THAT PROTECTS THIS VILLAGE.
THINK OF IT AS AN HONOR!
...THE CEREMONY.
IT HAPPENED ONCE EVERY FEW YEARS.
IT TOOK PLACE AT A RATH DEDICATED TO THE GUARDIAN GOD.
A SACRED PLACE WHERE THE VILLAGERS WERE RARELY ALLOWED.

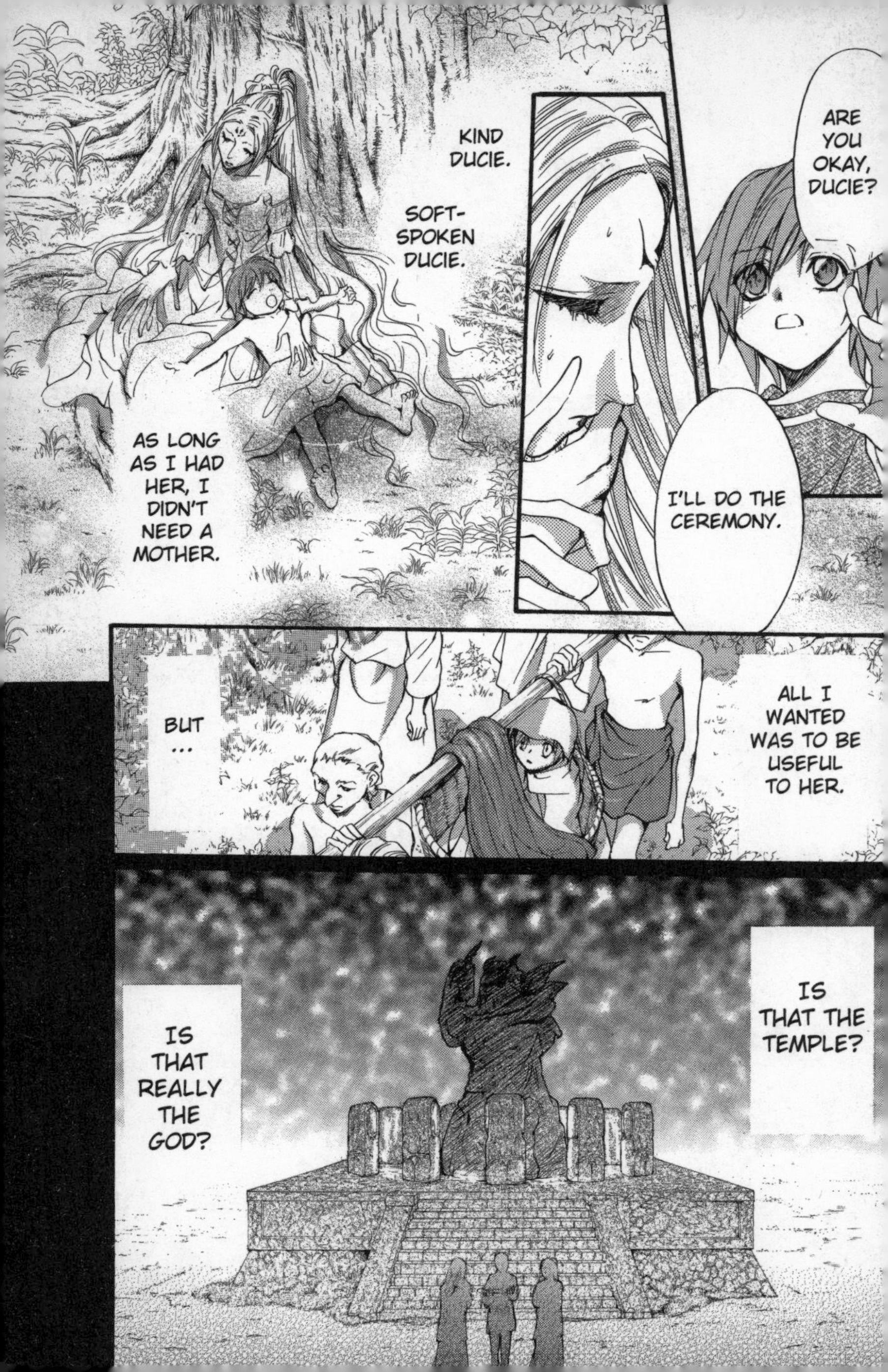
ARE YOU OKAY, DUCIE?
I'LL DO THE CEREMONY.
KIND DUCIE.
SOFT-SPOKEN DUCIE.
AS LONG AS I HAD HER, I DIDN'T NEED A MOTHER.
ALL I WANTED WAS TO BE USEFUL TO HER.
BUT ...
IS THAT THE TEMPLE?
IS THAT REALLY THE GOD?

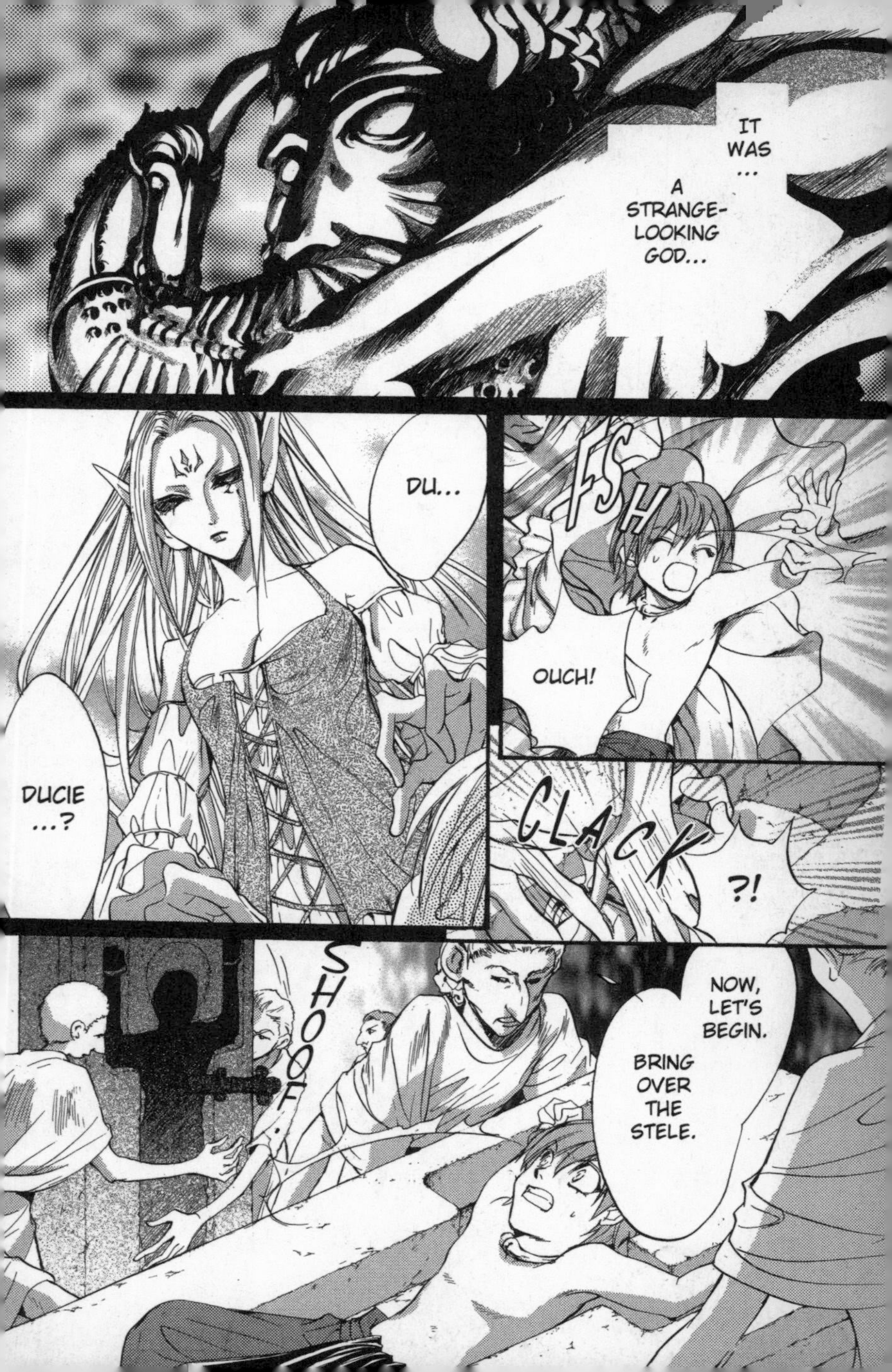
IT WAS ...
A STRANGE-LOOKING GOD...
FSH
OUCH!
CLACK
?!
DU...
DUCIE ...?
NOW, LET'S BEGIN.
BRING OVER THE STELE.
SHOOOF

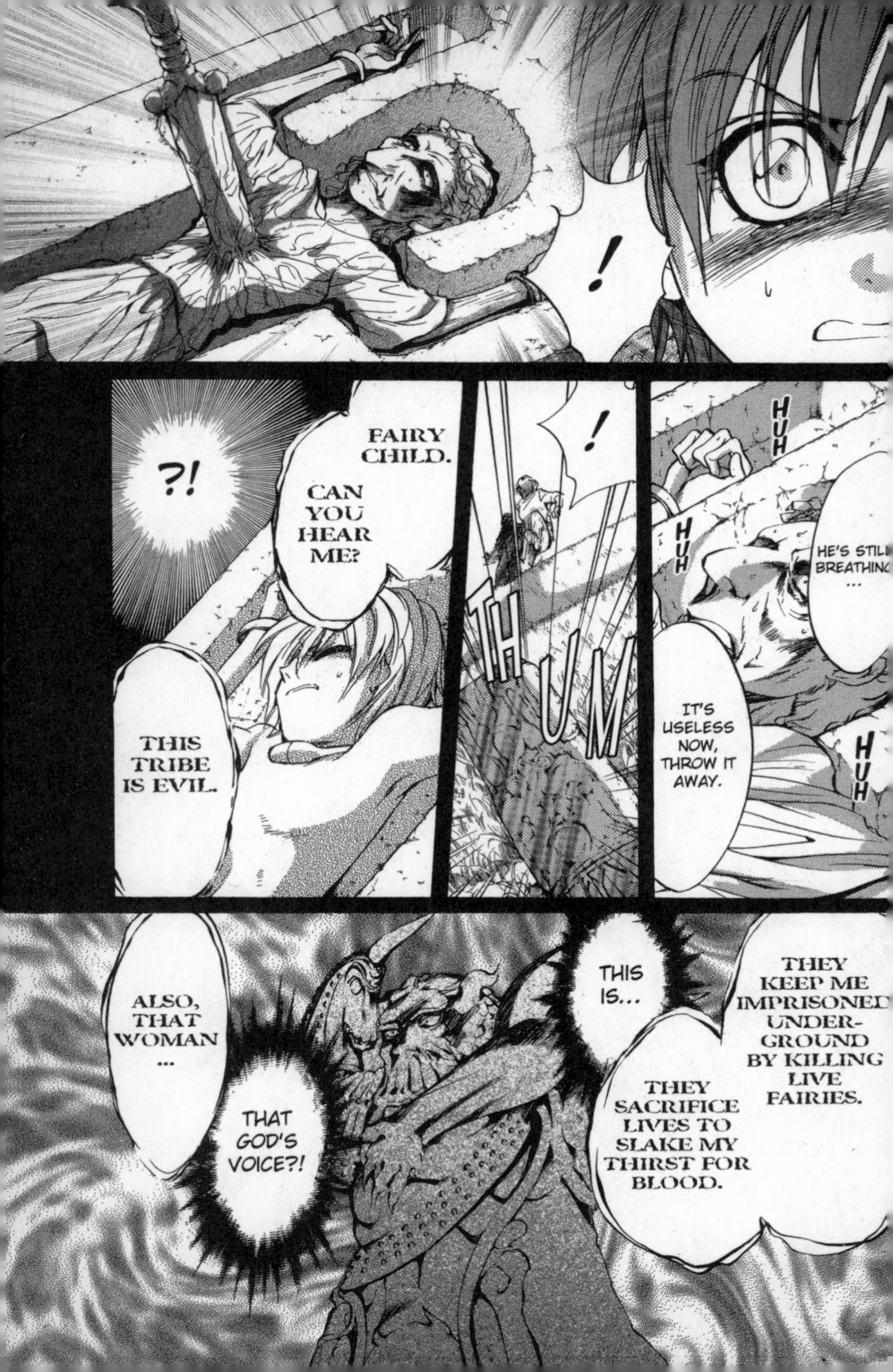
!
HUH
HUH
HE'S STILL BREATHING ...
IT'S USELESS NOW, THROW IT AWAY.
HUH
HUH
!
THUM
?!
FAIRY CHILD.
CAN YOU HEAR ME?
THIS TRIBE IS EVIL.
THEY KEEP ME IMPRISONED UNDER-GROUND BY KILLING LIVE FAIRIES.
THEY SACRIFICE LIVES TO SLAKE MY THIRST FOR BLOOD.
THIS IS...
THAT GOD'S VOICE?!
ALSO, THAT WOMAN ...

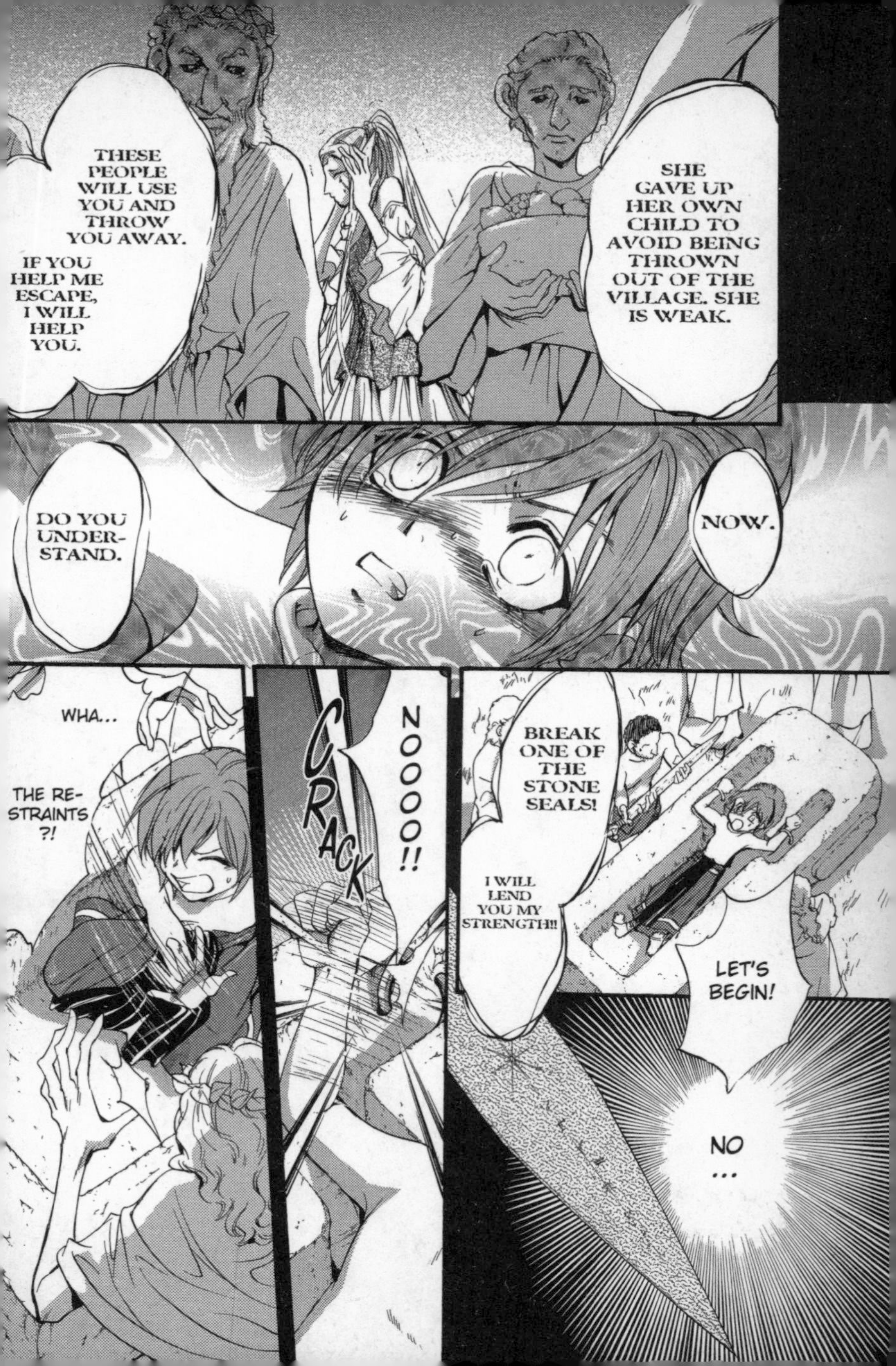
SHE GAVE UP HER OWN CHILD TO AVOID BEING THROWN OUT OF THE VILLAGE. SHE IS WEAK.
THESE PEOPLE WILL USE YOU AND THROW YOU AWAY.
IF YOU HELP ME ESCAPE, I WILL HELP YOU.
NOW.
DO YOU UNDER-STAND.
BREAK ONE OF THE STONE SEALS!
I WILL LEND YOU MY STRENGTH!!
LET'S BEGIN!
NO...
NOOOOO!!
CRACK
WHA...
THE RE-STRAINTS ?!

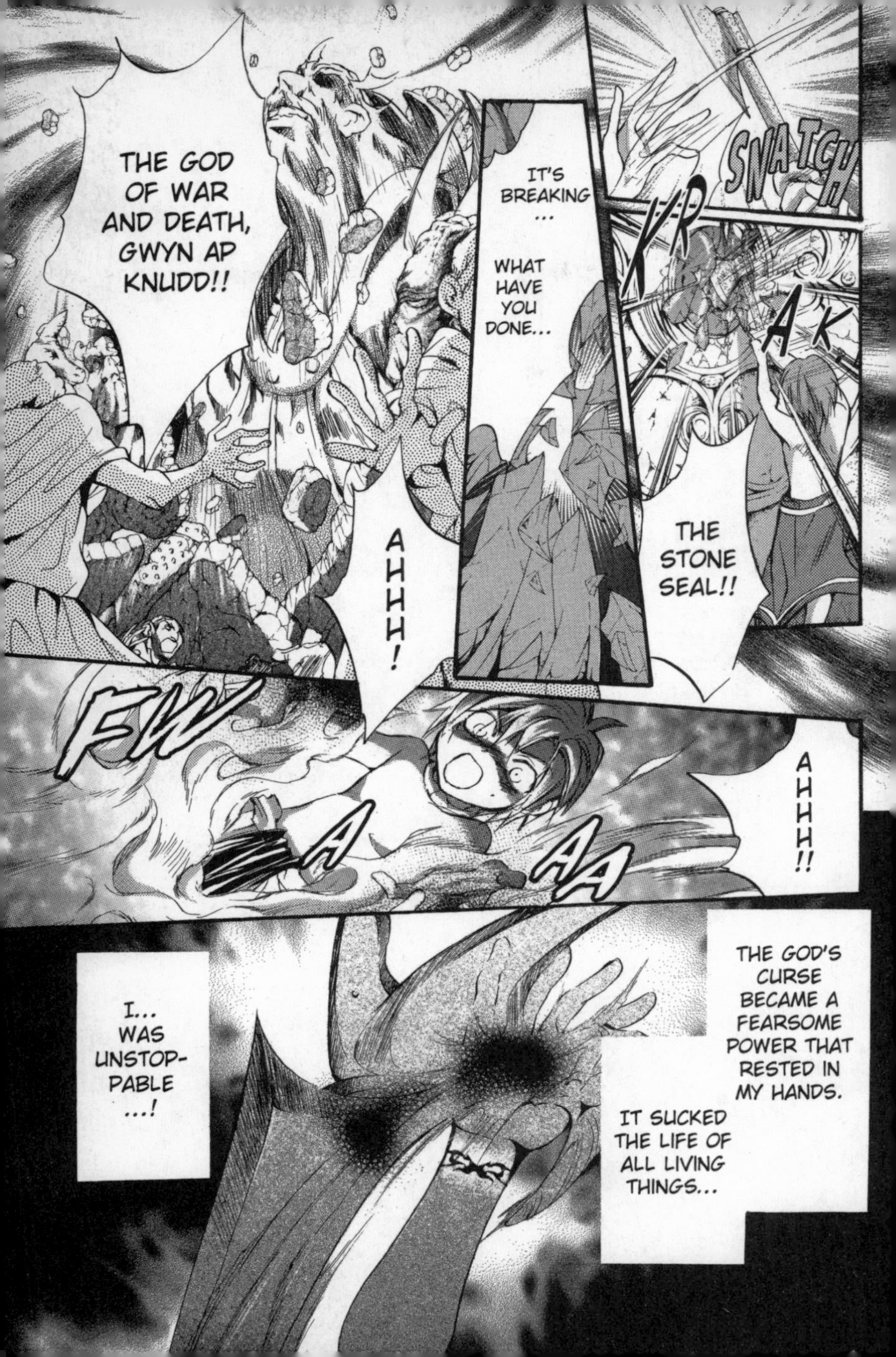
SNATCH
KRAK
THE STONE SEAL!!
IT'S BREAKING...
WHAT HAVE YOU DONE...
THE GOD OF WAR AND DEATH, GWYN AP KNUDD!!
AHHHH!
AHHHH!!
FW
A
AA
THE GOD'S CURSE BECAME A FEARSOME POWER THAT RESTED IN MY HANDS.
IT SUCKED THE LIFE OF ALL LIVING THINGS...
I... WAS UNSTOP-PABLE...!

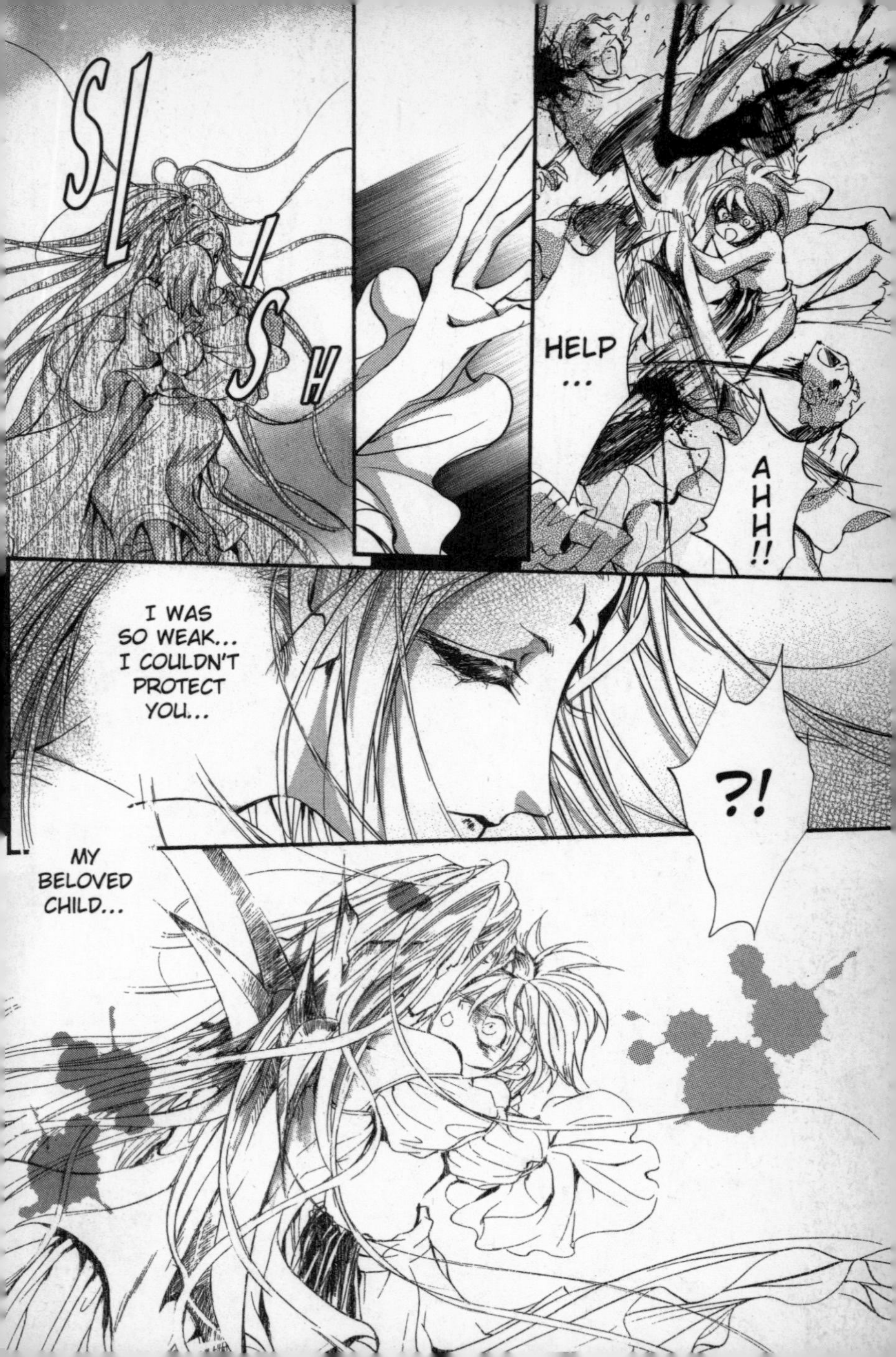
HELP ...
AHH!!
SLISH
?!
I WAS SO WEAK... I COULDN'T PROTECT YOU...
MY BELOVED CHILD...

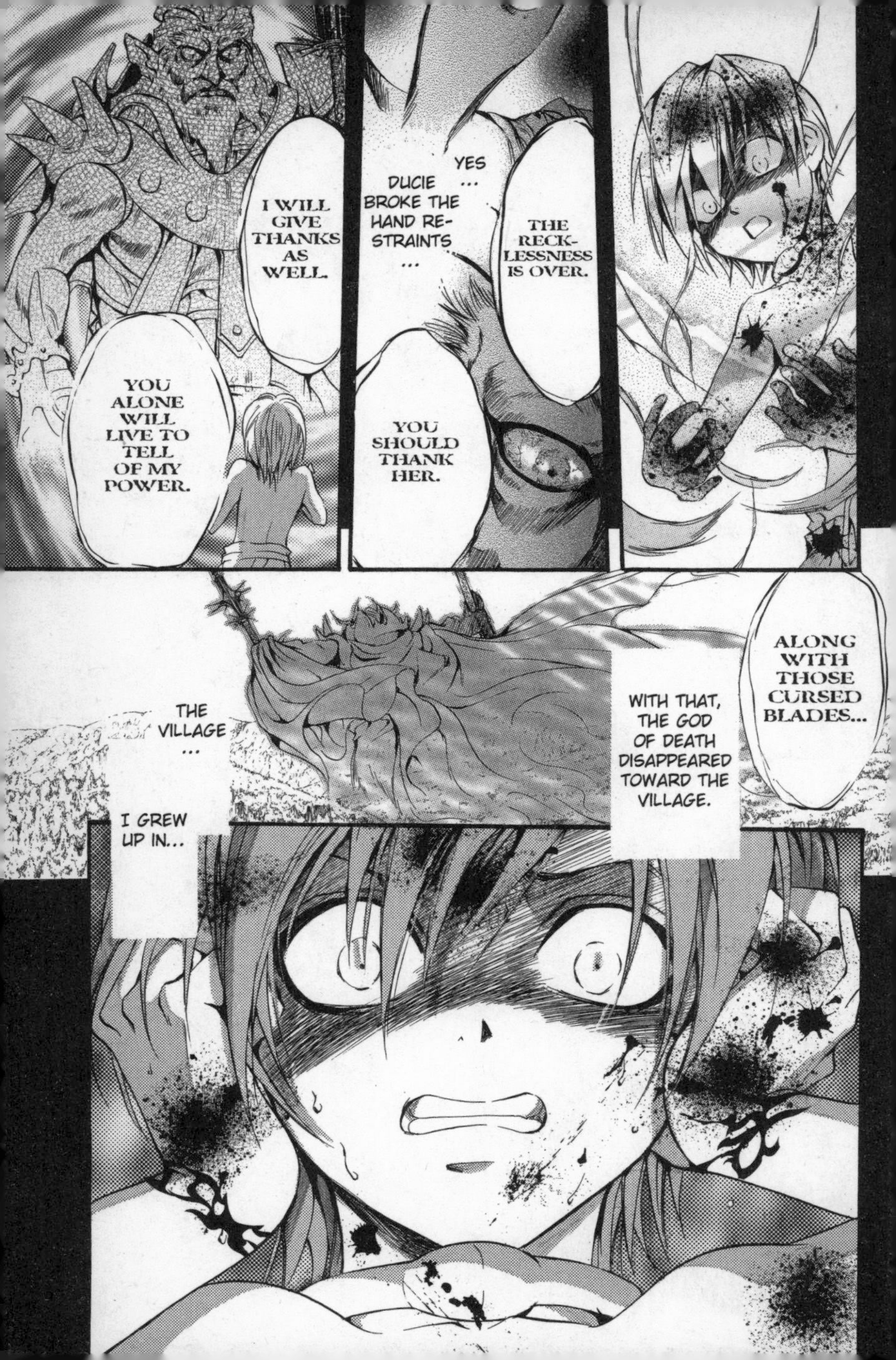
THE RECKLESSNESS IS OVER.
YES... DUCIE BROKE THE HAND RESTRAINTS...
YOU SHOULD THANK HER.
I WILL GIVE THANKS AS WELL.
YOU ALONE WILL LIVE TO TELL OF MY POWER.
ALONG WITH THOSE CURSED BLADES...
WITH THAT, THE GOD OF DEATH DISAPPEARED TOWARD THE VILLAGE.
THE VILLAGE...
I GREW UP IN...

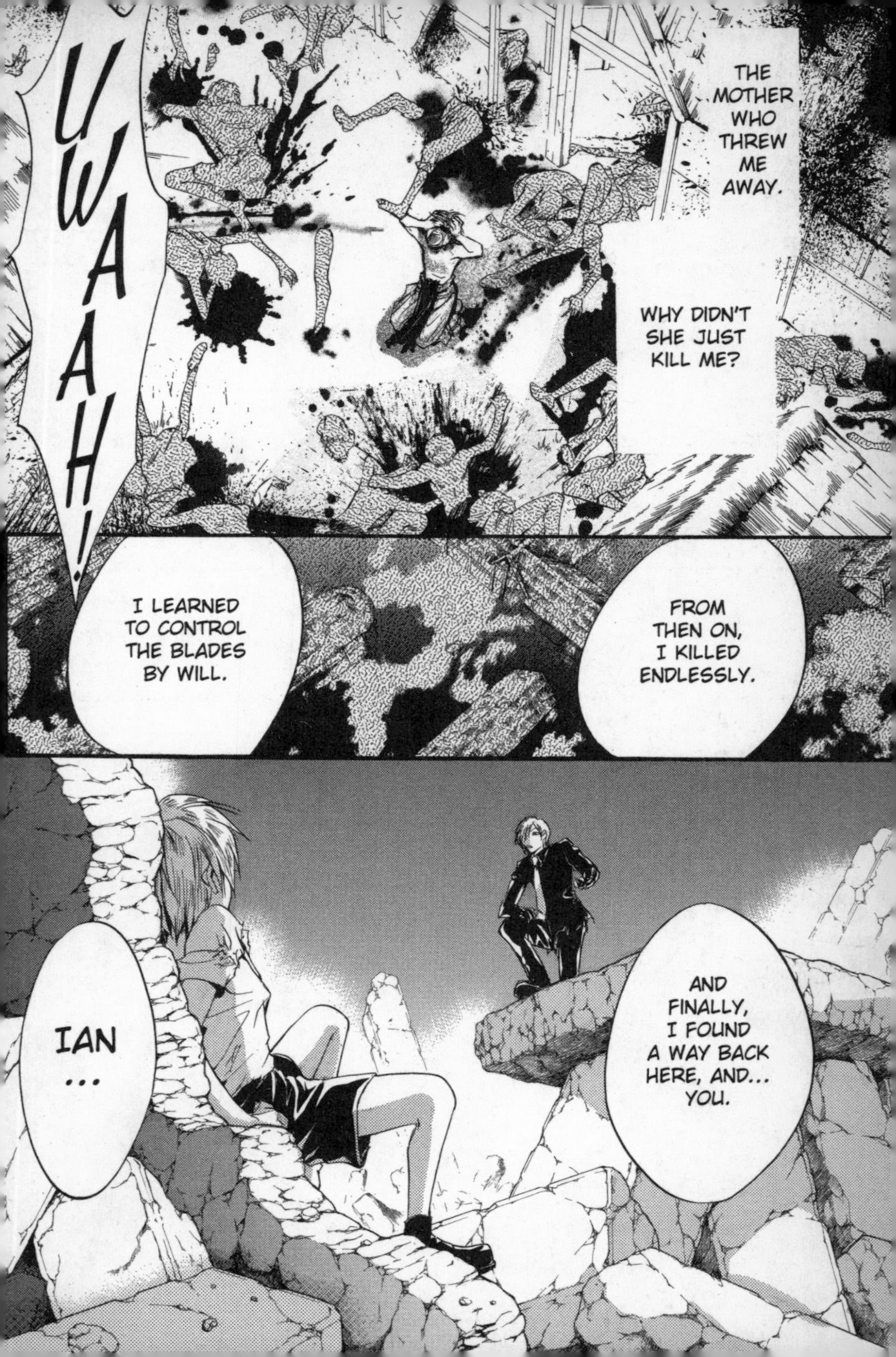
THE MOTHER WHO THREW ME AWAY.
WHY DIDN'T SHE JUST KILL ME?
UWAAH!!
FROM THEN ON, I KILLED ENDLESSLY.
I LEARNED TO CONTROL THE BLADES BY WILL.
AND FINALLY, I FOUND A WAY BACK HERE, AND... YOU.
IAN ...

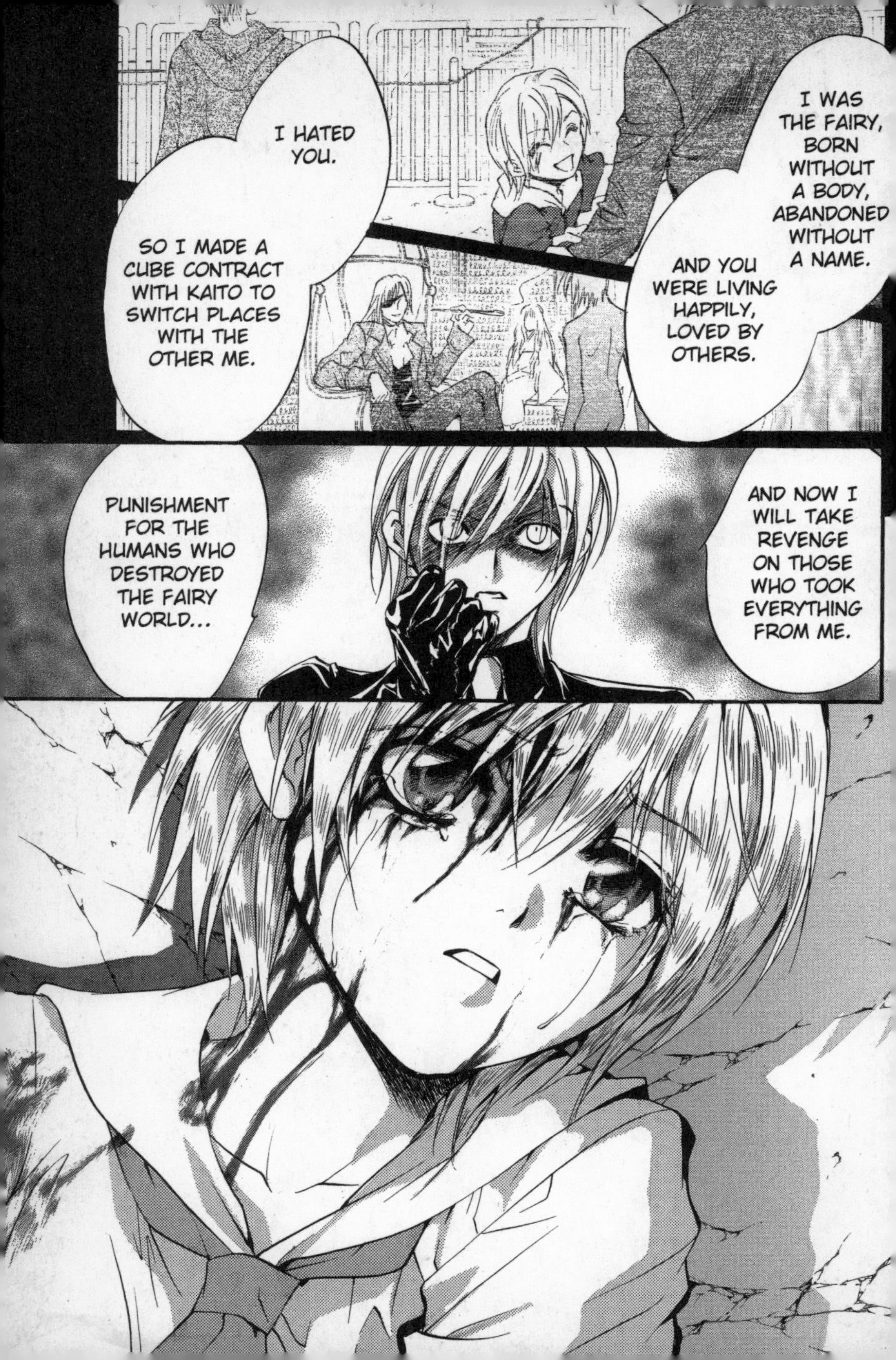

I WAS THE FAIRY, BORN WITHOUT A BODY, ABANDONED WITHOUT A NAME.
AND YOU WERE LIVING HAPPILY, LOVED BY OTHERS.
I HATED YOU.
SO I MADE A CUBE CONTRACT WITH KAITO TO SWITCH PLACES WITH THE OTHER ME.
AND NOW I WILL TAKE REVENGE ON THOSE WHO TOOK EVERYTHING FROM ME.
PUNISHMENT FOR THE HUMANS WHO DESTROYED THE FAIRY WORLD...

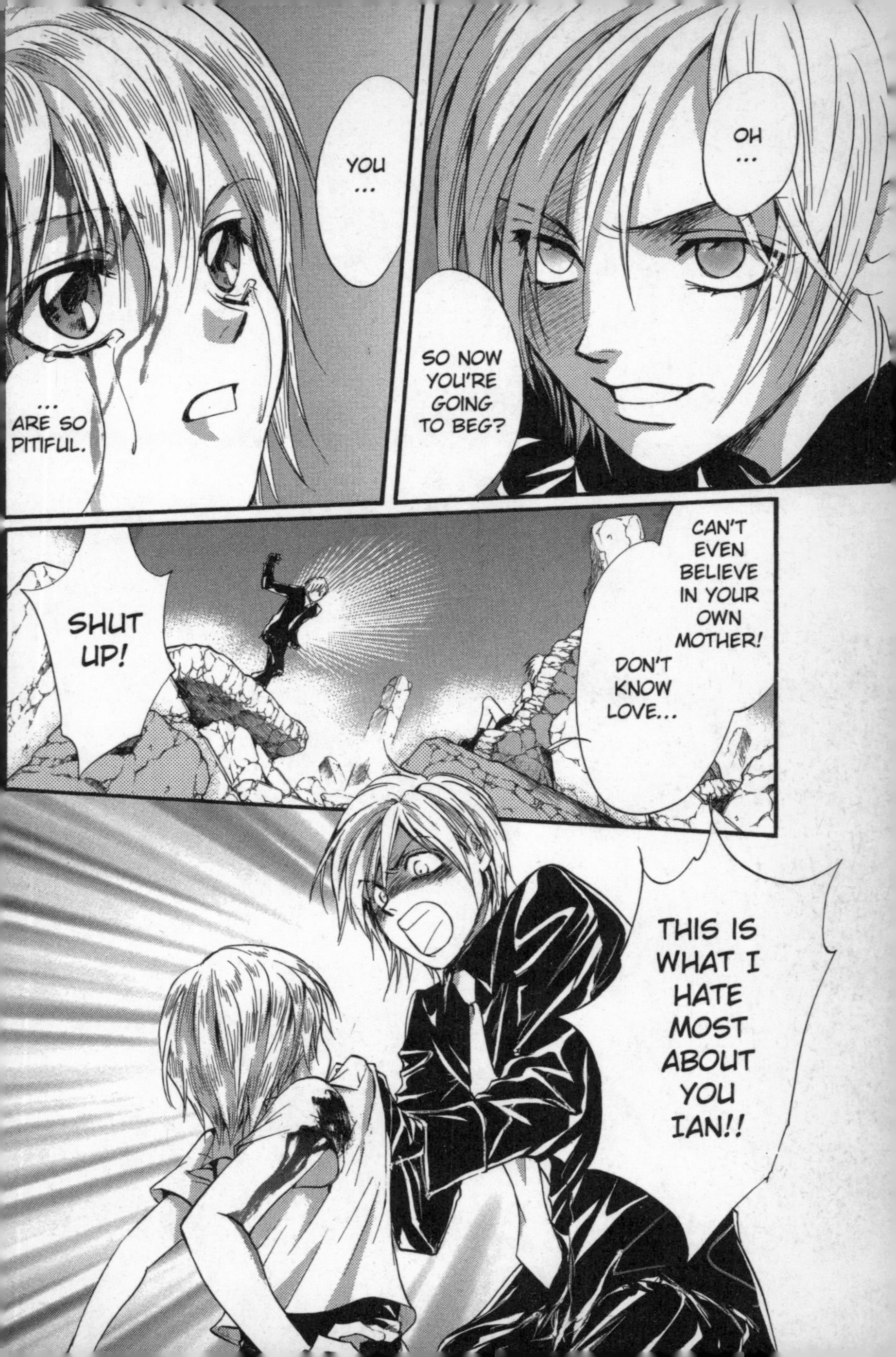
OH ...
SO NOW YOU'RE GOING TO BEG?
YOU ...
... ARE SO PITIFUL.
CAN'T EVEN BELIEVE IN YOUR OWN MOTHER!
DON'T KNOW LOVE...
SHUT UP!
THIS IS WHAT I HATE MOST ABOUT YOU IAN!!

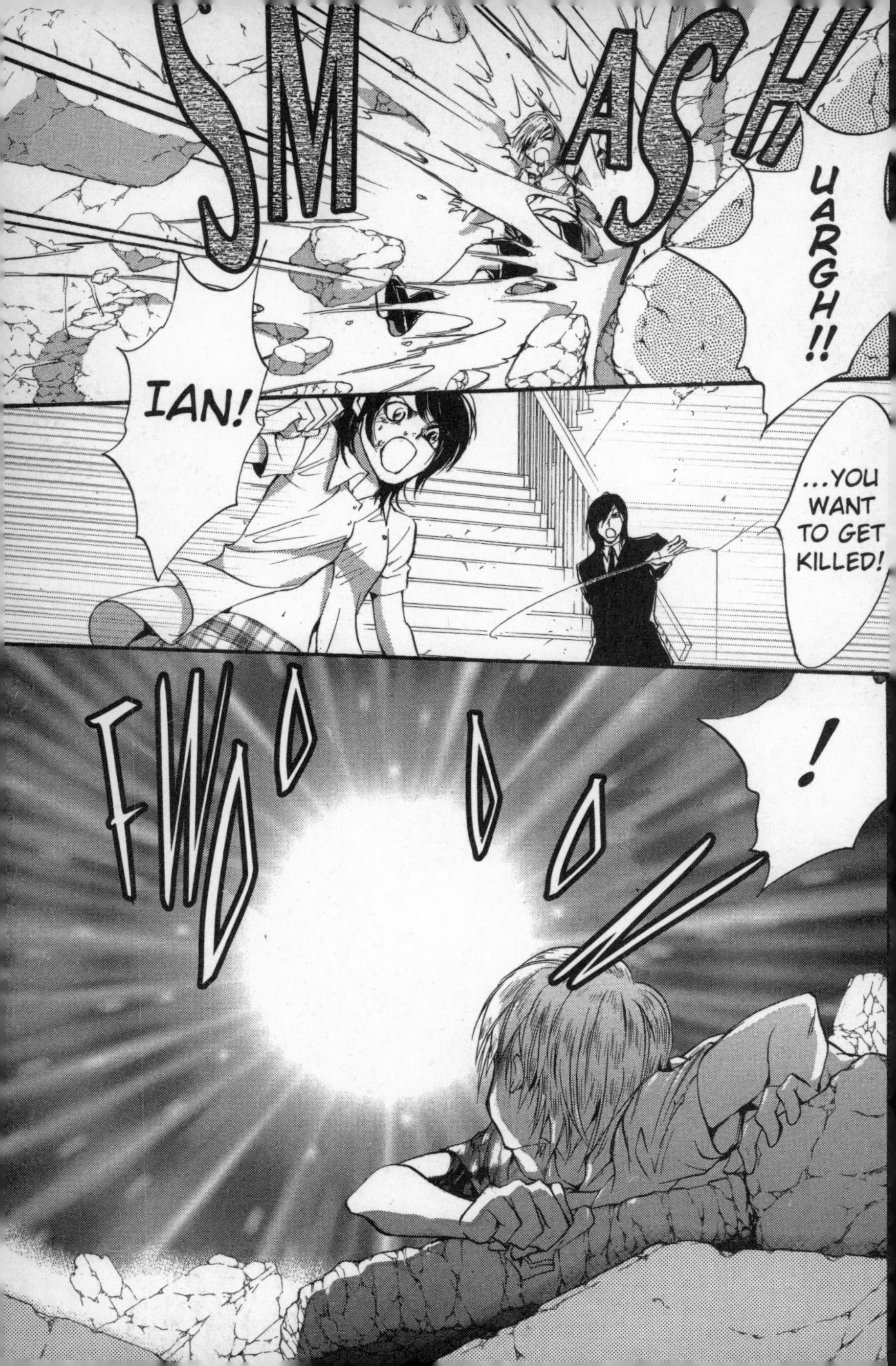
SMASH
UARGH!!
...YOU WANT TO GET KILLED!
IAN!
!
FWOOOO

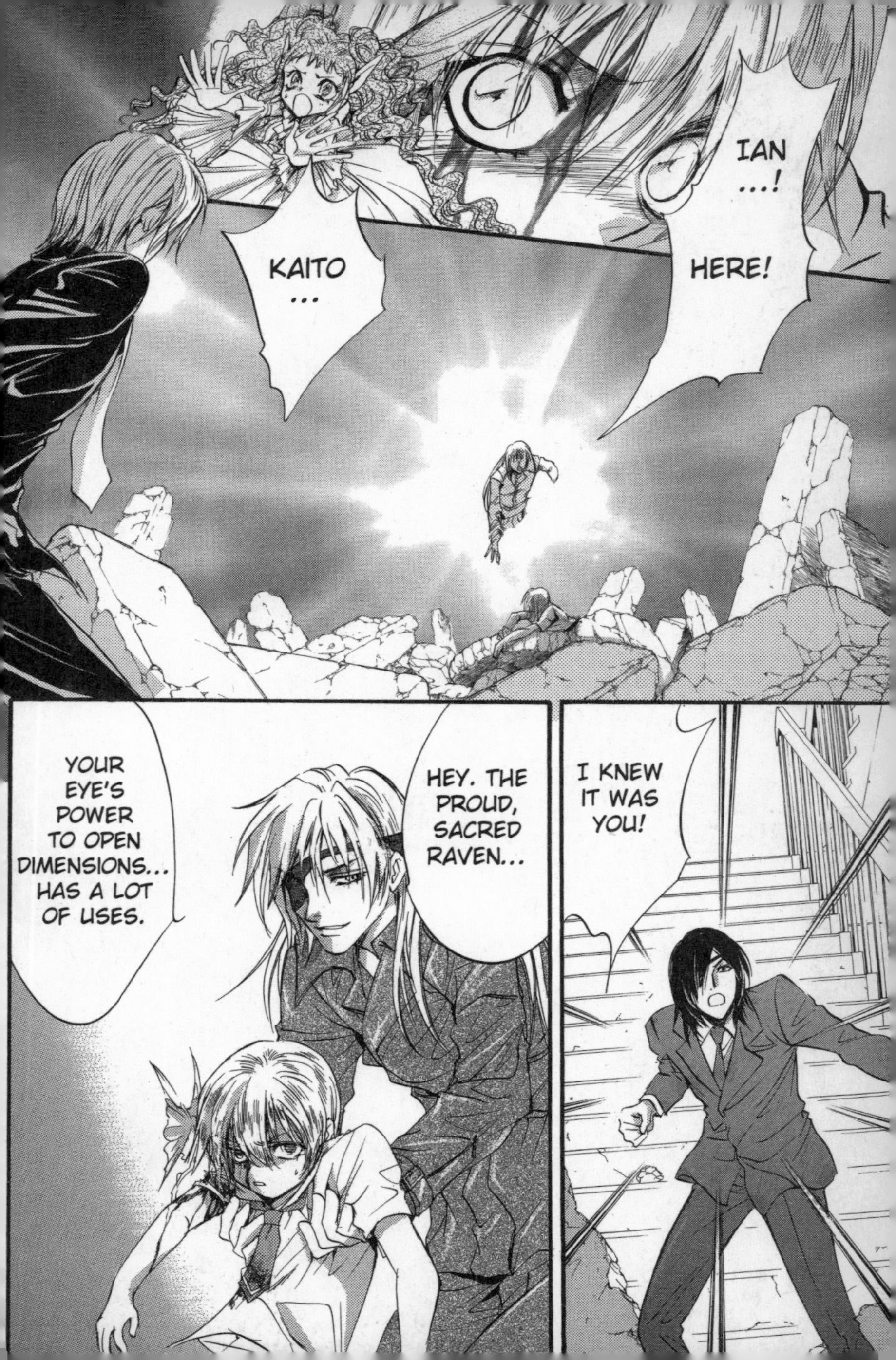
IAN ...!
HERE!
KAITO ...
I KNEW IT WAS YOU!
HEY. THE PROUD, SACRED RAVEN...
YOUR EYE'S POWER TO OPEN DIMENSIONS... HAS A LOT OF USES.

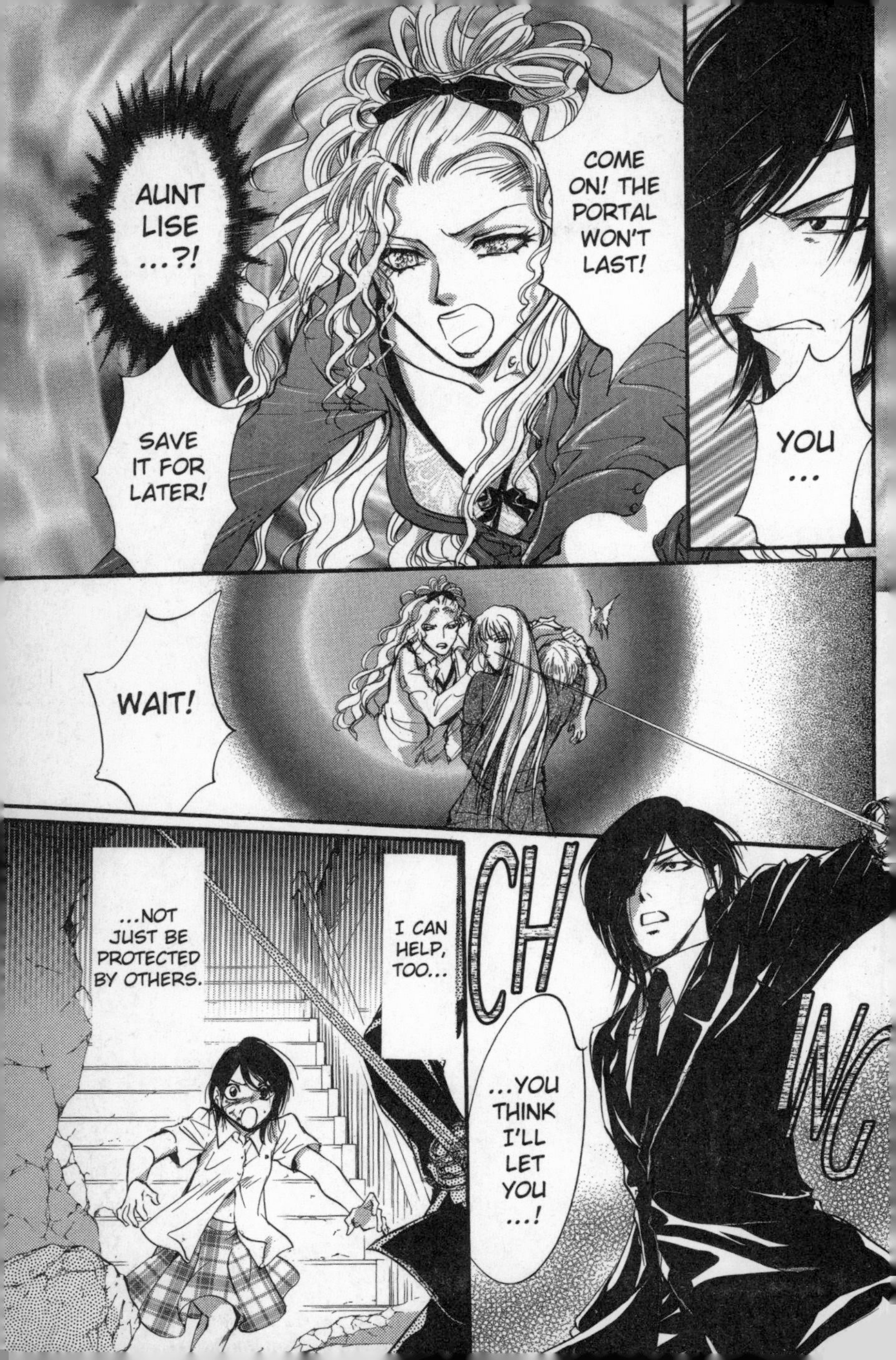
YOU ...
COME ON! THE PORTAL WON'T LAST!
AUNT LISE ...?!
SAVE IT FOR LATER!
WAIT!
CH
...YOU THINK I'LL LET YOU ...!
I CAN HELP, TOO...
...NOT JUST BE PROTECTED BY OTHERS.

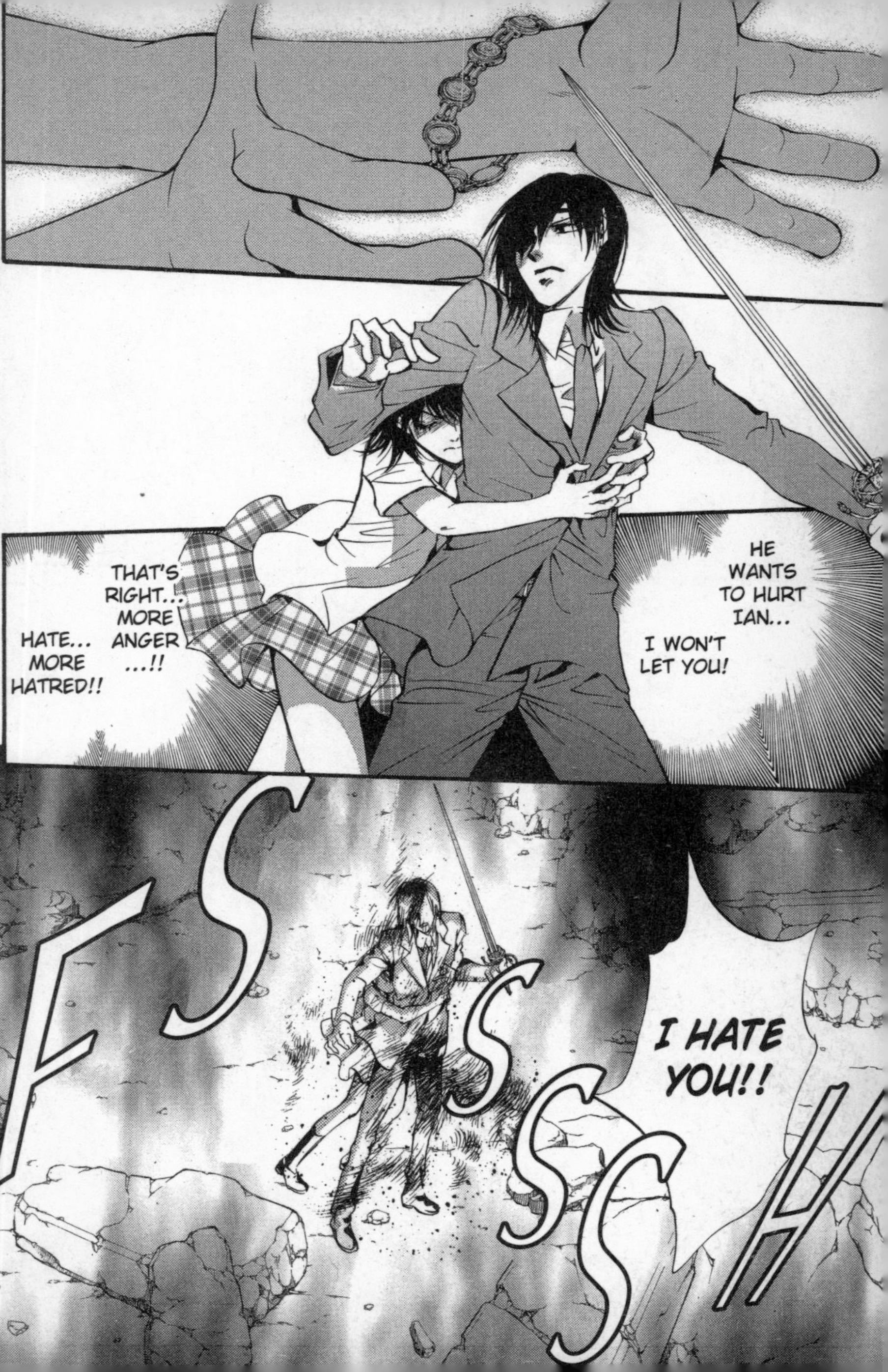
HE WANTS TO HURT IAN...
I WON'T LET YOU!
THAT'S RIGHT... MORE ANGER ...!!
HATE... MORE HATRED!!
I HATE YOU!!
FSSSCH

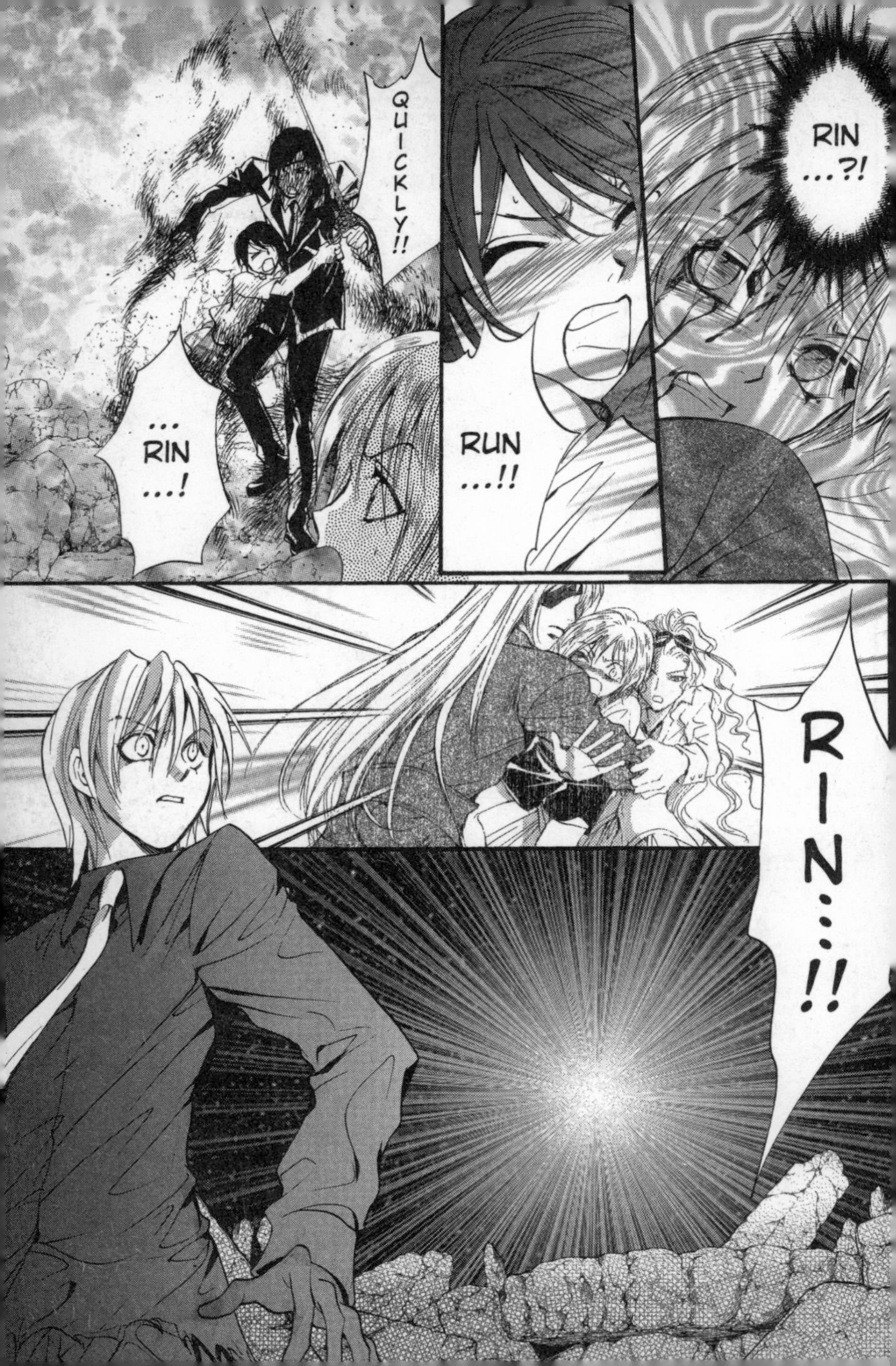
RIN ...?!
RUN ...!!
QUICKLY!!
... RIN ...!
RIN...!!

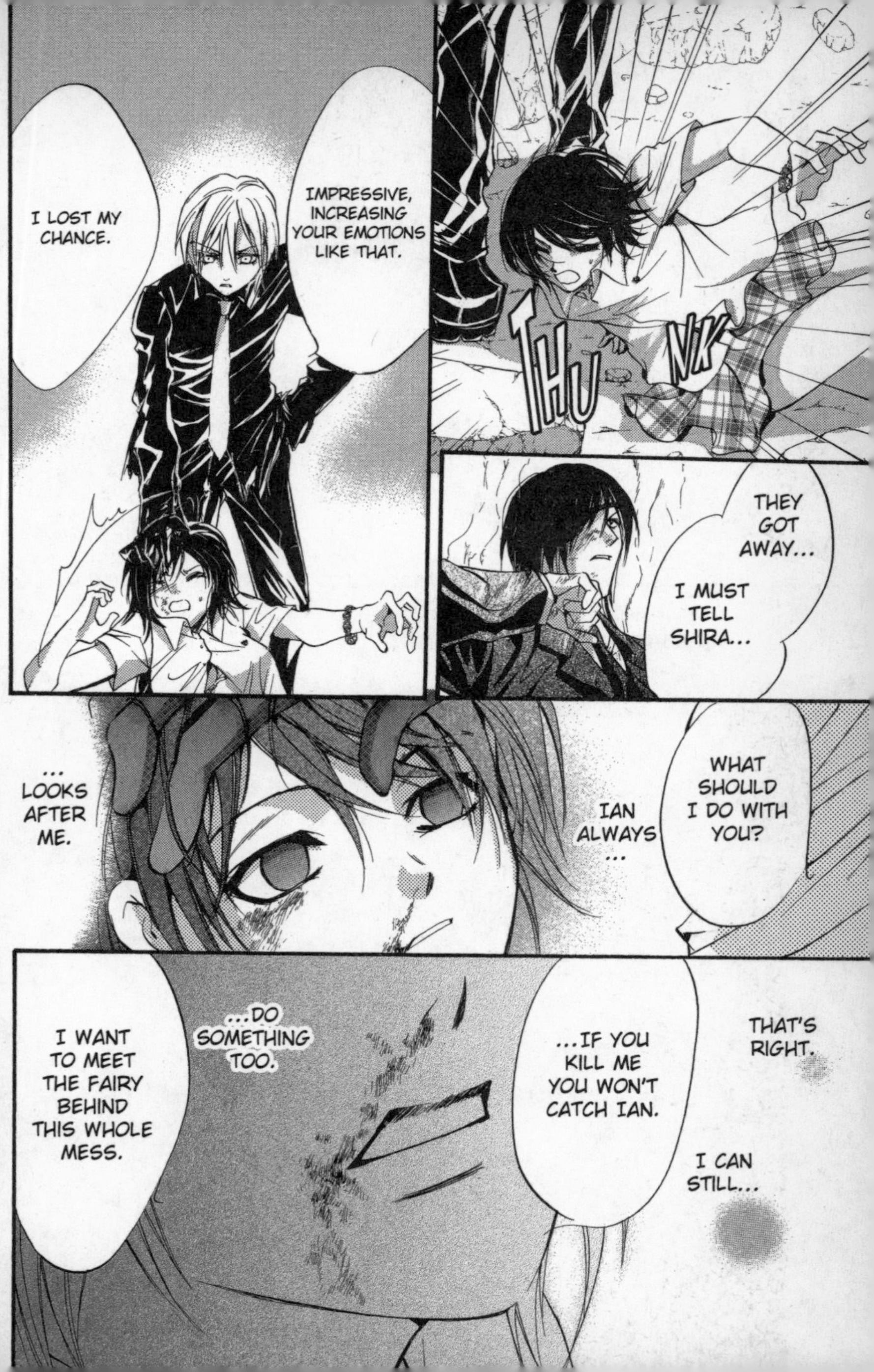
THUNK
THEY GOT AWAY...
I MUST TELL SHIRA...
IMPRESSIVE, INCREASING YOUR EMOTIONS LIKE THAT.
I LOST MY CHANCE.
WHAT SHOULD I DO WITH YOU?
IAN ALWAYS...
...LOOKS AFTER ME.
THAT'S RIGHT.
...IF YOU KILL ME YOU WON'T CATCH IAN.
I CAN STILL...
...DO SOMETHING TOO.
I WANT TO MEET THE FAIRY BEHIND THIS WHOLE MESS.

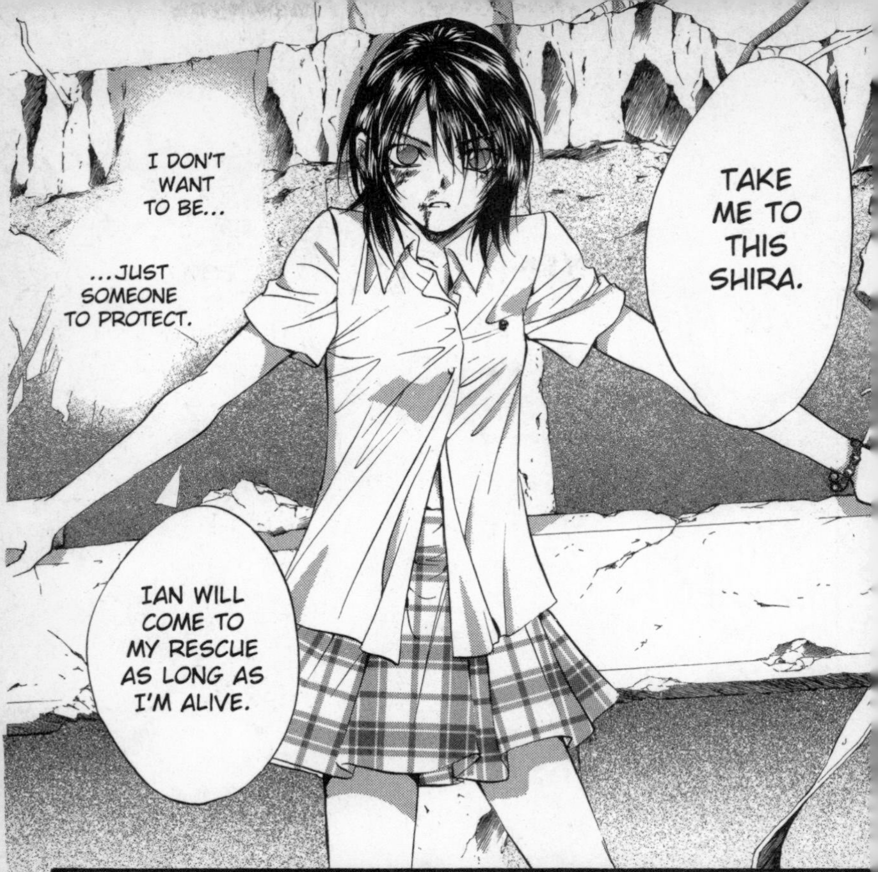
TAKE ME TO THIS SHIRA.
I DON'T WANT TO BE...
...JUST SOMEONE TO PROTECT.
IAN WILL COME TO MY RESCUE AS LONG AS I'M ALIVE.

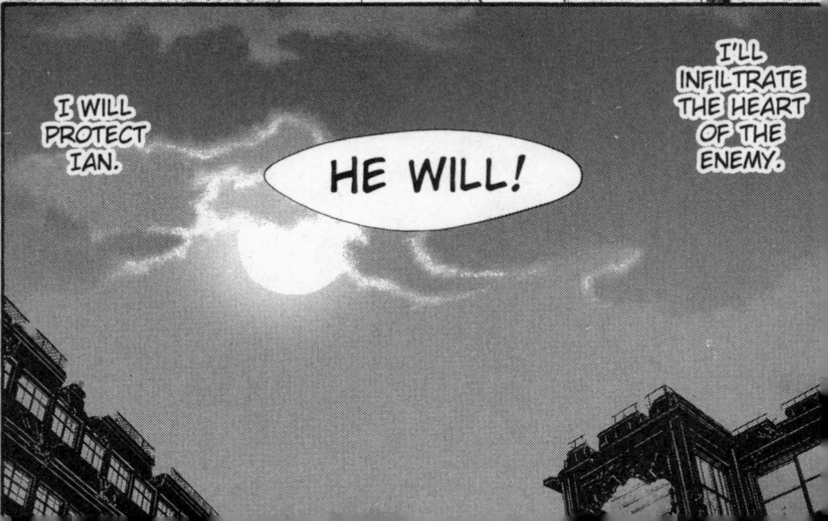
I'LL INFILTRATE THE HEART OF THE ENEMY.
HE WILL!
I WILL PROTECT IAN.

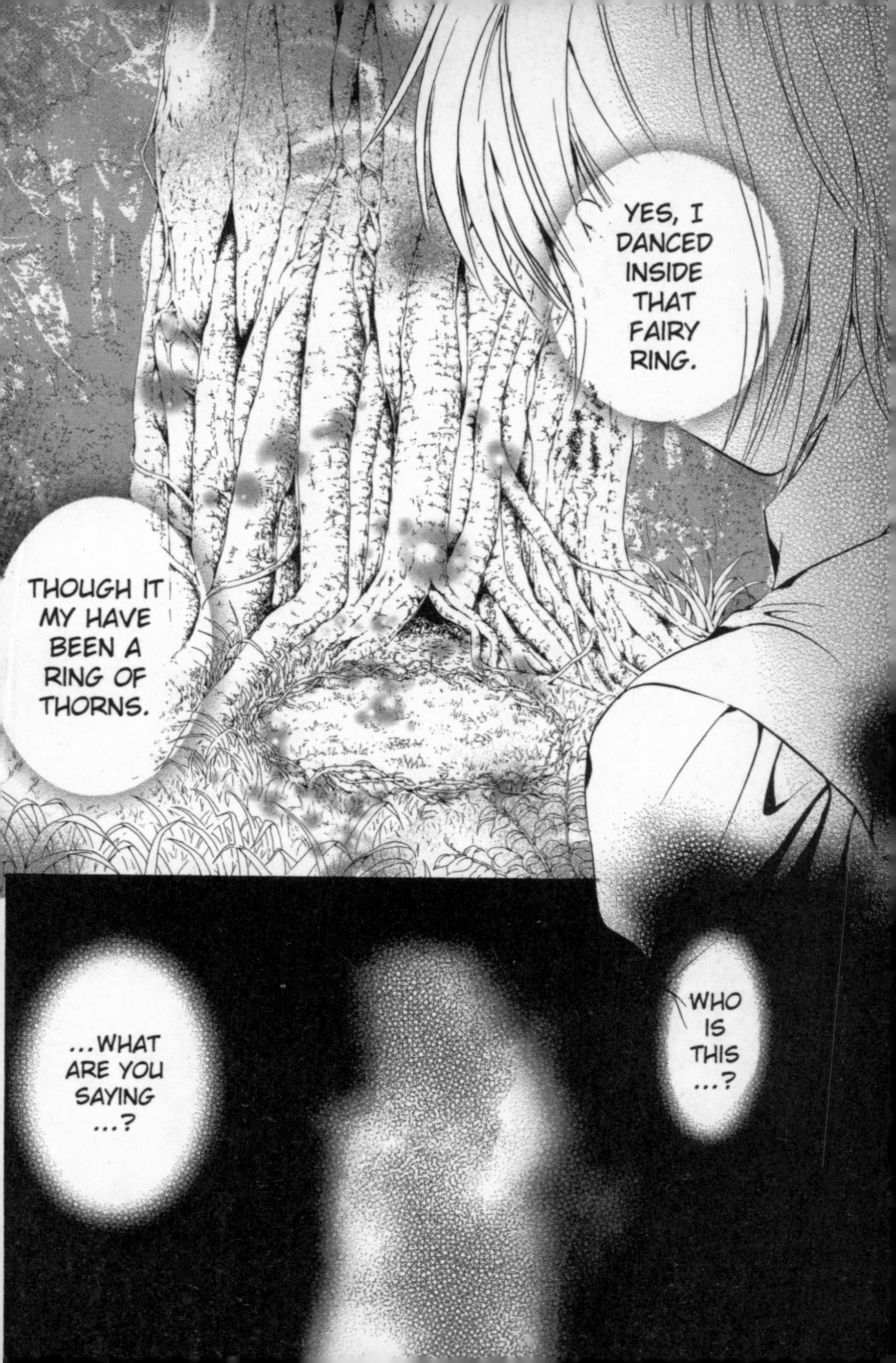
YES, I DANCED INSIDE THAT FAIRY RING.
THOUGH IT MY HAVE BEEN A RING OF THORNS.
WHO IS THIS ...?
...WHAT ARE YOU SAYING ...?

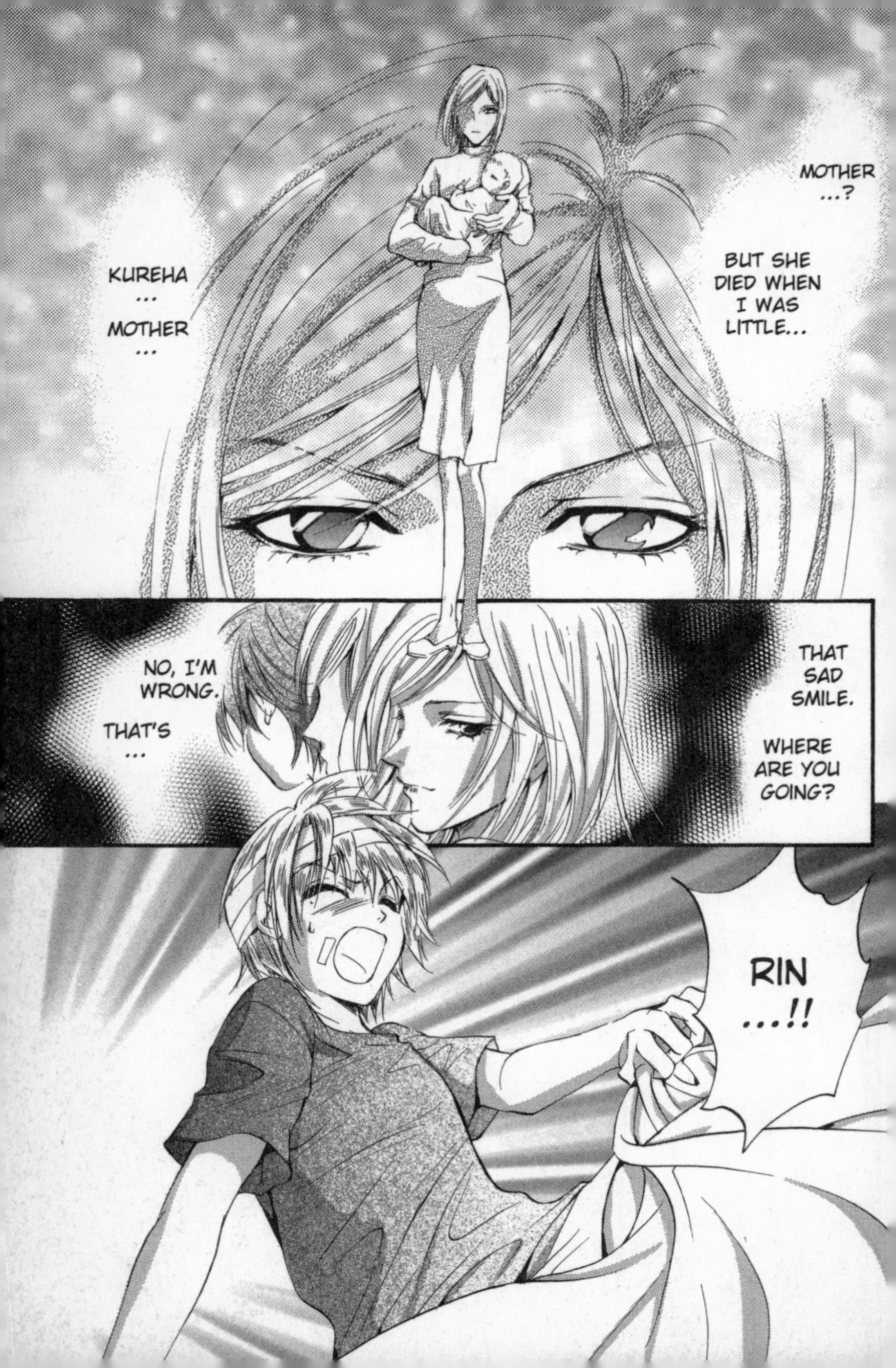
MOTHER ...?
BUT SHE DIED WHEN I WAS LITTLE...
KUREHA ...
MOTHER ...
THAT SAD SMILE.
WHERE ARE YOU GOING?
NO, I'M WRONG.
THAT'S ...
RIN ...!!

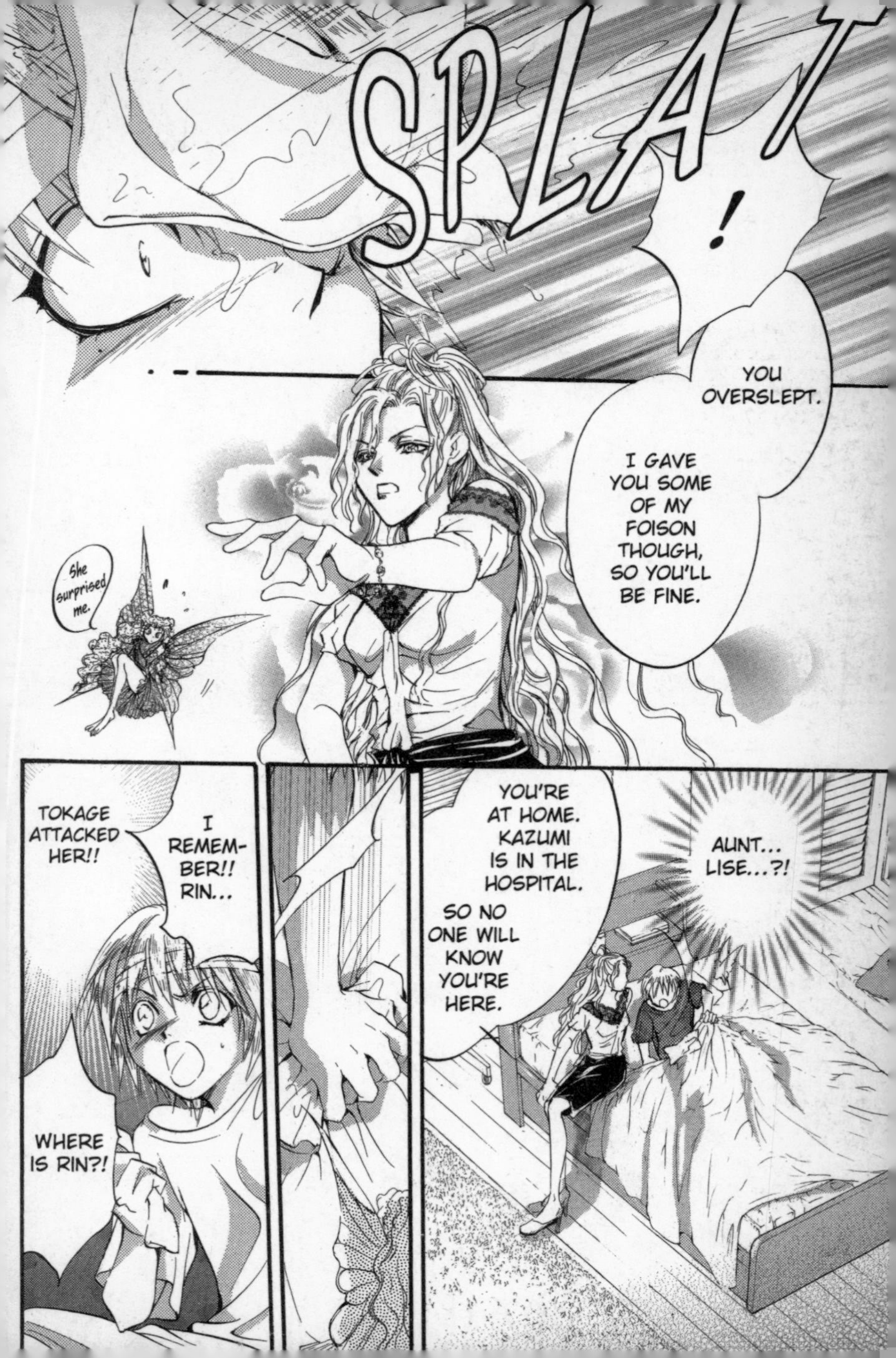
SPLAT!
YOU OVERSLEPT.
I GAVE YOU SOME OF MY FOISON THOUGH, SO YOU'LL BE FINE.
She surprised me.
AUNT... LISE...?!
YOU'RE AT HOME. KAZUMI IS IN THE HOSPITAL.
SO NO ONE WILL KNOW YOU'RE HERE.
I REMEMBER!! RIN...
TOKAGE ATTACKED HER!!
WHERE IS RIN?!

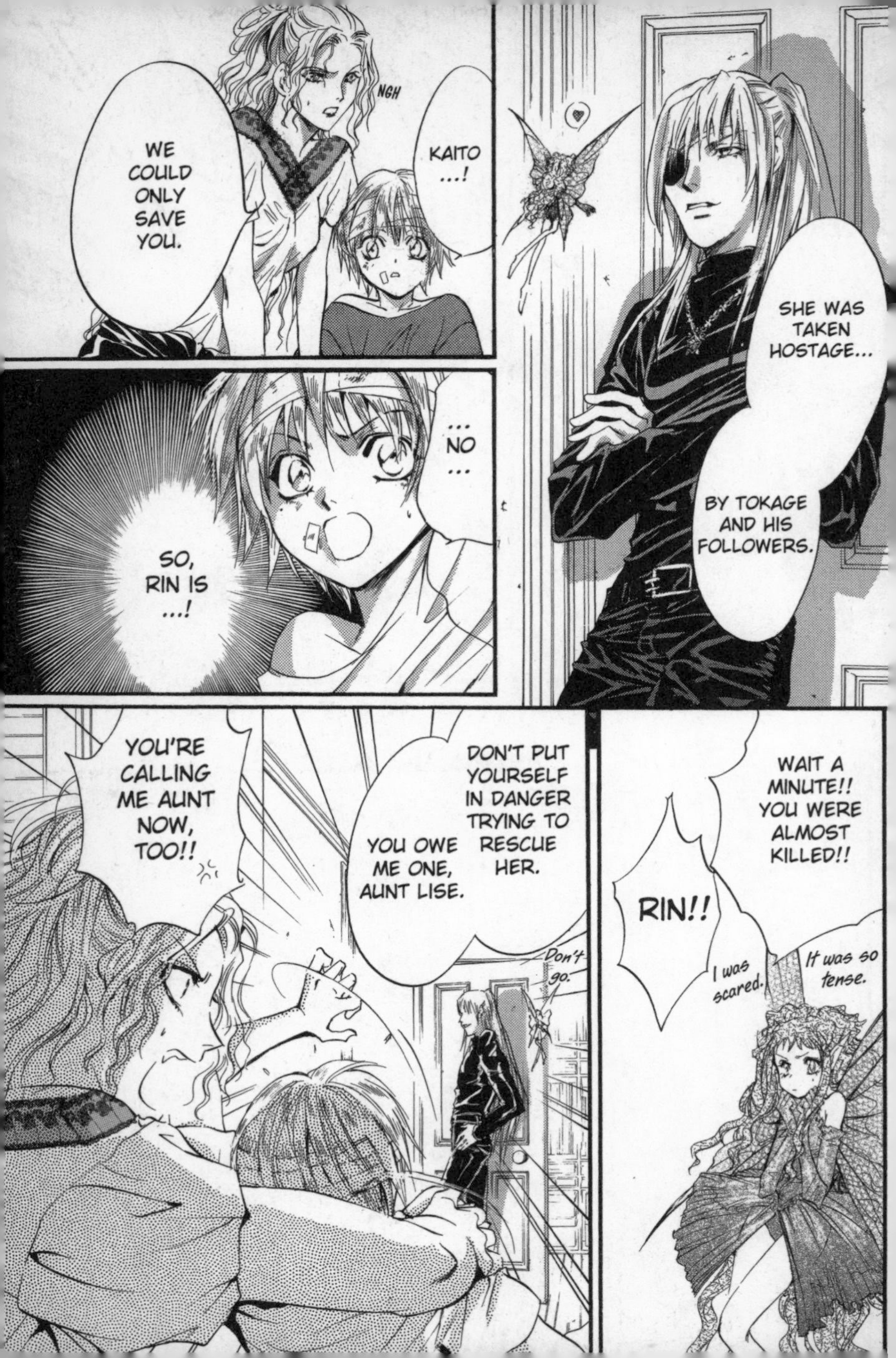
SHE WAS TAKEN HOSTAGE...
BY TOKAGE AND HIS FOLLOWERS.
NGH
KAITO ...!
WE COULD ONLY SAVE YOU.
... NO ...
SO, RIN IS ...!
WAIT A MINUTE!! YOU WERE ALMOST KILLED!!
RIN!!
It was so tense.
I was scared.
DON'T PUT YOURSELF IN DANGER TRYING TO RESCUE HER.
YOU OWE ME ONE, AUNT LISE.
YOU'RE CALLING ME AUNT NOW, TOO!!
Don't go.

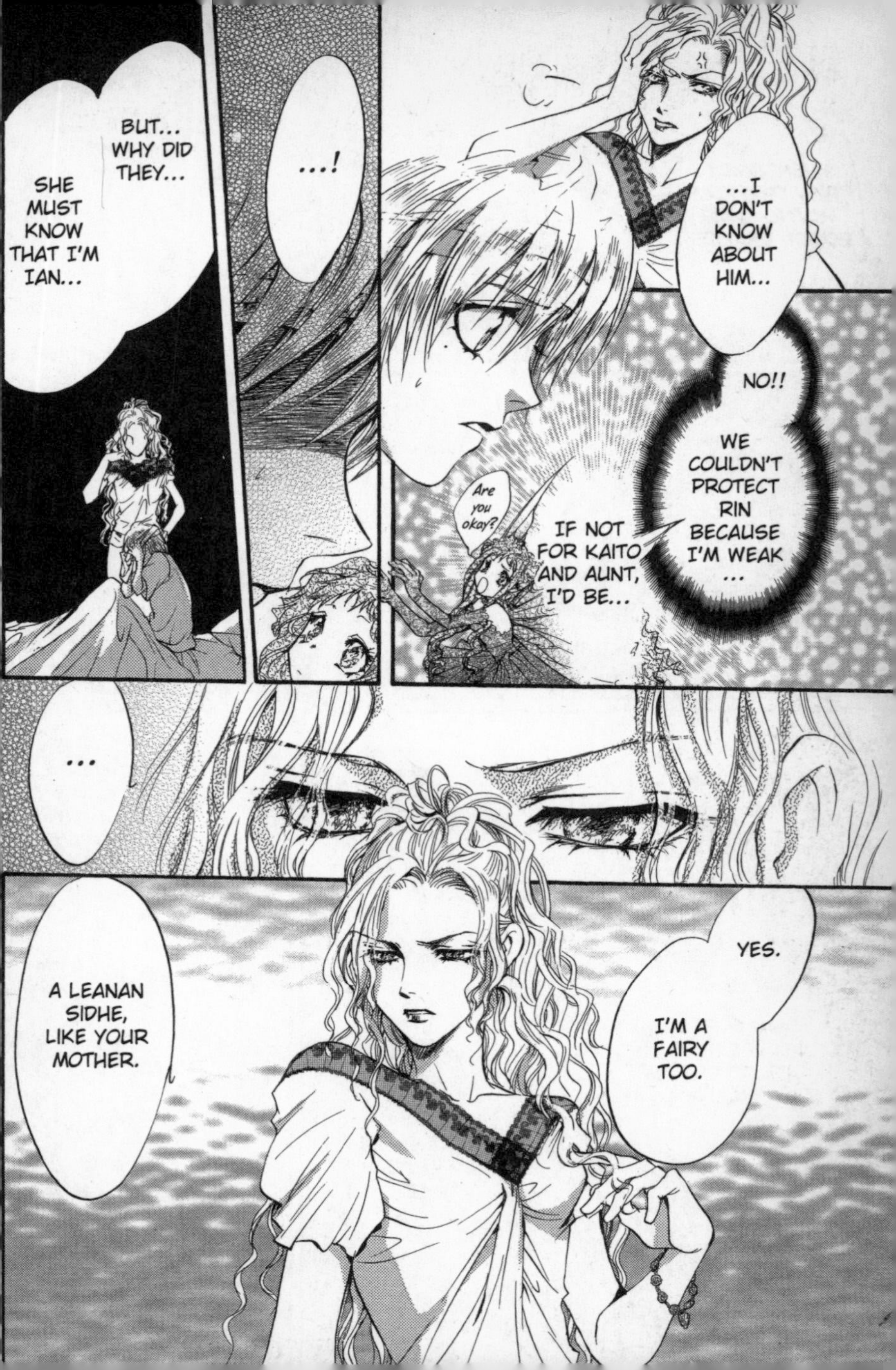
...I DON'T KNOW ABOUT HIM...
NO!!
WE COULDN'T PROTECT RIN BECAUSE I'M WEAK...
IF NOT FOR KAITO AND AUNT, I'D BE...
Are you okay?
...!
BUT... WHY DID THEY...
SHE MUST KNOW THAT I'M IAN...
...
YES.
I'M A FAIRY TOO.
A LEANAN SIDHE, LIKE YOUR MOTHER.

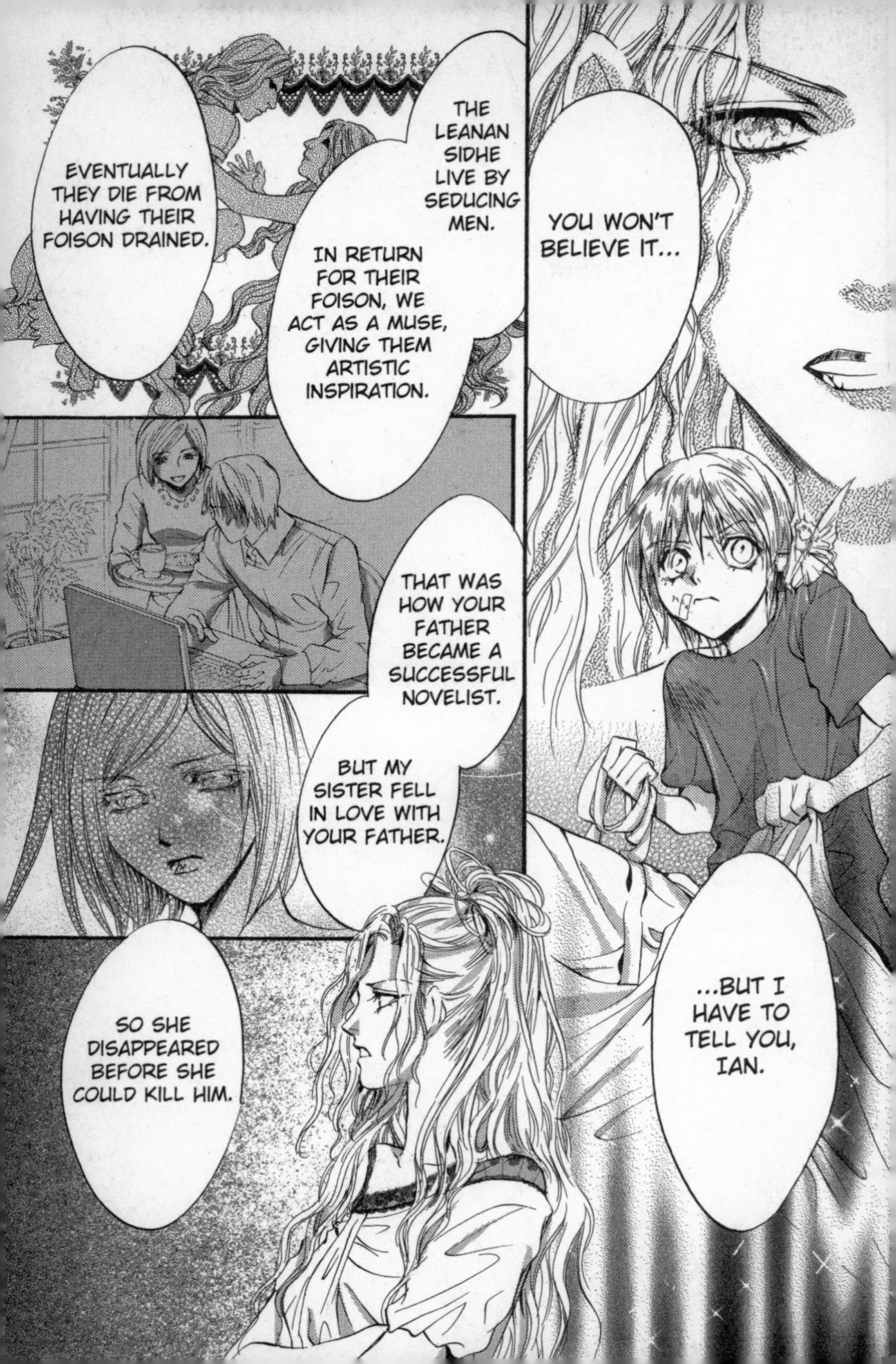
YOU WON'T BELIEVE IT...
...BUT I HAVE TO TELL YOU, IAN.
THE LEANAN SIDHE LIVE BY SEDUCING MEN.
IN RETURN FOR THEIR FOISON, WE ACT AS A MUSE, GIVING THEM ARTISTIC INSPIRATION.
EVENTUALLY THEY DIE FROM HAVING THEIR FOISON DRAINED.
THAT WAS HOW YOUR FATHER BECAME A SUCCESSFUL NOVELIST.
BUT MY SISTER FELL IN LOVE WITH YOUR FATHER.
SO SHE DISAPPEARED BEFORE SHE COULD KILL HIM.

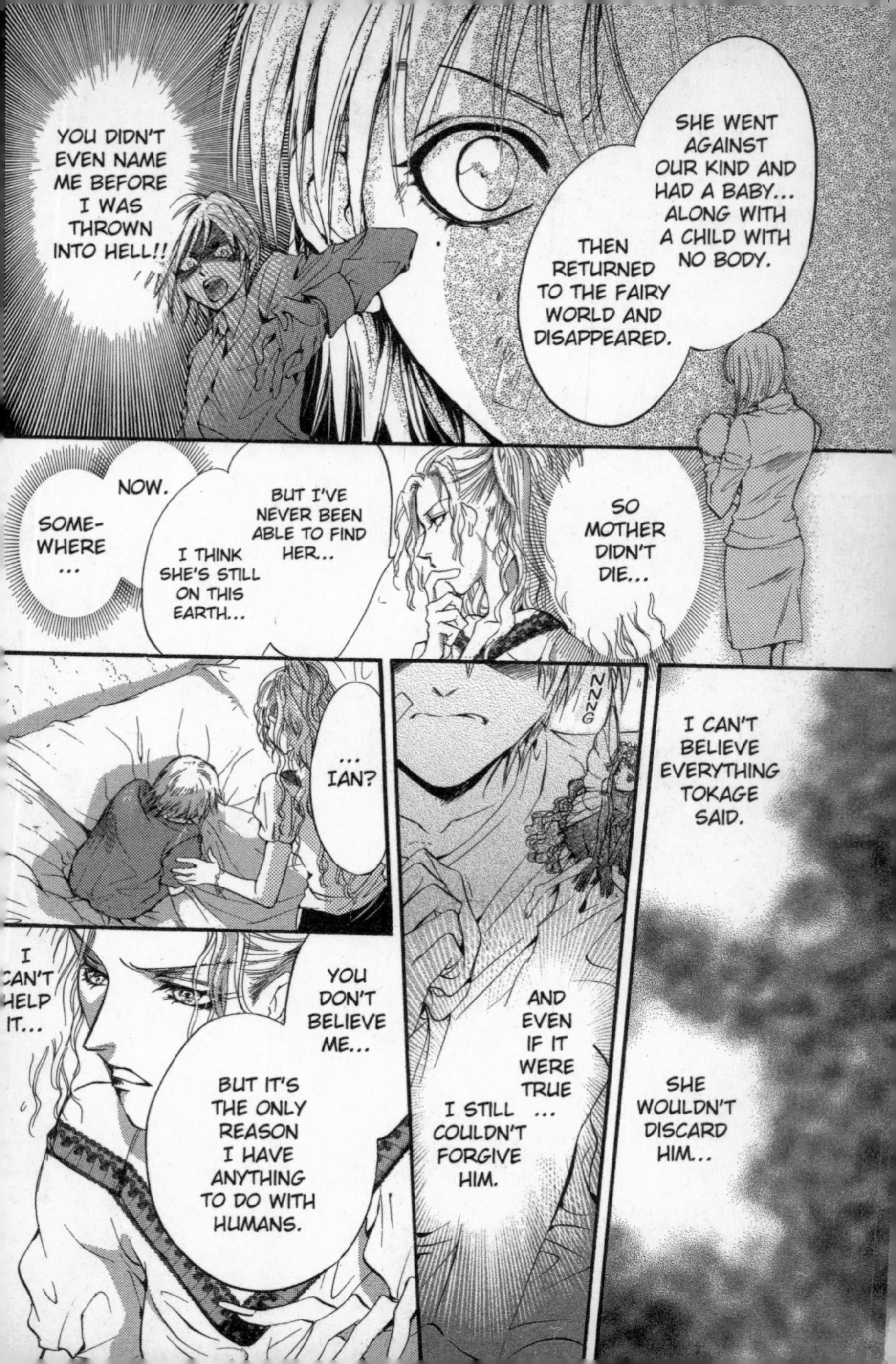
SHE WENT AGAINST OUR KIND AND HAD A BABY... ALONG WITH A CHILD WITH NO BODY.
THEN RETURNED TO THE FAIRY WORLD AND DISAPPEARED.
YOU DIDN'T EVEN NAME ME BEFORE I WAS THROWN INTO HELL!!
SO MOTHER DIDN'T DIE...
BUT I'VE NEVER BEEN ABLE TO FIND HER...
I THINK SHE'S STILL ON THIS EARTH...
NOW.
SOME-WHERE ...
I CAN'T BELIEVE EVERYTHING TOKAGE SAID.
SHE WOULDN'T DISCARD HIM...
NNNG
AND EVEN IF IT WERE TRUE ...
I STILL COULDN'T FORGIVE HIM.
... IAN?
YOU DON'T BELIEVE ME...
BUT IT'S THE ONLY REASON I HAVE ANYTHING TO DO WITH HUMANS.
I CAN'T HELP IT...

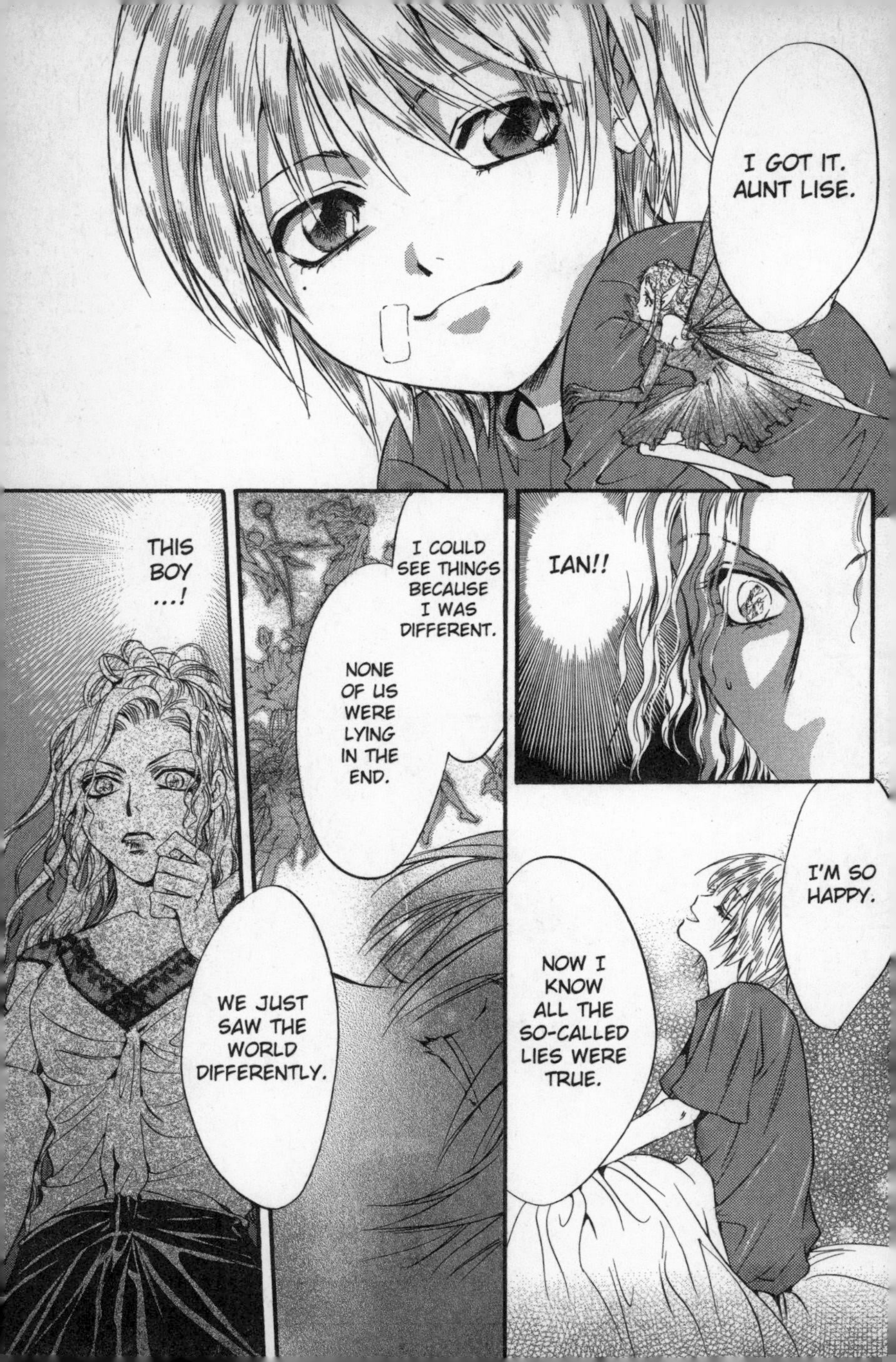
I GOT IT. AUNT LISE.
IAN!!
I'M SO HAPPY.
NOW I KNOW ALL THE SO-CALLED LIES WERE TRUE.
I COULD SEE THINGS BECAUSE I WAS DIFFERENT.
NONE OF US WERE LYING IN THE END.
WE JUST SAW THE WORLD DIFFERENTLY.
THIS BOY ...!

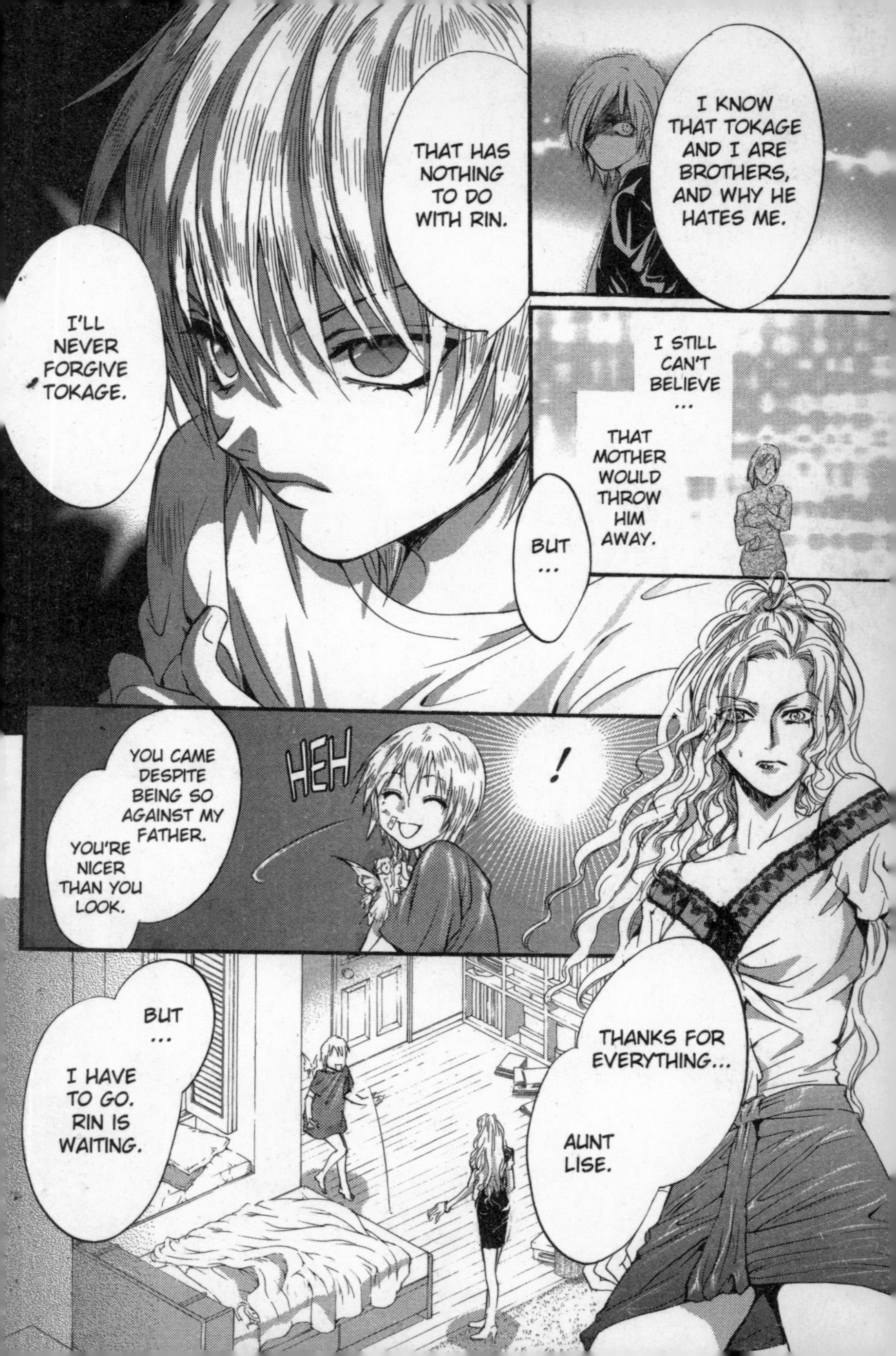
I KNOW THAT TOKAGE AND I ARE BROTHERS, AND WHY HE HATES ME.
I STILL CAN'T BELIEVE ...
THAT MOTHER WOULD THROW HIM AWAY.
BUT ...
THAT HAS NOTHING TO DO WITH RIN.
I'LL NEVER FORGIVE TOKAGE.
!
HEH
YOU CAME DESPITE BEING SO AGAINST MY FATHER.
YOU'RE NICER THAN YOU LOOK.
THANKS FOR EVERYTHING...
AUNT LISE.
BUT ...
I HAVE TO GO. RIN IS WAITING.

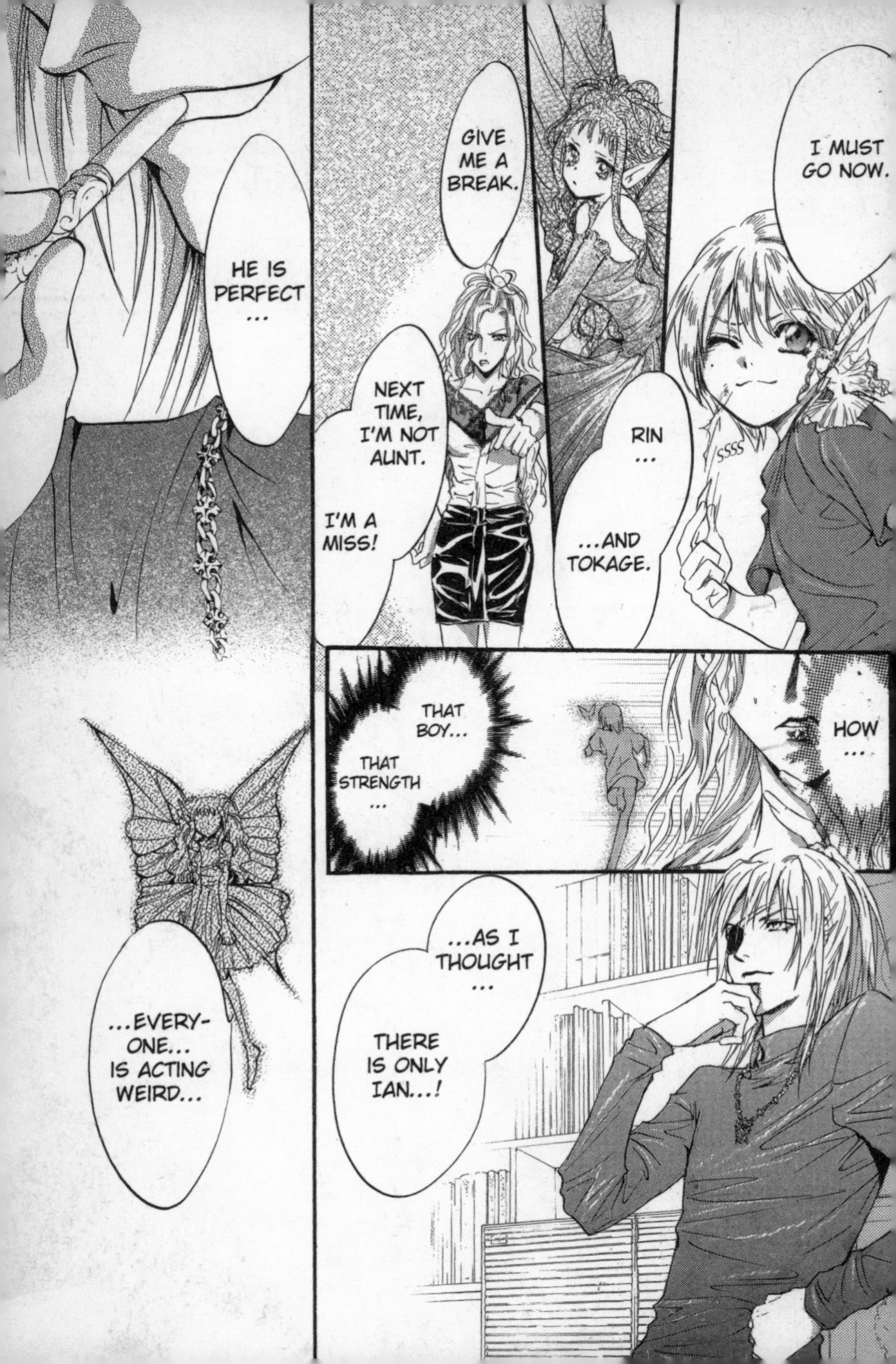
I MUST GO NOW.
RIN ...
...AND TOKAGE.
SSSS
GIVE ME A BREAK.
NEXT TIME, I'M NOT AUNT.
I'M A MISS!
HOW ...
THAT BOY...
THAT STRENGTH ...
...AS I THOUGHT ...
THERE IS ONLY IAN...!
HE IS PERFECT ...
...EVERY-ONE... IS ACTING WEIRD...

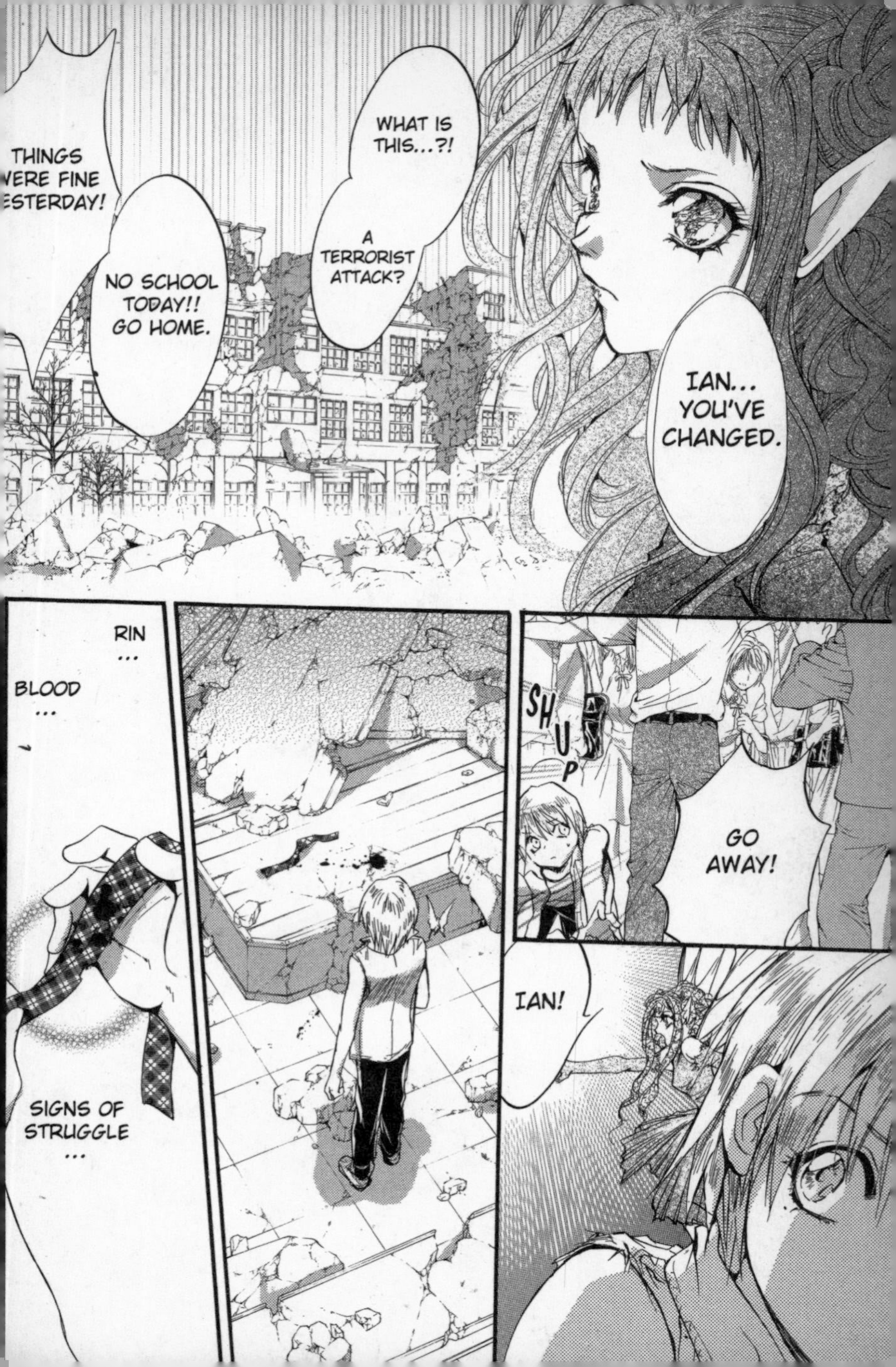
IAN... YOU'VE CHANGED.
WHAT IS THIS...?!
A TERRORIST ATTACK?
NO SCHOOL TODAY!! GO HOME.
THINGS ERE FINE ESTERDAY!
SHUP
GO AWAY!
IAN!
RIN...
BLOOD...
SIGNS OF STRUGGLE...

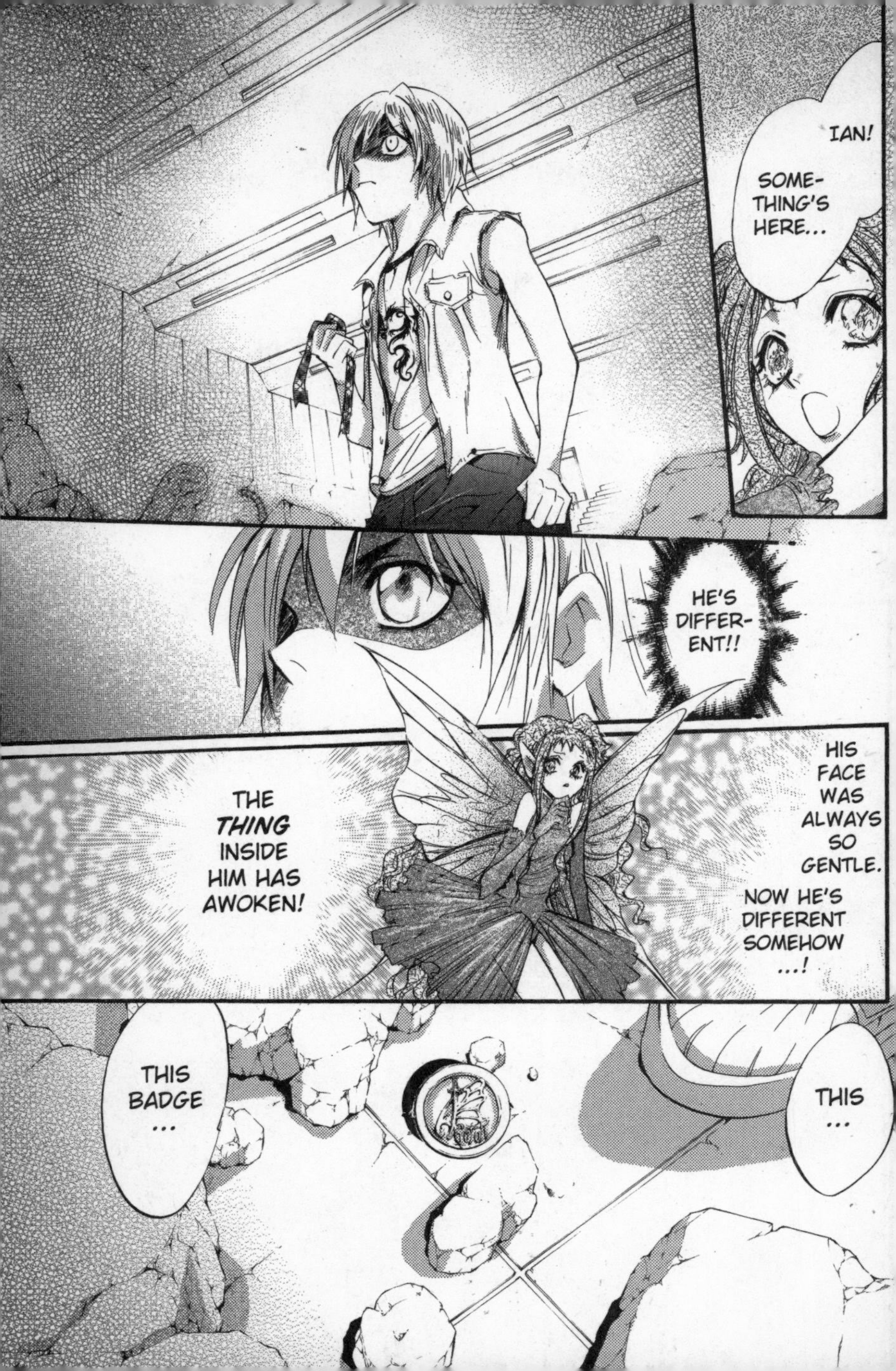
IAN!
SOMETHING'S HERE...
HE'S DIFFERENT!!
HIS FACE WAS ALWAYS SO GENTLE.
NOW HE'S DIFFERENT SOMEHOW...!
THE *THING* INSIDE HIM HAS AWOKEN!
THIS...
THIS BADGE...

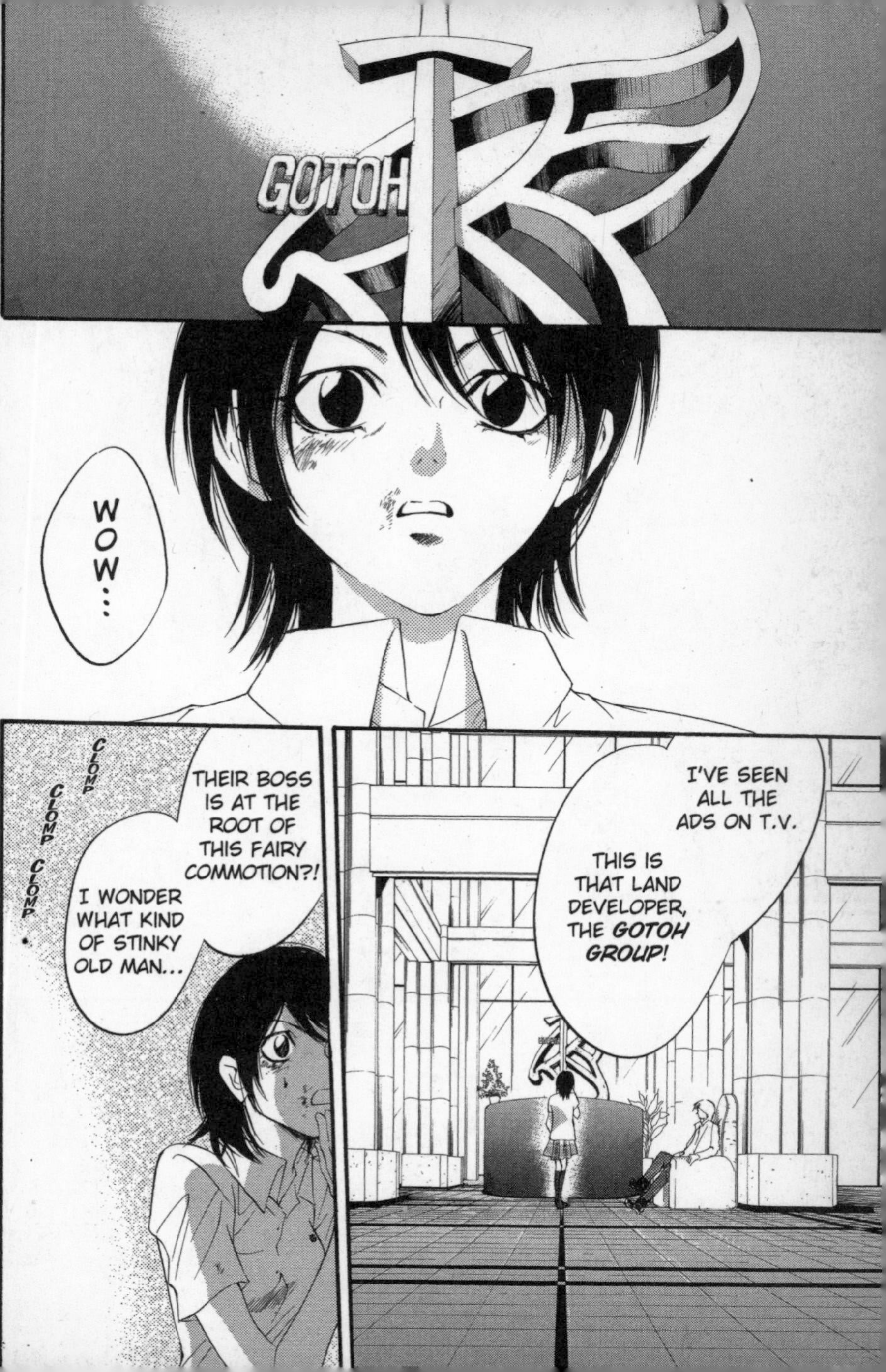
GOTOH
WOW...
I'VE SEEN ALL THE ADS ON T.V.
THIS IS THAT LAND DEVELOPER, THE *GOTOH GROUP!*
THEIR BOSS IS AT THE ROOT OF THIS FAIRY COMMOTION?!
I WONDER WHAT KIND OF STINKY OLD MAN...
CLOMP CLOMP CLOMP

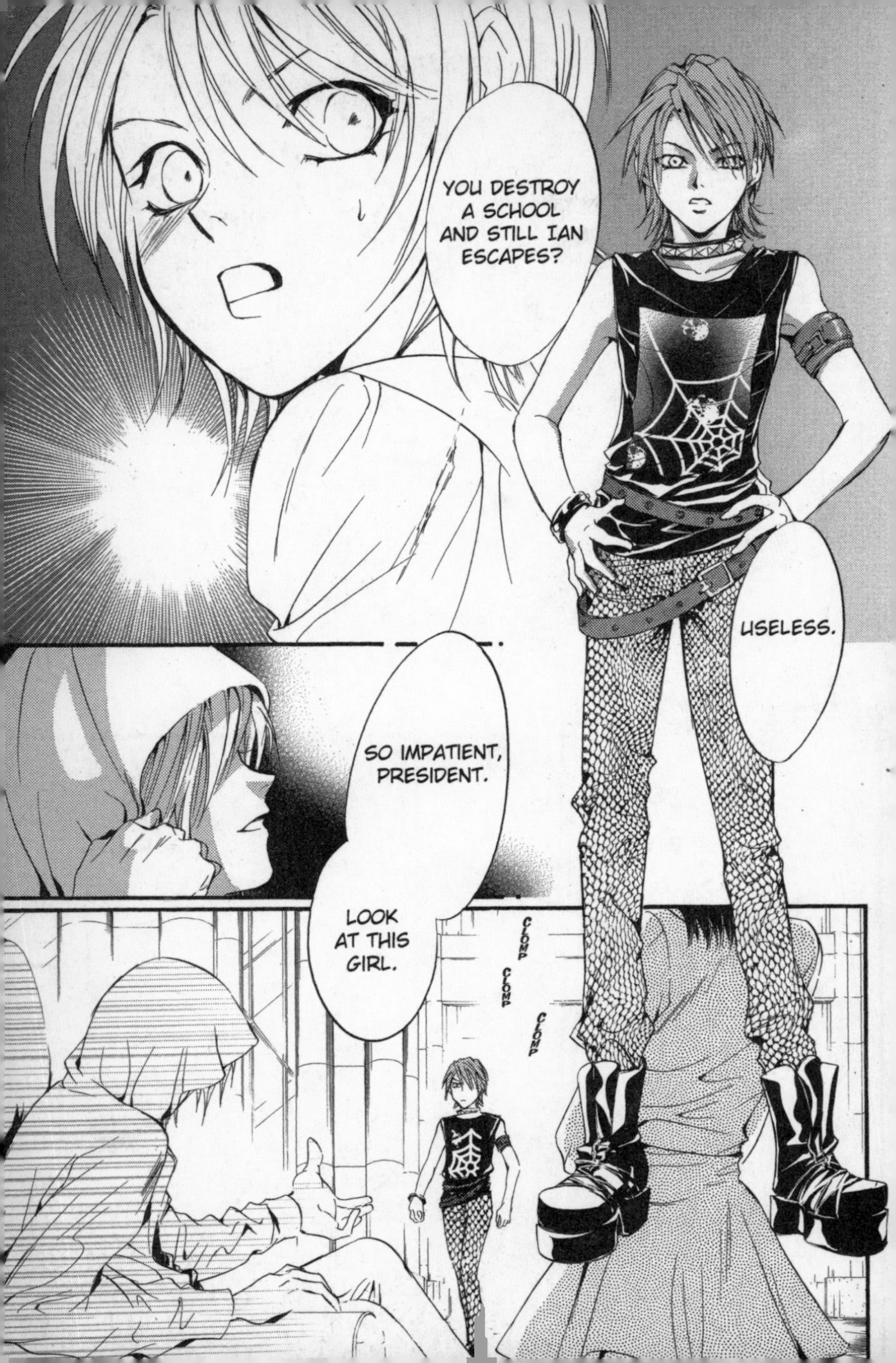
YOU DESTROY A SCHOOL AND STILL IAN ESCAPES?
USELESS.
SO IMPATIENT, PRESIDENT.
LOOK AT THIS GIRL.
CLOMP
CLOMP
CLOMP

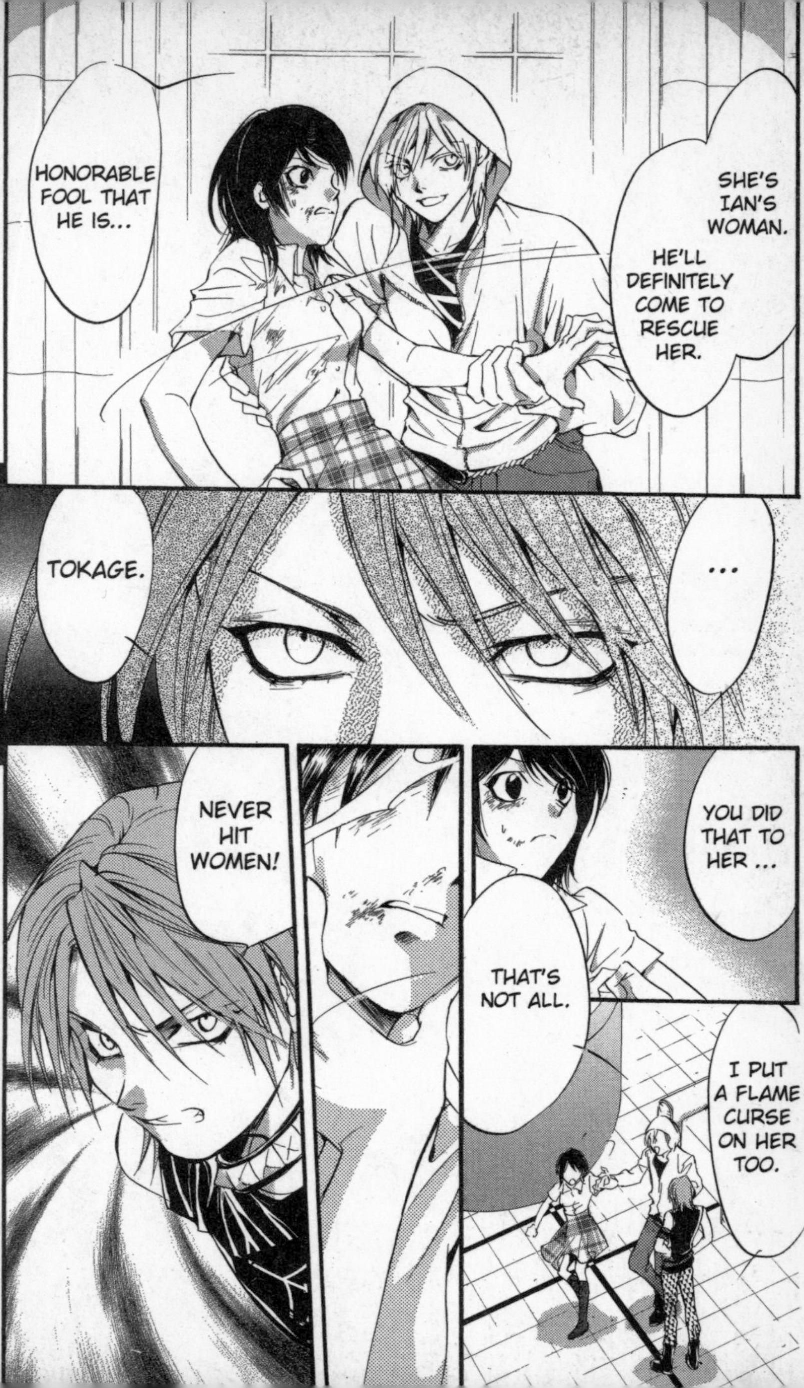
SHE'S IAN'S WOMAN.
HE'LL DEFINITELY COME TO RESCUE HER.
HONORABLE FOOL THAT HE IS...
...
TOKAGE.
YOU DID THAT TO HER ...
THAT'S NOT ALL.
I PUT A FLAME CURSE ON HER TOO.
NEVER HIT WOMEN!

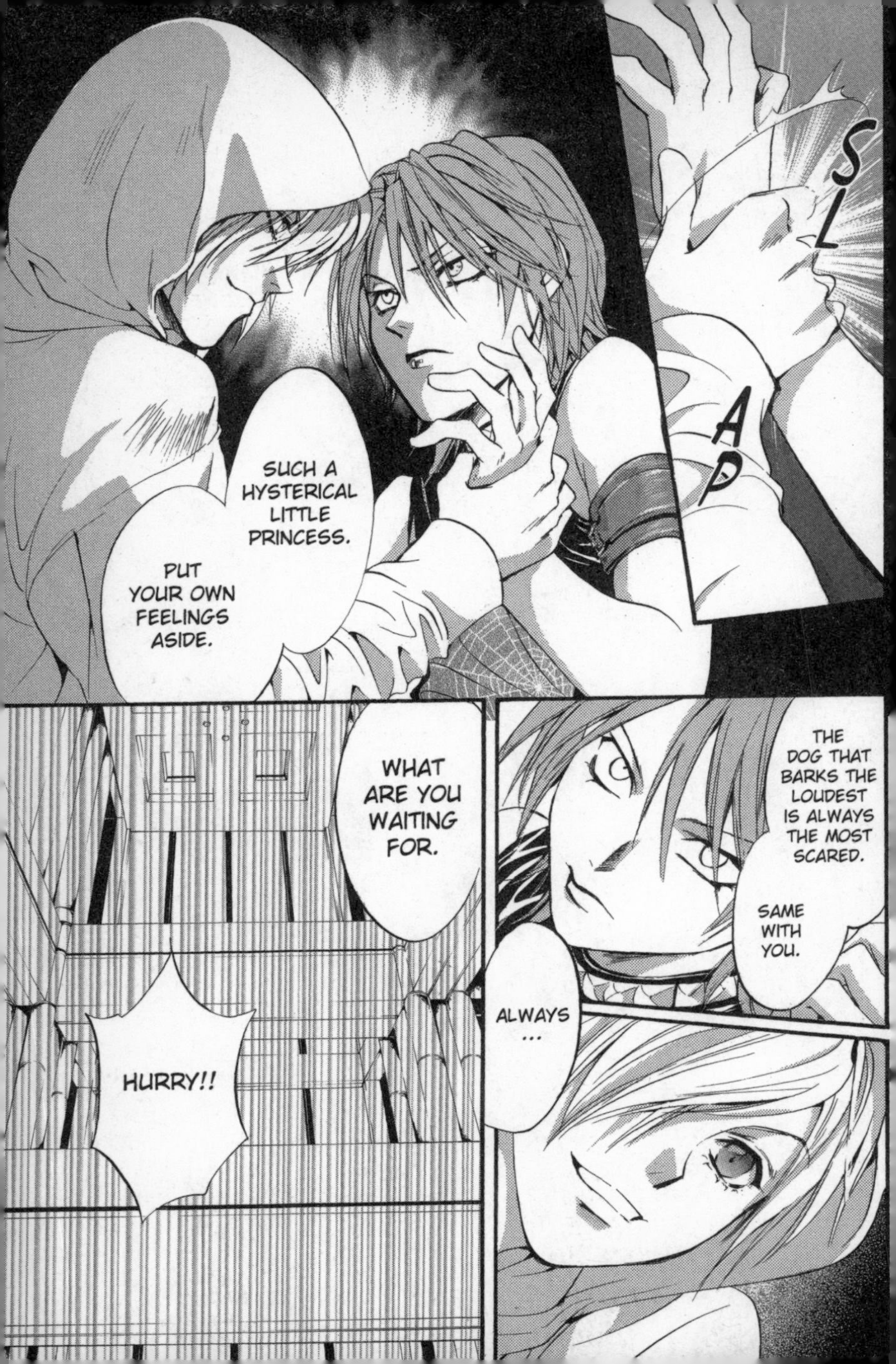
SLAP
SUCH A HYSTERICAL LITTLE PRINCESS.
PUT YOUR OWN FEELINGS ASIDE.
THE DOG THAT BARKS THE LOUDEST IS ALWAYS THE MOST SCARED.
SAME WITH YOU.
ALWAYS...
WHAT ARE YOU WAITING FOR.
HURRY!!

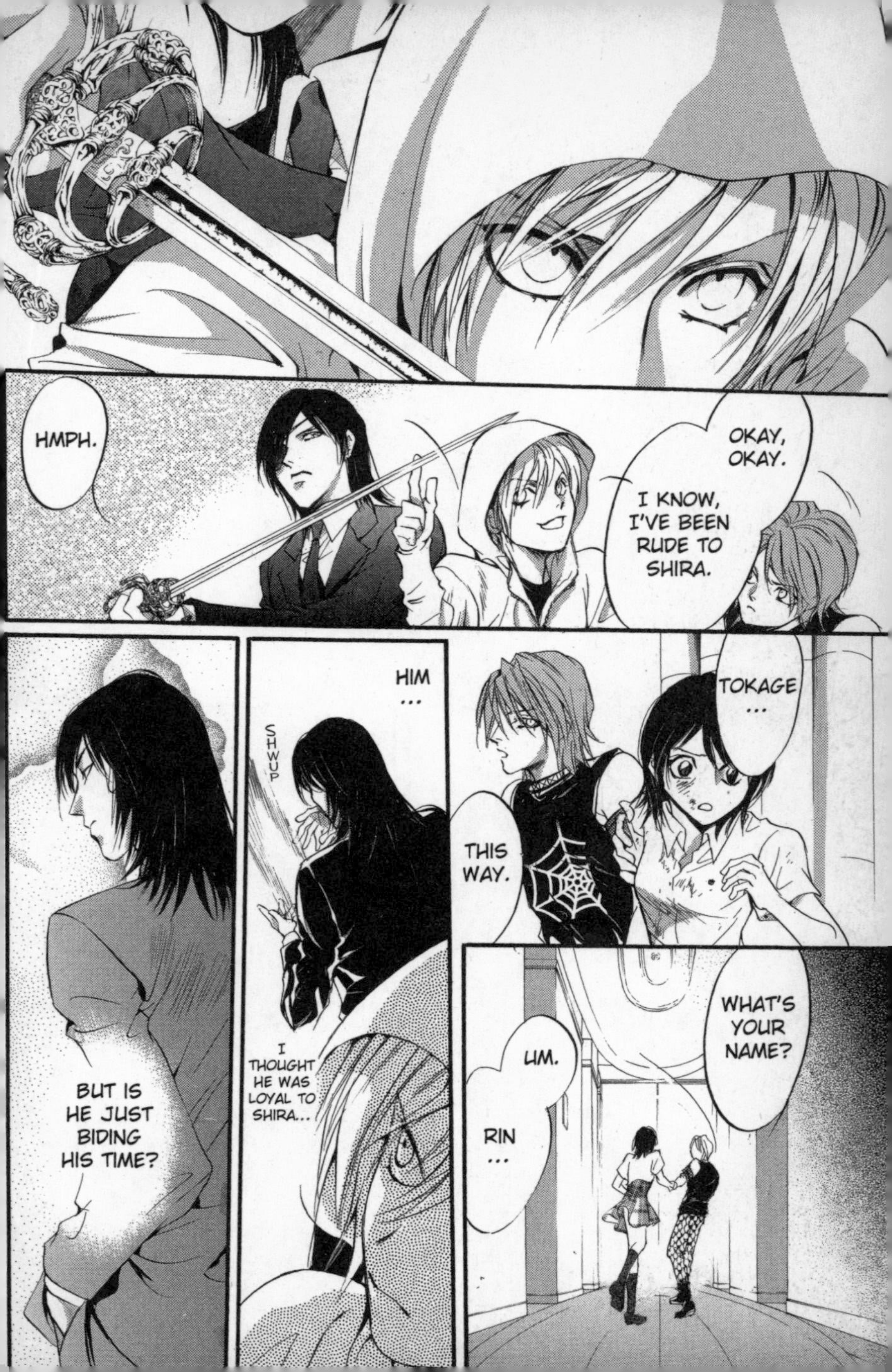
OKAY, OKAY.
I KNOW, I'VE BEEN RUDE TO SHIRA.
HMPH.
TOKAGE...
THIS WAY.
WHAT'S YOUR NAME?
UM.
RIN...
HIM...
SHWUP
I THOUGHT HE WAS LOYAL TO SHIRA...
BUT IS HE JUST BIDING HIS TIME?

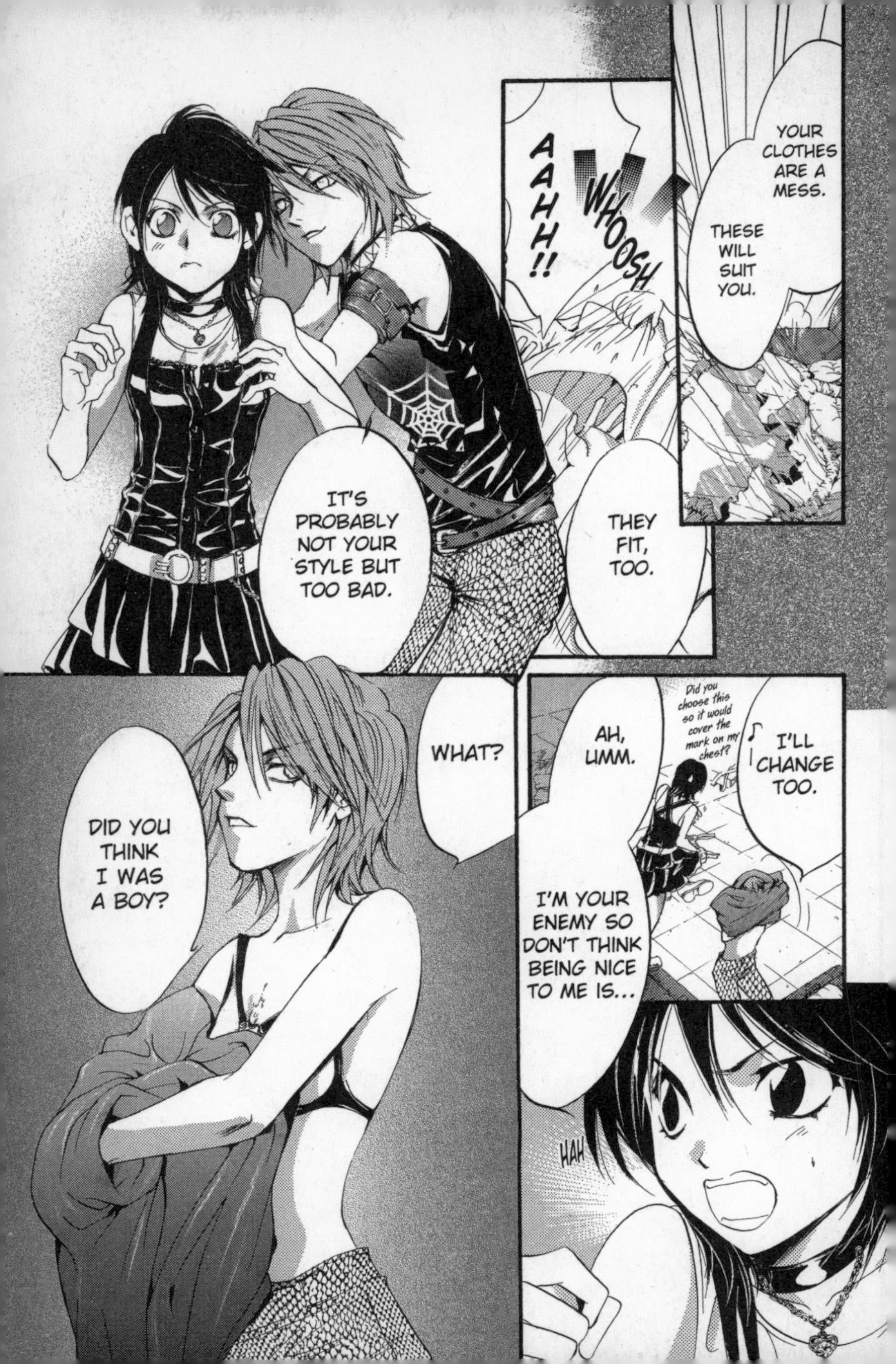
YOUR CLOTHES ARE A MESS.
THESE WILL SUIT YOU.
AAHH!!
WHOOSH
THEY FIT, TOO.
IT'S PROBABLY NOT YOUR STYLE BUT TOO BAD.
I'LL CHANGE TOO.
Did you choose this so it would cover the mark on my chest?
AH, UMM.
I'M YOUR ENEMY SO DON'T THINK BEING NICE TO ME IS...
HAH
WHAT?
DID YOU THINK I WAS A BOY?

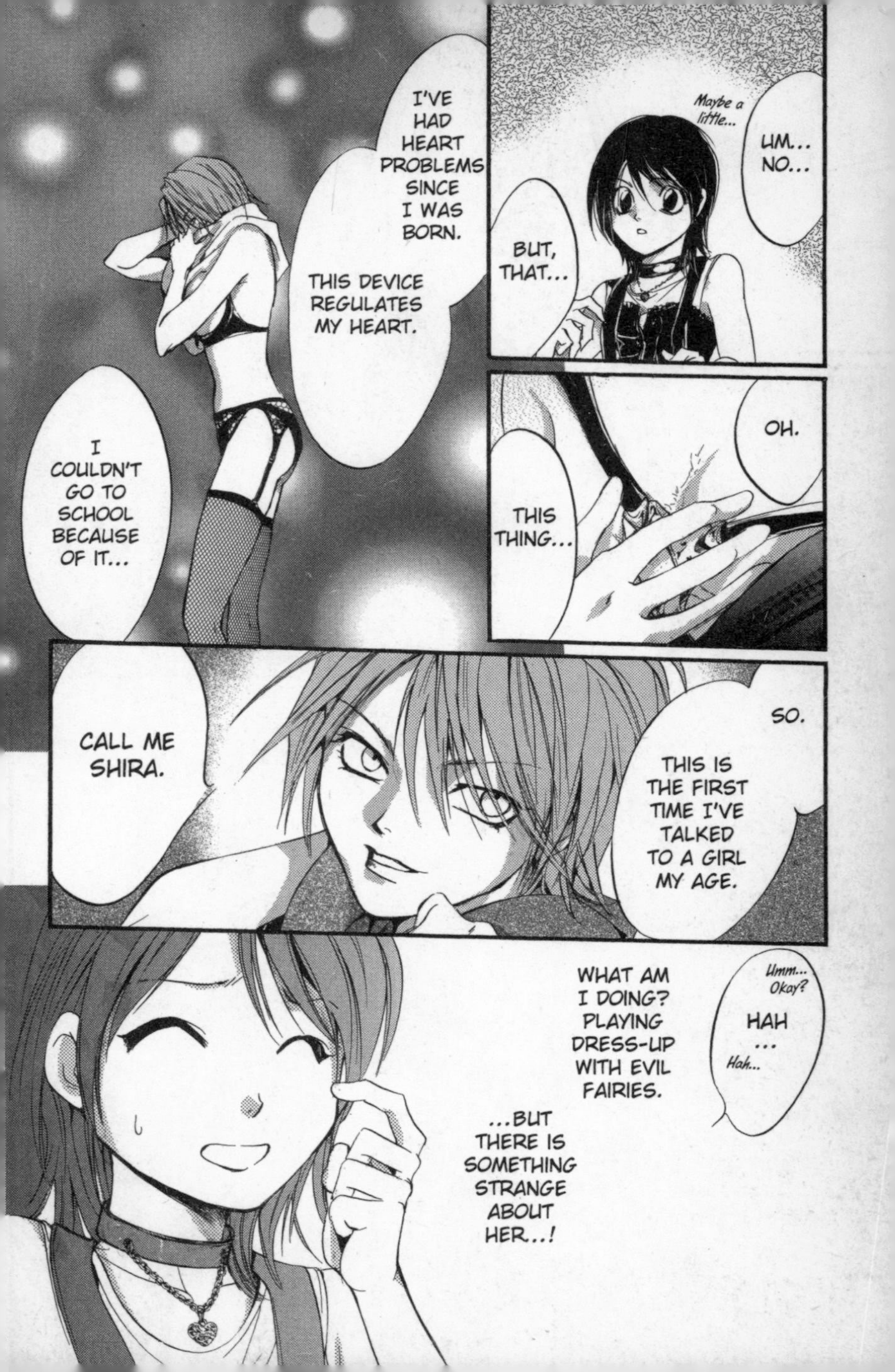
UM... NO...
Maybe a little...
BUT, THAT...
OH.
THIS THING...
I'VE HAD HEART PROBLEMS SINCE I WAS BORN.
THIS DEVICE REGULATES MY HEART.
I COULDN'T GO TO SCHOOL BECAUSE OF IT...
SO.
THIS IS THE FIRST TIME I'VE TALKED TO A GIRL MY AGE.
CALL ME SHIRA.
Umm... Okay?
HAH ...
Hah...
WHAT AM I DOING? PLAYING DRESS-UP WITH EVIL FAIRIES.
...BUT THERE IS SOMETHING STRANGE ABOUT HER...!

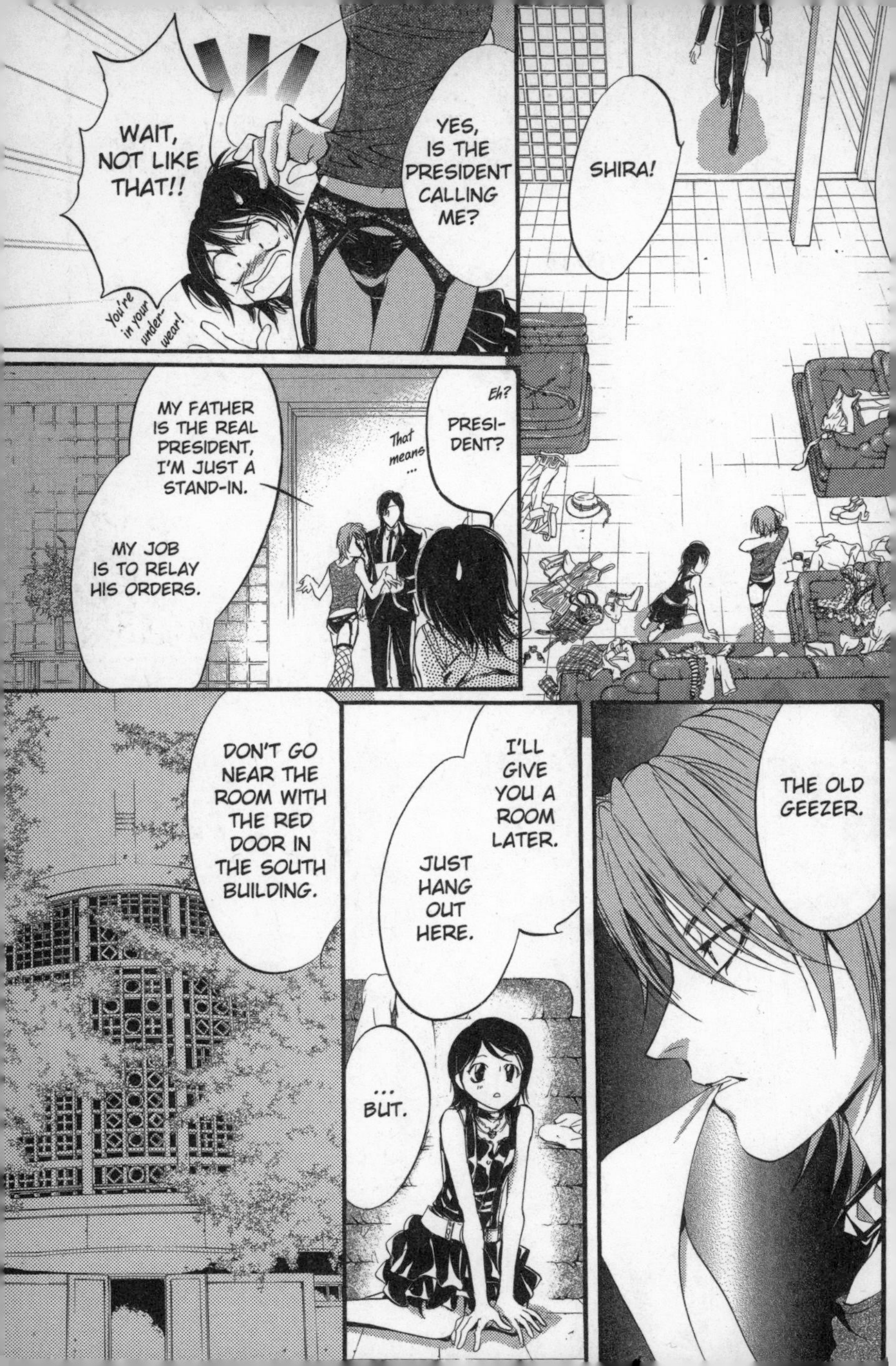

SHIRA!
YES, IS THE PRESIDENT CALLING ME?
WAIT, NOT LIKE THAT!!
You're in your under-wear!
Eh? PRESI-DENT?
That means ...
MY FATHER IS THE REAL PRESIDENT, I'M JUST A STAND-IN.
MY JOB IS TO RELAY HIS ORDERS.
THE OLD GEEZER.
I'LL GIVE YOU A ROOM LATER.
JUST HANG OUT HERE.
... BUT.
DON'T GO NEAR THE ROOM WITH THE RED DOOR IN THE SOUTH BUILDING.

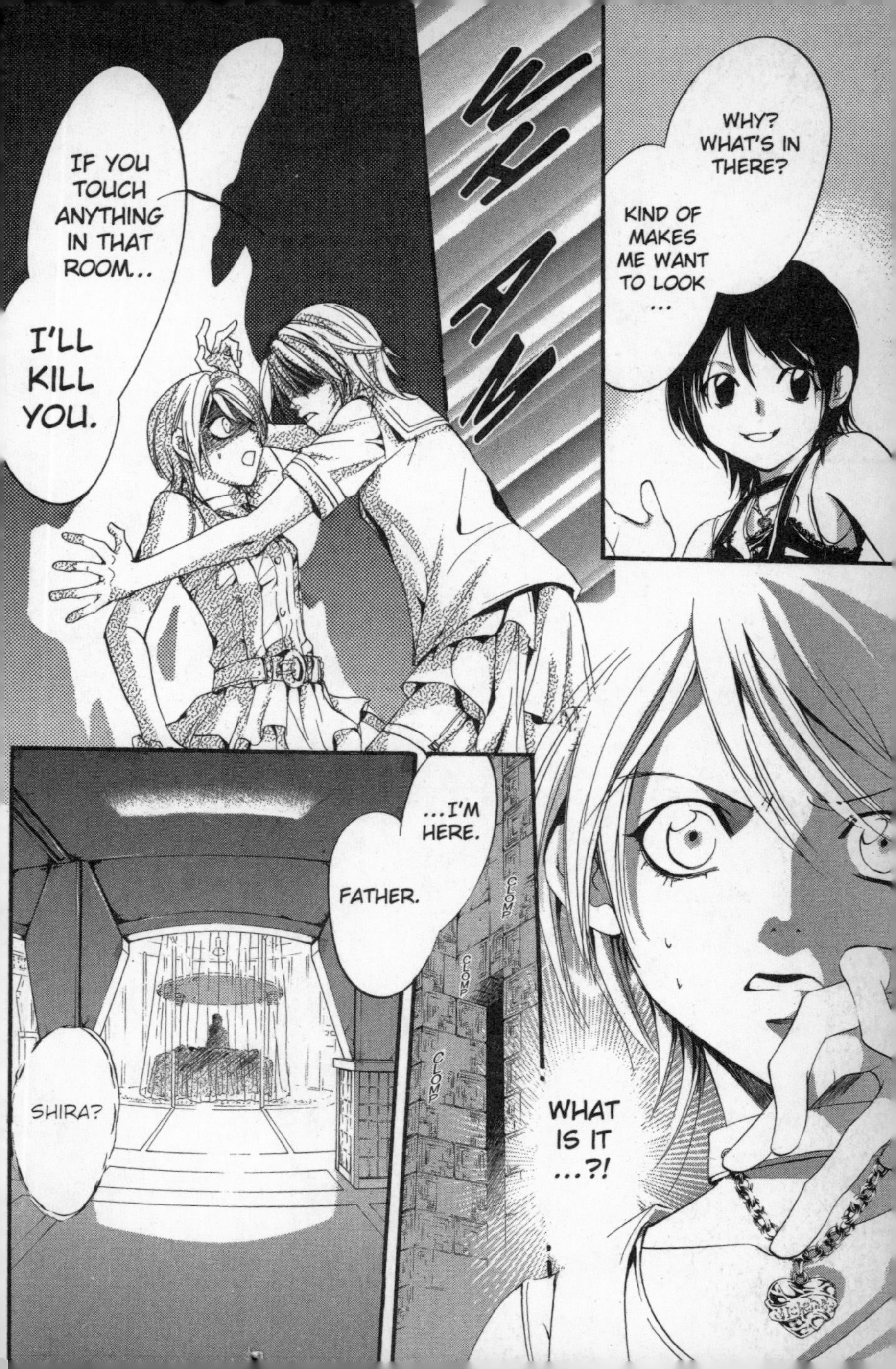
WHY? WHAT'S IN THERE?
KIND OF MAKES ME WANT TO LOOK ...
WHAM
IF YOU TOUCH ANYTHING IN THAT ROOM...
I'LL KILL YOU.
WHAT IS IT ...?!
...I'M HERE.
FATHER.
CLOMP
CLOMP
CLOMP
SHIRA?

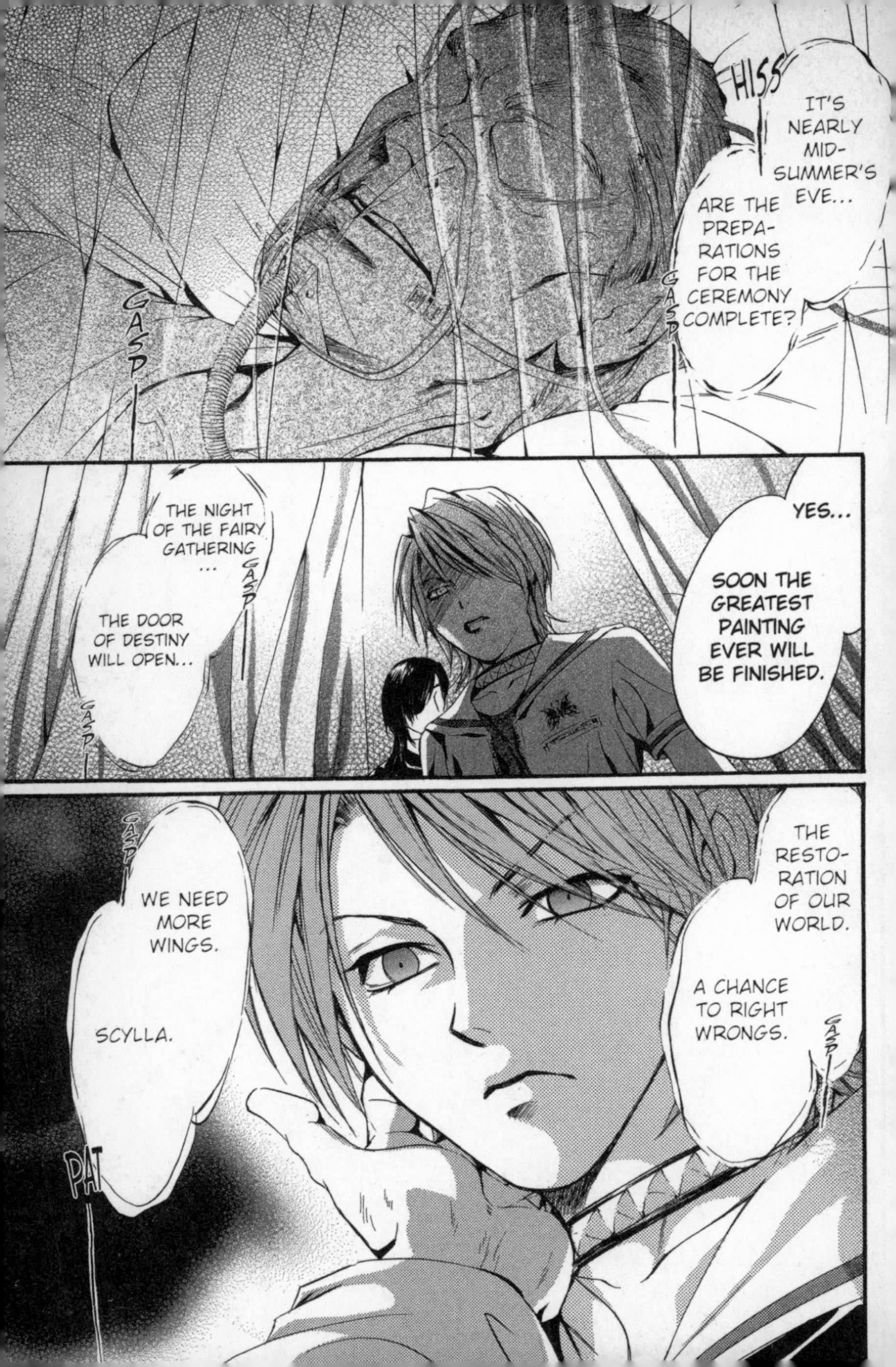
HISS
IT'S NEARLY MID-SUMMER'S EVE...
ARE THE PREPARATIONS FOR THE CEREMONY COMPLETE?
GASP
GASP
YES...
SOON THE GREATEST PAINTING EVER WILL BE FINISHED.
THE NIGHT OF THE FAIRY GATHERING...
GASP
THE DOOR OF DESTINY WILL OPEN...
GASP
THE RESTORATION OF OUR WORLD.
A CHANCE TO RIGHT WRONGS.
GASP
GASP
WE NEED MORE WINGS.
SCYLLA.
PAT

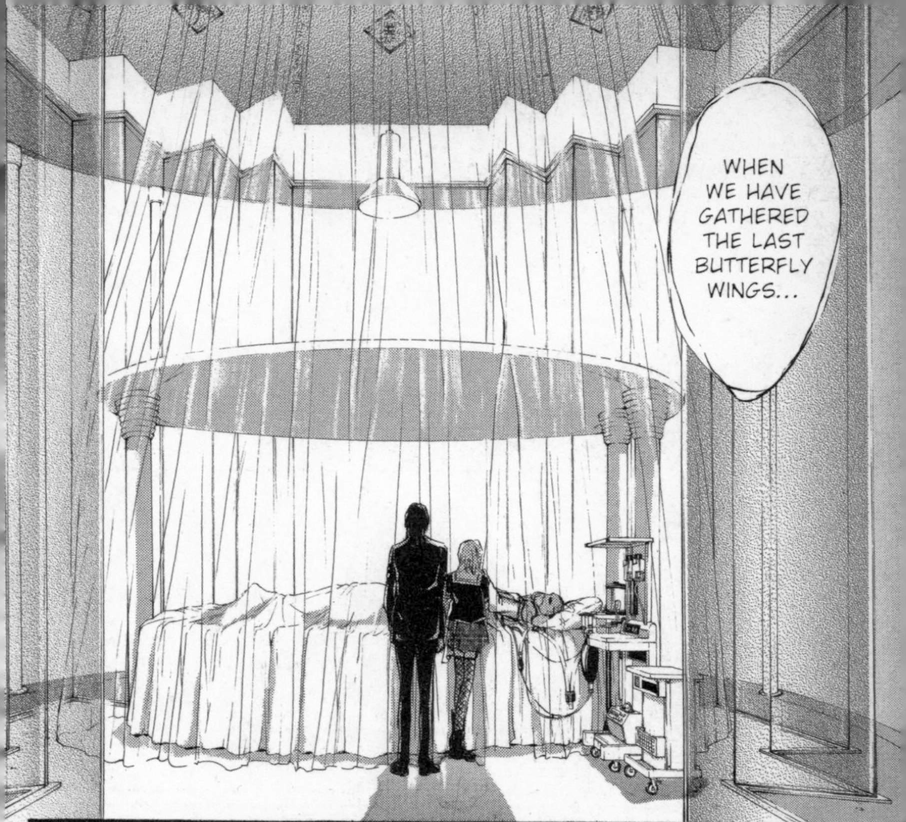
WHEN WE HAVE GATHERED THE LAST BUTTERFLY WINGS...

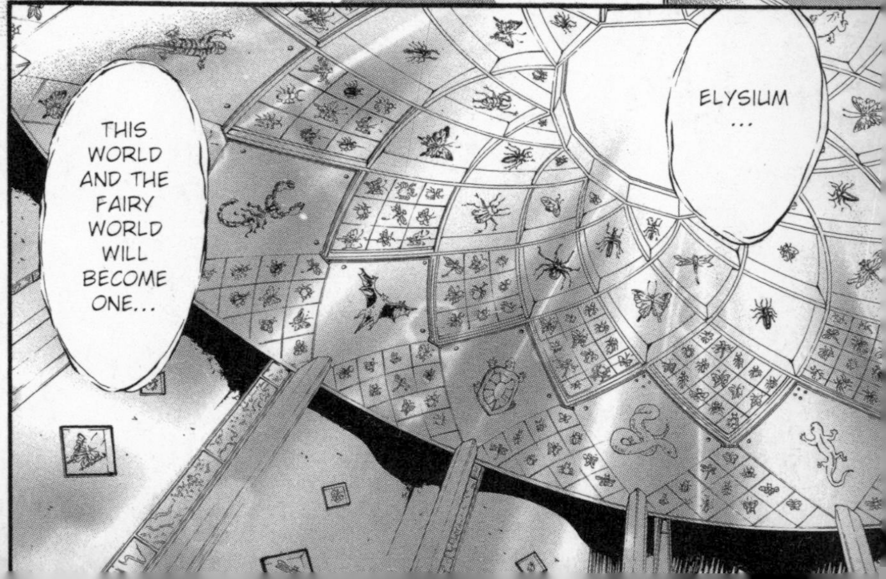
ELYSIUM ...
THIS WORLD AND THE FAIRY WORLD WILL BECOME ONE...

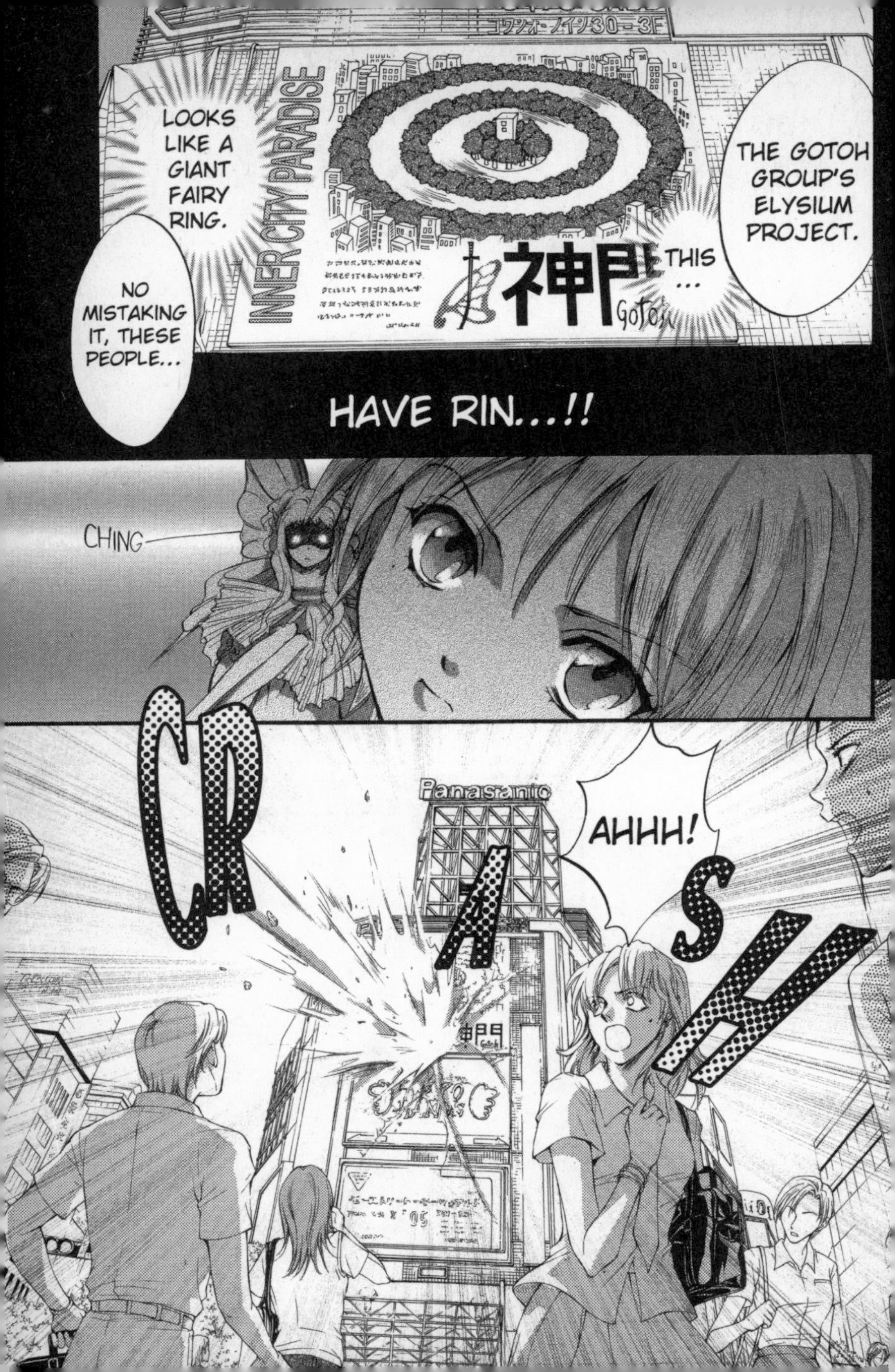
THE GOTOH GROUP'S ELYSIUM PROJECT.
THIS...
INNER CITY PARADISE
Gotoh
LOOKS LIKE A GIANT FAIRY RING.
NO MISTAKING IT, THESE PEOPLE...
HAVE RIN...!!
CHING
AHHH!
Panasanic
CRASH

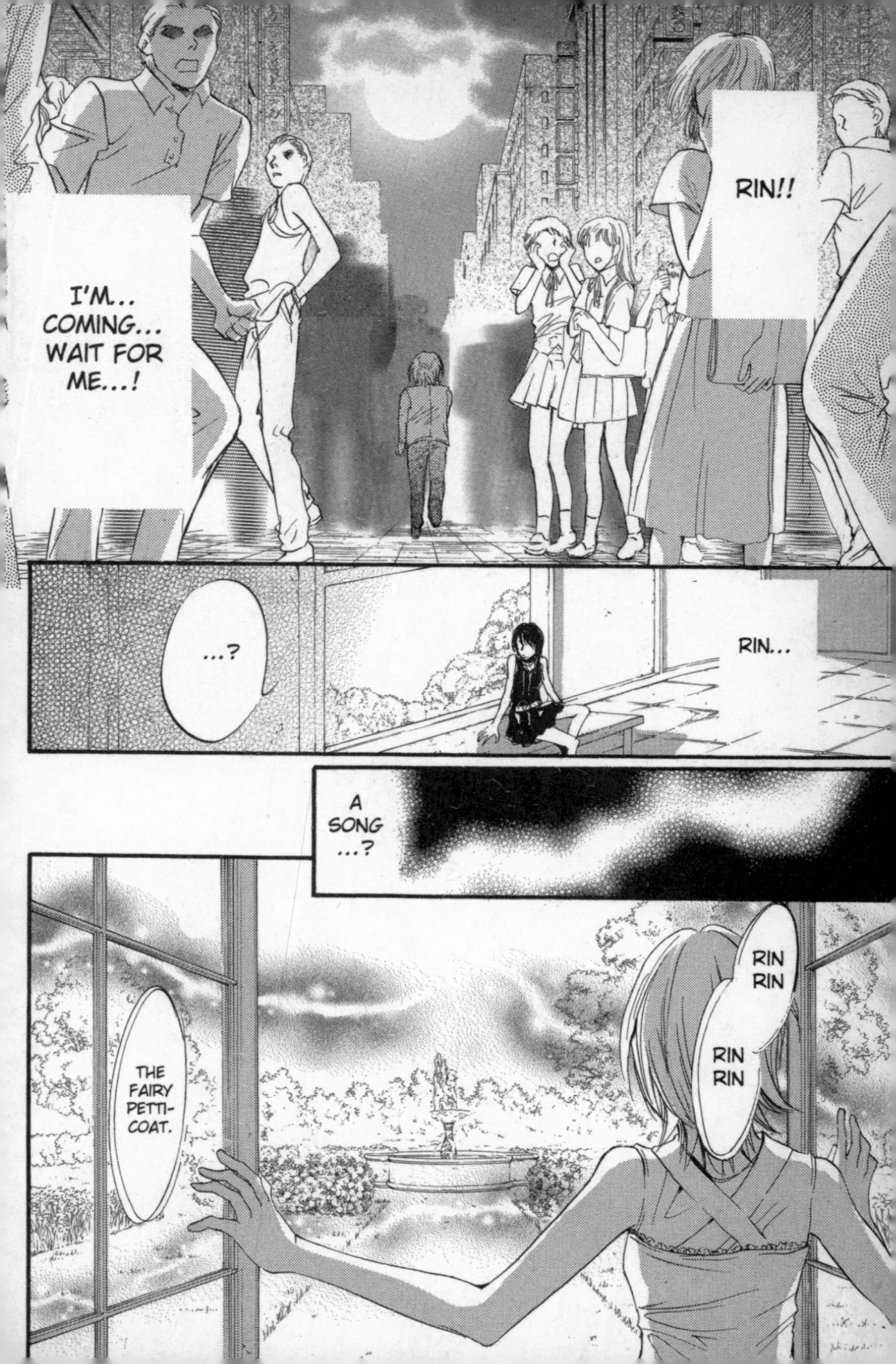
RIN!!
I'M... COMING... WAIT FOR ME...!
RIN...
...?
A SONG ...?
RIN RIN
RIN RIN
THE FAIRY PETTI-COAT.

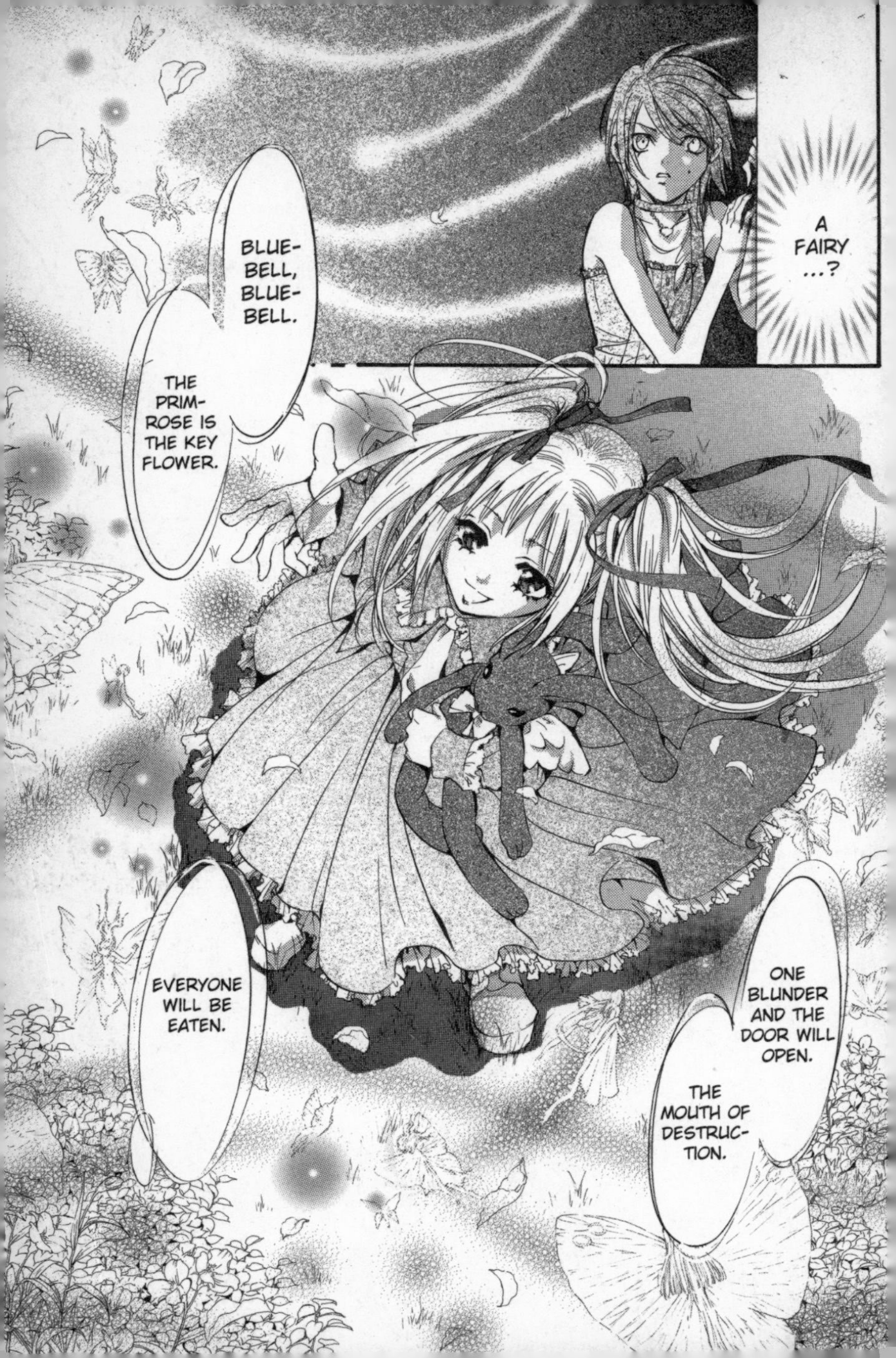
A FAIRY ...?
BLUE-BELL, BLUE-BELL.
THE PRIM-ROSE IS THE KEY FLOWER.
ONE BLUNDER AND THE DOOR WILL OPEN.
THE MOUTH OF DESTRUC-TION.
EVERYONE WILL BE EATEN.

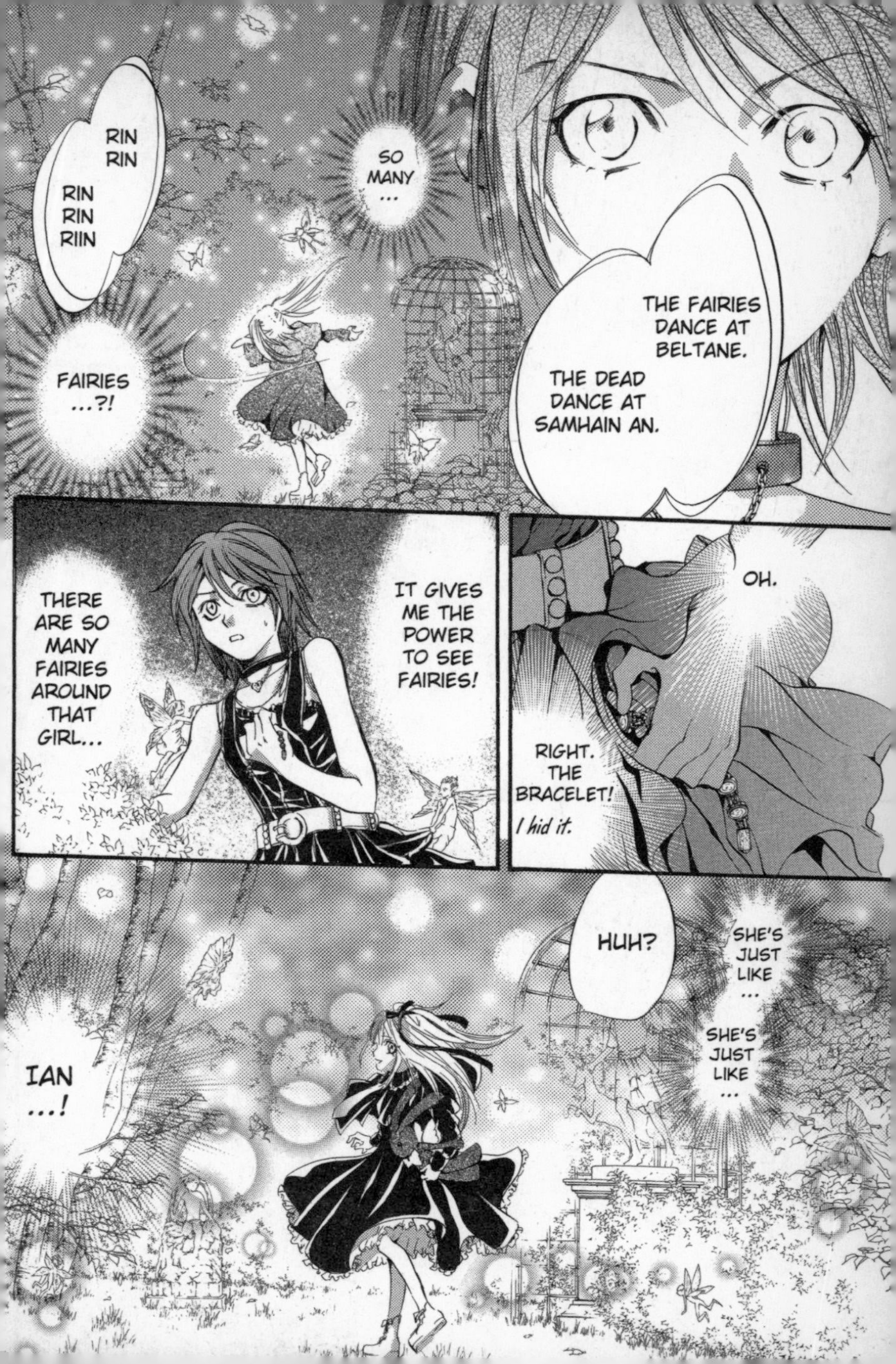
THE FAIRIES DANCE AT BELTANE.
THE DEAD DANCE AT SAMHAIN AN.
SO MANY...
RIN RIN
RIN RIN RIIN
FAIRIES...?!
OH.
RIGHT. THE BRACELET!
I hid it.
IT GIVES ME THE POWER TO SEE FAIRIES!
THERE ARE SO MANY FAIRIES AROUND THAT GIRL...
HUH?
SHE'S JUST LIKE...
SHE'S JUST LIKE...
IAN...!

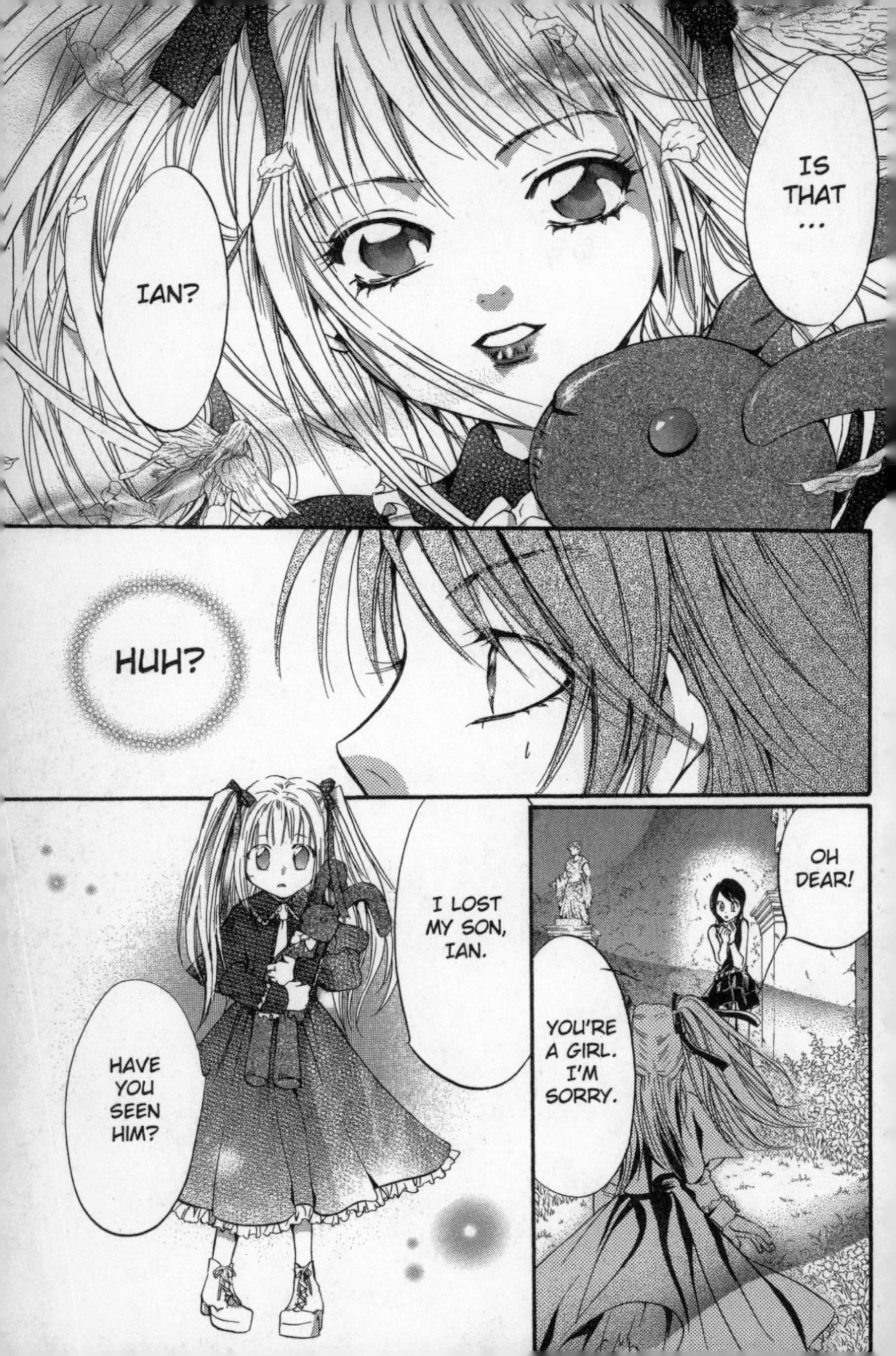
IS THAT ...
IAN?
HUH?
OH DEAR!
YOU'RE A GIRL. I'M SORRY.
I LOST MY SON, IAN.
HAVE YOU SEEN HIM?

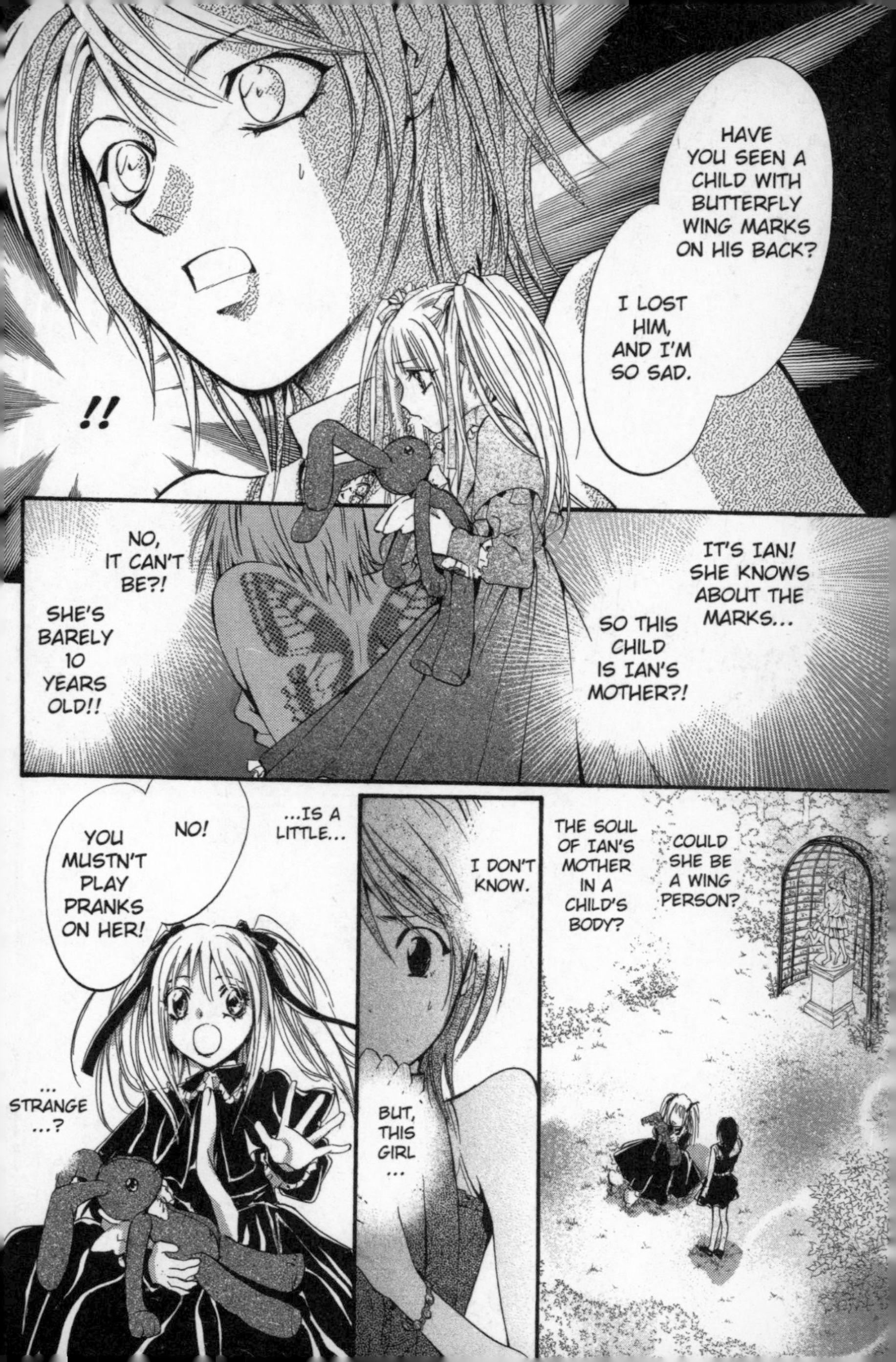

HAVE YOU SEEN A CHILD WITH BUTTERFLY WING MARKS ON HIS BACK?
I LOST HIM, AND I'M SO SAD.
!!
IT'S IAN! SHE KNOWS ABOUT THE MARKS...
SO THIS CHILD IS IAN'S MOTHER?!
NO, IT CAN'T BE?!
SHE'S BARELY 10 YEARS OLD!!
COULD SHE BE A WING PERSON?
THE SOUL OF IAN'S MOTHER IN A CHILD'S BODY?
I DON'T KNOW.
BUT, THIS GIRL ...
...IS A LITTLE...
...STRANGE ...?
NO!
YOU MUSTN'T PLAY PRANKS ON HER!

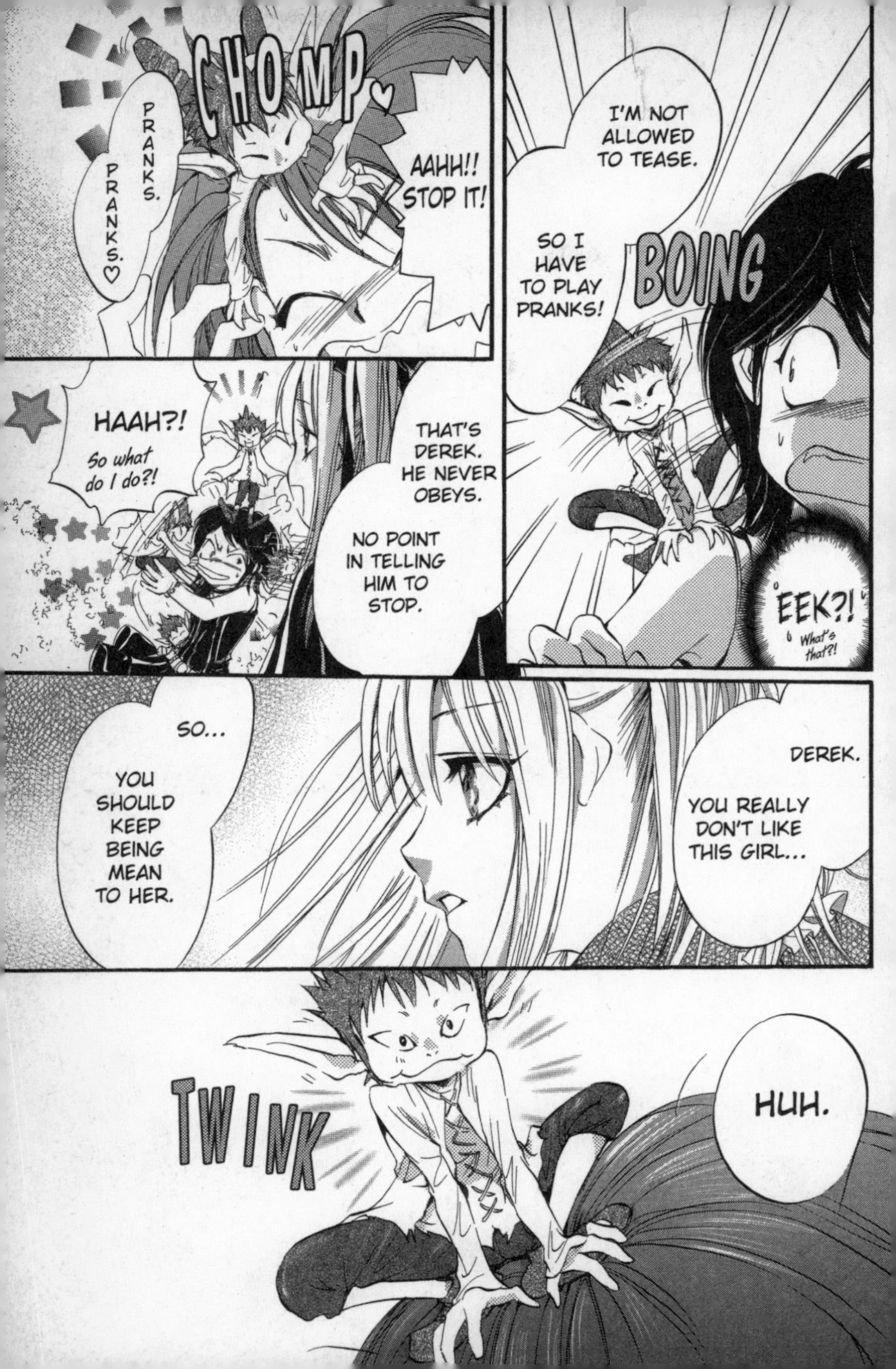
I'M NOT ALLOWED TO TEASE.
SO I HAVE TO PLAY PRANKS!
BOING
EEK?!
What's that?!
CHOMP♡
AAHH!! STOP IT!
PRANKS. PRANKS.♡
THAT'S DEREK. HE NEVER OBEYS.
NO POINT IN TELLING HIM TO STOP.
HAAH?!
So what do I do?!
DEREK.
YOU REALLY DON'T LIKE THIS GIRL...
SO...
YOU SHOULD KEEP BEING MEAN TO HER.
HUH.
TWINK

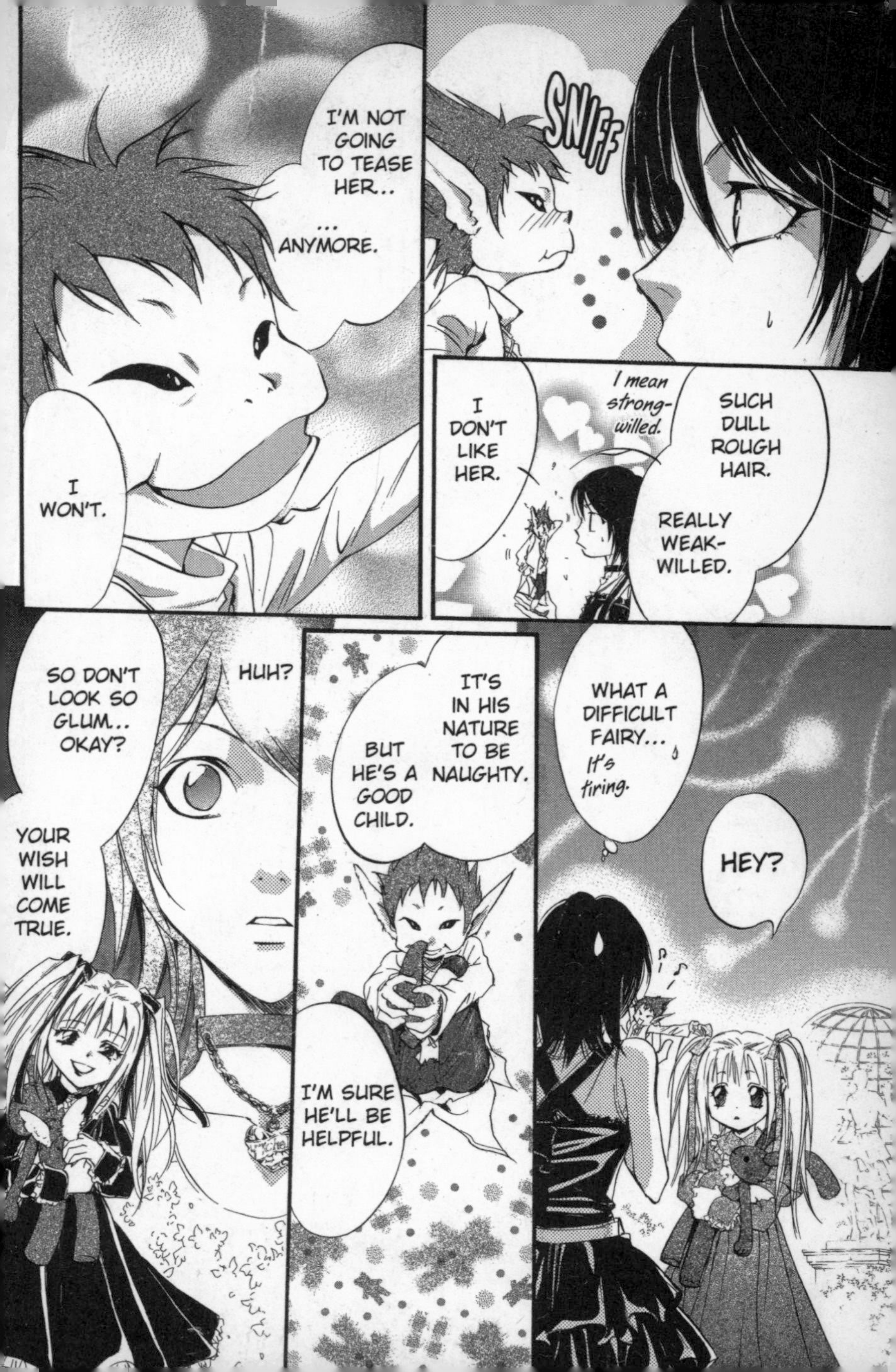
SNIFF
SUCH DULL ROUGH HAIR.
I mean strong-willed.
REALLY WEAK-WILLED.
I DON'T LIKE HER.
I'M NOT GOING TO TEASE HER...
... ANYMORE.
I WON'T.
WHAT A DIFFICULT FAIRY... It's tiring.
HEY?
IT'S IN HIS NATURE TO BE NAUGHTY.
BUT HE'S A GOOD CHILD.
I'M SURE HE'LL BE HELPFUL.
HUH?
SO DON'T LOOK SO GLUM... OKAY?
YOUR WISH WILL COME TRUE.

Derek the Naughty Fairy

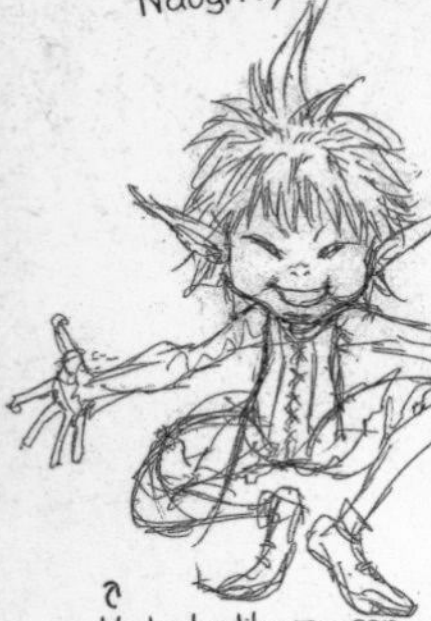

He looks like my son, the way he smiles as he pesters.

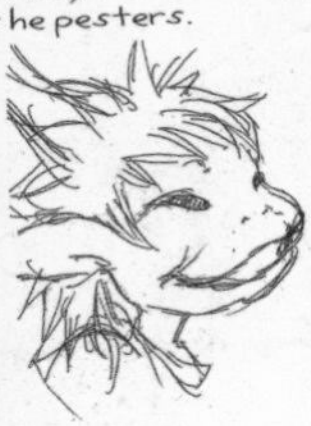

I couldn't find anything in all my research, so I made this design up myself.
...But.

When I went to Karaoke with some co-workers I thought I saw a song titled "Fairy Derek"... an illusion?!

Is there an anime with a fairy hero, however minor, as a character?? Perhaps not so minor??

If anyone knows, please tell me!

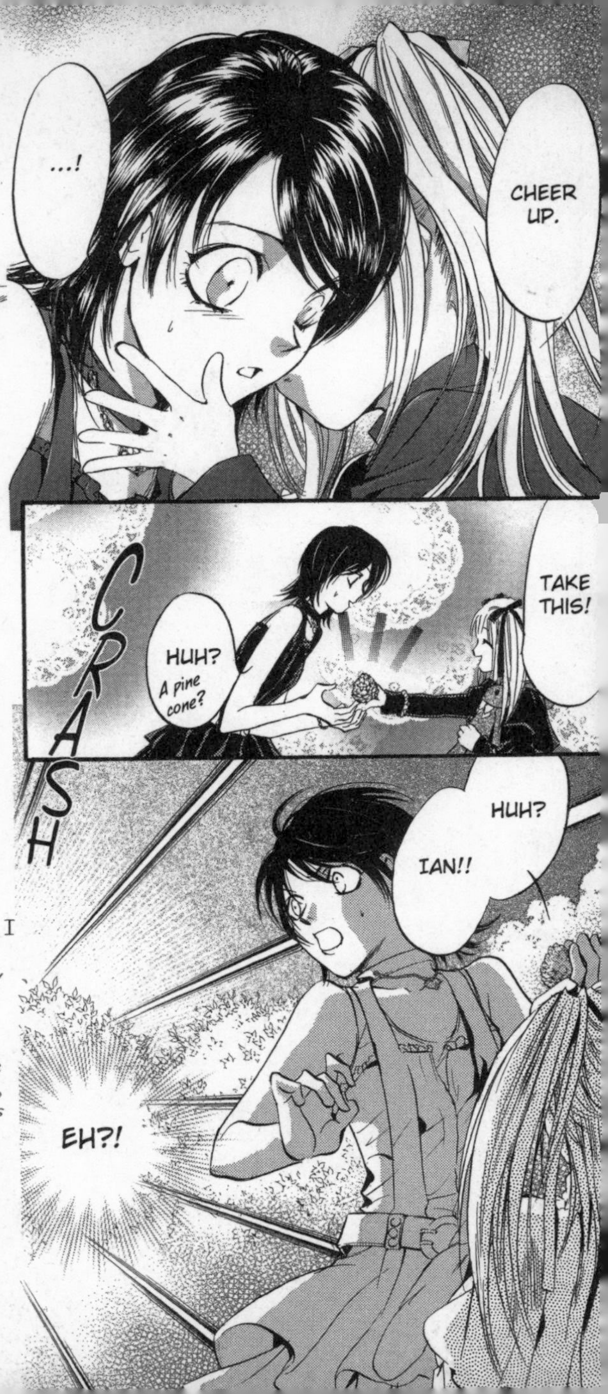
CHEER UP.
...!
TAKE THIS!
HUH? A pine cone?
CRASH
HUH?
IAN!!
EH?!

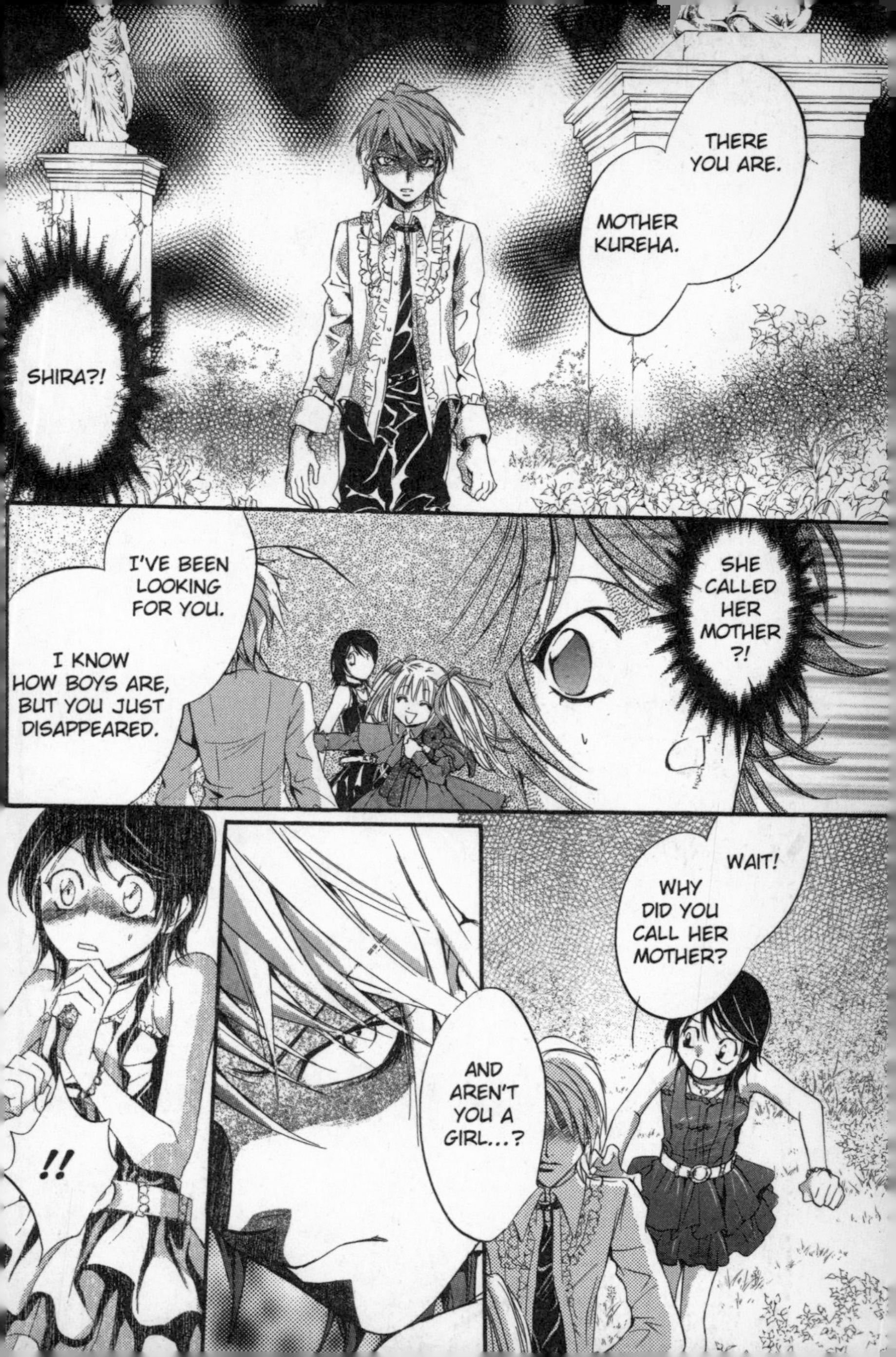
THERE YOU ARE.
MOTHER KUREHA.
SHIRA?!
SHE CALLED HER MOTHER?!
I'VE BEEN LOOKING FOR YOU.
I KNOW HOW BOYS ARE, BUT YOU JUST DISAPPEARED.
WAIT!
WHY DID YOU CALL HER MOTHER?
AND AREN'T YOU A GIRL...?
!!

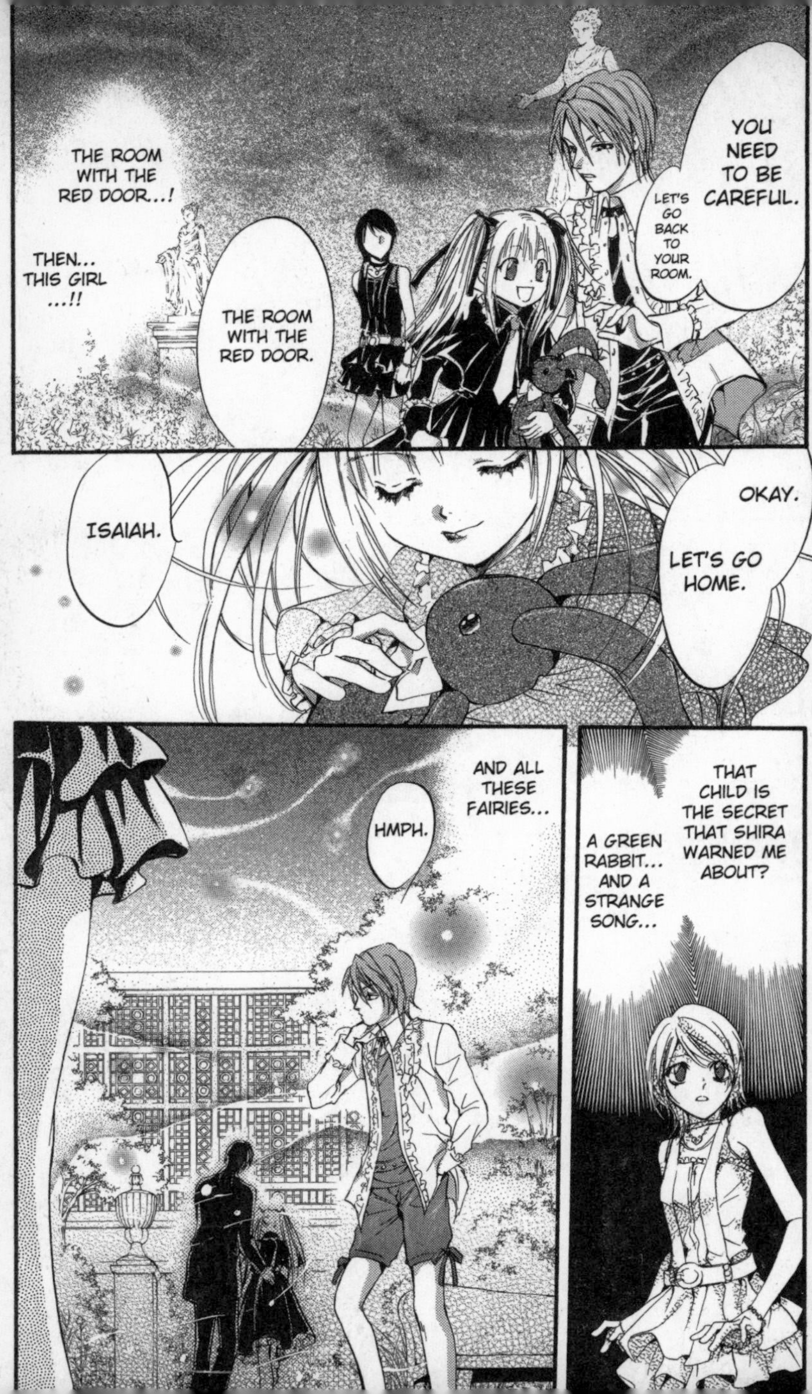
YOU NEED TO BE CAREFUL.
LET'S GO BACK TO YOUR ROOM.
THE ROOM WITH THE RED DOOR.
THE ROOM WITH THE RED DOOR...!
THEN... THIS GIRL ...!!
OKAY.
LET'S GO HOME.
ISAIAH.
THAT CHILD IS THE SECRET THAT SHIRA WARNED ME ABOUT?
A GREEN RABBIT... AND A STRANGE SONG...
AND ALL THESE FAIRIES...
HMPH.

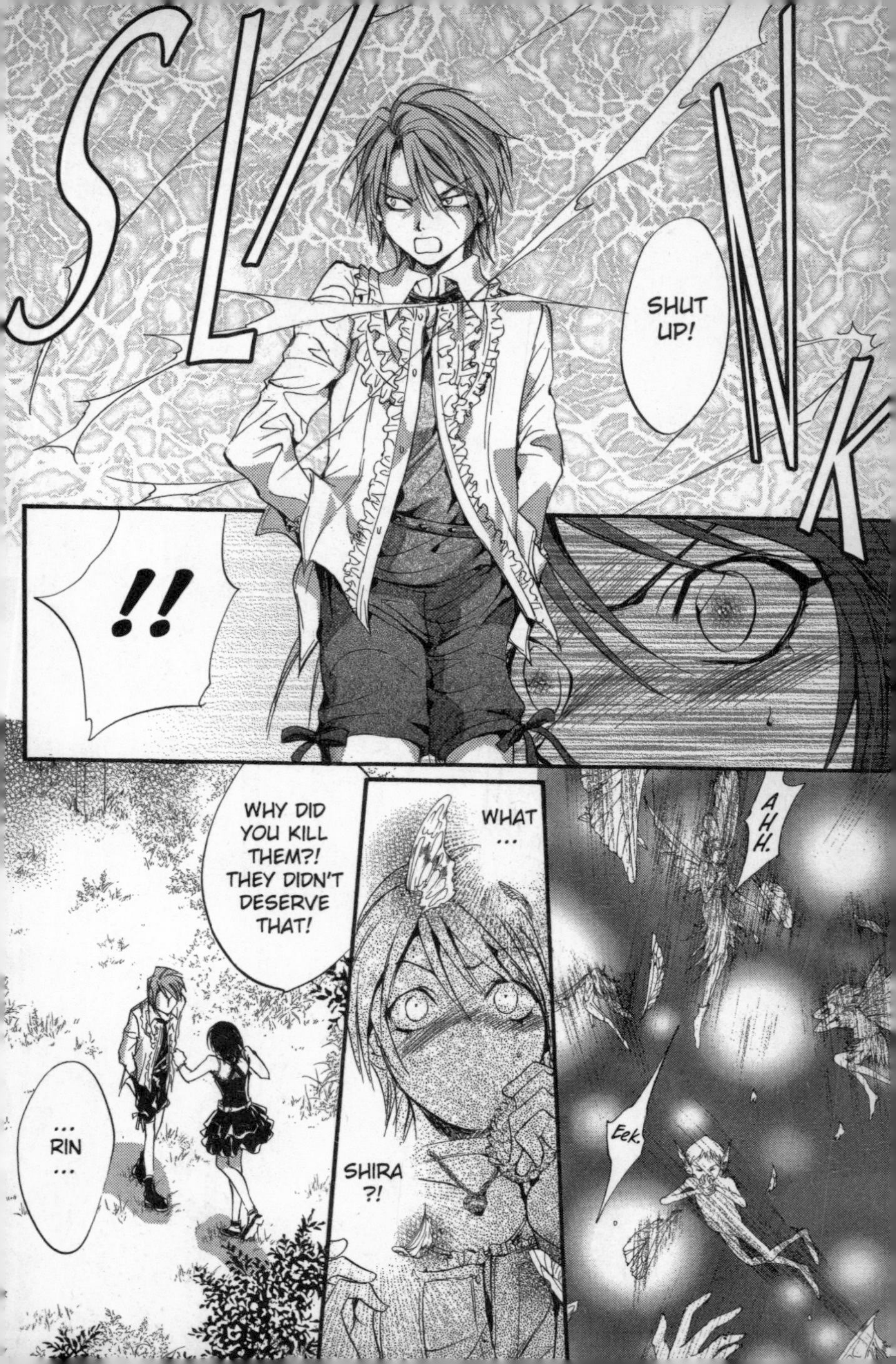
SLINK
SHUT UP!
!!
AHH.
Eek.
WHAT ...
SHIRA ?!
WHY DID YOU KILL THEM?! THEY DIDN'T DESERVE THAT!
... RIN ...

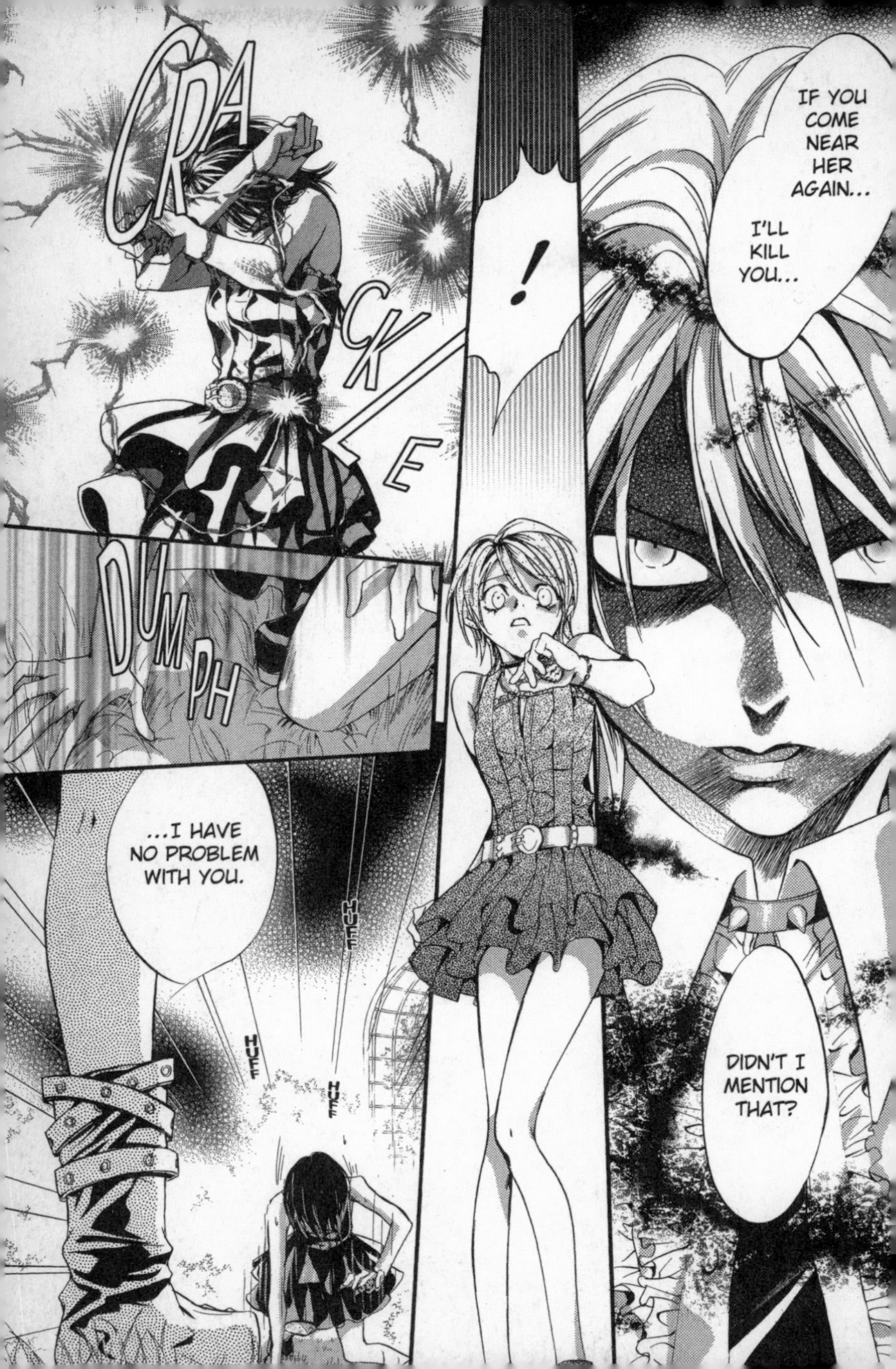
IF YOU COME NEAR HER AGAIN...
I'LL KILL YOU...
DIDN'T I MENTION THAT?
!
CRACKLE
DUMPH
...I HAVE NO PROBLEM WITH YOU.
HUFF
HUFF
HUFF

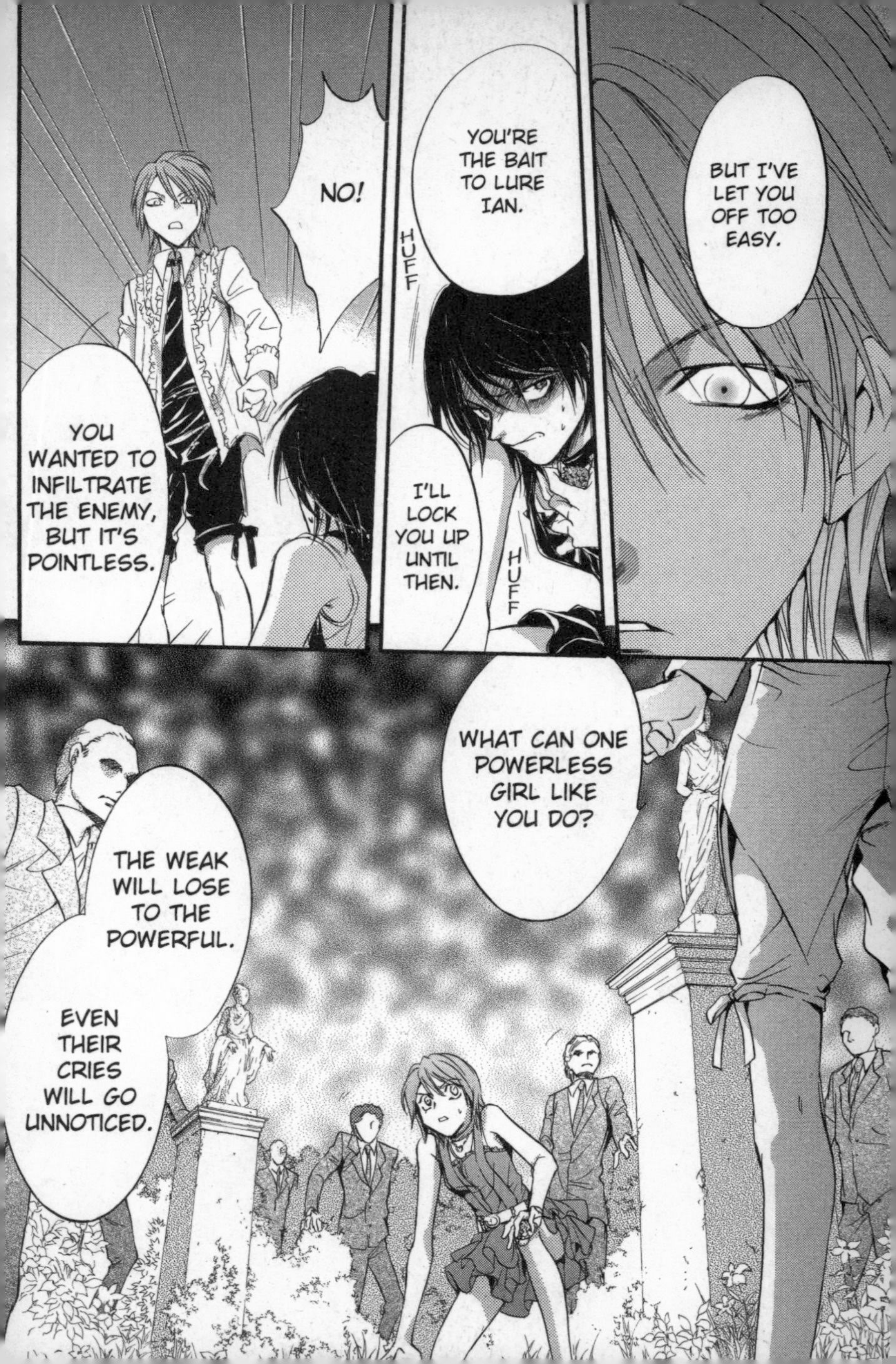
BUT I'VE LET YOU OFF TOO EASY.
YOU'RE THE BAIT TO LURE IAN.
HUFF
I'LL LOCK YOU UP UNTIL THEN.
HUFF
NO!
YOU WANTED TO INFILTRATE THE ENEMY, BUT IT'S POINTLESS.
WHAT CAN ONE POWERLESS GIRL LIKE YOU DO?
THE WEAK WILL LOSE TO THE POWERFUL.
EVEN THEIR CRIES WILL GO UNNOTICED.

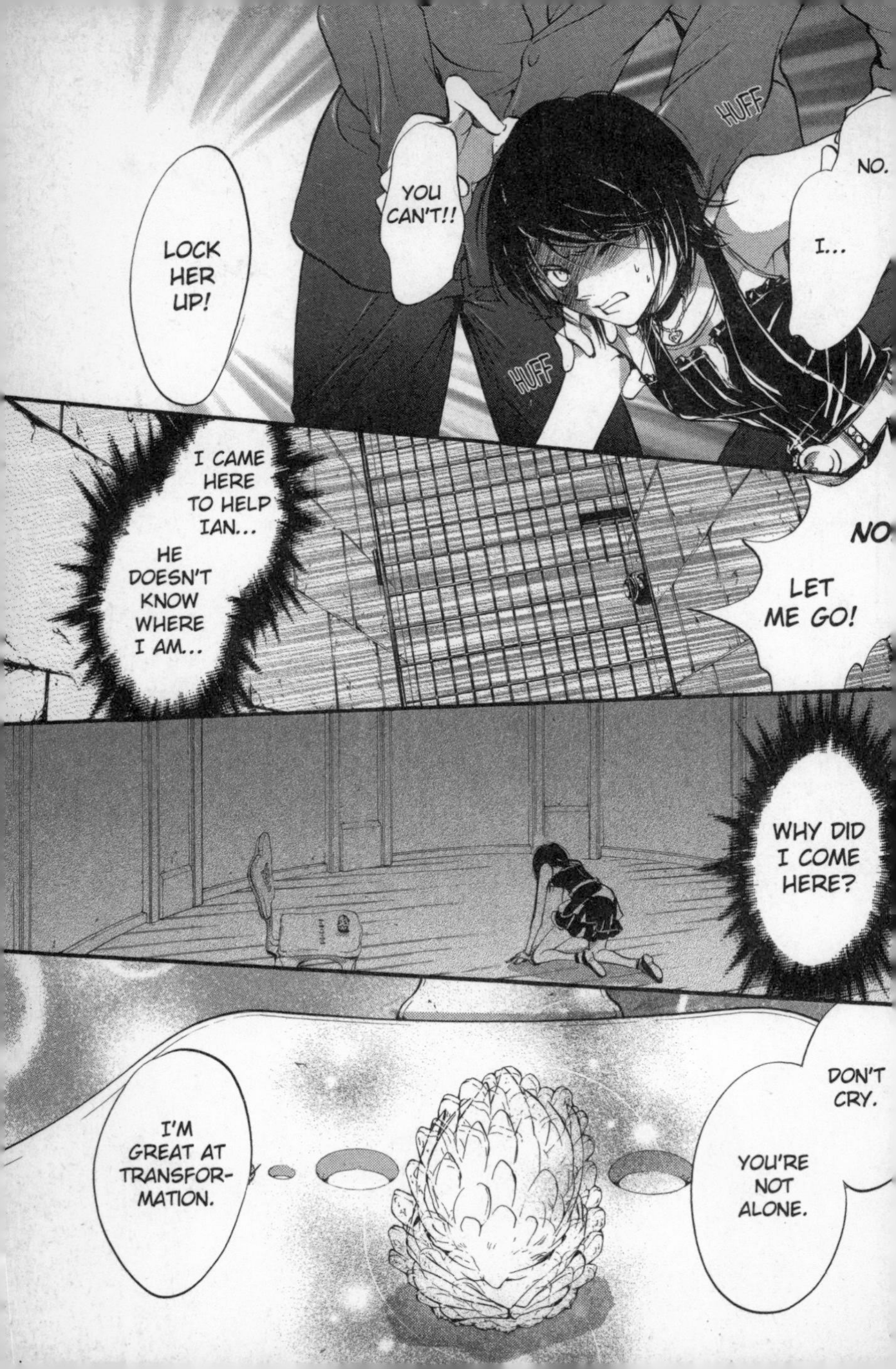
NO.
HUFF
I...
YOU CAN'T!!
LOCK HER UP!
HUFF
NO
LET ME GO!
I CAME HERE TO HELP IAN...
HE DOESN'T KNOW WHERE I AM...
WHY DID I COME HERE?
DON'T CRY.
YOU'RE NOT ALONE.
I'M GREAT AT TRANSFORMATION.

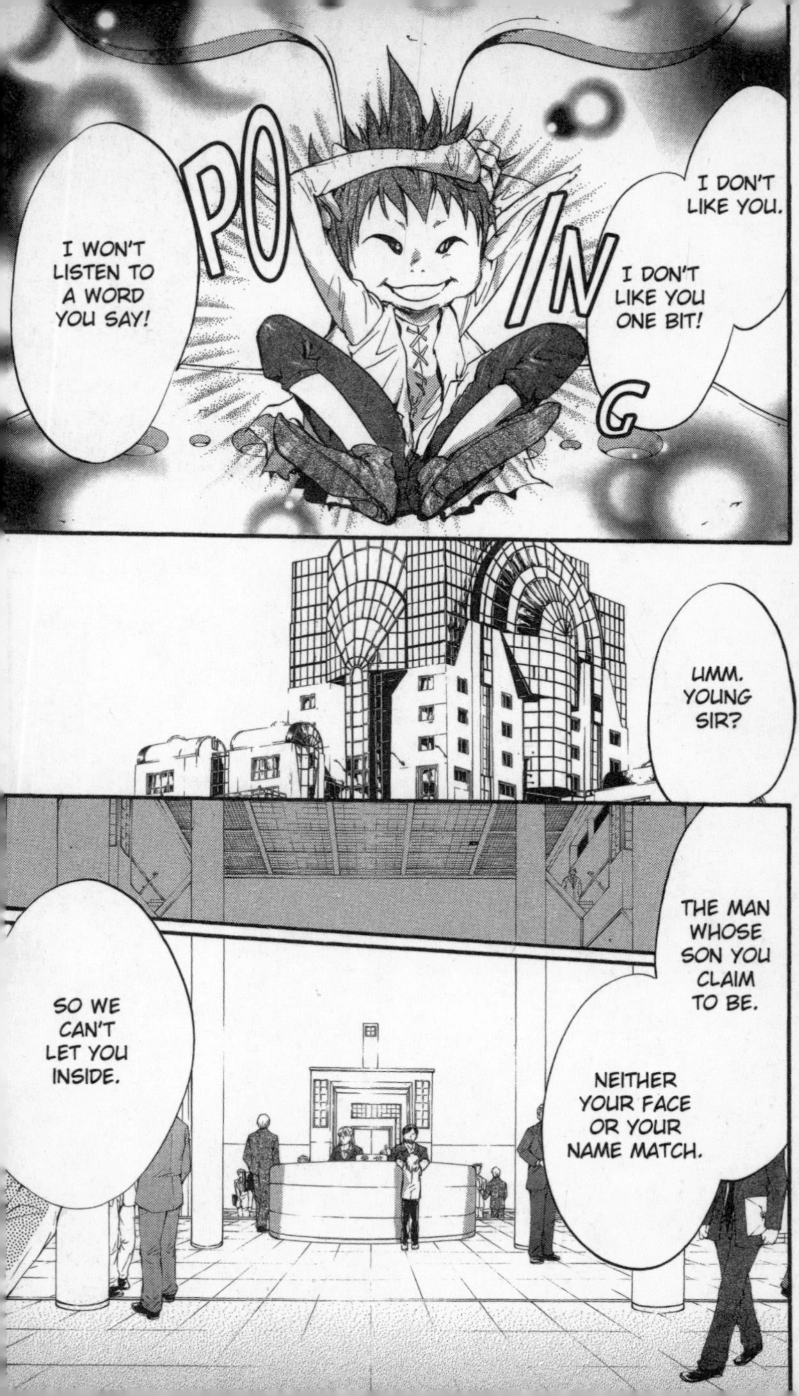
I DON'T LIKE YOU.
I DON'T LIKE YOU ONE BIT!
POING
I WON'T LISTEN TO A WORD YOU SAY!
UMM. YOUNG SIR?
THE MAN WHOSE SON YOU CLAIM TO BE.
NEITHER YOUR FACE OR YOUR NAME MATCH.
SO WE CAN'T LET YOU INSIDE.

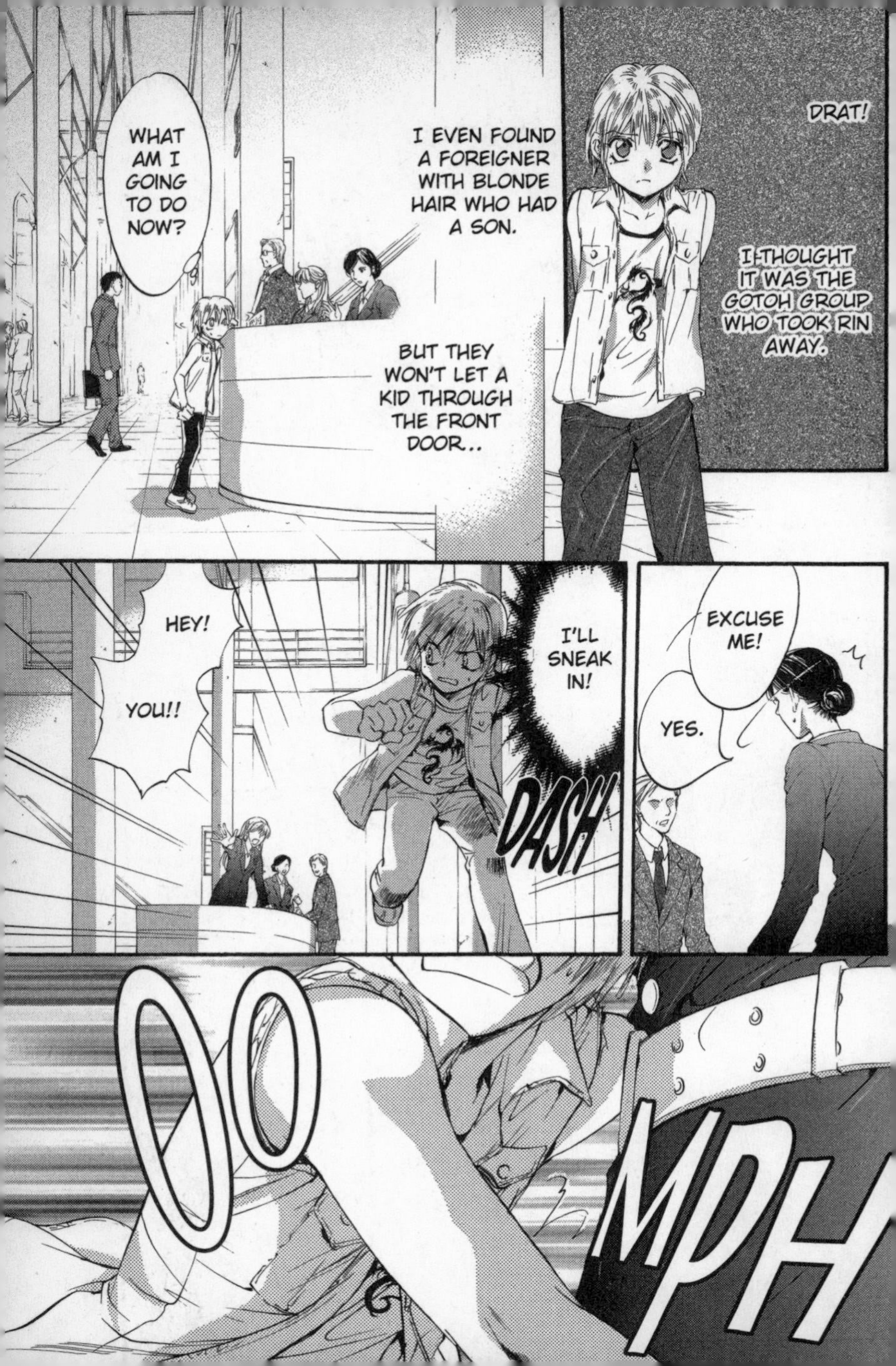
DRAT!
I THOUGHT IT WAS THE GOTOH GROUP WHO TOOK RIN AWAY.
I EVEN FOUND A FOREIGNER WITH BLONDE HAIR WHO HAD A SON.
BUT THEY WON'T LET A KID THROUGH THE FRONT DOOR...
WHAT AM I GOING TO DO NOW?
EXCUSE ME!
YES.
I'LL SNEAK IN!
DASH
HEY!
YOU!!
MPH

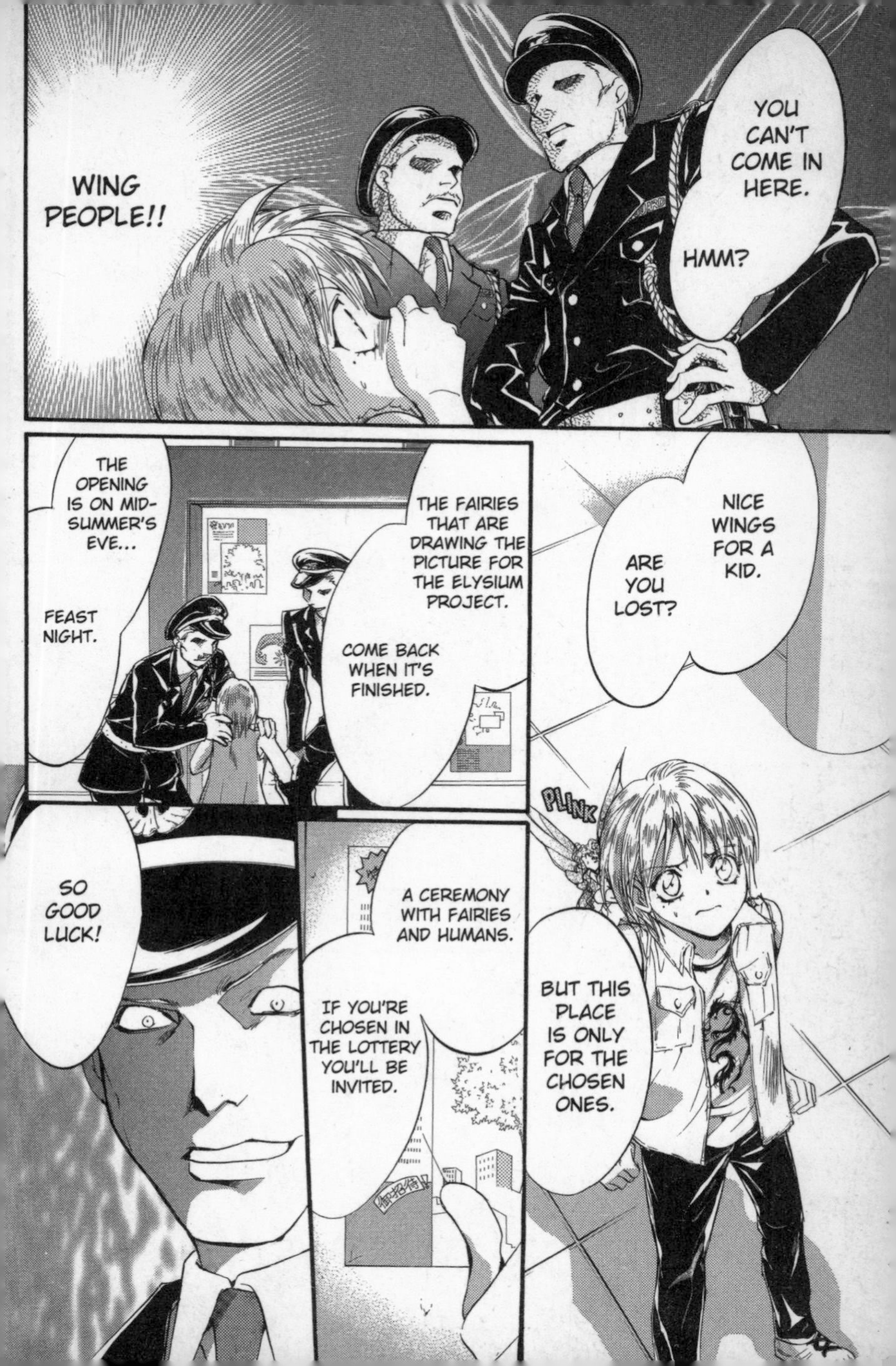

YOU CAN'T COME IN HERE.
HMM?
WING PEOPLE!!
NICE WINGS FOR A KID.
ARE YOU LOST?
PLINK
BUT THIS PLACE IS ONLY FOR THE CHOSEN ONES.
THE FAIRIES THAT ARE DRAWING THE PICTURE FOR THE ELYSIUM PROJECT.
COME BACK WHEN IT'S FINISHED.
THE OPENING IS ON MID-SUMMER'S EVE...
FEAST NIGHT.
A CEREMONY WITH FAIRIES AND HUMANS.
IF YOU'RE CHOSEN IN THE LOTTERY YOU'LL BE INVITED.
SO GOOD LUCK!

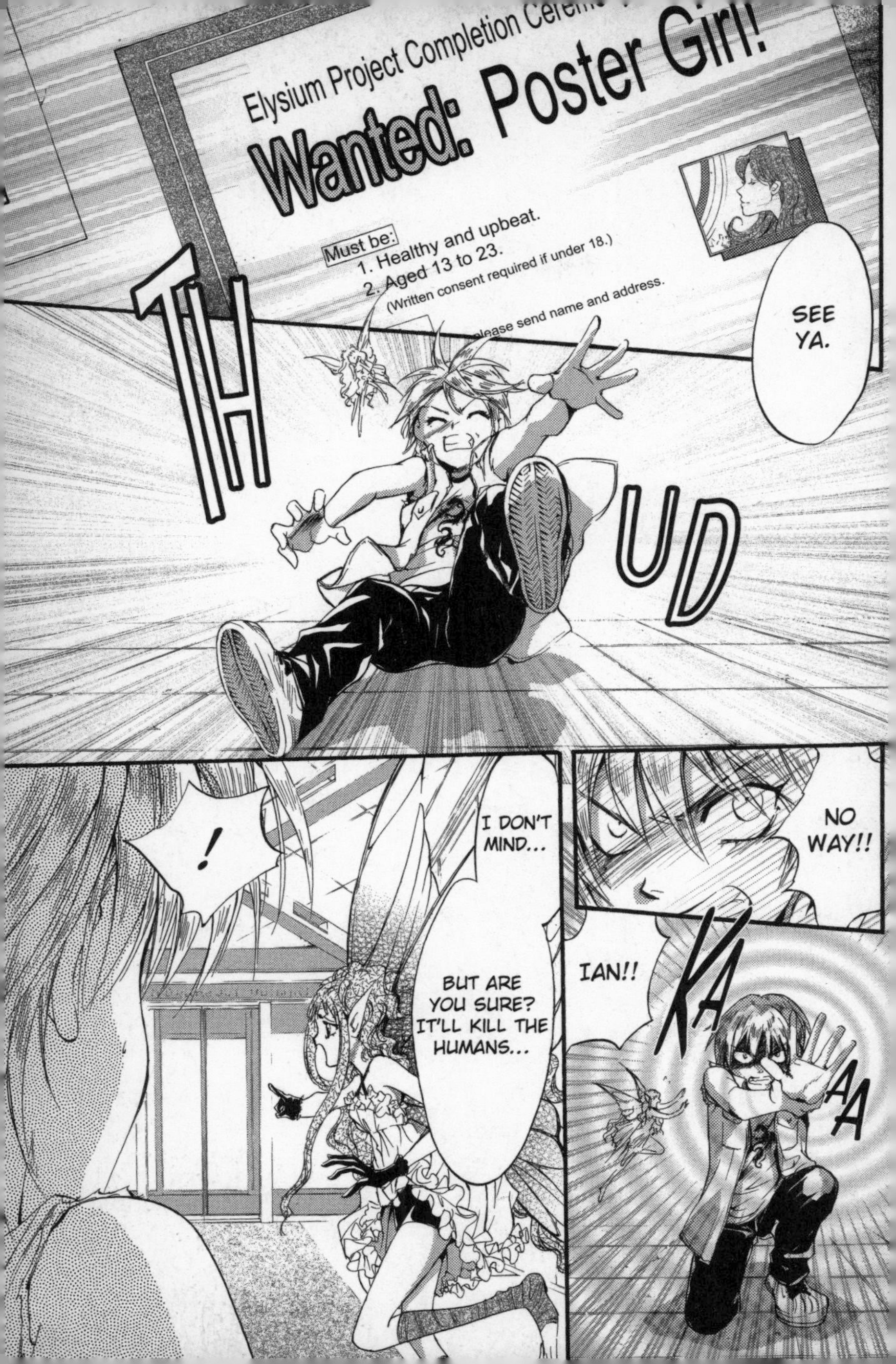
Elysium Project Completion Cerem
Wanted: Poster Girl!
Must be:
1. Healthy and upbeat.
2. Aged 13 to 23.
(Written consent required if under 18.)
please send name and address.
SEE YA.
THUD
NO WAY!!
IAN!!
KAAA
!
I DON'T MIND...
BUT ARE YOU SURE? IT'LL KILL THE HUMANS...

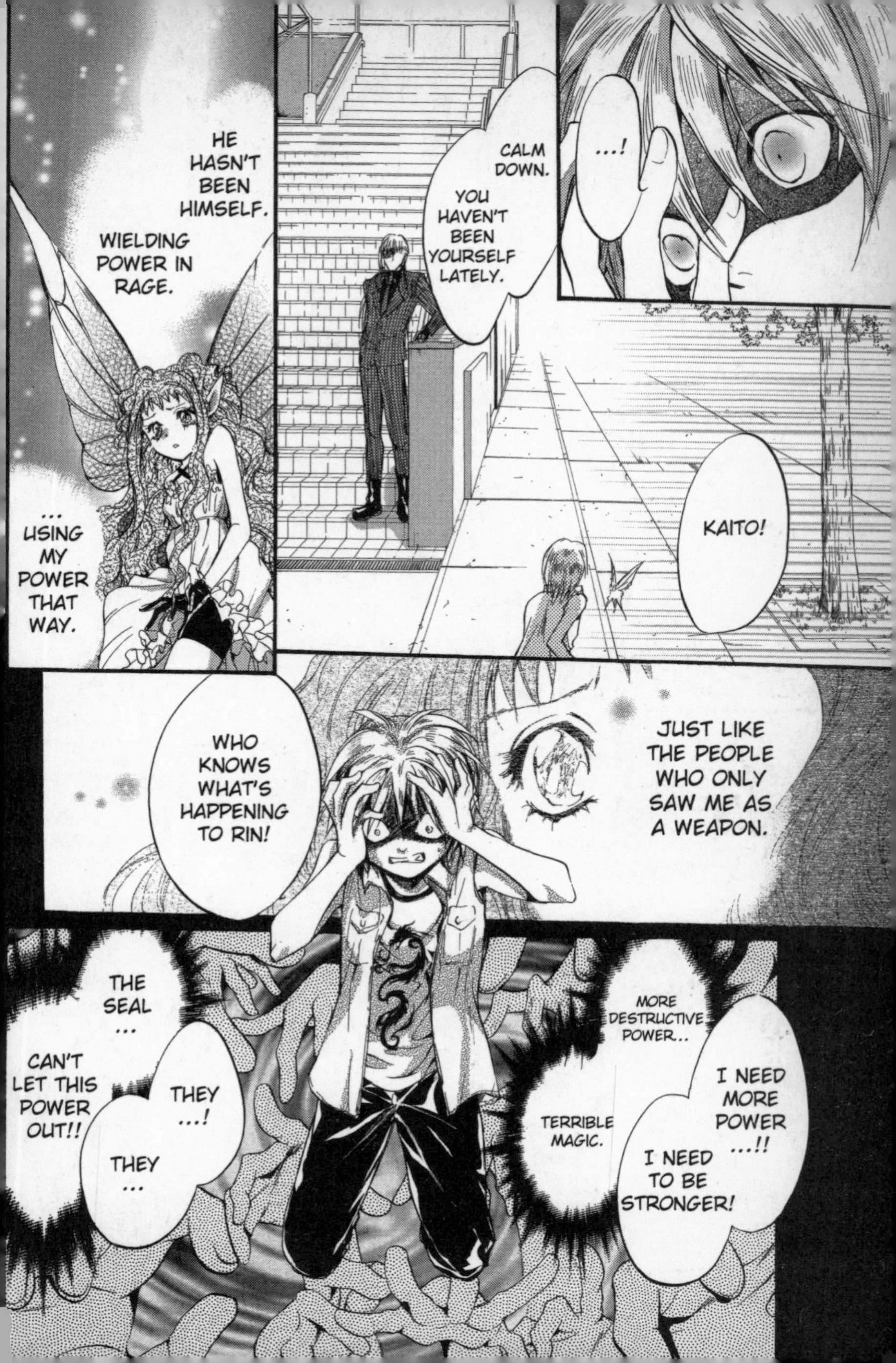
...!
KAITO!
CALM DOWN.
YOU HAVEN'T BEEN YOURSELF LATELY.
HE HASN'T BEEN HIMSELF.
WIELDING POWER IN RAGE.
...USING MY POWER THAT WAY.
JUST LIKE THE PEOPLE WHO ONLY SAW ME AS A WEAPON.
WHO KNOWS WHAT'S HAPPENING TO RIN!
MORE DESTRUCTIVE POWER...
I NEED MORE POWER ...!!
I NEED TO BE STRONGER!
TERRIBLE MAGIC.
THE SEAL...
THEY ...!
THEY ...
CAN'T LET THIS POWER OUT!!

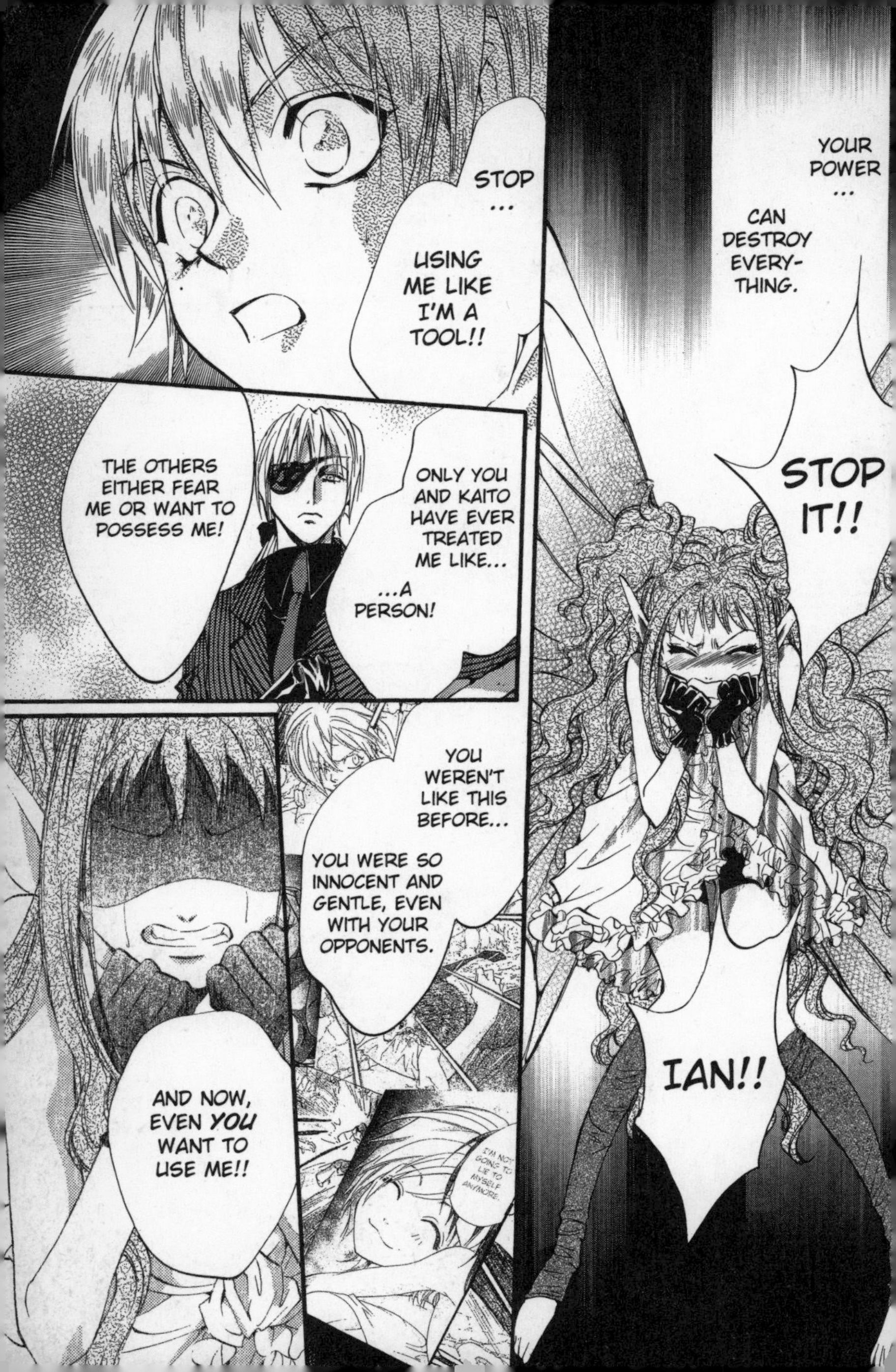
YOUR POWER ...
CAN DESTROY EVERY-THING.
STOP IT!!
IAN!!
STOP ...
USING ME LIKE I'M A TOOL!!
THE OTHERS EITHER FEAR ME OR WANT TO POSSESS ME!
ONLY YOU AND KAITO HAVE EVER TREATED ME LIKE...
...A PERSON!
YOU WEREN'T LIKE THIS BEFORE...
YOU WERE SO INNOCENT AND GENTLE, EVEN WITH YOUR OPPONENTS.
I'M NOT GOING TO LIE TO MYSELF ANYMORE.
AND NOW, EVEN *YOU* WANT TO USE ME!!

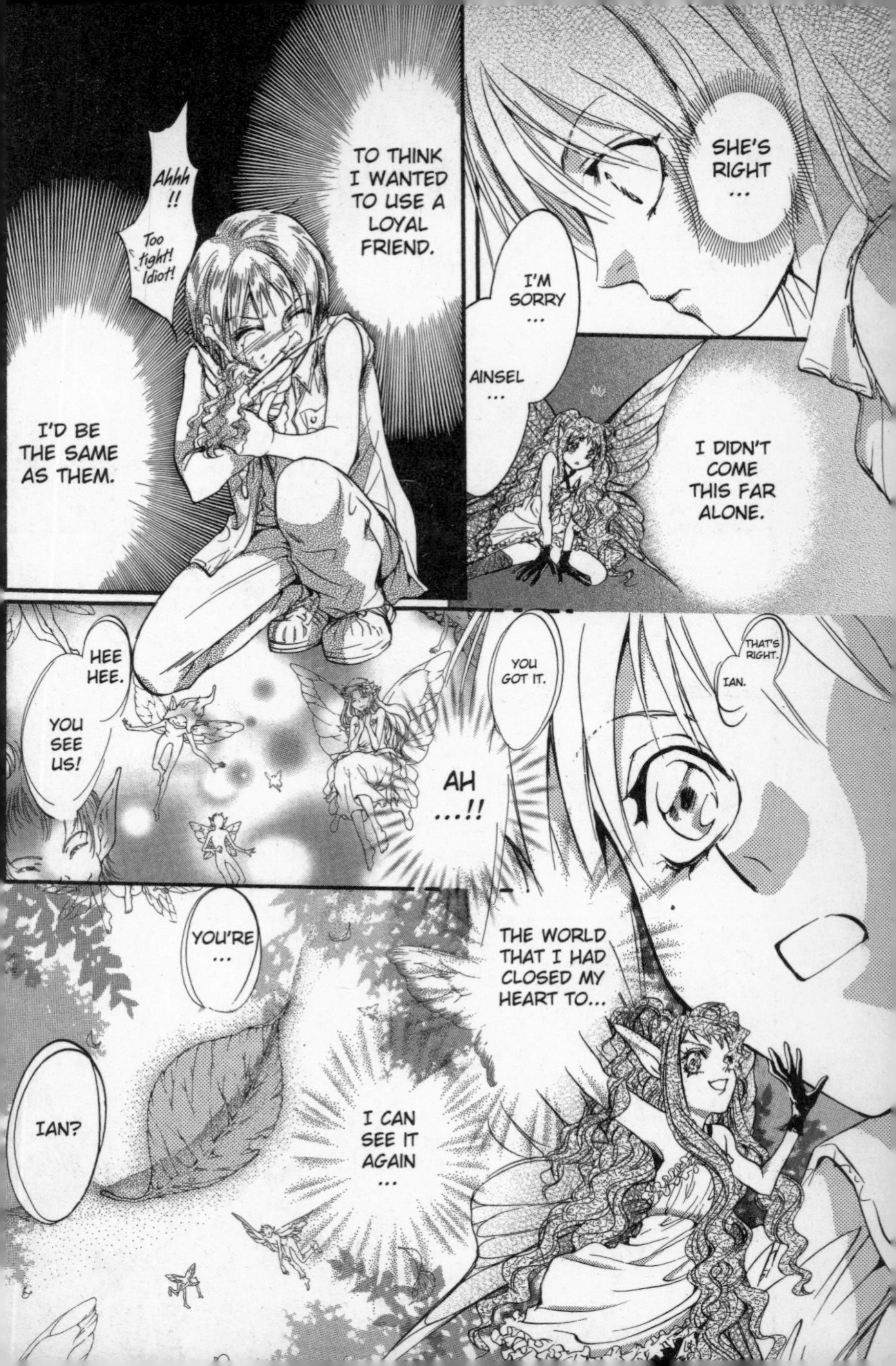

SHE'S RIGHT ...
I'M SORRY ...
AINSEL ...
I DIDN'T COME THIS FAR ALONE.
TO THINK I WANTED TO USE A LOYAL FRIEND.
Ahhh !!
Too tight! Idiot!
I'D BE THE SAME AS THEM.
THAT'S RIGHT.
IAN.
YOU GOT IT.
AH ...!!
HEE HEE.
YOU SEE US!
THE WORLD THAT I HAD CLOSED MY HEART TO...
I CAN SEE IT AGAIN ...
YOU'RE ...
IAN?

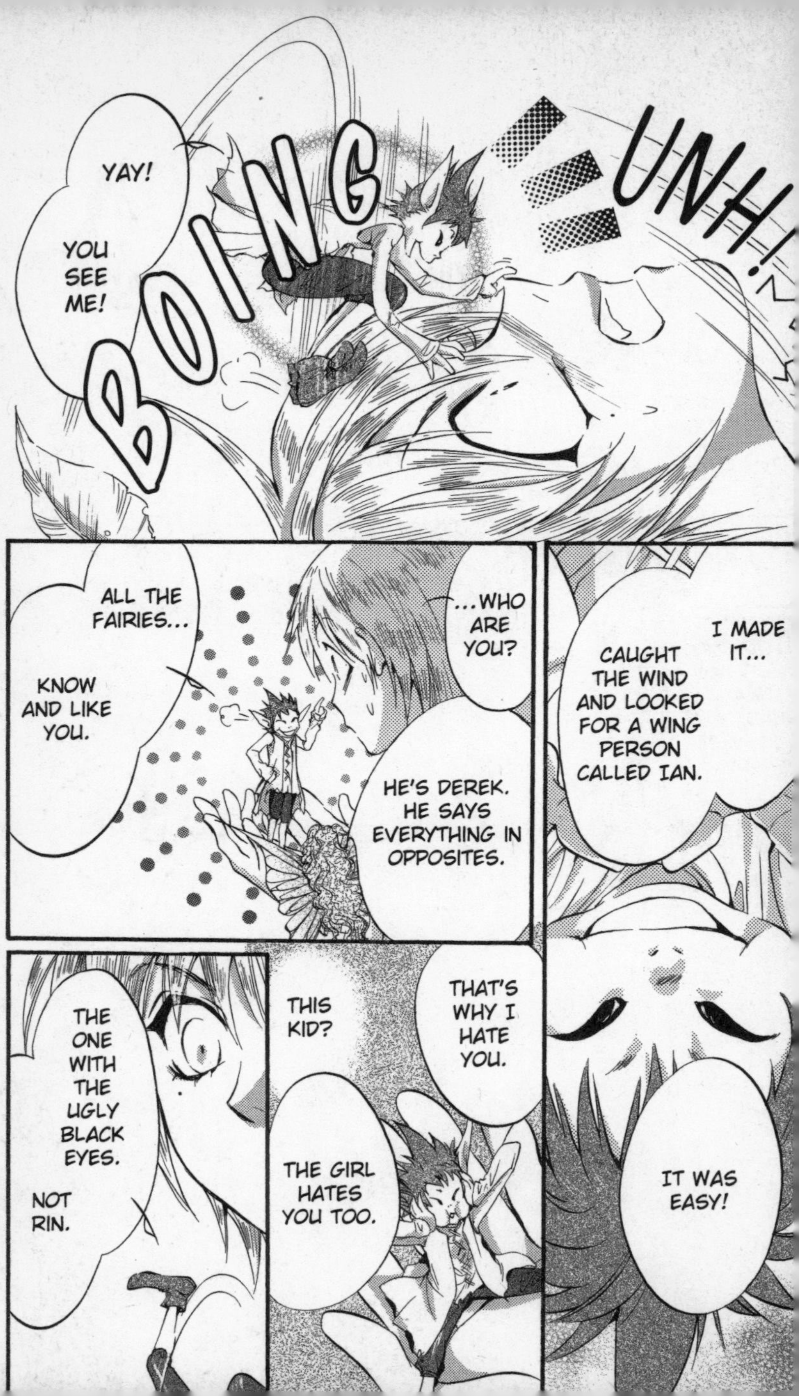
UNH!!
BOING
YAY!
YOU SEE ME!
I MADE IT...
CAUGHT THE WIND AND LOOKED FOR A WING PERSON CALLED IAN.
IT WAS EASY!
...WHO ARE YOU?
HE'S DEREK. HE SAYS EVERYTHING IN OPPOSITES.
ALL THE FAIRIES...
KNOW AND LIKE YOU.
THAT'S WHY I HATE YOU.
THIS KID?
THE GIRL HATES YOU TOO.
THE ONE WITH THE UGLY BLACK EYES.
NOT RIN.

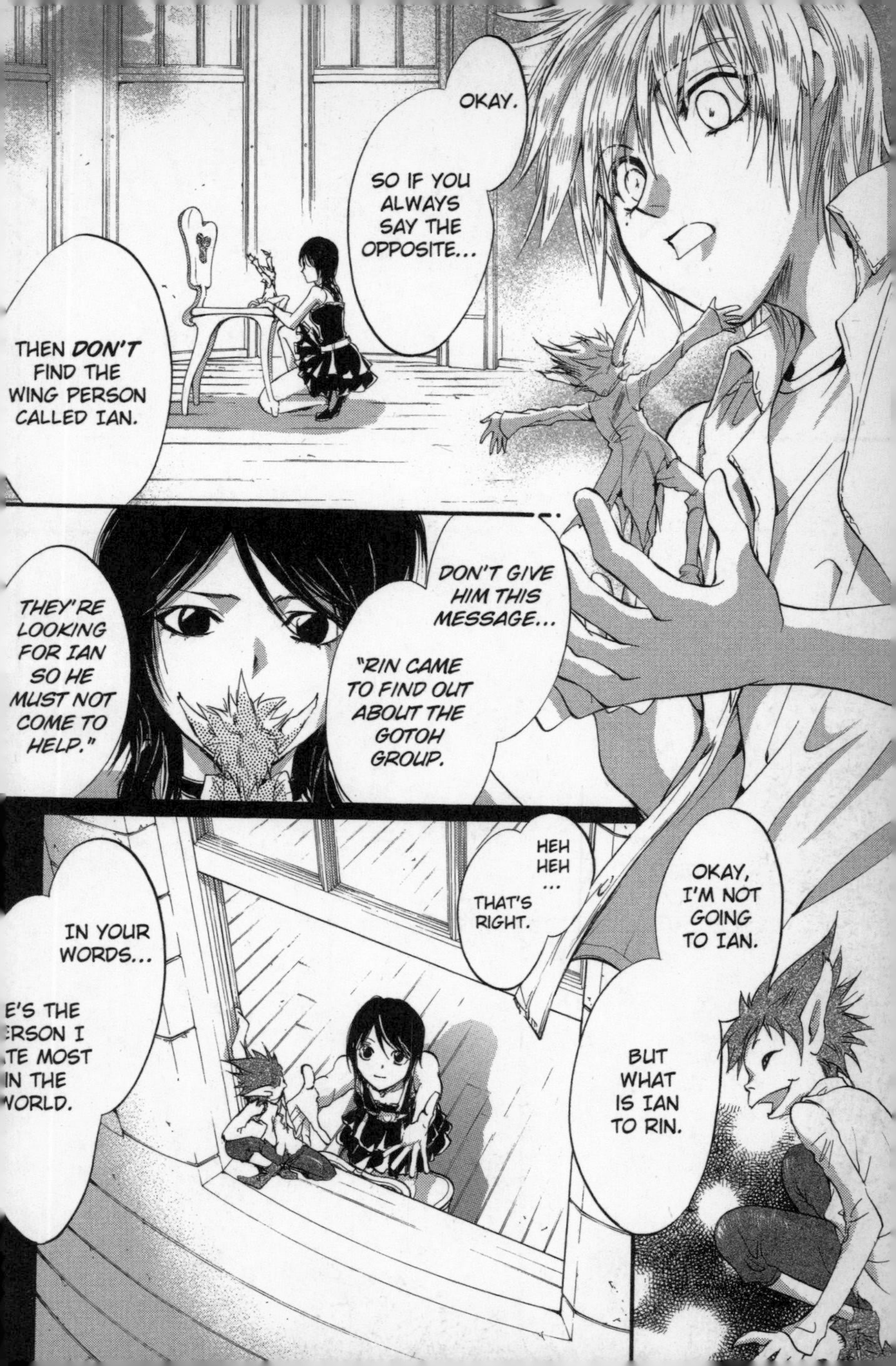
OKAY.
SO IF YOU ALWAYS SAY THE OPPOSITE...
THEN *DON'T* FIND THE WING PERSON CALLED IAN.
DON'T GIVE HIM THIS MESSAGE...
"RIN CAME TO FIND OUT ABOUT THE GOTOH GROUP.
THEY'RE LOOKING FOR IAN SO HE MUST NOT COME TO HELP."
OKAY, I'M NOT GOING TO IAN.
BUT WHAT IS IAN TO RIN.
HEH HEH ...
THAT'S RIGHT.
IN YOUR WORDS...
E'S THE ERSON I TE MOST IN THE ORLD.

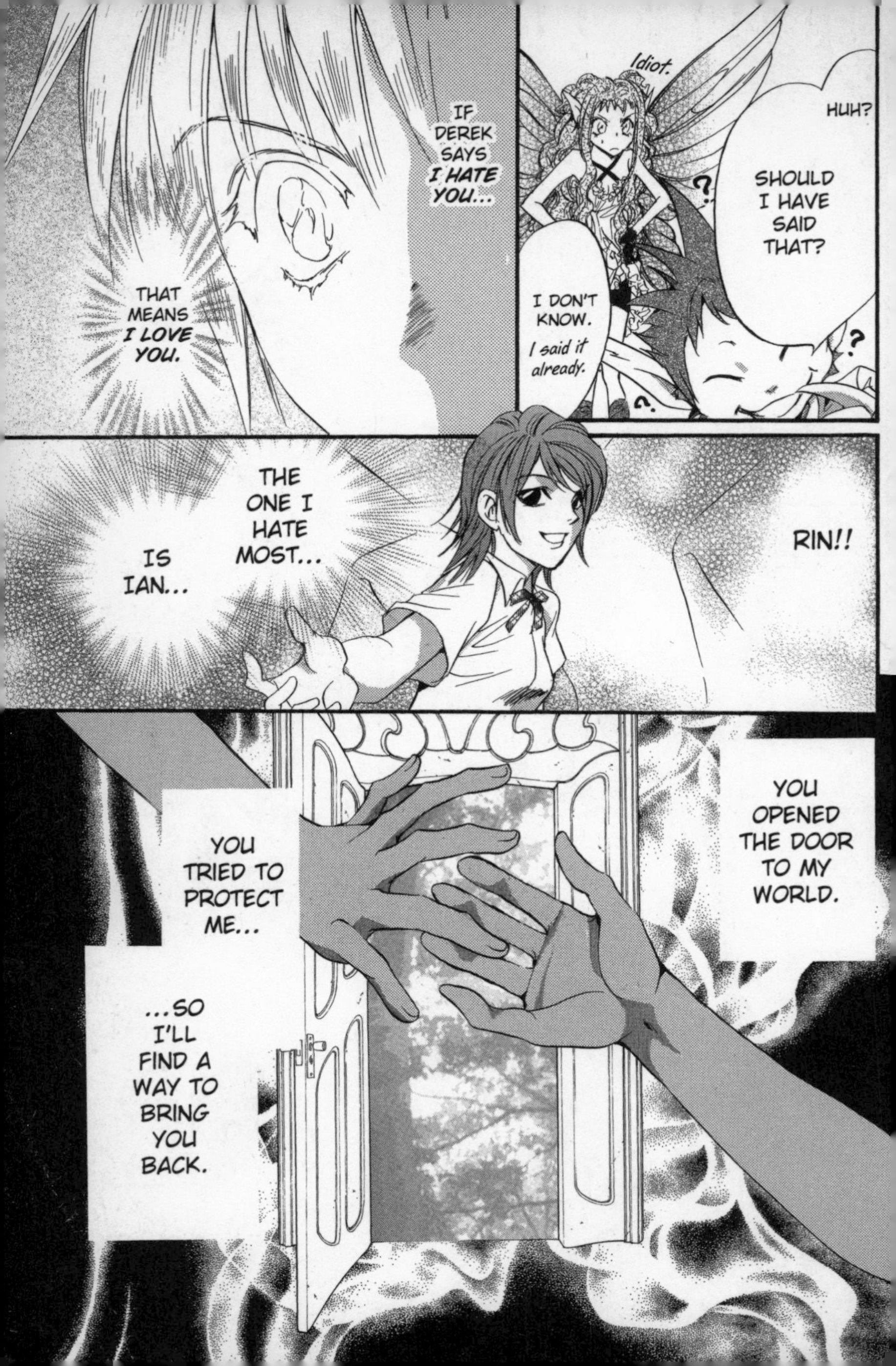
HUH?
SHOULD I HAVE SAID THAT?
Idiot.
I DON'T KNOW.
I said it already.
IF DEREK SAYS I HATE YOU...
THAT MEANS I LOVE YOU.
RIN!!
THE ONE I HATE MOST...
IS IAN...
YOU OPENED THE DOOR TO MY WORLD.
YOU TRIED TO PROTECT ME...
...SO I'LL FIND A WAY TO BRING YOU BACK.

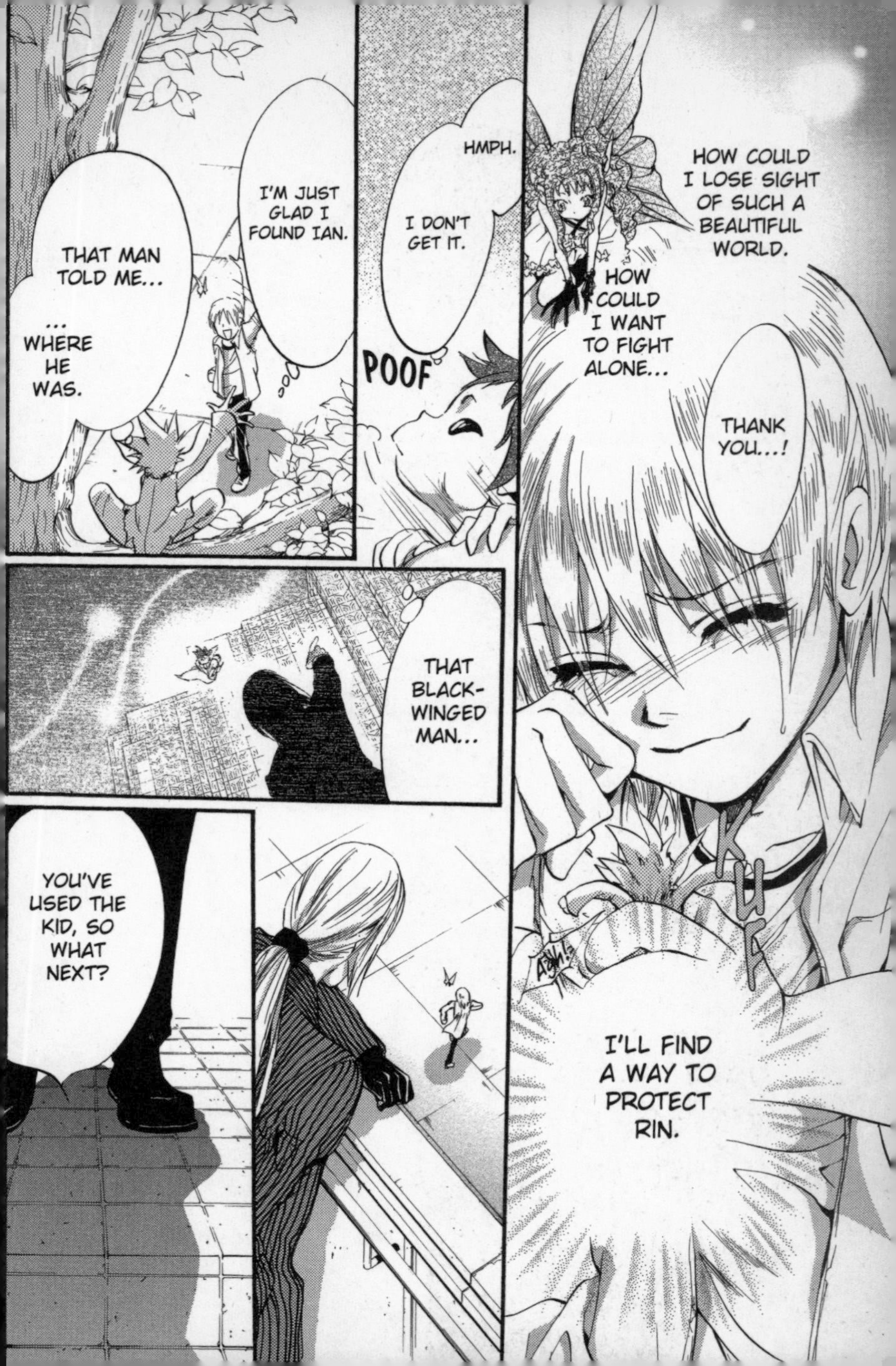
HOW COULD I LOSE SIGHT OF SUCH A BEAUTIFUL WORLD.
HOW COULD I WANT TO FIGHT ALONE...
THANK YOU...!
KUF
Agh!
I'LL FIND A WAY TO PROTECT RIN.
HMPH.
I DON'T GET IT.
POOF
I'M JUST GLAD I FOUND IAN.
THAT MAN TOLD ME...
...WHERE HE WAS.
THAT BLACK-WINGED MAN...
YOU'VE USED THE KID, SO WHAT NEXT?

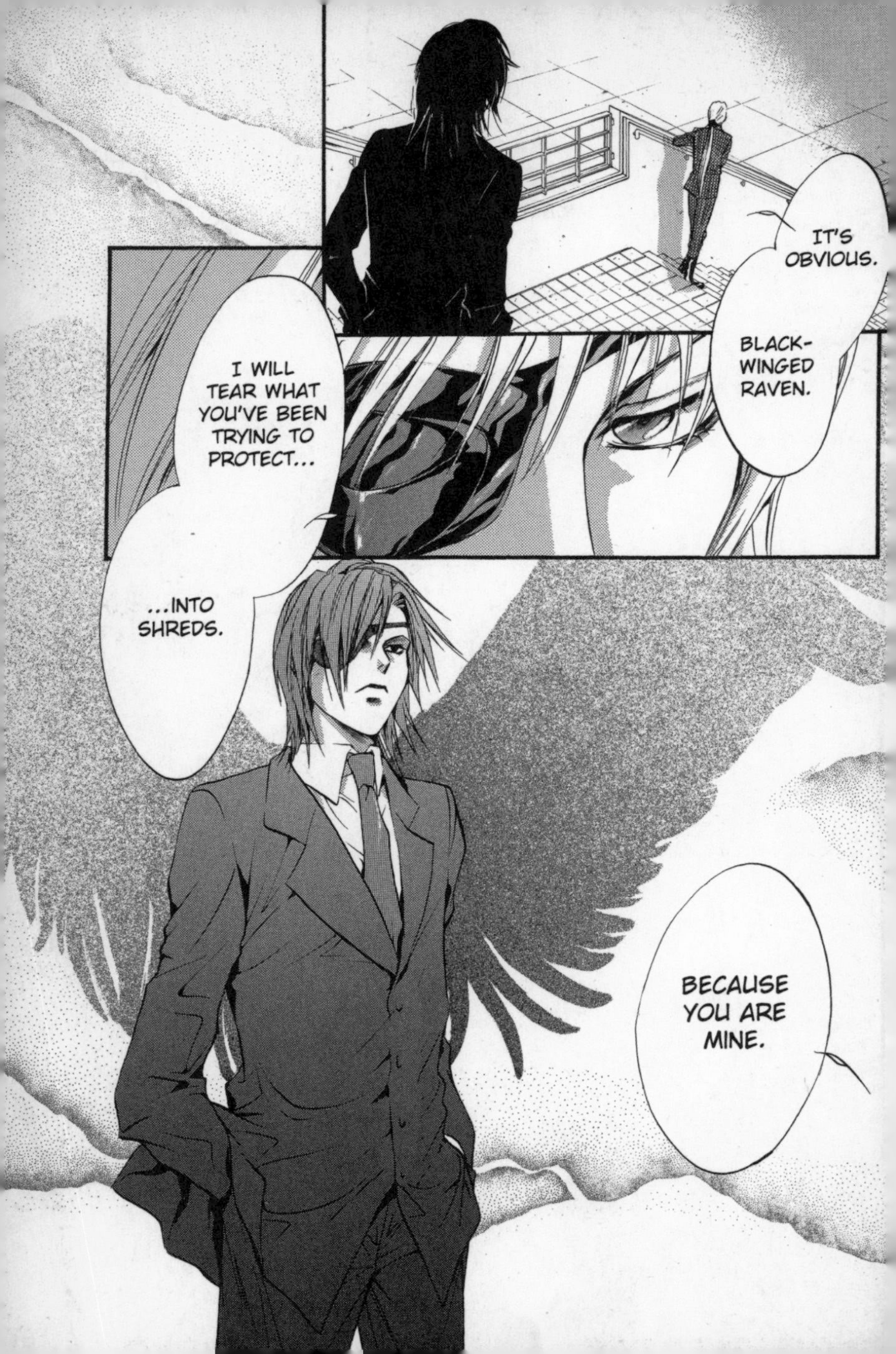
IT'S OBVIOUS.
BLACK-WINGED RAVEN.
I WILL TEAR WHAT YOU'VE BEEN TRYING TO PROTECT...
...INTO SHREDS.
BECAUSE YOU ARE MINE.

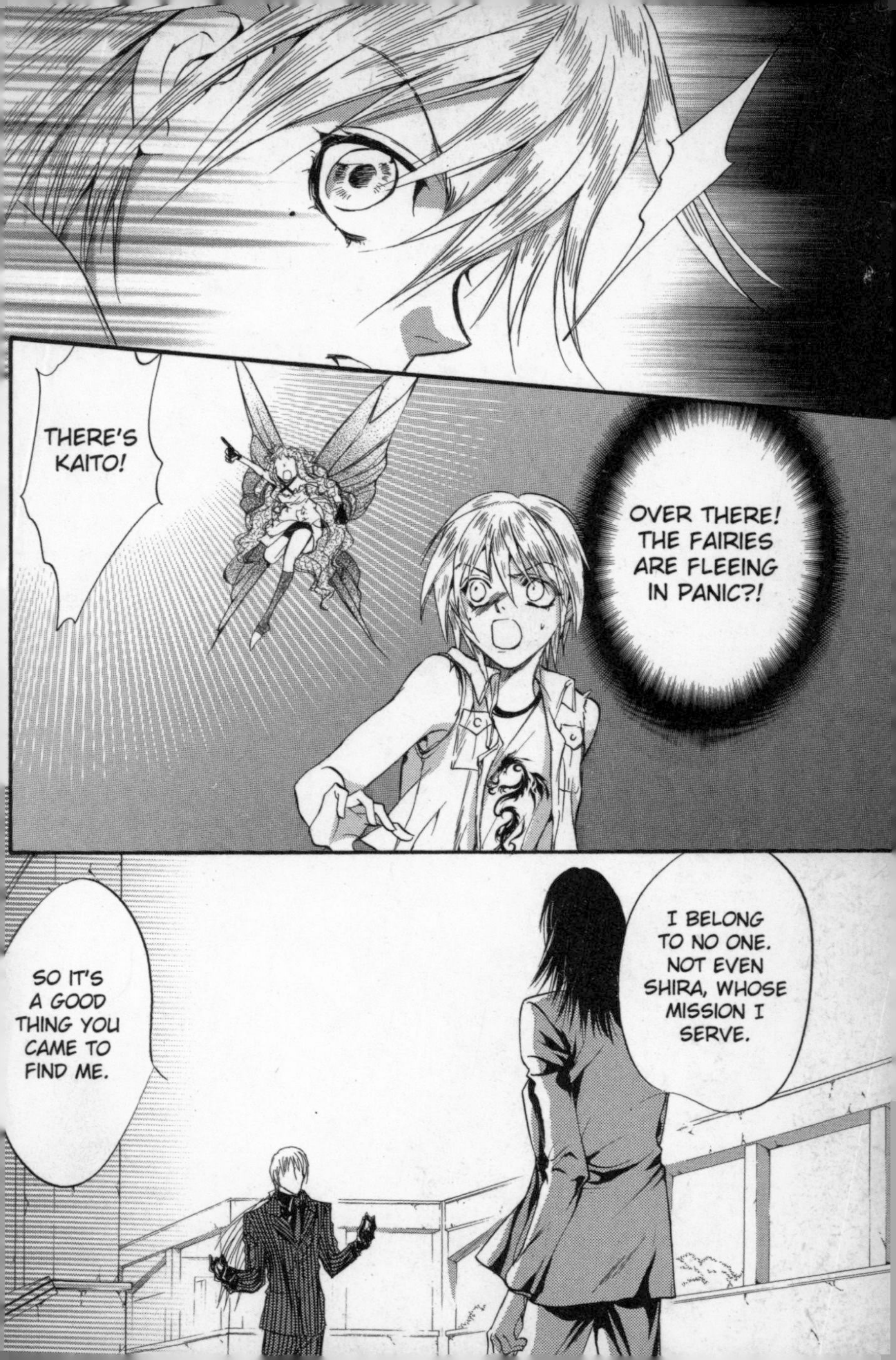
OVER THERE! THE FAIRIES ARE FLEEING IN PANIC?!
THERE'S KAITO!
I BELONG TO NO ONE. NOT EVEN SHIRA, WHOSE MISSION I SERVE.
SO IT'S A GOOD THING YOU CAME TO FIND ME.

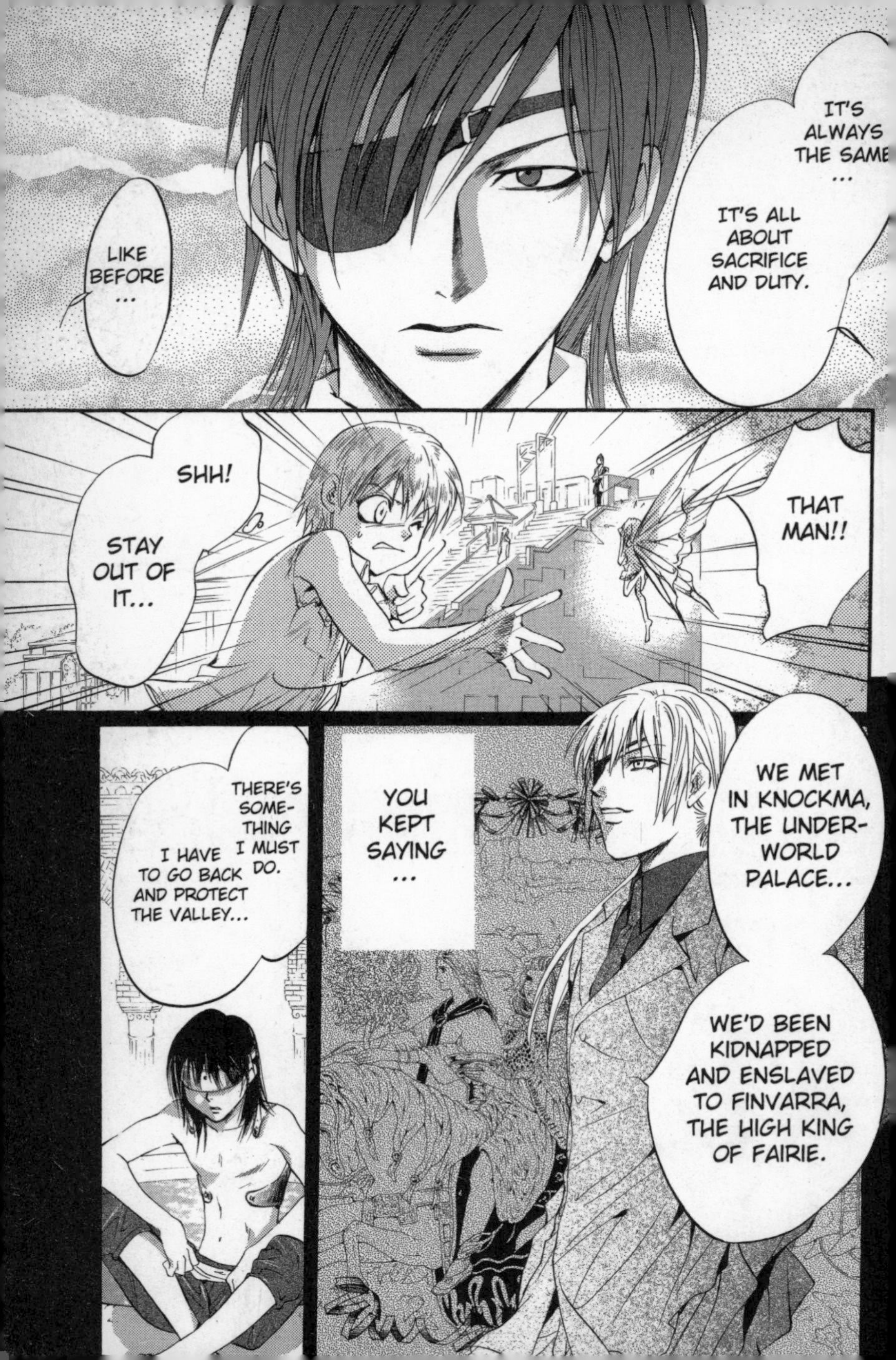
IT'S ALWAYS THE SAME ...
IT'S ALL ABOUT SACRIFICE AND DUTY.
LIKE BEFORE ...
THAT MAN!!
SHH!
STAY OUT OF IT...
WE MET IN KNOCKMA, THE UNDER-WORLD PALACE...
WE'D BEEN KIDNAPPED AND ENSLAVED TO FINVARRA, THE HIGH KING OF FAIRIE.
YOU KEPT SAYING ...
THERE'S SOME-THING I MUST DO.
I HAVE TO GO BACK AND PROTECT THE VALLEY...

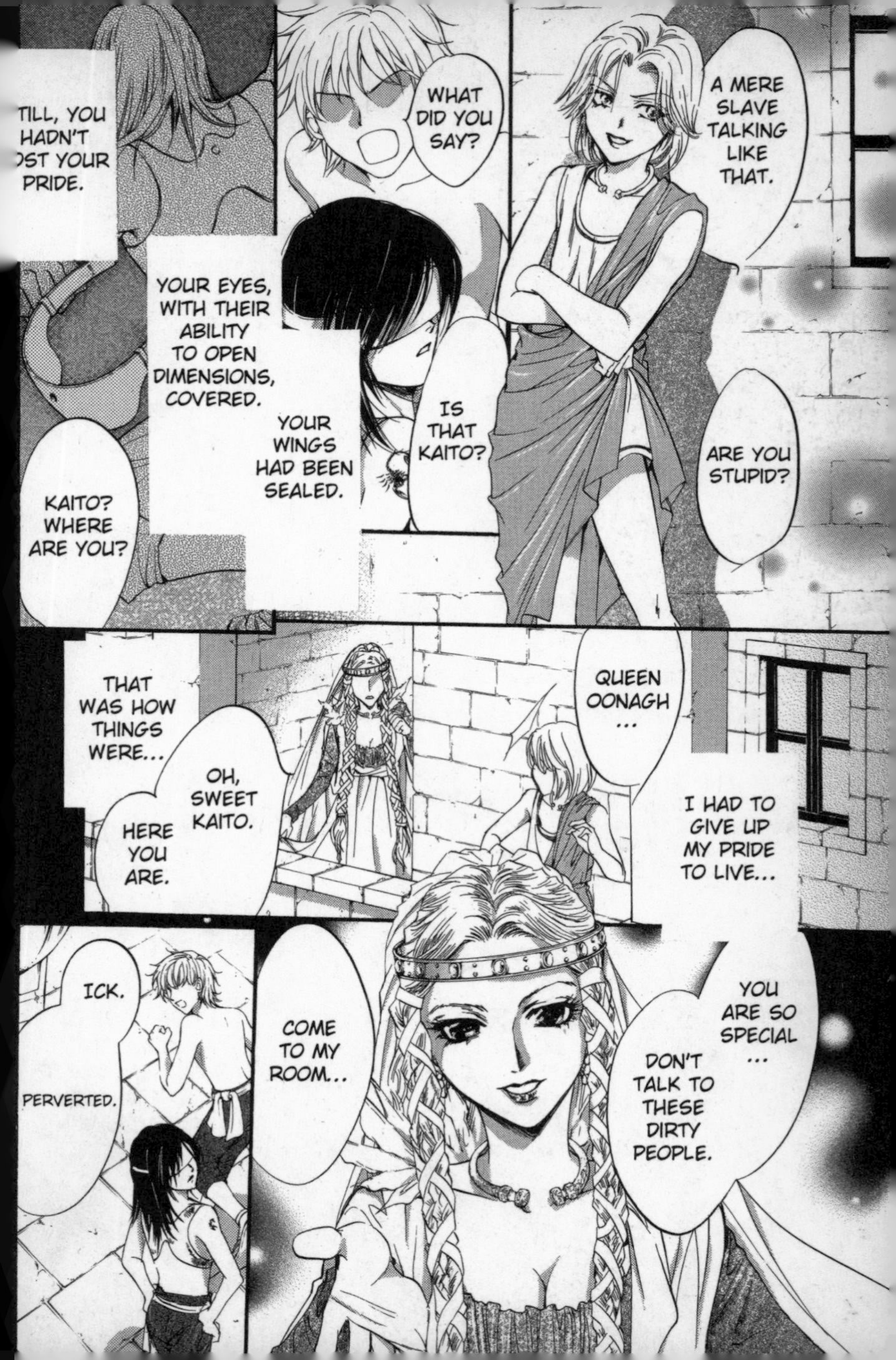
A MERE SLAVE TALKING LIKE THAT.
WHAT DID YOU SAY?
ARE YOU STUPID?
IS THAT KAITO?
TILL, YOU HADN'T OST YOUR PRIDE.
YOUR EYES, WITH THEIR ABILITY TO OPEN DIMENSIONS, COVERED.
YOUR WINGS HAD BEEN SEALED.
KAITO? WHERE ARE YOU?
QUEEN OONAGH ...
I HAD TO GIVE UP MY PRIDE TO LIVE...
OH, SWEET KAITO.
THAT WAS HOW THINGS WERE...
HERE YOU ARE.
YOU ARE SO SPECIAL ...
DON'T TALK TO THESE DIRTY PEOPLE.
COME TO MY ROOM...
ICK.
PERVERTED.

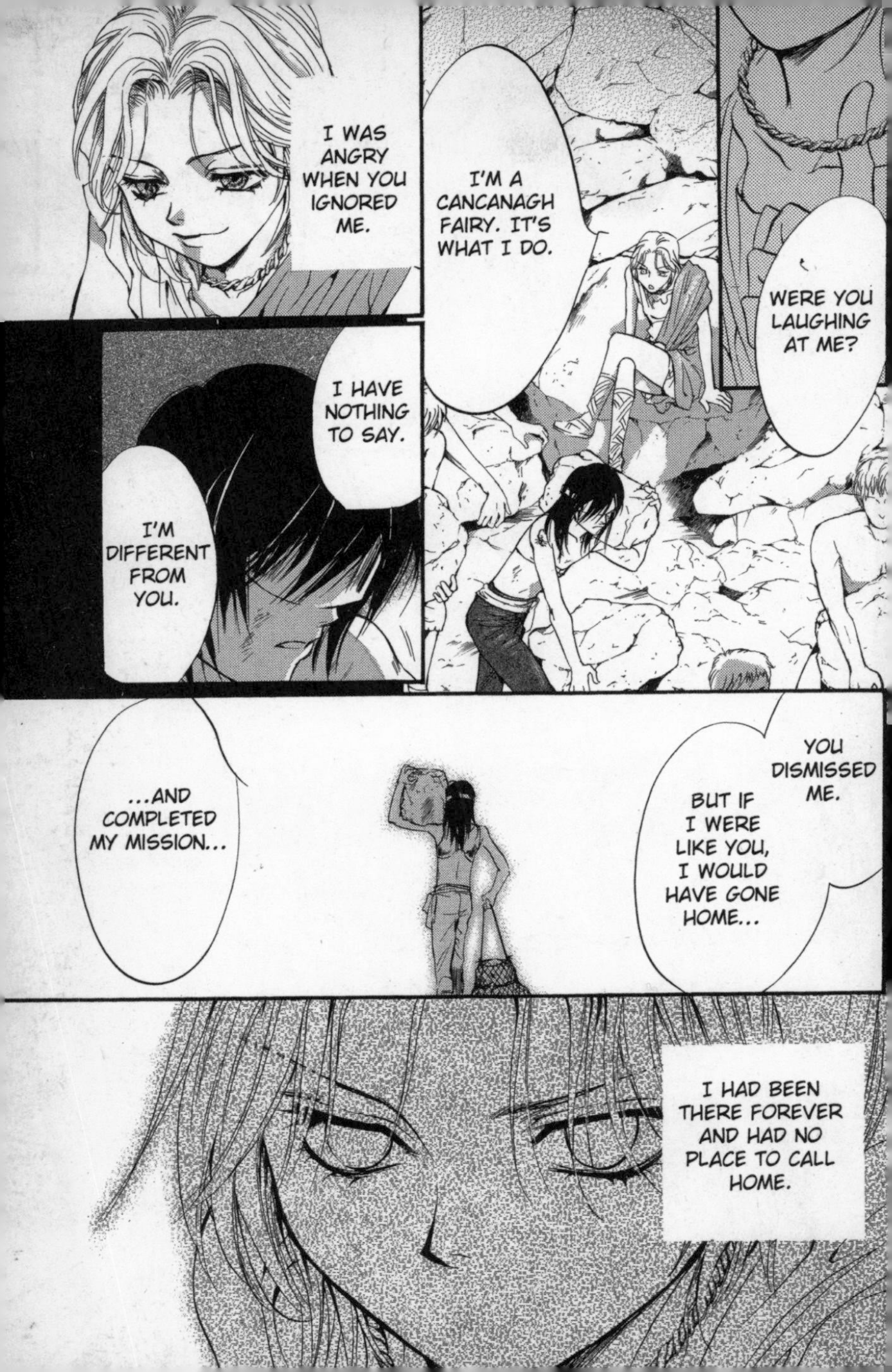
WERE YOU LAUGHING AT ME?
I'M A CANCANAGH FAIRY. IT'S WHAT I DO.
I WAS ANGRY WHEN YOU IGNORED ME.
I HAVE NOTHING TO SAY.
I'M DIFFERENT FROM YOU.
YOU DISMISSED ME.
BUT IF I WERE LIKE YOU, I WOULD HAVE GONE HOME...
...AND COMPLETED MY MISSION...
I HAD BEEN THERE FOREVER AND HAD NO PLACE TO CALL HOME.

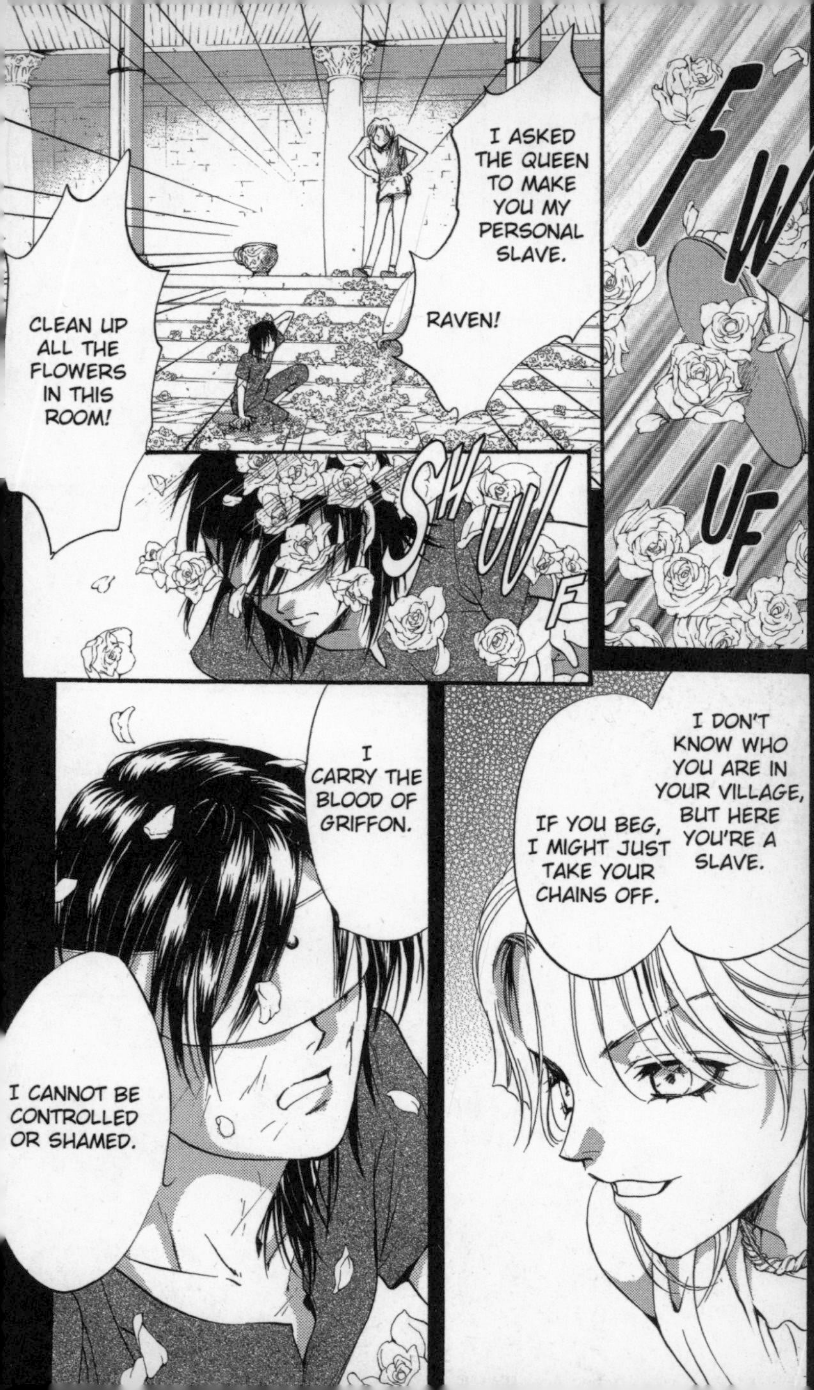
FWUF
I ASKED THE QUEEN TO MAKE YOU MY PERSONAL SLAVE.
RAVEN!
CLEAN UP ALL THE FLOWERS IN THIS ROOM!
SHUUF
I DON'T KNOW WHO YOU ARE IN YOUR VILLAGE, BUT HERE YOU'RE A SLAVE.
IF YOU BEG, I MIGHT JUST TAKE YOUR CHAINS OFF.
I CARRY THE BLOOD OF GRIFFON.
I CANNOT BE CONTROLLED OR SHAMED.

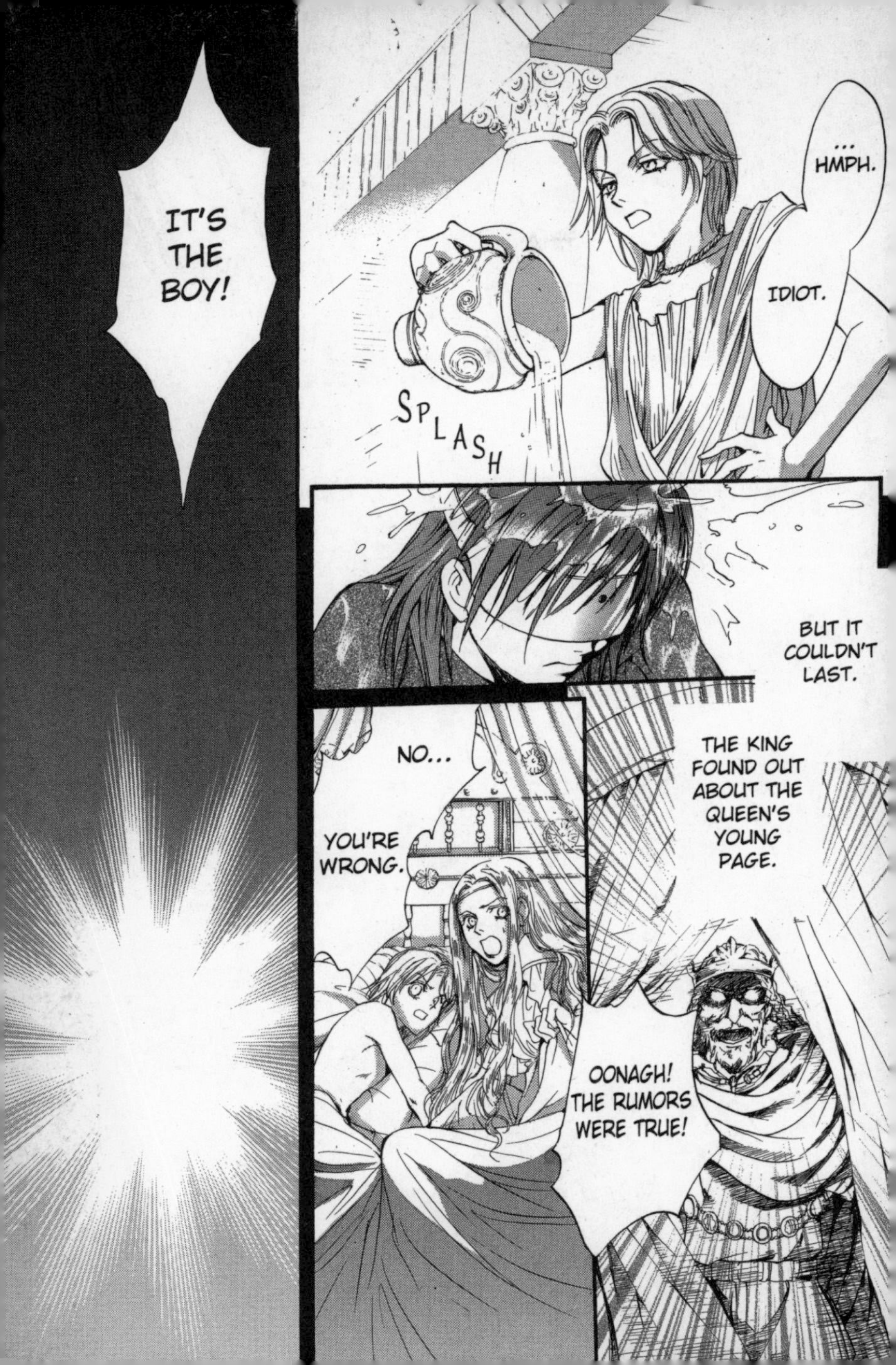
...HMPH.
IDIOT.
SPLASH
BUT IT COULDN'T LAST.
THE KING FOUND OUT ABOUT THE QUEEN'S YOUNG PAGE.
OONAGH! THE RUMORS WERE TRUE!
NO...
YOU'RE WRONG.
IT'S THE BOY!

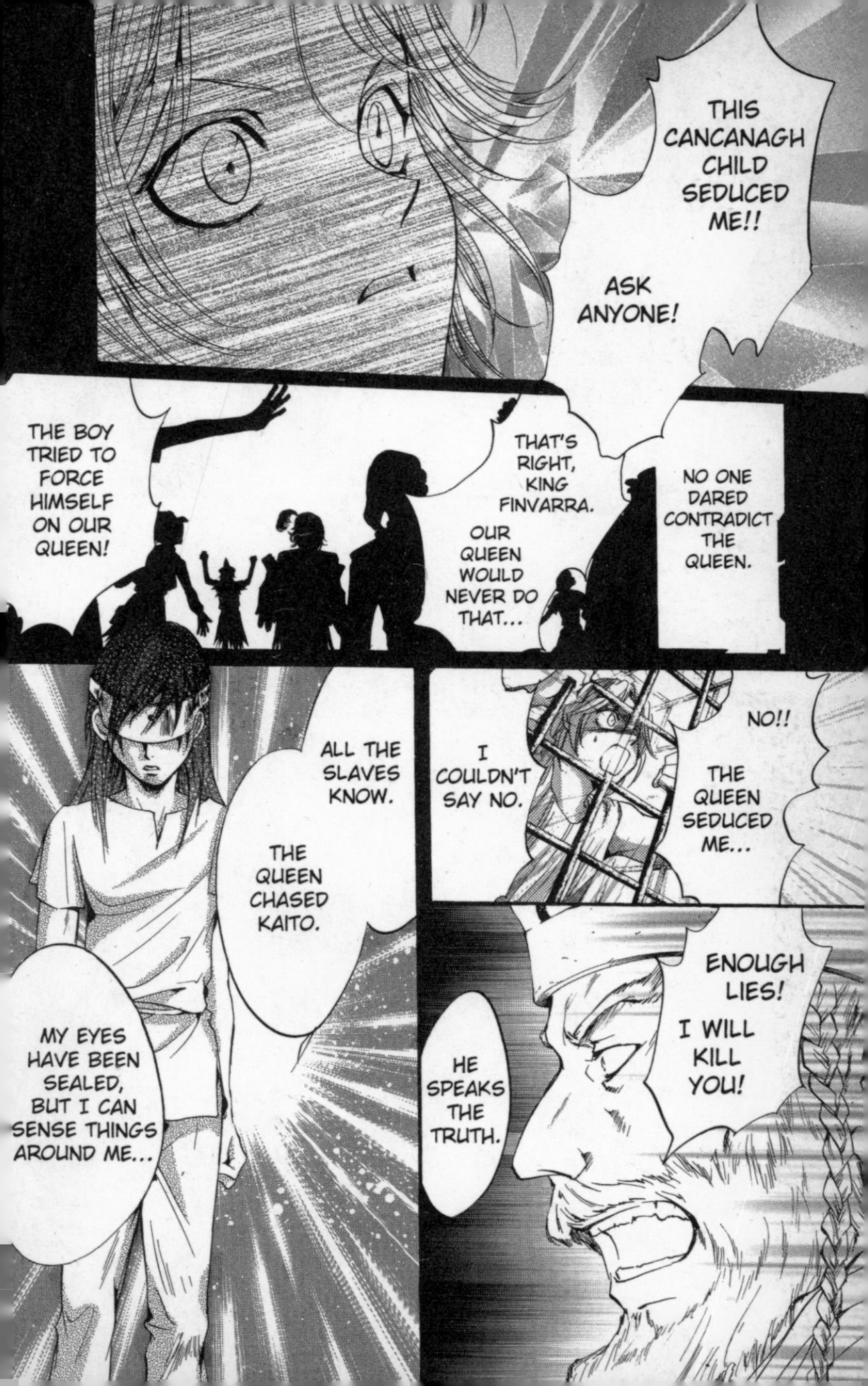
THIS CANCANAGH CHILD SEDUCED ME!!
ASK ANYONE!
NO ONE DARED CONTRADICT THE QUEEN.
THAT'S RIGHT, KING FINVARRA.
OUR QUEEN WOULD NEVER DO THAT...
THE BOY TRIED TO FORCE HIMSELF ON OUR QUEEN!
NO!!
THE QUEEN SEDUCED ME...
I COULDN'T SAY NO.
ENOUGH LIES!
I WILL KILL YOU!
HE SPEAKS THE TRUTH.
ALL THE SLAVES KNOW.
THE QUEEN CHASED KAITO.
MY EYES HAVE BEEN SEALED, BUT I CAN SENSE THINGS AROUND ME...

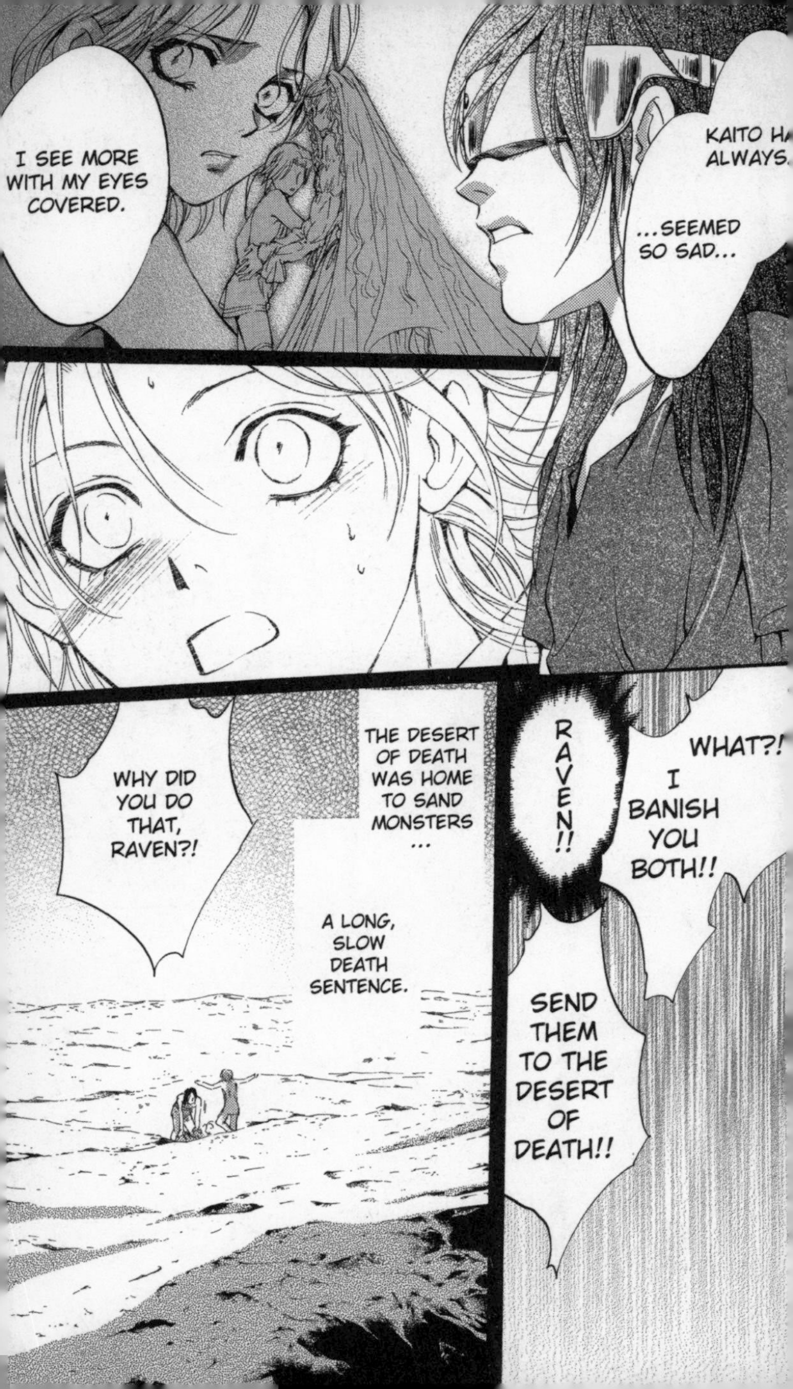
KAITO HA ALWAYS.
...SEEMED SO SAD...
I SEE MORE WITH MY EYES COVERED.
WHAT?!
I BANISH YOU BOTH!!
RAVEN!!
SEND THEM TO THE DESERT OF DEATH!!
THE DESERT OF DEATH WAS HOME TO SAND MONSTERS ...
WHY DID YOU DO THAT, RAVEN?!
A LONG, SLOW DEATH SENTENCE.

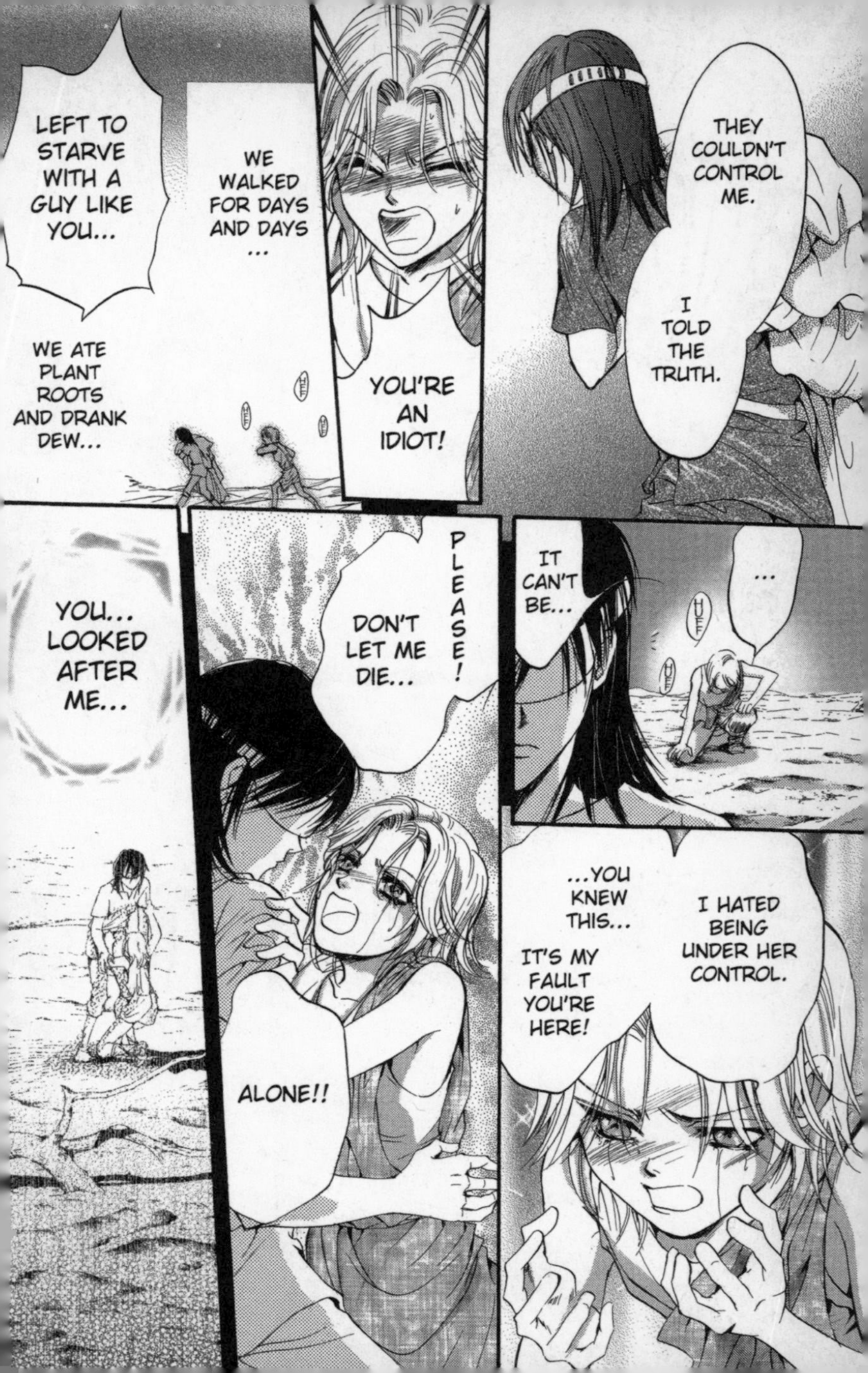
THEY COULDN'T CONTROL ME.
I TOLD THE TRUTH.
YOU'RE AN IDIOT!
LEFT TO STARVE WITH A GUY LIKE YOU...
WE WALKED FOR DAYS AND DAYS ...
HUF
HUF
HUF
WE ATE PLANT ROOTS AND DRANK DEW...
...
IT CAN'T BE...
HUF
HUF
I HATED BEING UNDER HER CONTROL.
...YOU KNEW THIS...
IT'S MY FAULT YOU'RE HERE!
PLEASE!
DON'T LET ME DIE...
ALONE!!
YOU... LOOKED AFTER ME...

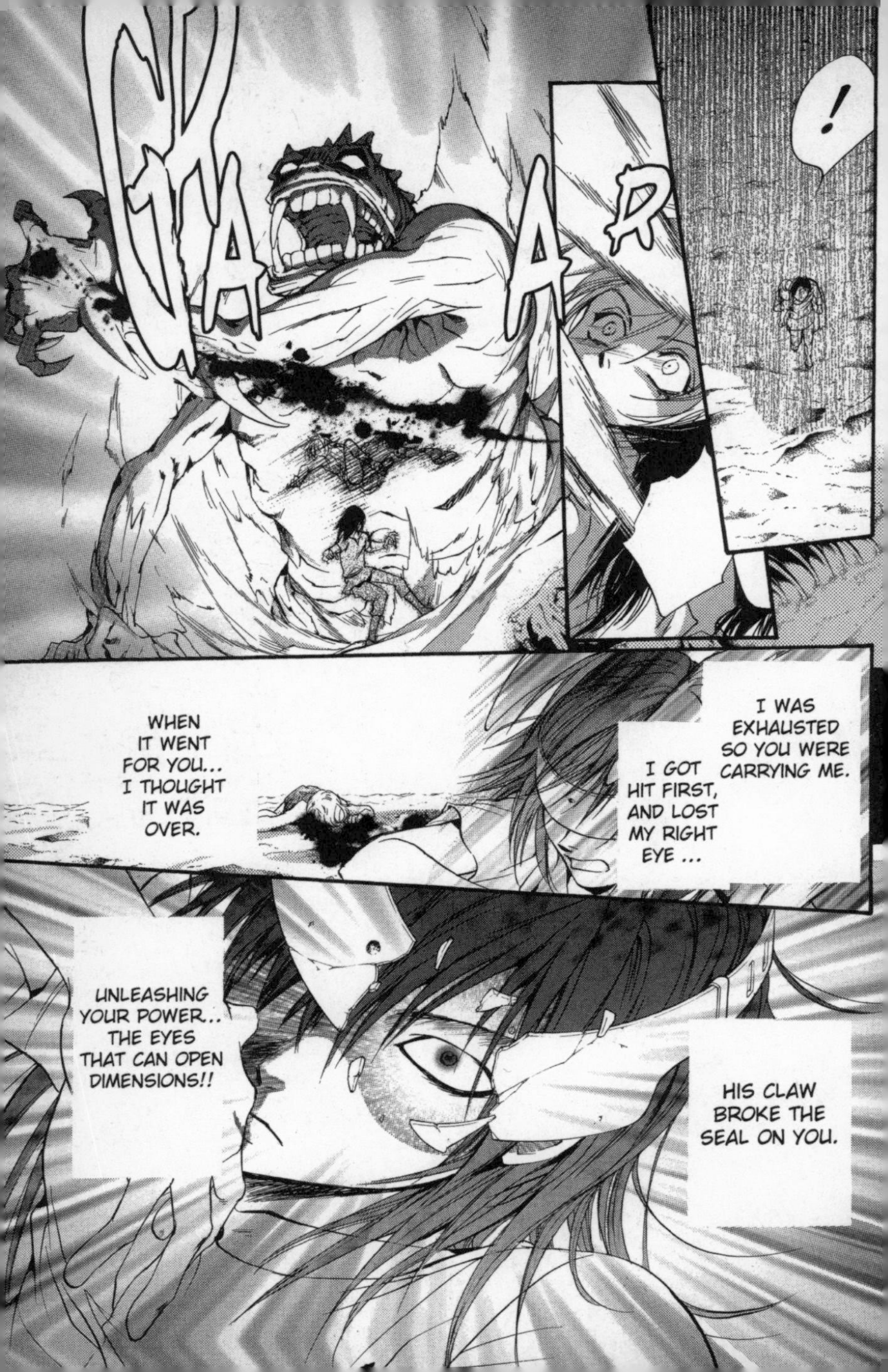
!
GWAAR
I WAS EXHAUSTED SO YOU WERE CARRYING ME.
I GOT HIT FIRST, AND LOST MY RIGHT EYE ...
WHEN IT WENT FOR YOU... I THOUGHT IT WAS OVER.
HIS CLAW BROKE THE SEAL ON YOU.
UNLEASHING YOUR POWER... THE EYES THAT CAN OPEN DIMENSIONS!!

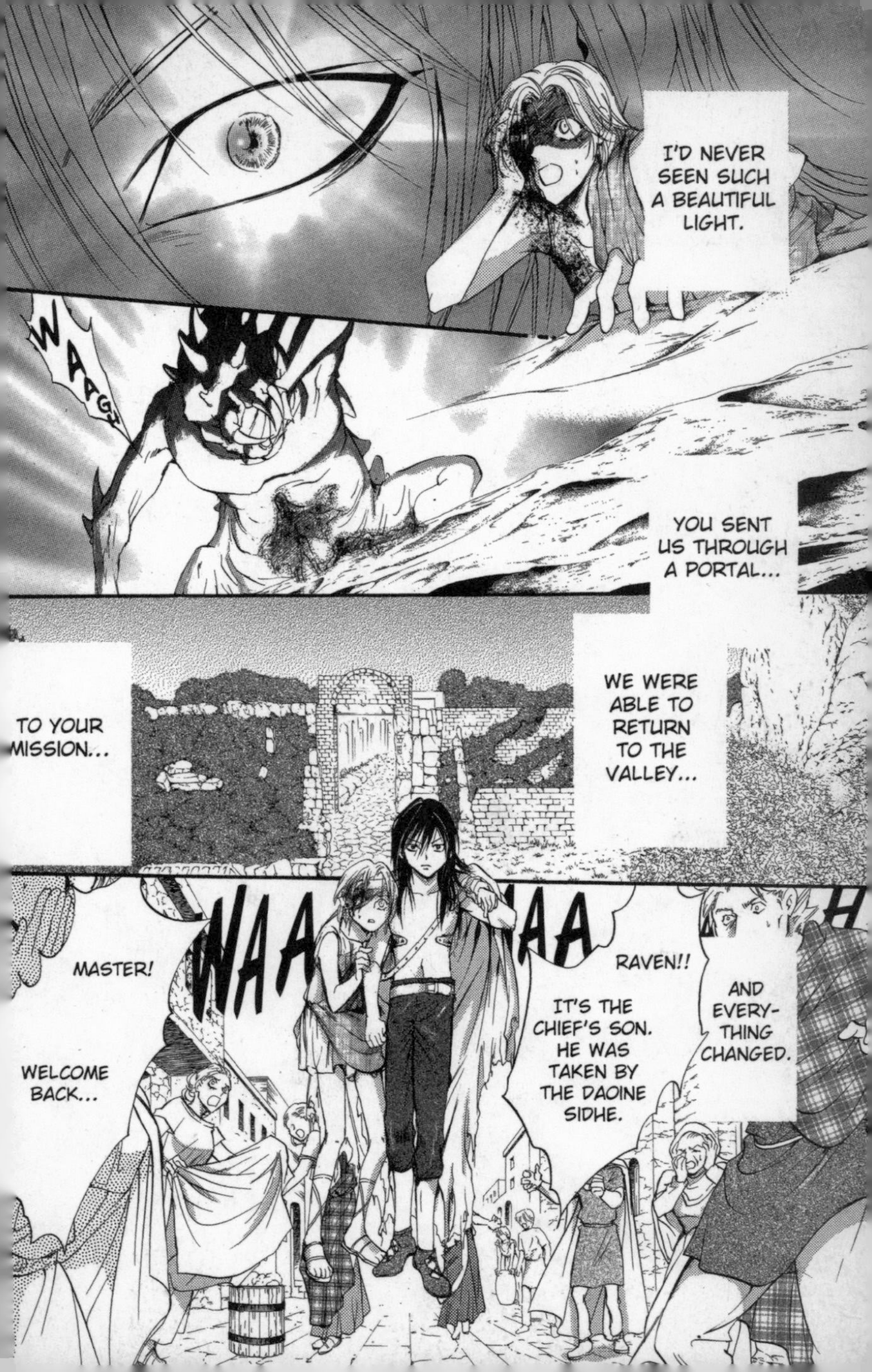
I'D NEVER SEEN SUCH A BEAUTIFUL LIGHT.
WAAAGH!
YOU SENT US THROUGH A PORTAL...
WE WERE ABLE TO RETURN TO THE VALLEY...
TO YOUR MISSION...
AND EVERYTHING CHANGED.
RAVEN!!
IT'S THE CHIEF'S SON. HE WAS TAKEN BY THE DAOINE SIDHE.
WAA
WAA
MASTER!
WELCOME BACK...

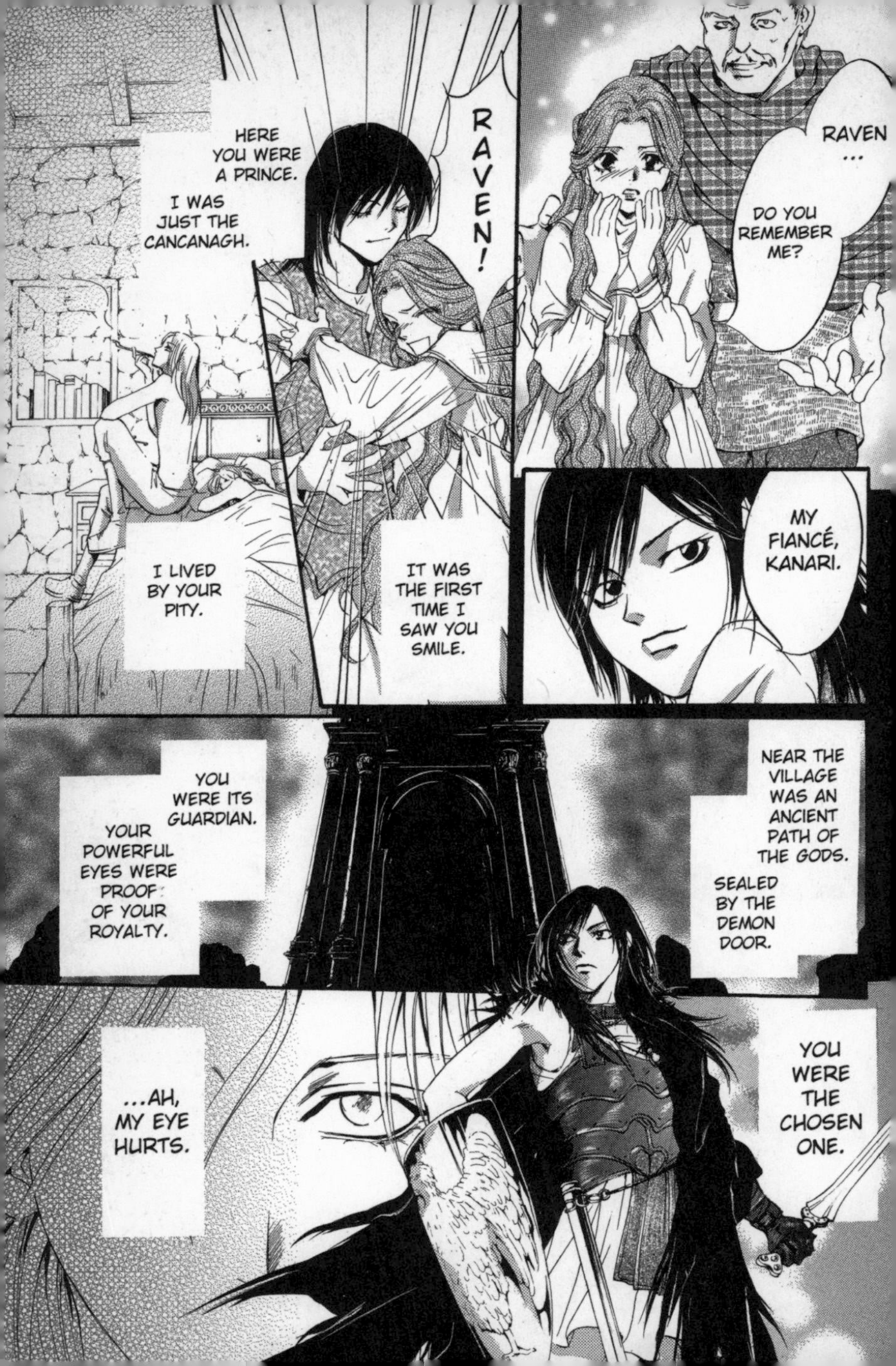
RAVEN ...
DO YOU REMEMBER ME?
MY FIANCÉ, KANARI.
RAVEN!
IT WAS THE FIRST TIME I SAW YOU SMILE.
HERE YOU WERE A PRINCE.
I WAS JUST THE CANCANAGH.
I LIVED BY YOUR PITY.
NEAR THE VILLAGE WAS AN ANCIENT PATH OF THE GODS.
SEALED BY THE DEMON DOOR.
YOU WERE ITS GUARDIAN.
YOUR POWERFUL EYES WERE PROOF OF YOUR ROYALTY.
YOU WERE THE CHOSEN ONE.
...AH, MY EYE HURTS.

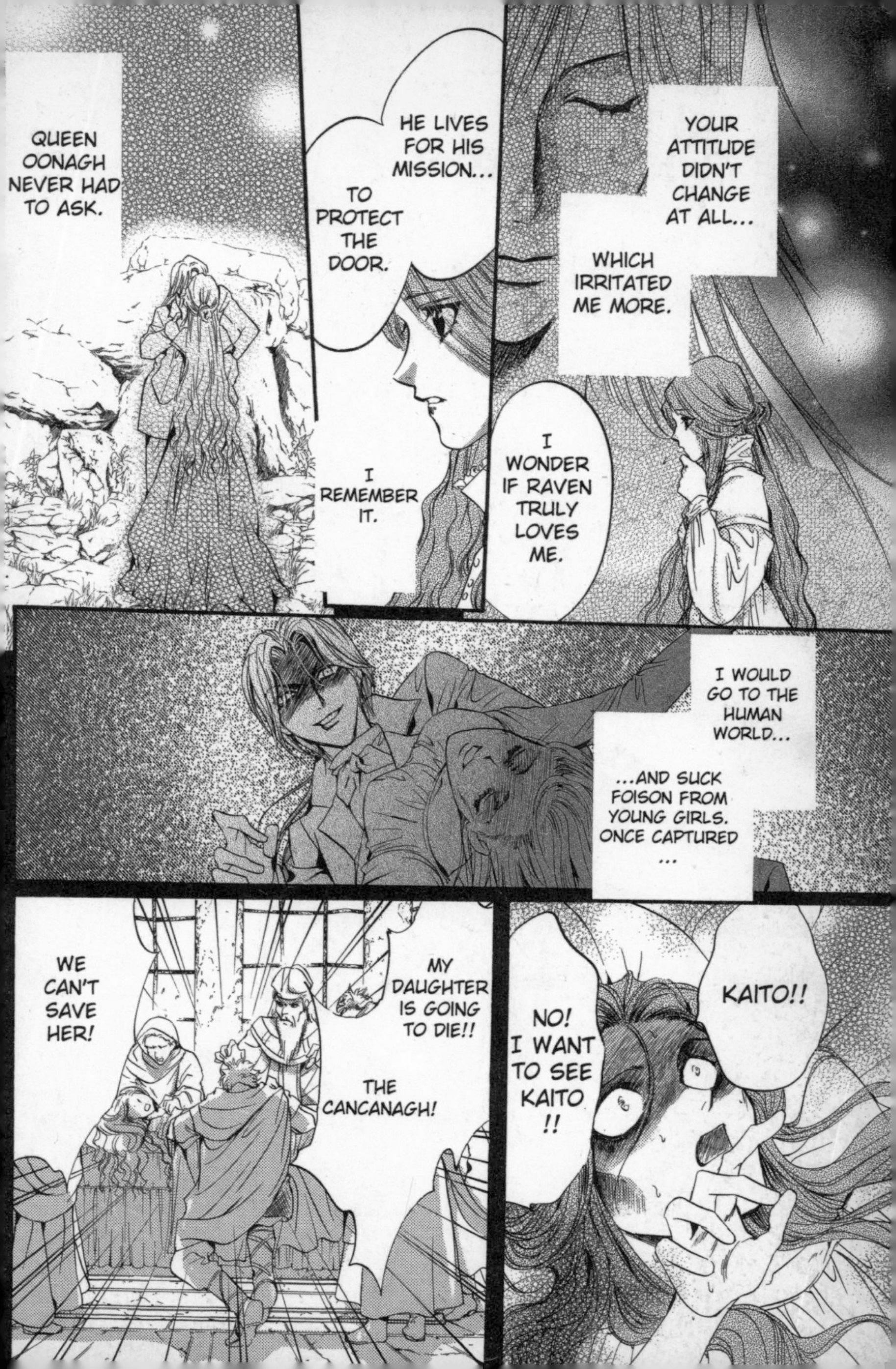
YOUR ATTITUDE DIDN'T CHANGE AT ALL...
WHICH IRRITATED ME MORE.
I WONDER IF RAVEN TRULY LOVES ME.
HE LIVES FOR HIS MISSION...
TO PROTECT THE DOOR.
I REMEMBER IT.
QUEEN OONAGH NEVER HAD TO ASK.
I WOULD GO TO THE HUMAN WORLD...
...AND SUCK FOISON FROM YOUNG GIRLS. ONCE CAPTURED ...
KAITO!!
NO! I WANT TO SEE KAITO !!
MY DAUGHTER IS GOING TO DIE!!
THE CANCANAGH!
WE CAN'T SAVE HER!

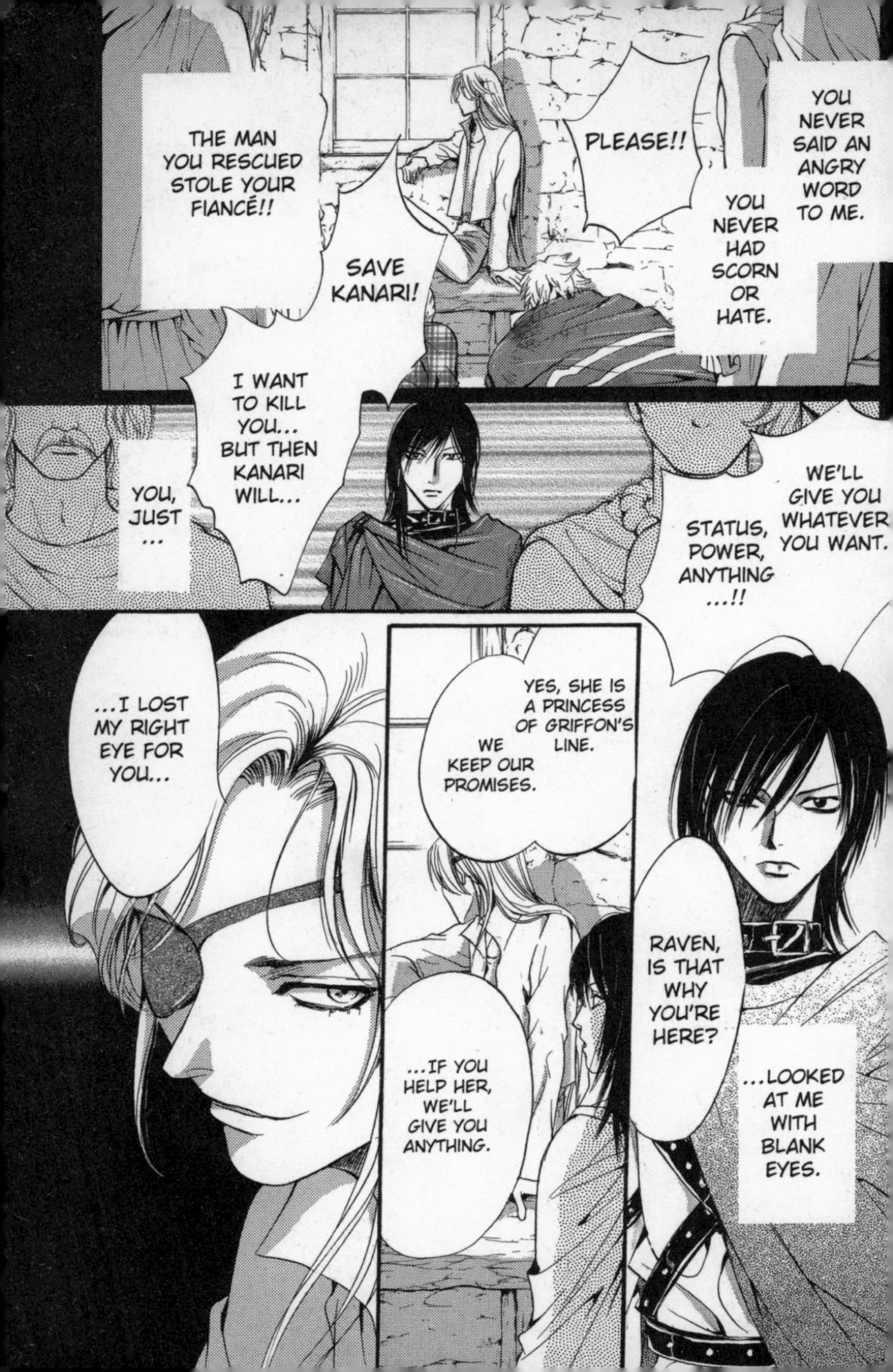
YOU NEVER SAID AN ANGRY WORD TO ME.
YOU NEVER HAD SCORN OR HATE.
PLEASE!!
THE MAN YOU RESCUED STOLE YOUR FIANCÉ!!
SAVE KANARI!
WE'LL GIVE YOU WHATEVER YOU WANT.
STATUS, POWER, ANYTHING ...!!
I WANT TO KILL YOU... BUT THEN KANARI WILL...
YOU, JUST ...
RAVEN, IS THAT WHY YOU'RE HERE?
...LOOKED AT ME WITH BLANK EYES.
YES, SHE IS A PRINCESS OF GRIFFON'S LINE.
WE KEEP OUR PROMISES.
...IF YOU HELP HER, WE'LL GIVE YOU ANYTHING.
...I LOST MY RIGHT EYE FOR YOU...

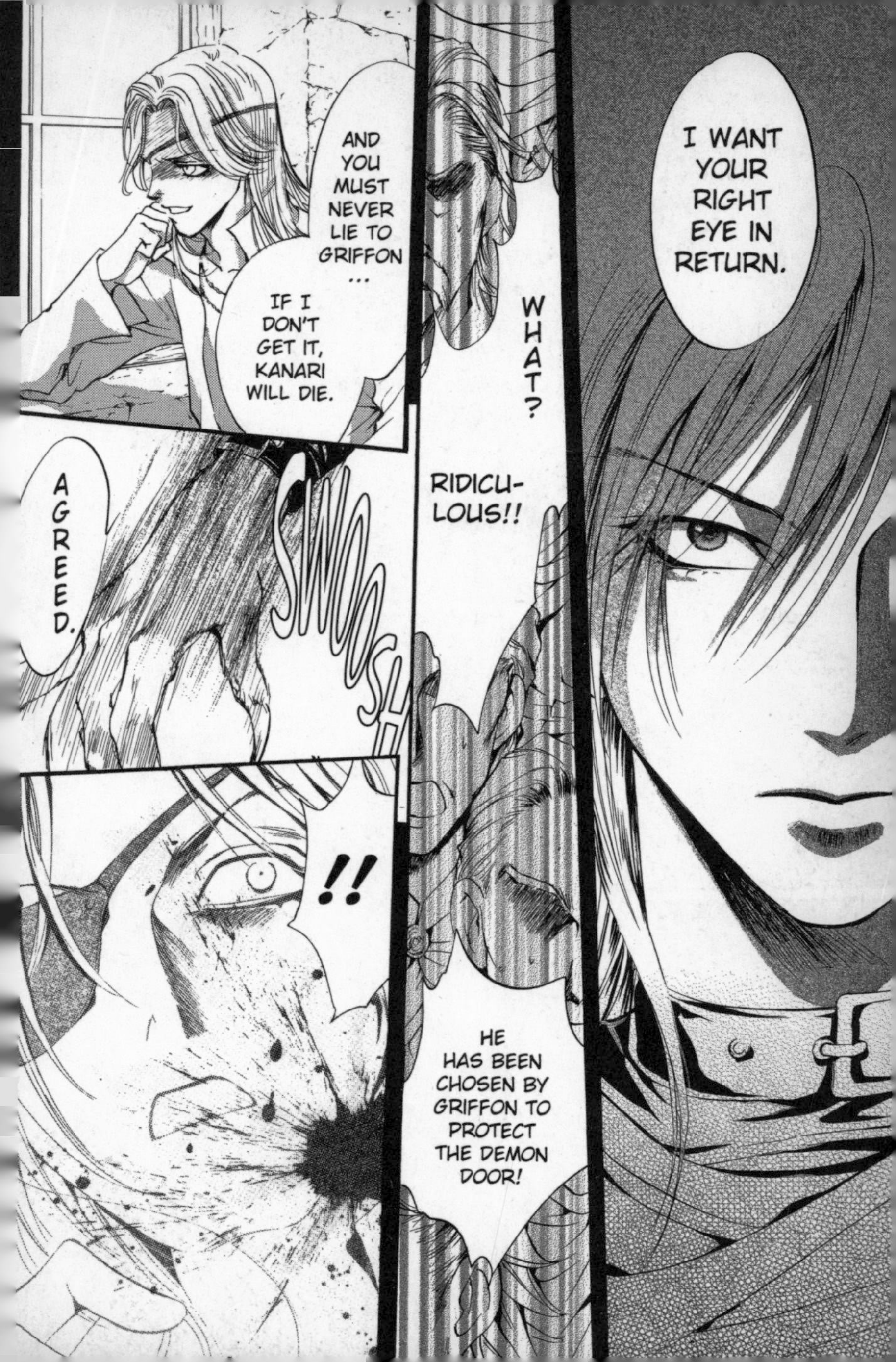
I WANT YOUR RIGHT EYE IN RETURN.
WHAT?
RIDICULOUS!!
HE HAS BEEN CHOSEN BY GRIFFON TO PROTECT THE DEMON DOOR!
AND YOU MUST NEVER LIE TO GRIFFON...
IF I DON'T GET IT, KANARI WILL DIE.
AGREED.
SWOOSH
!!

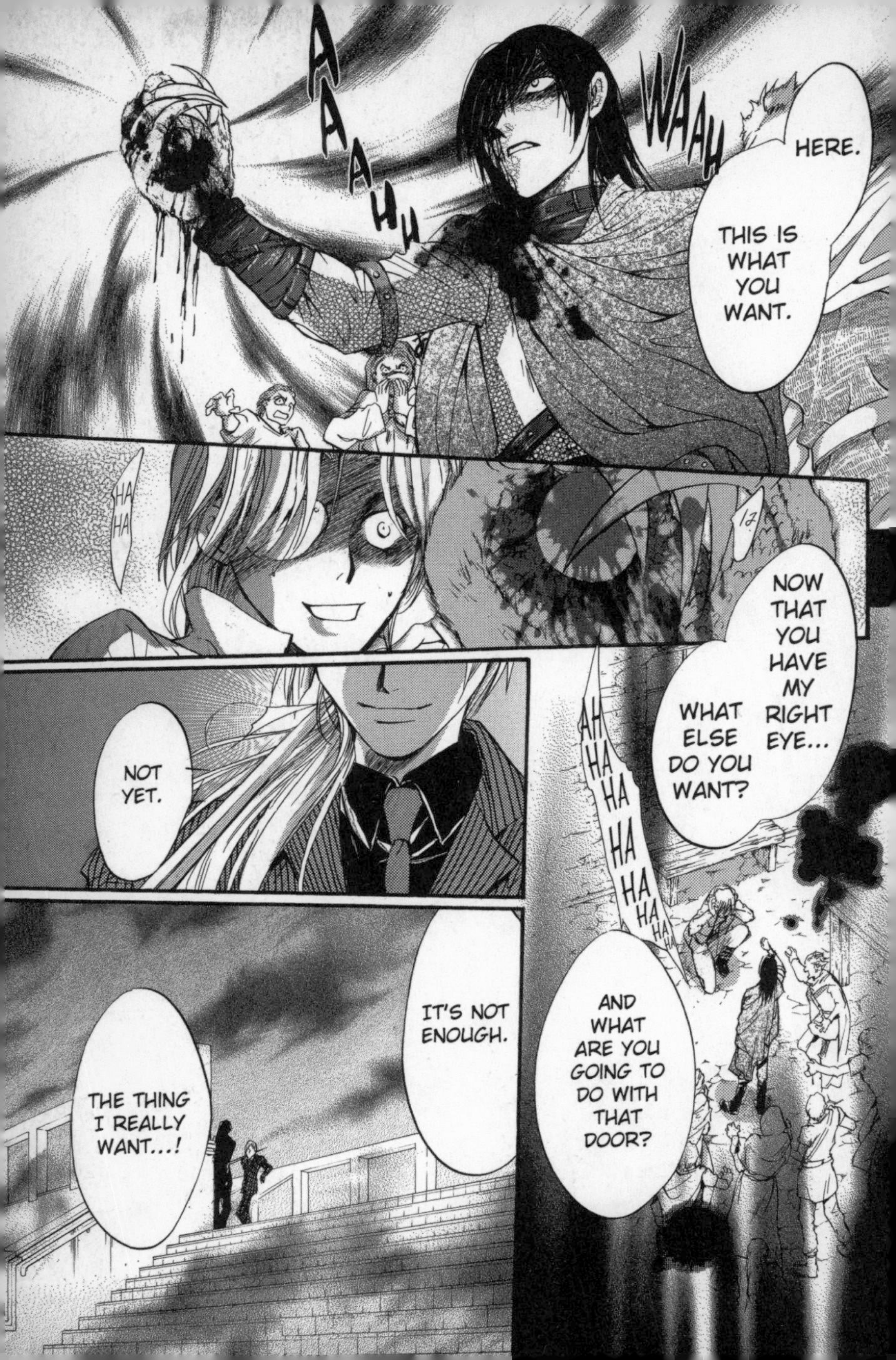

HERE.
THIS IS WHAT YOU WANT.
WAAH
AAAAHHH
HA HA
NOW THAT YOU HAVE MY RIGHT EYE...
WHAT ELSE DO YOU WANT?
AH HA HA HA HA HA HA HA HA
NOT YET.
AND WHAT ARE YOU GOING TO DO WITH THAT DOOR?
IT'S NOT ENOUGH.
THE THING I REALLY WANT...!

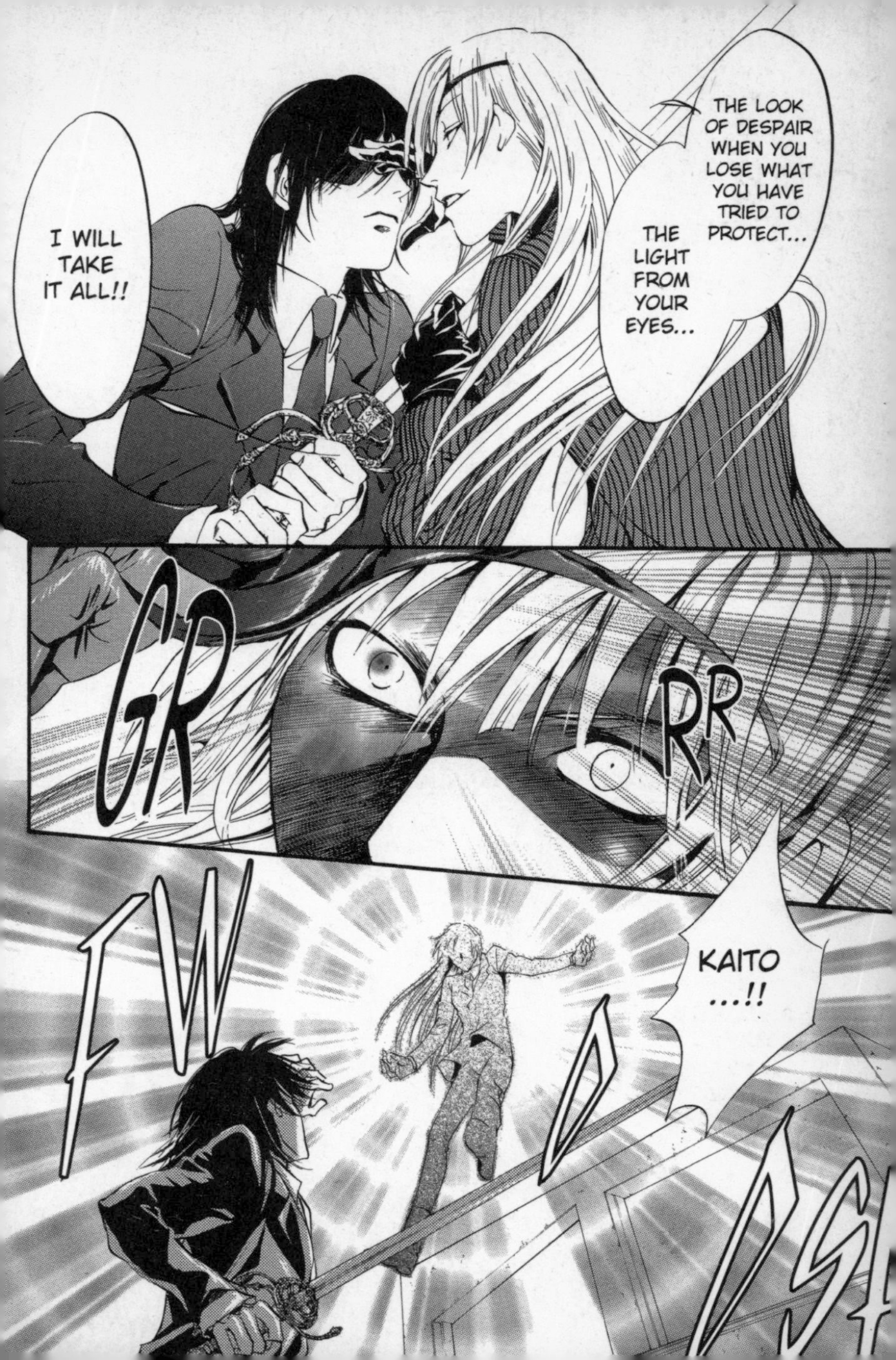
THE LOOK OF DESPAIR WHEN YOU LOSE WHAT YOU HAVE TRIED TO PROTECT...
THE LIGHT FROM YOUR EYES...
I WILL TAKE IT ALL!!
GR
RR
KAITO ...!!
FW

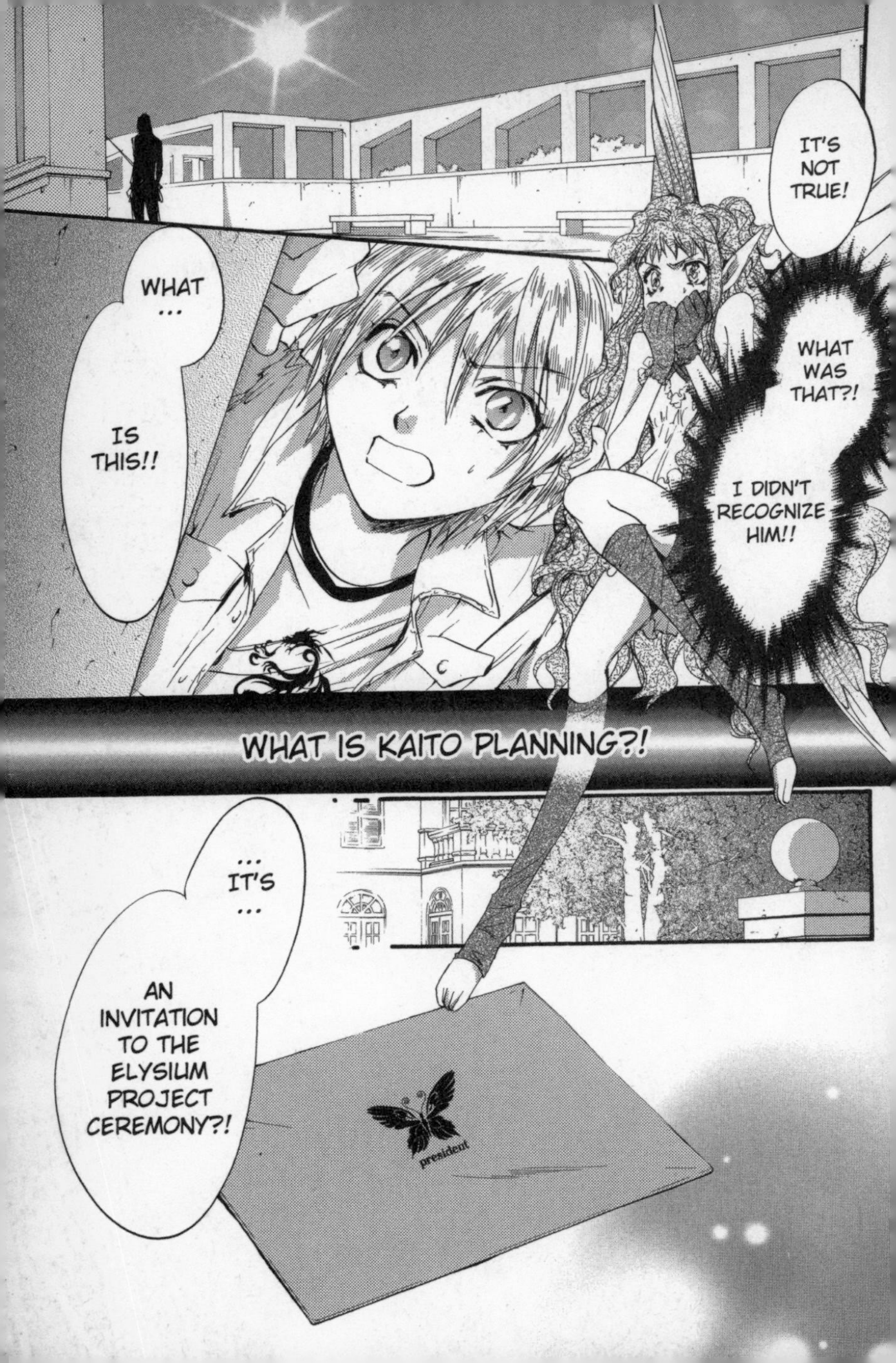
IT'S NOT TRUE!
WHAT WAS THAT?!
I DIDN'T RECOGNIZE HIM!!
WHAT ...
IS THIS!!
WHAT IS KAITO PLANNING?!
... IT'S ...
AN INVITATION TO THE ELYSIUM PROJECT CEREMONY?!
president

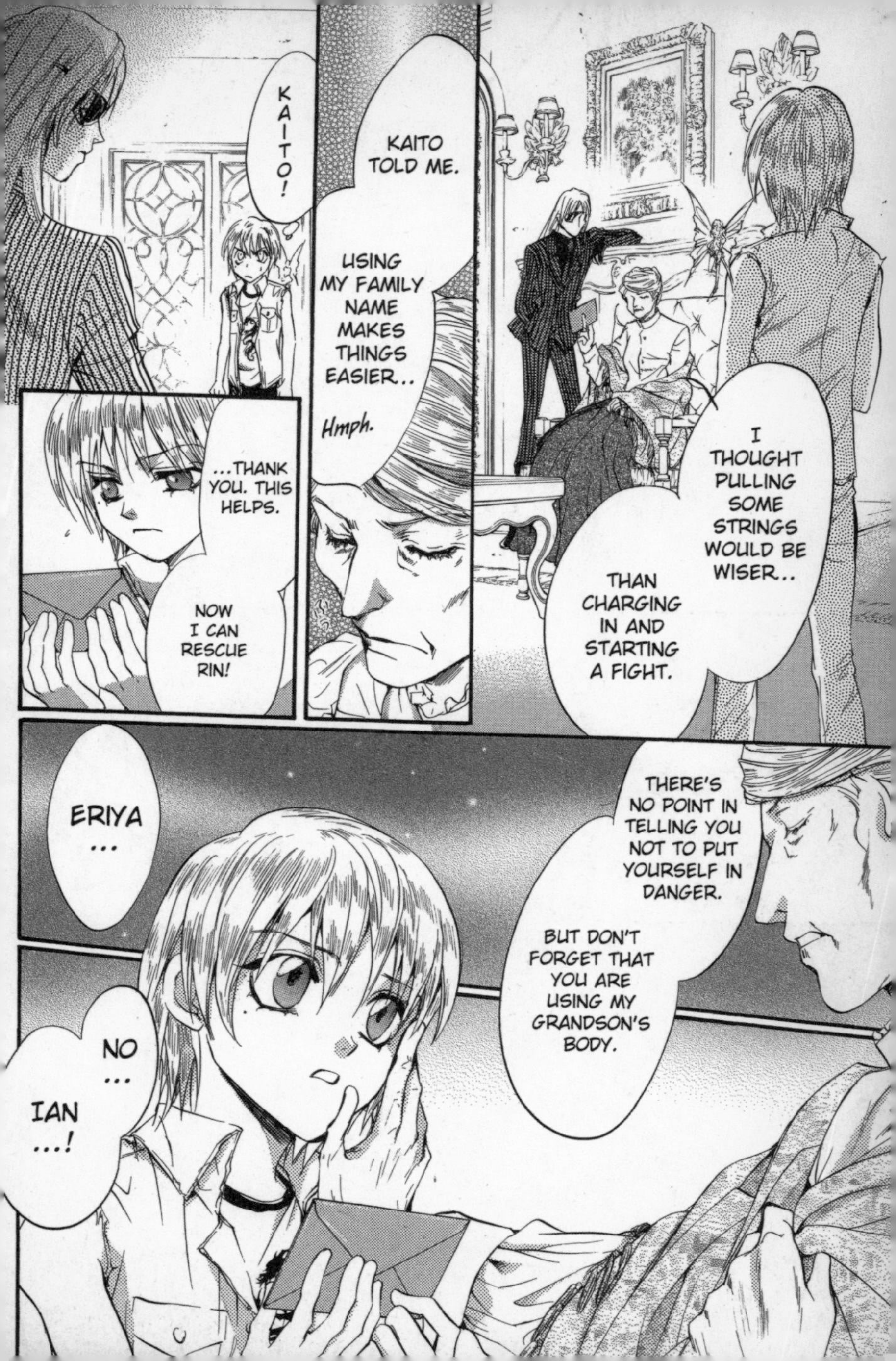
I THOUGHT PULLING SOME STRINGS WOULD BE WISER...
THAN CHARGING IN AND STARTING A FIGHT.
KAITO TOLD ME.
USING MY FAMILY NAME MAKES THINGS EASIER...
Hmph.
KAITO!
...THANK YOU. THIS HELPS.
NOW I CAN RESCUE RIN!
THERE'S NO POINT IN TELLING YOU NOT TO PUT YOURSELF IN DANGER.
BUT DON'T FORGET THAT YOU ARE USING MY GRANDSON'S BODY.
ERIYA...
NO... IAN...!

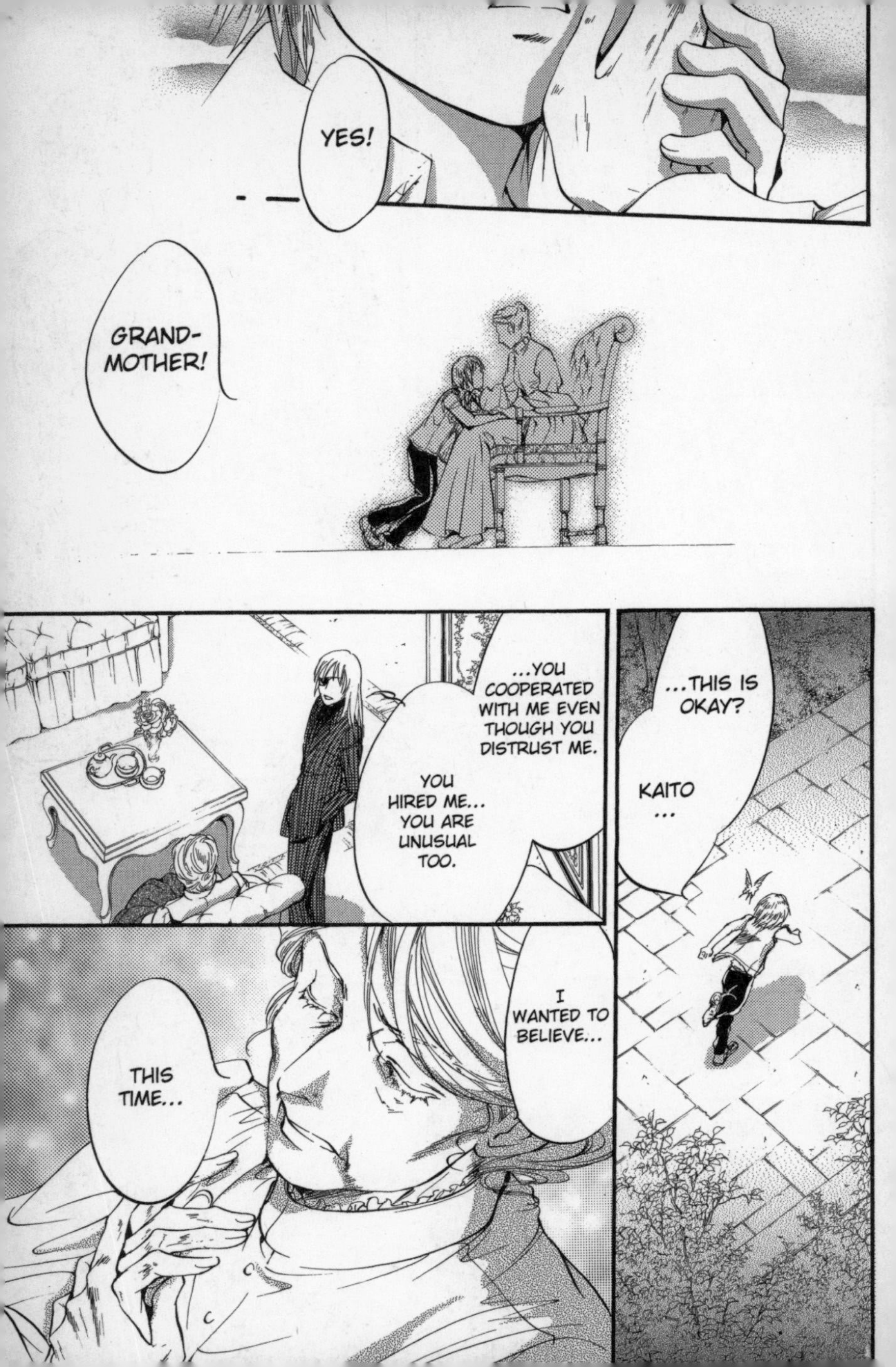
YES!
GRAND-MOTHER!
...THIS IS OKAY?
KAITO ...
...YOU COOPERATED WITH ME EVEN THOUGH YOU DISTRUST ME.
YOU HIRED ME... YOU ARE UNUSUAL TOO.
I WANTED TO BELIEVE...
THIS TIME...

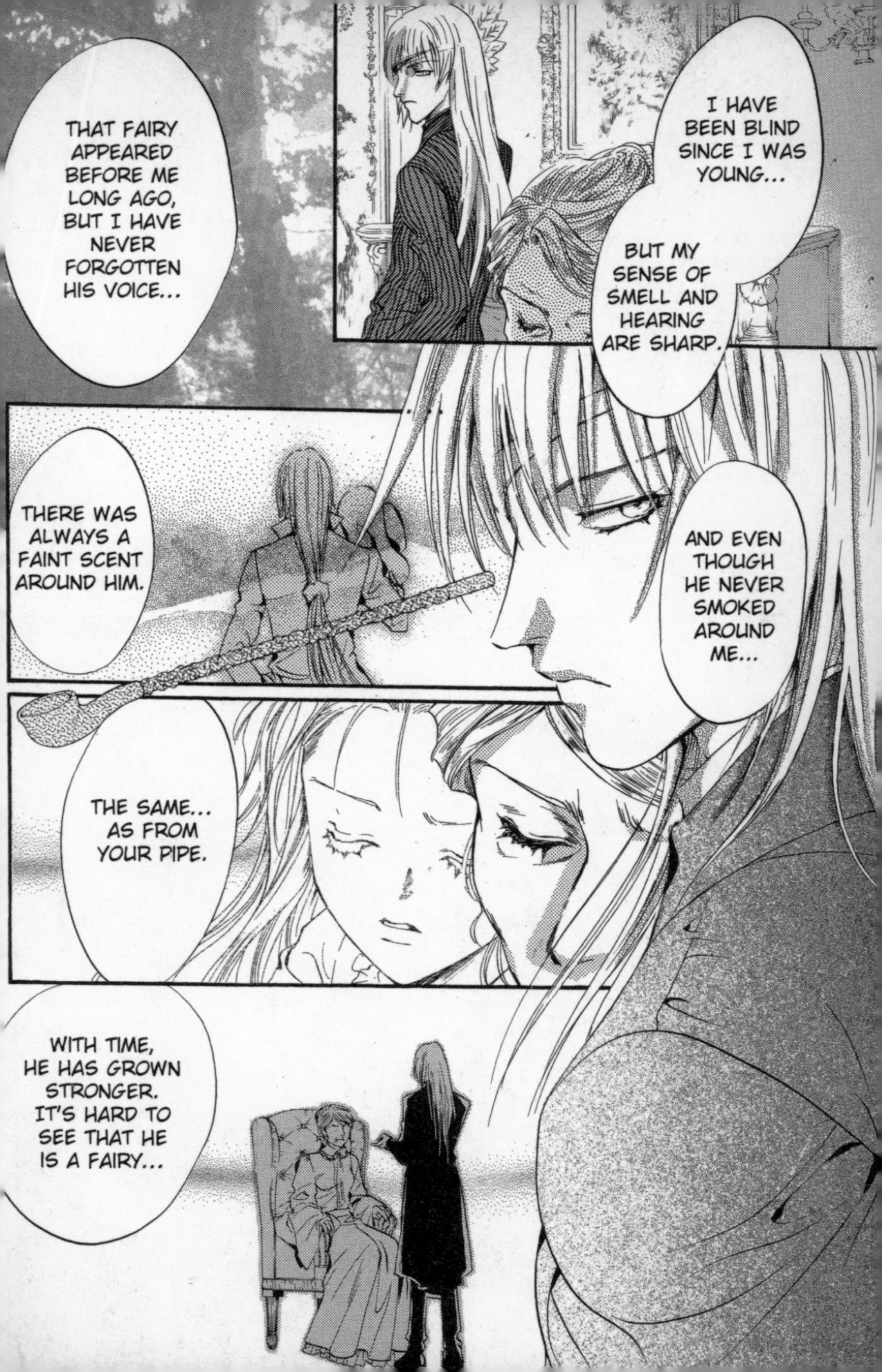
I HAVE BEEN BLIND SINCE I WAS YOUNG...
BUT MY SENSE OF SMELL AND HEARING ARE SHARP.
THAT FAIRY APPEARED BEFORE ME LONG AGO, BUT I HAVE NEVER FORGOTTEN HIS VOICE...
AND EVEN THOUGH HE NEVER SMOKED AROUND ME...
THERE WAS ALWAYS A FAINT SCENT AROUND HIM.
THE SAME... AS FROM YOUR PIPE.
WITH TIME, HE HAS GROWN STRONGER. IT'S HARD TO SEE THAT HE IS A FAIRY...

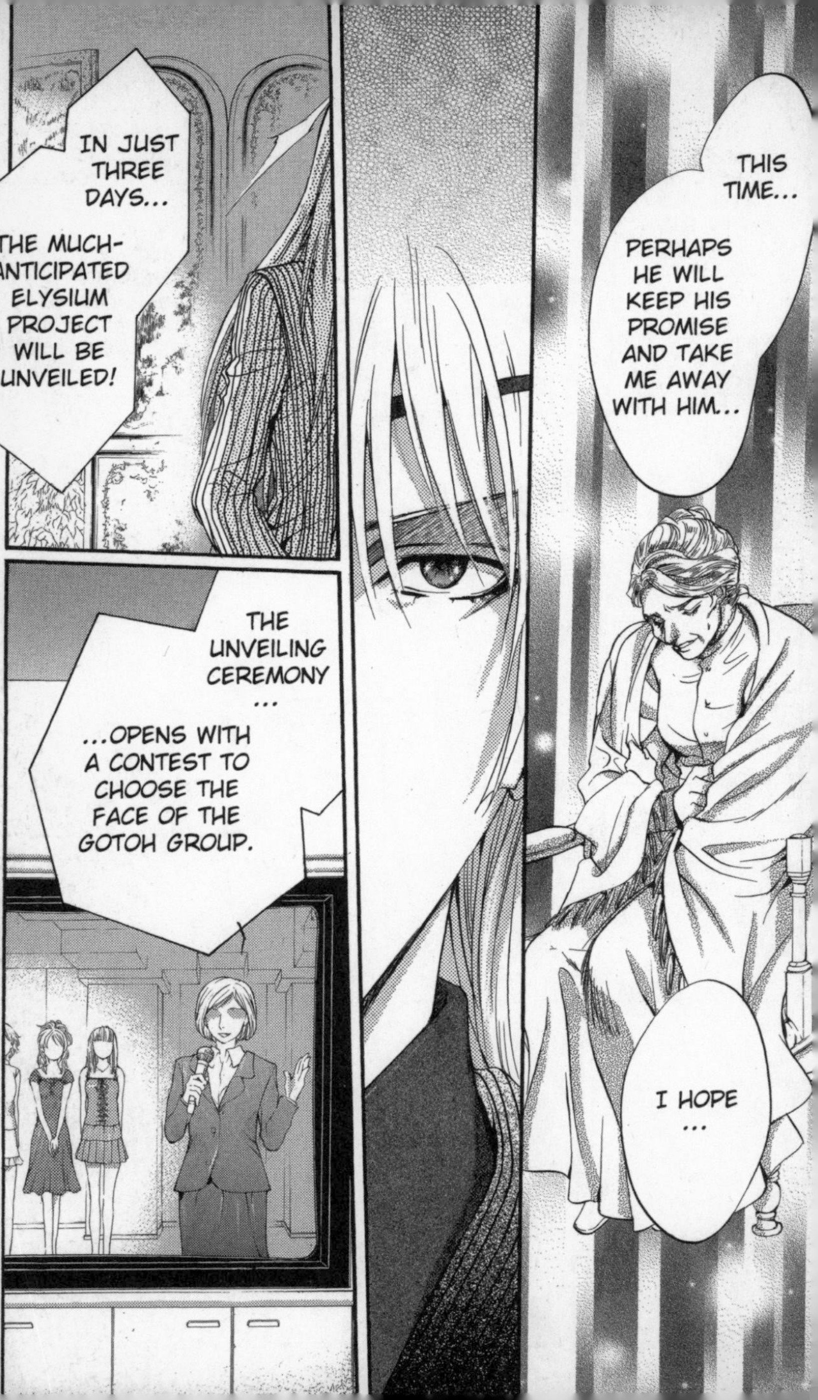
THIS TIME...
PERHAPS HE WILL KEEP HIS PROMISE AND TAKE ME AWAY WITH HIM...
I HOPE...
IN JUST THREE DAYS...
THE MUCH-ANTICIPATED ELYSIUM PROJECT WILL BE UNVEILED!
THE UNVEILING CEREMONY...
...OPENS WITH A CONTEST TO CHOOSE THE FACE OF THE GOTOH GROUP.

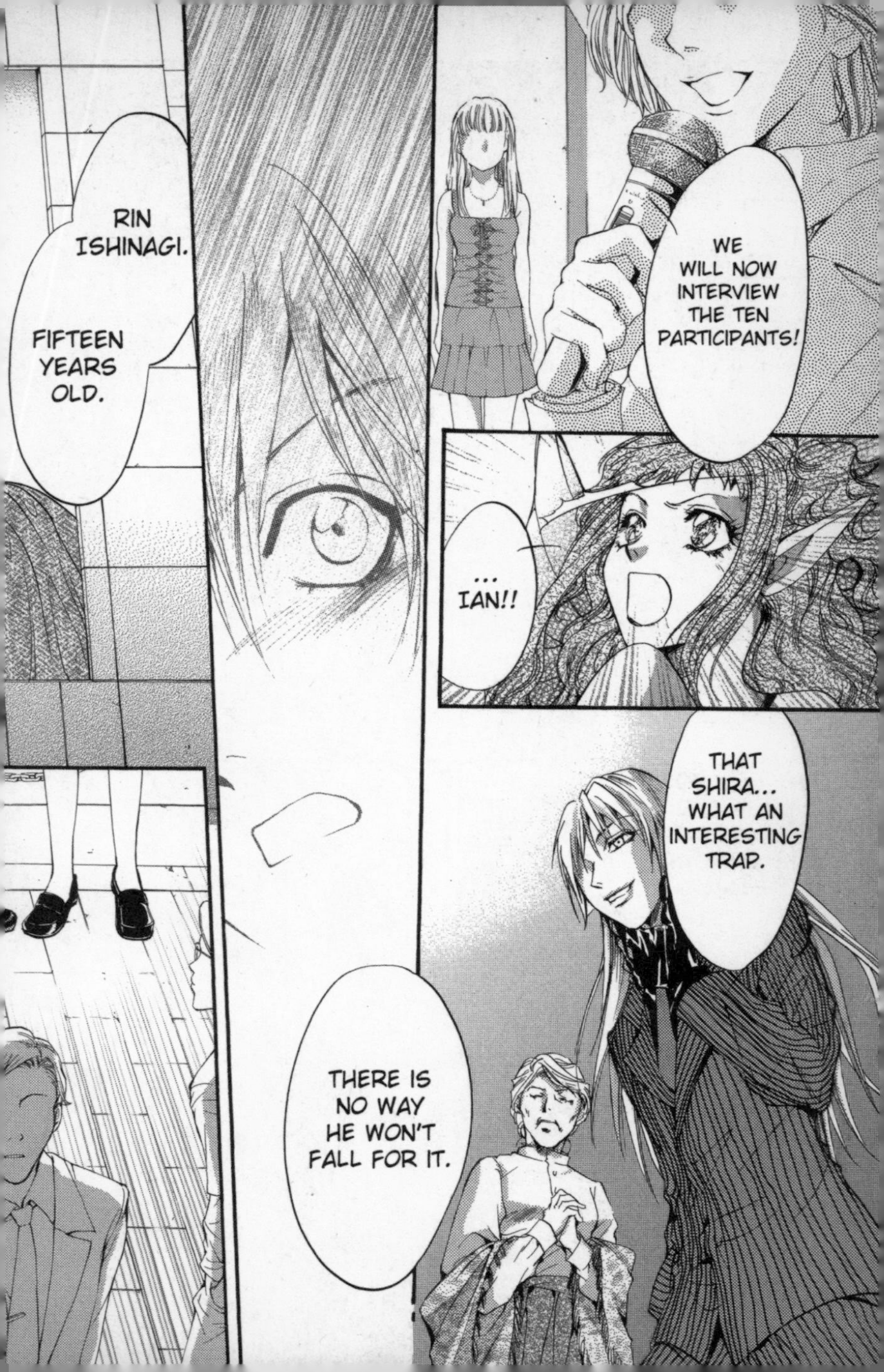
WE WILL NOW INTERVIEW THE TEN PARTICIPANTS!
... IAN!!
THAT SHIRA... WHAT AN INTERESTING TRAP.
THERE IS NO WAY HE WON'T FALL FOR IT.
RIN ISHINAGI.
FIFTEEN YEARS OLD.

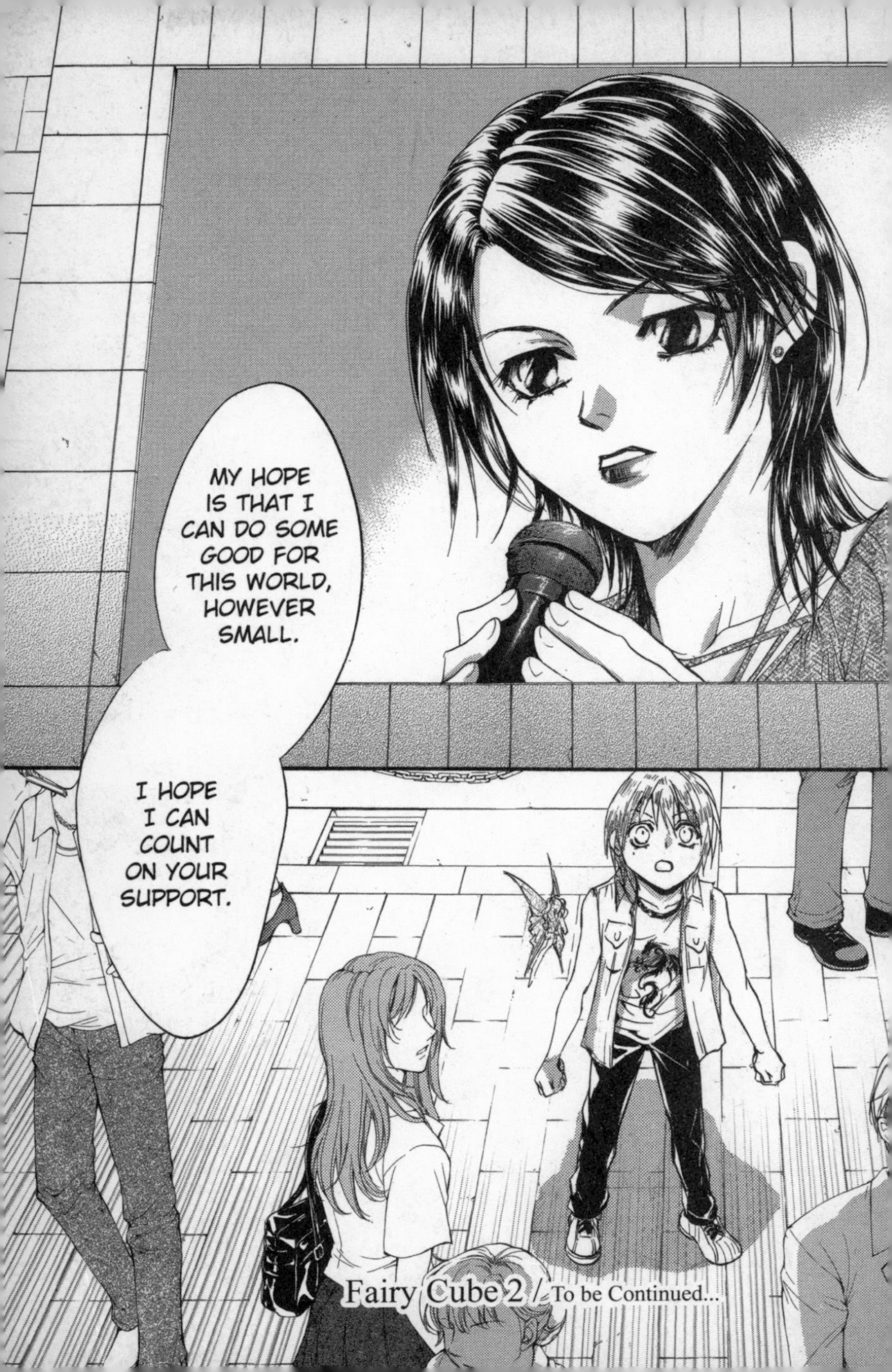
MY HOPE IS THAT I CAN DO SOME GOOD FOR THIS WORLD, HOWEVER SMALL.
I HOPE I CAN COUNT ON YOUR SUPPORT.
Fairy Cube 2 / To be Continued...

BONUS ILLUSTRATIONS

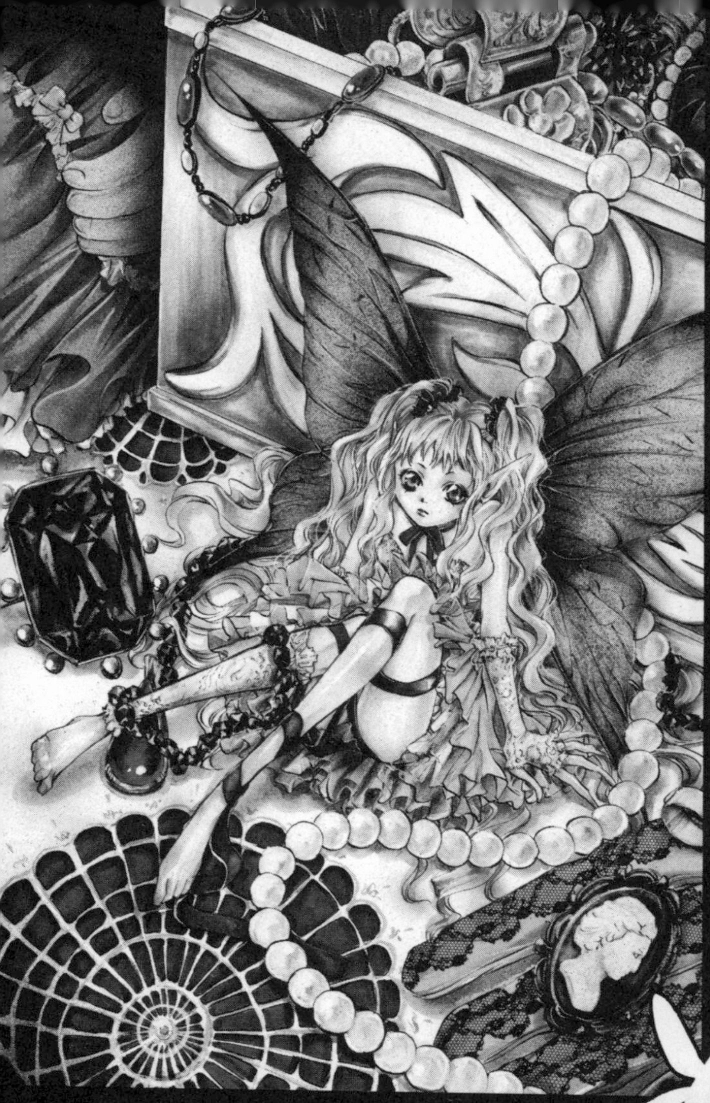

CHAPTER EIGHT

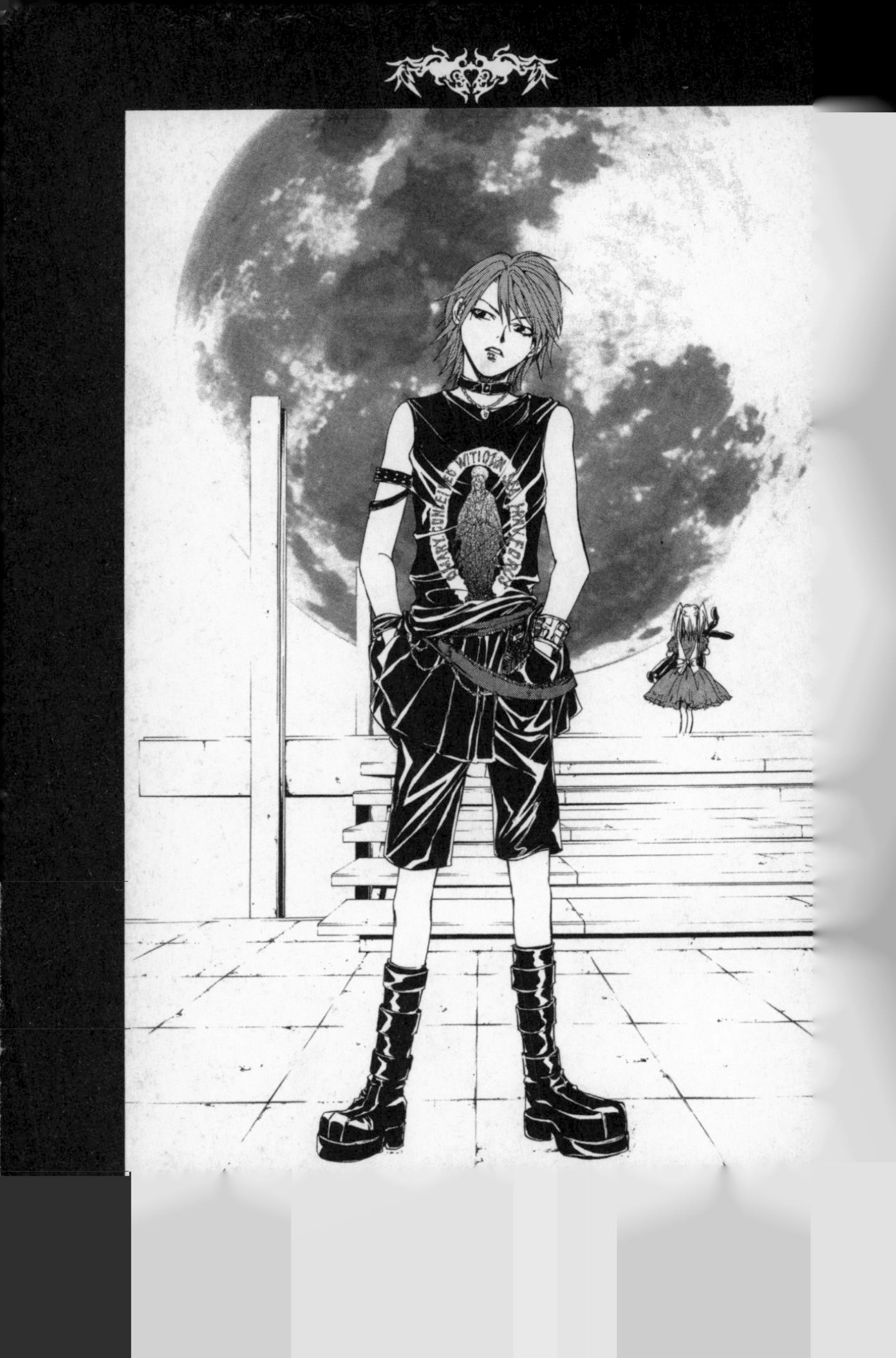

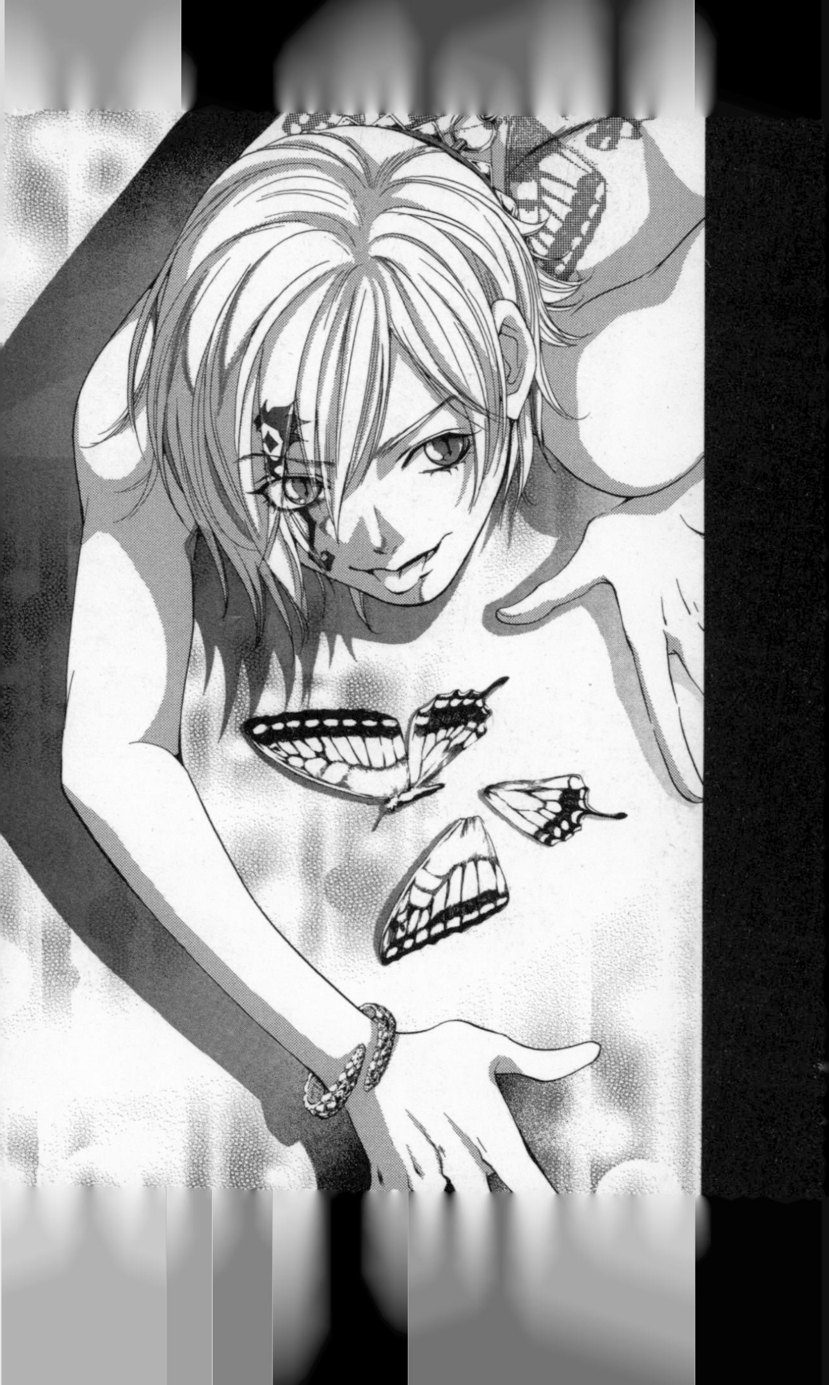

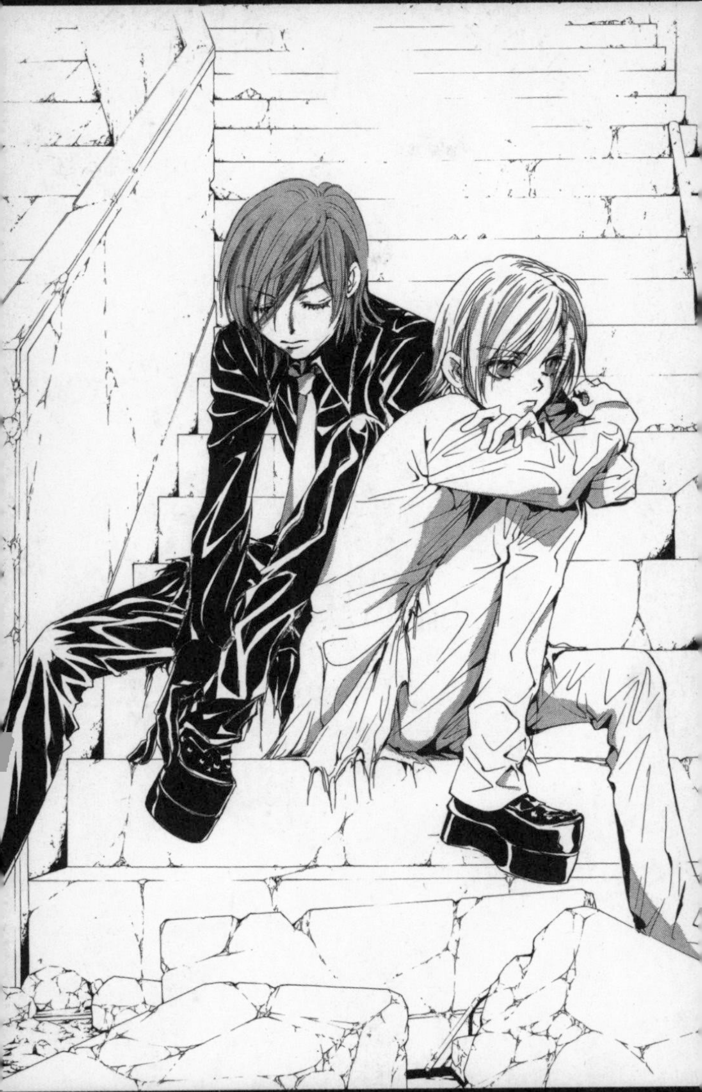

CHAPTER ELEVEN

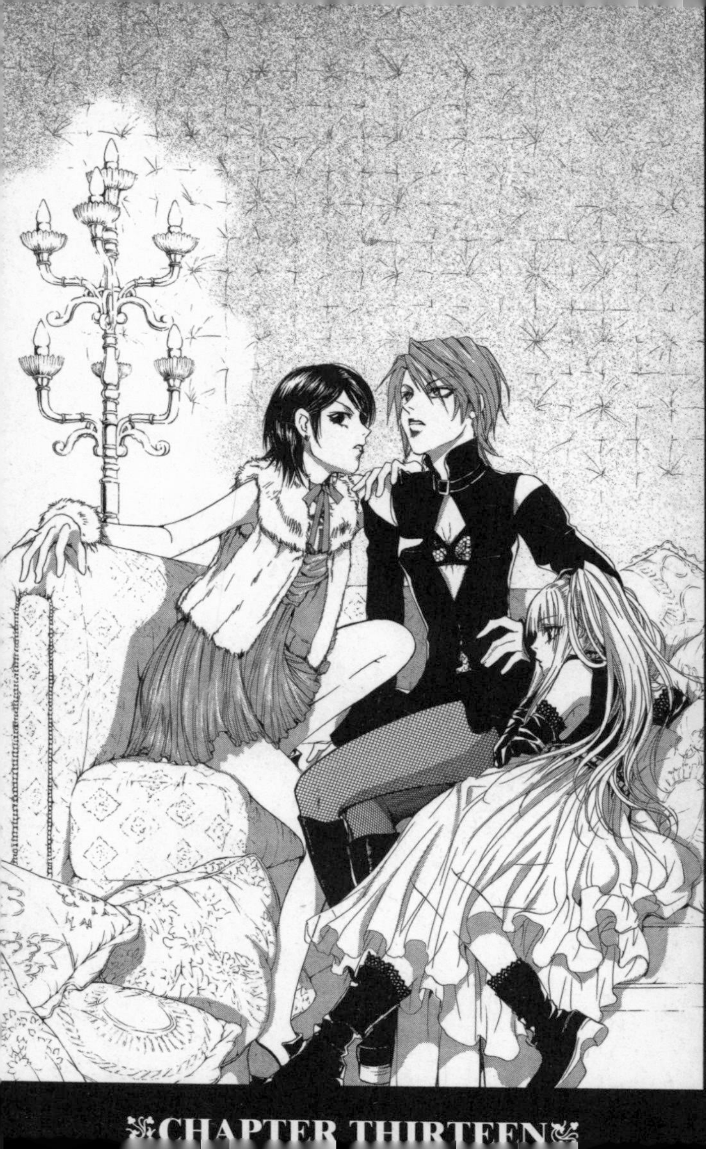

CHAPTER THIRTEEN

CHAPTER FOURTEEN

Creator: Kaori Yuki
Date of Birth: December 18
Blood Type: B
Major Works: *Angel Sanctuary* and *Godchild*

Kaori Yuki was born in Tokyo and started drawing at a very early age. Following her debut work *Natsufuku no Erie* (Ellie in Summer Clothes) in the Japanese magazine *Bessatsu Hana to Yume* (1987), she wrote a compelling series of short stories: *Zankoku na Douwatachi* (Cruel Fairy Tales), *Neji* (Screw), and *Sareki Ōkoku* (Gravel Kingdom).

As proven by her best-selling series *Angel Sanctuary* and *Godchild*, her celebrated body of work has etched an indelible mark on the gothic comics genre. She likes mysteries and British films and is a fan of the movie *Dead Poets Society* and the television show *Twin Peaks*.

FAIRY CUBE

VOL. 2
The Shojo Beat Manga Edition

STORY AND ART BY KAORI YUKI

Translation/Gemma Collinge
English Adaptation/Kristina Blachere
Touch-up Art & Lettering/James Gaubatz
Design/Courtney Utt
Editor/Joel Enos

Editor in Chief, Books/Alvin Lu
Editor in Chief, Magazines/Marc Weidenbaum
VP of Publishing Licensing/Rika Inouye
VP of Sales/Gonzalo Ferreyra
Sr. VP of Marketing/Liza Coppola
Publisher/Hyoe Narita

Printed in Canada

Published by VIZ Media, LLC
P.O. Box 77010
San Francisco, CA 94107

Shojo Beat Manga Edition
10 9 8 7 6 5 4 3 2 1

First printing, August 2008

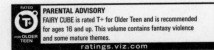

Love Kaori Yuki?
Read the rest of VIZ Media's Kaori Yuki Collection!

Angel Sanctuary
Rated T+ for Older Teen
20 Volumes

The angel Alexiel loved God, but she rebelled against Heaven when she saw how disgracefully the other angels were behaving. She was finally captured and, as punishment, sent to Earth to live an endless series of tragic lives. She now inhabits the body of Setsuna Mudo, a troubled teen in love with his sister Sara.

The Cain Saga
Rated M for Mature Readers
5 Volumes

Delve into the tortured past of Earl Cain C. Hargreaves, charismatic heir to a wealthy family full of secrets, lies and unthinkable crimes. The prequel to the *Godchild* series, *The Cain Saga* follows the young Cain as he attempts to unravel the secrets of his birth, all the while solving each new mystery that comes his way.

Godchild
Rated T+ for Older Teen
8 Volumes

In 19th century London, dashing young nobleman Earl Cain Hargreaves weaves his way through the shadowy cobblestone streets that hide the dark secrets of aristocratic society. With his young sister Mary Weather and his constant companion Riff, Cain sets out to solve the dangerous mystery of his disturbing lineage.

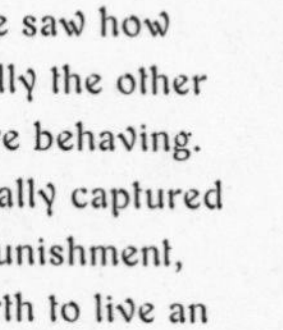

The Art of Angel Sanctuary:
Angel Cage

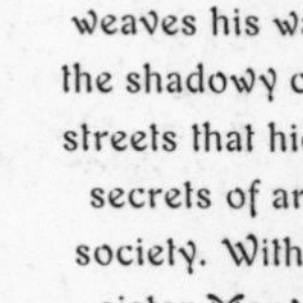

The Art of Angel Sanctuary 2:
Lost Angel

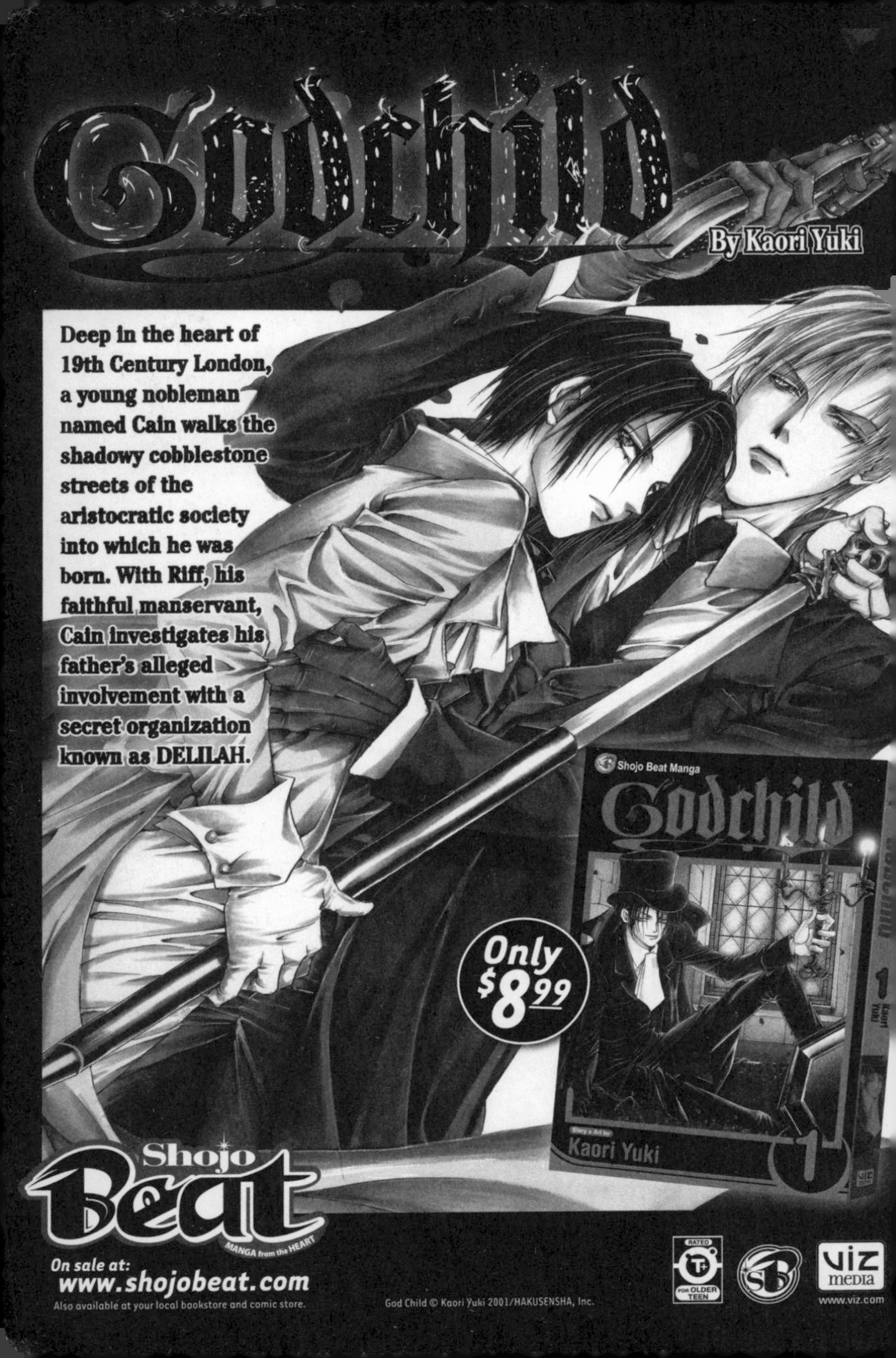
Godchild
By Kaori Yuki
Deep in the heart of 19th Century London, a young nobleman named Cain walks the shadowy cobblestone streets of the aristocratic society into which he was born. With Riff, his faithful manservant, Cain investigates his father's alleged involvement with a secret organization known as DELILAH.
Shojo Beat Manga
Godchild
Kaori Yuki
1
Only $8.99
Shojo Beat
MANGA from the HEART
On sale at:
www.shojobeat.com
Also available at your local bookstore and comic store.
God Child © Kaori Yuki 2001/HAKUSENSHA, Inc.
RATED T+ FOR OLDER TEEN
VIZ media
www.viz.com

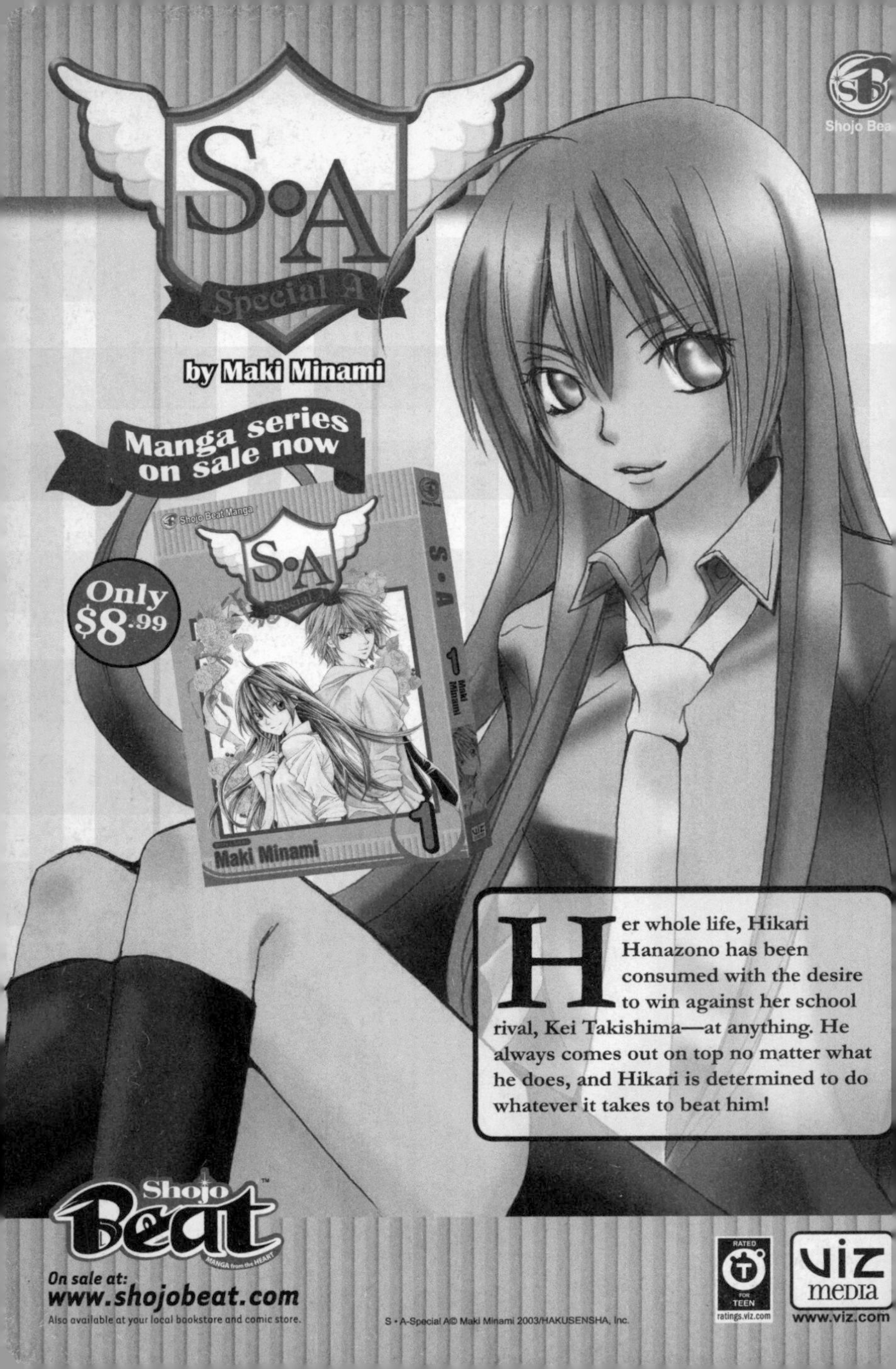
Shojo Beat
S•A
Special A
by Maki Minami
Manga series on sale now
Only $8.99
Shojo Beat Manga
S•A
1
Maki Minami
Her whole life, Hikari Hanazono has been consumed with the desire to win against her school rival, Kei Takishima—at anything. He always comes out on top no matter what he does, and Hikari is determined to do whatever it takes to beat him!
Shojo Beat™
MANGA from the HEART
On sale at:
www.shojobeat.com
Also available at your local bookstore and comic store.
S • A-Special A© Maki Minami 2003/HAKUSENSHA, Inc.
RATED T FOR TEEN
ratings.viz.com
VIZ media
www.viz.com